Romanticism and Women Poets

Romanticism
and
Women Poets

Opening the Doors of Reception

Harriet Kramer Linkin
and Stephen C. Behrendt
Editors

THE UNIVERSITY PRESS OF KENTUCKY

Publication of this volume was made possible in part
by a grant from the National Endowment for the Humanities.

Scholarly publisher for the Commonwealth,
serving Bellarmine College, Berea College, Centre
College of Kentucky, Eastern Kentucky University,
The Filson Club Historical Society, Georgetown College,
Kentucky Historical Society, Kentucky State University,
Morehead State University, Murray State University,
Northern Kentucky University, Transylvania University,
University of Kentucky, University of Louisville,
and Western Kentucky University.
All rights reserved.

Editorial and Sales Offices: The University Press of Kentucky
663 South Limestone Street, Lexington, Kentucky 40508-4008

03 02 01 00 99   1 2 3 4 5

Library of Congress Cataloging-in-Publication Data

Romanticism and women poets : opening the doors of reception /
Harriet Kramer Linkin and Stephen C. Behrendt, editors.
p.   cm.
Includes bibliographical references and index.
ISBN 0-8131-2107-8 (alk. paper)
1. English poetry—Women authors—History and criticism. 2. Feminism and
literature—Great Britain—History—19th century. 3. Women and literature—Great
Britain—History—19th century. 4. English poetry—19th century—History and
criticism. 5. Romanticism—Great Britain. 6. Canon (Literature).   I. Linkin,
Harriet Kramer, 1956–   . II. Behrendt, Stephen C., 1947–   .
PR585.W6R66   1999
821'.709145'082—dc21   98-48349

Manufactured in the United States of America

Contents

~ Part Three: Reconstructing Reception ~

Illustrations

Acknowledgments

A volume such as this incurs so many debts in its making that it would be impossible to list all the acknowledgments owed, and thus the editors would like to point to the list of works cited as offering many of the names and works that we acknowledge with gratitude and great respect. We would like to give more direct thanks to our companion contributors to the collection, whose energy, enthusiasm, commitment, generosity, and patience made the process of collaboration pleasurable, instructive, and thoroughly rewarding. Kevin Binfield, Elizabeth Fay, Melissa Davis Parks, and John Rieder provided critical support, as did our home institutions, New Mexico State University and the University of Nebraska. Harriet Kramer Linkin thanks the Interlibrary Loan Department at New Mexico State University's Branson Memorial Library, the College of Arts and Sciences for summer research funds, and *European Romantic Review*.

Introduction

Recovering Romanticism and Women Poets

❦

Harriet Kramer Linkin and Stephen C. Behrendt

If the doors of perception were cleansed every thing would appear to man as it is, infinite.

> *William Blake,* The Marriage of Heaven and Hell

Bursting the fetters and breaking the bars.

> *Emily Brontë, "High Waving Heather"*

Ten years ago this would have been a very different introduction. Anna Letitia Barbauld, Charlotte Smith, Mary Tighe, Amelia Opie, Mary Lamb, Fanny Kemble, Caroline Bowles Southey, Felicia Hemans, Letitia Elizabeth Landon: many of these names—and others as well—are now familiar to us. Ten years ago they were new to many, even among Romanticists. All this has changed. Today it is almost a truism that the Romantic literary community—and the subset of Romantic poets in particular—was populated by active and widely known women and men alike; ten years ago that too was a relatively novel idea. And though even now comparatively few know the names (or the poems) of poets such as Eliza Daye, Anne Candler, Charlotte Richardson, Anne Batten Cristall, Anna Maria Smallpiece, Caroline Norton, and Isabella Lickbarrow, the names of women poets have in the past decade or so nevertheless become increasingly familiar in discussions at conferences, in articles and books, and in anthologies. What has transpired in this short space is no less than a wholesale rethinking of British Romanticism, both as an intellectual and cultural phenomenon and as a site of literary production. Even poets such as Hemans and Landon, who never entirely disappeared from traditional literary history, are being reassessed not in terms of how well they conform to—or fail to conform to—paradigms associated for more than a century with a small group of canonical male poets, but rather in terms of the particular literary, cultural, social, intellectual, and aesthetic dynamic that informs their writing. What emerges from this broader, revisionist view of a Romantic poetic community is a clearer sense of a functioning dynamic: these writers knew one another, in many cases, knew one another's work, and knew how it was being received and interpreted in both the literary and the broader public audience. Moreover, they often used that knowledge, as Smith, Opie, and Landon did, for instance, to manipulate the sensibilities—and the critical responses—of those audiences.

The recovery and repositioning of British women poets of the Romantic period have challenged many of our received notions about British Romanticism. Moreover, the process has prompted important questions that may never receive full, unanimous, or entirely satisfying answers but which need to be asked nevertheless. Who were those poets, most fundamentally, what did they produce, what do we know about them, why for so long did we know so little (and, frequently, even less that was accurate) about them, and how are we coming to know them once again? Equally important, what did they think about themselves, their work, and their place in the contemporary literary scene and in the broad expanse of literary history as a whole? How did they envision their relationship to their audiences and to one another? And how does our greater knowledge of their poetic production in the later eighteenth and early nineteenth centuries modify our understanding of literary periods—and indeed of periodicity generally—and of literary and critical history? Finally, what can the recovery of their work—and the circumstances in which it is now occurring—teach us about current and past theoretical and critical frameworks that have been brought to bear upon their poetry and that of their contemporaries?

The essays in this volume wrestle with questions like these in examining how the historical reception of Romantic women poets has complicated our understanding of their achievement. *Reception* is itself a vexed term, involving as it does an often diverse array of literary markets, readerships, and cultural conditions that affect the way literary works are read and interpreted. Closely related is *reputation,* which has historically indicated the more protracted, less momentary form that reception assumes within the continuum of history. Like their male counterparts, the women poets appreciated that the latter depended upon the volatile former. Unlike them, however, the literary production of the women poets was carried on in a less stable and generally less hospitable environment, especially when they opted for subjects and forms traditionally associated with the male poetic tradition. Just as the reception accorded their poetry in their own time was various and often frankly contradictory, so in our own time the judgments and conclusions being reached by scholars are often at odds. What remains as consistent now as it was two centuries ago is the enthusiasm of writers on all sides of the questions.

Much current critical discourse on women writers of the Romantic period may be traced to the influential work of Anne Mellor, Stuart Curran, and Marlon Ross in particular, who cast new light upon matters explored earlier by Ellen

Moers, Mary Poovey, Margaret Homans, and others.[1] The essays collected here challenge many of the major currents in this scholarly discourse, even as they build upon the foundations laid by earlier critical inquiry. Three examples help to illustrate how this is so. Adriana Craciun, for instance, reformulates both the place of violence and the popular *and* critical response to it in the case of Mary Lamb, in the process making a case for the necessity of reconsidering the place of other sorts of nonconventional and even deviant behavior in the lives and works of the women poets. Indeed, Craciun disrupts what she regards as "gender complementary feminist poetics," which disregard the violence that women may themselves perform—or wish to perform. Violence, as Craciun re-views it, proves not to be the exclusive masculine province it is often reductively seen as being. Roxanne Eberle deconstructs Amelia Opie's abolitionist politics, leaving us to wonder why Opie's canny manipulation of voices in poems on these (and other) subjects failed to save her from the derision of much of twentieth-century criticism. Eberle's rich analysis provides a bracing corrective to overly simplistic ideological critiques of women writers' complicated relations with abolitionist discourse while probing the broader issue of justice in ways that are as relevant to literary criticism as they are to abolitionist politics. And in yet another example, Tricia Lootens's reading of Letitia Landon provides an equally salutary corrective not only to those critics who insist on making the woman poet "feminine" in all her concerns (the line taken with numbing frequency in the Victorian period), but also to those who routinely segregate poetry from fiction in women's writing. Like the writers of all the other essays here, Lootens reminds us that the contemporary reception and the ongoing reputation of writers involves the intersection of many and various "narratives" that both disguise and reveal cultural patterns, and that we must therefore constantly guard against clinging too tightly to *any* particular narrative or (hi)story.

The questions asked individually and in the aggregate by the essays that follow are important ones to ask right now, before any dust settles on the current flux in British Romanticism studies and we find ourselves confronting some seeming consensus view of a "new" list—if not a new canon (to use the *C* word)—of noteworthy Romantic poets. We are, after all, a list-making species, and even if we believe we have jettisoned the apparently outworn notion of canons, in Romanticism and elsewhere, there has nevertheless existed for at least the past century a list of writers who have been variously identified as Romantic. The list has changed from decade to decade, of course (witness the shifting fortune of Walter Scott or Felicia Hemans), but it has been there, in one form or another, explicit or implicit, for most of the century and two thirds that have followed what we typically think of as the Romantic period in England.

If we are list-makers, we are also simplifiers; we found it both practical and convenient to define a Romantic poetic canon around certain key principles and the figures who epitomized them and then to reduce the list to a few major poets and a surrounding constellation of minor poets. This made "Romantic poetry" both manageable and identifiable, because it simply excluded what did not fit the paradigm. In Romanticism that has meant, most obviously, eliminating women writers—and women poets in particular. Their elimination was accelerated during the crucial period of the first half of the twentieth century by the rise of modernism and the institutionalization of New Criticism, both of which privileged the esoteric and the coolly intellectual over the quotidian and the expressive and both of which in fact depressed the stock of *all* Romantic writers. When it came to reclaiming Romantic poets generally, as Paula Feldman and Theresa Kelley have argued, it was neither conspiracy nor deliberate silencing that kept the women out, but rather "an absence of sufficient curiosity and advocacy" combined with "an absence of the political power and energy to break the silence" where they were concerned.[2] Just as writing for publication was for women during the Romantic period an especially and often overtly political act, so too has their recovery proven to be a political activity in several senses, as is clear both in the essays of this book and in the often controversial reformulations of "Romantic poetry" to be found today in print and in the classroom.

Our reference above to the stock market is not merely gratuitous. The history of any author's reception is not unlike the history of any particular stock's performance on the market: like the stock, the author's reception and reputation fluctuate according to the effects of causes that may (and in fact usually do) have comparatively little to do with the author herself. "Market factors" are typically invoked as the cause for the rise and fall of stocks: nebulous, shady, undefinable, they resist particularization and so are especially convenient shadows with which to delude the insecure and the uncurious alike. And just as the history of a particular stock (or a related group of stocks) may be read against the broader picture of market activity generally (which is itself a reflector of cultural as well as economic phenomena), in an analogous fashion the history of the reputation of Barbauld or Tighe or Hemans—or of them and their female contemporaries taken collectively—may be read as a reflector of phenomena that are both literary and cultural—including social, political, intellectual, and economic.

Now that the renewed scholarly interest in women poets of the Romantic period has proven to be no mere flash in the pan, commercial publishers (and some academic ones) have moved to capitalize on the new market options this "new" Romanticism has opened up for them. Within the past several years, new anthologies have begun to appear that contain an increasingly familiar set of names and works when it comes to women poets. Although the greater critical attention that follows from this increased exposure is crucial to the larger enterprise of revaluation, there exists a perhaps inevitable danger that these expanded parameters may themselves encourage the imposition of an artificial and limiting (and therefore oversimplifying) closure to the set of women poets being considered. That is a very real danger, and one that will be familiar to anyone who has felt a bit overwhelmed when it comes to keeping up with her or his professional field in the face of exponentially expanding fields of new knowledge. In the face of that possibility, it is best to take the more confident line and regard it not as a danger but as both a challenge and an opportunity.

That is one reason why the essays in this collection insist on keeping open the doors of reception, on keeping fluid our consideration of the categories (aesthetic, cultural, and gender in particular) that construct our sense of value, and on keeping open the ways in which we think about historical and theoretical conditions that shape reception and reputation. That is why we have adapted for our title the words of the great Romantic iconoclast Blake, who appreciated that embracing truth (with or without a capital *T*) is more a matter of seeing correctly for oneself, with eyes cleansed by the exertions of what in *Milton* he called "Mental Fight," than of merely accepting without question the received notions of one's predecessors or contemporaries. Hence this collection is grounded in our conviction of the continuing need for reassessment not only of the works of the women poets themselves, but also of the conditions that governed their production, their consumption, and their contemporary reception and influence. This is why the contributors have not hesitated to interrogate and to challenge much of what has been written in recent years and to advance new and sometimes frankly controversial readings of poets and reception. This sustained commitment to the spirit of inquiry is absolutely necessary if the study of women writers of the Romantic period is to have a vital intellectual future. We cannot go backward, nor can we risk merely going in circles.

This collection is the first to look exclusively at the *poetry* produced by women writers in the Romantic era, as opposed to the work women were producing in all the literary and extraliterary genres at the time.[3] Poetry, after all, was the arena in which British Romanticism staked its canonical claims for so long. It was no small arena, either, as is evident from the remarkable numbers of volumes of poetry published annually during the years spanning 1780 and 1835 and from the astonishing numbers of poems that appeared in other venues such as the periodical press.[4] Because poetry clearly commanded considerable public attention, it was no small matter that women engaged in this most esteemed genre in very considerable numbers: James Robert de J. Jackson has identified more than eight hundred women poets in England and America during this period. As writers addressing audiences, they surely identified with the position articulated by their aristocratic French contemporary, Isabelle de Charriére, who wrote in 1794 that "in speaking one must be, or believe oneself to be, heard."[5] Consequently, they wrote. That they did so in remarkably large numbers is in itself striking; that their reputations were often wide and their influence considerable is likewise noteworthy. That traditional literary history has largely ignored both these indisputable facts tells us perhaps more about the conditions governing reception, valuation, and reputation in our own times (and in those generations preceding ours) than it does about the actual conditions under which these poets wrote and published. In looking specifically at the matters of reception, valuation, and reputation, therefore, the contributors to this volume help us both to reimagine the Romantic literary community and to rediscover the circumstances and values that characterized it. That the focus is specifically upon the women poets need not exclude consideration of the male, however; indeed, their presence is inevitable and should not in any case become the target of a new marginalization that would merely replicate old errors under the guise of repayment in kind. Rather, the really pressing need is to rediscover the dynamic of the English Romantic poetic milieu, a dynamic that has remained hidden—both by omission and by design—for much of the post-Romantic era. The picture that emerges from this project is one that paints British Romanticism in new and exciting ways, as a literary and cultural phenomenon characterized by a dynamic community of ideas and voices in conversation with one another and with their audiences.

Reflecting the several primary threads to the argument sketched out here, our volume is divided into three principal sections, each taking a slightly different perspective upon the central issue of reception and reputation. As a prologue to these more sharply critical examinations, Paula Feldman offers a remarkable personal reminiscence of "what was"—of how we used to think about Romantic poetry—and of how radical and ultimately deeply professional were the consequences for contemporary Romanticists of the wholesale rethinking of Romanticism brought about by the recovery of historically marginalized or ignored women poets.

Three essays then take up the obligation of questioning reception by interrogating the received wisdom about Romantic poetry, its authors, its themes and preoccupations, and its audiences. Stephen C. Behrendt examines in particular detail the period from 1802 to 1812, demonstrating how publication history reveals that this telling decade—often regarded as a fallow one among Romanticists because of the relative inactivity of the principal male poets—was an especially productive one for women poets, who were in fact prominent on the literary scene. The familiar Romantic truism of "two generations" is problematized, in other words, by consideration of the larger poetic scene. This is a watershed period for women poets, we discover, who were shifting their emphasis from an often very visible social and political radicalism that largely ends with the deaths of Mary Robinson and Charlotte Smith to the heightened domesticity that would flourish particularly in Felicia Hemans and Letitia Landon. The evolution of this shift, which is documented in contemporary critical commentary on individual poets and their works, Behrendt argues, helps us better to appreciate the nature of the transition between what are often loosely labeled the "first generation" and the "second generation" Romantics. It also reveals the surprisingly frequent extent to which male and female poets were in close accord during this period when it came to subjects, themes, and poetic forms.

Adriana Craciun examines the case of a single much-maligned (and misrepresented) writer, the familiar sister of "gentle-hearted" Charles Lamb. Whereas early writing about Mary Lamb generally suppressed discussion of her murder of her mother, more recent work emphasizes Lamb's attempts to stifle her own critical or violent emotions. Craciun argues, though, that failing to confront the facts of Lamb's violent behavior itself constitutes an act of violence against the full range of Lamb's experience, subjectivity, and agency. Craciun's discussion therefore questions the adequacy of programmatic modern critical formulations like "feminine Romanticism" when it comes to representing areas of women's experience—such as violent desires and actions—that do not fit neatly within the benevolent and nurturant model of interpersonal behavior implied in such formulations.

Roxanne Eberle next considers Amelia Alderson Opie, examining some of the ways in which Opie refuses to conveniently fix herself in a single consistent identity. An ardent supporter of the abolitionist movement throughout her life, Opie nevertheless shifted the narrative poetics of her works over her career from the revolutionary feminism and heightened sentimentalism of early poems like "The Negro Boy's Tale" (1804) to a no less eloquent but far less sentimental and more pragmatic socioeconomic discourse in later poems like "The Black Man's Lament; or, How to Make Sugar" (1826). Eberle argues that Opie's long career defies the easy categorizing that has historically beset many writers of the period—male and female—in part because of Opie's deliberate self-positioning in relation to her several publics, first as a radical, then as the witty but seemingly ephemeral Bluestocking, and finally as a devout Quaker abolitionist.

From these initial discussions about gaps between received notions and actual facts, the authors of the next three essays turn to self-positioning and in so doing pointedly reveal some of the complications that attend attempts to generalize about women poets of this period. Even as the first group of essays questions the operative categories and suggests that Romantic women poets cannot generally be fixed in stable positions, the next group looks at ways in which other individual women poets sought to establish just such stable positions and identities for themselves. Sarah Zimmerman explores some of the ways in which Charlotte Smith's lyrical self-presentation constituted a calculated rhetorical posture designed to enhance—even to mythologize—the highly personal manner that characterized her writing style and that as a consequence sharply defined her contemporary critical reception. Smith had determined that she was most successful with her intended audience when she adopted the rhetorical posture of turning her back on her readers and developing the figure we associate with her *Elegiac Sonnets*—the solitary speaker lost in private sorrows. This seemingly private figure, whose voice is heard also in *The Emigrants*, evoked strong sympathetic responses from Smith's contemporary readers and reviewers alike, a point that took on additional significance as Smith began to be perceived as a political and intellectual radical. In objectifying herself in her poetry, in other words, Smith established both a public presence and a public persona for herself.

Catherine B. Burroughs examines the poetry of Frances Anne Kemble against the context of her prose writings to argue for a more subtle understanding of the ideological conflicts Kemble expresses in her public configurations of herself. Burroughs observes that we currently know Kemble best as an actress whose journals describe the social and psychological difficulties she experienced in performing a sexually active woman, a performance her nonfiction writings often eschew and which she seeks to reconstruct through oratorical reading rather than acting. But Kemble positions herself precisely as that sensuous woman in her underexamined verse, where she unapologetically unleashes a sensual persona who revels in bodily joy. Thus the position as sexual being that Kemble constructs for herself in her poetry provides the romantic outlet and identity she does not or cannot locate in her representations of the female on stage, and which she seeks to regulate and even discipline through her oratorical efforts to "be good."

Finally, Harriet Kramer Linkin takes up the paradigmatic case of Mary Tighe, showing how Tighe confronts the characteristic male romantic representation of woman as fixed by presenting herself in her poetry as a romantic seeker after the sublime. Her enormously popular *Psyche* (1805) made Tighe a fixture of English literary history for much of the nineteenth century, but then her stock fell abruptly, along with that of her female contemporaries who were still known. Indeed, for most of the present century Tighe's claim to fame has lain not with the considerable merits of her own work, but rather with her early influence on Keats's work. Linkin argues not simply for the return of this important poet to the stature she held in her own time, but also, more importantly, for a concerted interrogation of the critical position occupied by "women" both within Tighe's long poem and within the Romantic aesthetic generally.

In considering both how Tighe represents herself in her poetry and how she is subsequently received, Linkin's essay provides a bridge to the third and final group of essays. These essays probe issues that have complicated the relation of various poets' reputations in their own times to what we have come to know—or have come to forget—about those reputations (and the poets and poems behind them) in the intervening years. William McCarthy, for instance, reviews the vexed history of Barbauld's reception, suggesting multiple causes for her disappearance from the mainstream of British literature. Poised, it seemed at her death, to be permanently enshrined in the canon, Barbauld instead suffered the fate of many middle-class Dissenters at the hands of Victorian literary historians like Matthew Arnold. Although her works for children remained visible throughout the century, her literary works for adults, including critical prose along with poetry, largely vanished, partly as a consequence of the image that was created of her as an icon of "Christian womanliness." Indeed, McCarthy argues, Barbauld's current reputation still does not accurately reflect the realities of either her writings as a whole or the historical and cultural context in which they were composed.

Kathleen Hickok traces the reputation of Caroline Bowles Southey, a varied and productive late Romantic poet whose works include not only early romances (e.g., *Ellen FitzArthur, A Metrical Tale,* 1820) but also collections of lyrics (e.g., *Solitary Hours,* 1826), poems of social protest (*Tales of the Factories,* 1833), and a long autobiographical poem, *The Birthday* (1836). Despite its varied and influential nature, however, in the twentieth century her work has routinely been devalued, even by feminist writers and critics, or unflatteringly compared to that of her poet laureate husband Robert Southey. Hickok argues that a proper assessment of Bowles and other female contemporaries sets this skewed record straight by reminding us of the centrality of her—and their— work to any historically balanced view of the later Romantic period.

Susan Wolfson next takes up the consequences of a different sort of misrepresentation, showing how Hemans's reputation as the ultimate in feminine decorousness has historically blunted her frequently sharp edges. Arguing that the famous 1829 *Edinburgh Review* essay in which Francis Jeffrey so designated her was intended as a gesture of support for women writers, Wolfson demonstrates that the "feminine" aspects of Hemans's work were nevertheless routinely set up as attractive alternatives (because they are appropriately "womanly") to the supposedly "masculine" (and therefore unacceptable) aspects of the work of other women, such as Hemans's friend Maria Jane Jewsbury. And yet, Wolfson shows us, even in the works in which Hemans's reviewers portrayed her emphases as pointedly "feminine," the poet is typically far more troubling, far more oppositional, in her representations of gender and gendered behavior than her contemporary critics seem to have been willing to acknowledge.

The final essay examines a poet whose place in the literary history of the later Romantic period remains problematic. Tricia Lootens's essay on Letitia Landon reconsiders the popular myth of "L.E.L."—already in place even before Landon died—as the melancholy, abandoned woman poet, a myth deliberately crafted by the poet to blur the boundaries between life and literary legend. Although Landon's poetry dramatizes a variety of creative self-pitying feminine anguish, Lootens argues, the very substantial power of that poetry cannot be contained within the sentimental paradigm of the "doomed poetess." Landon's work reminds us that no performance of femininity is ever seamless: the often disturbing strain of bleak rebelliousness in her poetry relates importantly not only to the stereotypical image of the doomed poetess (which it interrogates and finally rejects) but also to the work of women poets like Emily Brontë, Christina Rossetti, and Emily Dickinson who followed her.

When Lootens asks at the outset of her essay, "What happens if one sets out to read Letitia Elizabeth Landon as something other than a poet of ideal femininity or a primary source of the poetess tradition?" and furthermore, "Why challenge an approach that has been so successful?" she pointedly observes that "what critics rescue, we partly create; and the construction of our generation's 'Letitia Landon' is at a crucial stage." It is the larger implication of that observation—for the past, the present, and the future—that so productively haunts the personal reminiscence Feldman offers in her prologue to the essays in this collection, where she ruefully queries, "Who has time to question every truism?" If we lack time to question every truism, this volume offers a space to interrogate a near dozen such, as essays from Feldman to Lootens consider how reception continues to complicate the recovery of women poets of the British Romantic period.

Notes

1. Among their important and often groundbreaking works may be numbered especially the following: Mellor, *Romanticism and Gender;* Curran, *Poetic Form and British Romanticism;* M.B. Ross, *The Contours of Masculine Desire;* Moers, *Literary Women;* Poovey, *The Proper Lady and the Woman Writer;* Homans, *Bearing the Word.*

2. Kelley and Feldman, introduction to *Romantic Women Writers,* 3.

3. In this it differs particularly from Feldman and Kelley's *Romantic Women Writers* and Wilson and Haefner's *Re-Visioning Romanticism;* both of these address women's work in various literary genres. In its focus on a single genre, our collection is more like

the excellent volume on early women's fiction, *Fetter'd or Free?* edited by Schofield and Macheski.

4. The best indicator of the numbers of volumes published appears in Jackson's *Annals of English Verse.*

5. Jackson, *Romantic Poetry by Women.* Charriére, *Œuvres complètes,* 4:565. The comment comes in a letter to Benjamin Constant.

PROLOGUE

Endurance and Forgetting

What the Evidence Suggests

❦

Paula R. Feldman

> *Yet just as the generation of [women poets of] the 1790s had largely been forgotten
> by the 1830s, so too the generation of the 1820s and 1830s was largely disparaged
> and forgotten in the second half of the century. (Certain figures, such as Hemans,
> survived in popular taste, but were not canonical.)*
>
> *Andrew Ashfield*

I hold in my hands two books published in the Oxford Editions of Standard
Authors series from the early decades of the twentieth century. They are nearly
identical in physical appearance—octavo volumes, sturdy linen bindings, each
in a tastefully muted color, a small abstract gilt ornament on the front cover
and simple gilt lettering at the top of the backstrip naming the contents. "Ox-
ford" appears conspicuously at the base of the spine of both books; in fact, both
were produced by the official printer to Oxford University and both could be
procured in more expensive leather bindings, but in cloth each sold for four
shillings, sixpence. On my bookshelf, from a distance of just a few feet, the two
books appear indistinguishable.

One is *The Complete Poetical Works of Percy Bysshe Shelley;* the other is en-
titled *The Poetical Works of Mrs. Hemans.* According to the dust jacket on the
latter, published in 1914, there were fifty-three volumes in the Oxford Edi-
tions of Standard Authors series, which included, among others (in addition to
Shelley and Hemans), Arnold, Blake, Byron, Chaucer, Coleridge, Donne,
Dryden, Gay, Keats, Scott, Shakespeare, and Wordsworth.

Hemans, a standard author? Hemans, occupying a place with Byron, Keats,
and Shelley as late as the early twentieth century? How can this be? The Brit-
ish Library Catalogue and the National Union Catalogue confirm that my
eyes do not deceive me. Wasn't Hemans forgotten by this time or, if not forgot-
ten, merely popular? Is this 1914 volume some sort of aberration? Or might it
be documentary evidence of a status now forgotten or denied?

One index to literary stature in the late nineteenth century is a book series entitled *Moxon's Popular Poets*, originated by Edward Moxon in the 1870s and sold widely in the 1880s. It consisted of twenty-six volumes, edited with critical memoirs by William Michael Rossetti and published by Ward, Lock, and Company in London. The series, whose motto was "The power of English Literature is in its Poets," included Hemans along with Shakespeare, Byron, Wordsworth, Scott, Coleridge, Milton, Keats, and others. Like the Oxford University Press twins, on the shelf the Shelley and Hemans volumes of Moxon's Popular Poets resemble one another closely.[1] Hemans was also one of the two dozen poets included in Ward and Lock's *Moxon's Standard Poets* series, available for two shillings per volume, and she was one of fifteen authors included in *Moxon's Library Poets*, costing five shillings per volume and including Byron, Shelley, and Keats but not Wordsworth, Coleridge, or Blake. Ward and Lock had entirely reset the Hemans text by 1912. My copy of this 1912 edition was awarded to a child as a school prize in July 1920 for "excellent form work." It was not at all uncommon for collected editions of Hemans's poetry to be presented as prize books.[2]

Hemans was reprinted in America in the early twentieth century as well—her collected works were included as one of thirty-two volumes in *A Library of Poetical Literature* published in New York in 1902 by P.F. Collier and Son and by the American Home Library Company. What can we make of these books? How did Hemans's stature compare with, say, that of Shelley at the end of the nineteenth century and the beginning of the twentieth? The evidence strongly suggests that Hemans enjoyed the status of a standard poet into the twentieth century, until the advent of the modernist aesthetic, which so disparaged all of the poetry produced during the Romantic era, including that of Percy Bysshe Shelley.

Today the prevailing notion about Hemans is that she was popular but not part of the canon. How do we measure canonicity as the nineteenth century saw it? Influence? Interest? Readership? In her own time, Hemans was widely respected, widely read, and reviewed in some of the leading journals of her day, including the *Quarterly Review*, the *Gentleman's Magazine*, the *New Monthly Magazine*, *Blackwood's Edinburgh Magazine*, the *Eclectic Review*, the *Antijacobin Review*, the *Critical Review*, the *European Magazine*, and others.[3] Her poetry was admired by Byron, Shelley, Lady Morgan, Matthew Arnold, William Michael Rossetti, Marian Evans (George Eliot), Elizabeth Barrett, and countless other writers and literary critics of discerning taste. Although Walter Scott, Francis Jeffrey, and William Wordsworth expressed some reservations about her style, they each took her seriously as a major poet. Other critics, such as Andrews Norton, David M. Moir, and William Gifford, praised her highly. Many poetic tributes were written to her, even during her lifetime. Within several years of her death in 1835, three major Hemans biographies appeared. Other poets eulogized her, including Wordsworth in his "Epitaphs" (no. 12, stanza 10), Letitia Elizabeth Landon in "Stanzas on the Death of Mrs. Hemans," Maria Abdy in "Lines Written on the Death of Mrs. Hemans," and Lydia Sigourney in "Monody on Mrs. Hemans."

What is more surprising is that Hemans sold more books in her lifetime than Wordsworth, Coleridge, or Austen, not to mention Keats, Blake, or Shelley. Of her contemporaries well-known today, only Scott and Byron sold more books than she did.[4] Throughout the nineteenth century, dozens of publishers in America and in Britain reprinted her collected poems.[5] When most of her works went out of copyright in the 1870s, making them cheap to reprint, a surge of new collected editions appeared. She was a strong influence on such poets as Alfred Tennyson in Britain and Lydia Sigourney in America. Poems such as "Casabianca" ("The boy stood on the burning deck"), "The Stately Homes of England," "The Better Land," and "The Graves of a Household" were by this time standard English lyrics. "Casabianca," in fact, was so well-known that it was a common subject of school recitation well into the twentieth century. It was also, of course, a favorite subject for tasteless parody, but that is in itself a measure of how much a part of both British and American culture it had become. Her poetry was set to music, widely quoted, anthologized, illustrated by artists, and by the late 1870s, ensconced in leather bindings that sometimes make her volumes resemble Bibles. In many ways, for the Victorian reader, Hemans did author sacred texts. If she was not a canonical poet of the English Romantic period, who, other than Byron and Scott, was?

Though Hemans was unquestionably the most popular and best-selling woman poet of the Romantic era, she was, contrary to received opinion, by no means the only one with an enduring reputation. My survey of sixty poetry anthologies from 1803 to 1929 reveals that the reputations of a respectable number of women poets were not short-lived.[6] (One must bear in mind, of course, that, except for the few anthologies devoted specifically to poetry by women, no anthology published in the nineteenth century featured more than about 20 percent of its contents by women poets, either when measured by number of poems included or by number of pages. In most cases, and using either method of measurement, the representation of women poets was under 10 percent.) Anna Letitia Barbauld, like Hemans, continued to appear as a staple in poetry anthologies through the turn of the twentieth century. Also of the first generation of women poets of the Romantic era, that is, those who first established their names before 1800, Joanna Baillie; Carolina, Baroness Nairne; Amelia Opie; Lady Ann Lindsay; and Charlotte Smith could regularly be found in anthologies of the 1860s and 1870s.[7] Helen Maria Williams, Anna Seward, and Mary Robinson were still sometimes present. Of Hemans's contemporaries, Mary Howitt, Caroline Norton, and Letitia Elizabeth Landon were featured in the anthologies of the 1870s. Anthologies of the 1880s attest to the endurance of works by Joanna Baillie; Carolina, Baroness Nairne; Anna Letitia Barbauld; Mary Tighe; Susanna Blamire; Amelia Opie; Caroline Norton; Letitia Elizabeth Landon; Jane Taylor; Ann Grant; Mary Howitt; and Charlotte Smith.[8] Some anthologies, it is true, contained no women poets. But other often-reprinted anthologies from the latter half of the nineteenth century were devoted entirely to women and therefore contained, along with the usual suspects, some of their lesser known colleagues.[9] As late as 1929, Francis T. Palgrave's *Golden Treasury* still included selections from Anna Letitia Barbauld, Caroline Norton, Lady Ann Lindsay, and Carolina, Baroness Nairne. Even before the present resurgence of interest in nineteenth-century women writers, the twentieth century saw printings of books by and about Joanna Baillie; Anna Letitia Barbauld; the Countess of Blessington; Mary Howitt; Letitia Elizabeth Landon; Lady Ann Lindsay; Carolina, Baroness Nairne; Caroline Norton; Amelia Opie; Mary Robinson; Anna Seward; Charlotte Smith; Agnes Strickland; Jane Taylor; Mary Tighe; Helen Maria Williams; and others.

The establishment of a literary reputation and its maintenance require active championing and an ongoing effort to keep that reputation alive and prospering. It is easy to forget that authors such as William Shakespeare and John Donne once fell into disfavor and had to have their reputations resuscitated. Could Percy Bysshe Shelley have been a candidate for canonization had Mary Shelley not painstakingly edited his works and rehabilitated his public image through her notes to his poems? Would that reputation have continued to build without the enthusiasm of the Chartists and later the pre-Raphaelites and the Shelley Society? And, after having been eclipsed in the twentieth century, would that reputation have been revived without the efforts of such scholars as Newman Ivey White, with his monumental 1940 biography? In a similar way, in the year after Hemans's death, the critic David M. Moir edited and published her *Poetical Remains* (1836); within the next few years her siblings and children gathered her poems for an authorized seven-volume collection of her works, accompanied by a memoir by her sister, Harriet Hughes; two additional biographies were brought out by her friends Rose Lawrence and Henry F. Chorley. Hemans's reputation was boosted in America by Andrews Norton, a professor at Harvard University who, with the critic Andrew Peabody, ranked Hemans's work more highly than that of Milton and Homer and who edited her collected works in Boston.

But in the mid–twentieth century, when the time came to recuperate poets of the Romantic era, Shelley garnered champions, while no one advanced Hemans's cause. When the poetry of the Romantic era began to regain currency, why was it that Hemans and other women writers gained no following? Why were the only candidates for recanonization male? Elsewhere I have argued that there seems not to have been a deliberate conspiracy to exclude from the canon women of the Romantic era or to silence them. None was necessary. No one had been reading writers of that era for some years. For any literary reputation to be rehabilitated, there must first be curiosity about the writer's works and then an advocacy campaign on behalf of that author's writing. For Hemans and for other women poets of her age, that curiosity, that advocacy was absent. As a result, where the women were concerned, the silence already there remained unbroken.[10]

Was it sexism merely? Certainly the patriarchal power structure of the academic world and the deeply misogynist bent of New Criticism were significant factors. But they were not the only factors, as subsequent events in the 1970s demonstrate. For even then, with the advent of feminist efforts to rediscover and republish important women authors, women poets of the Romantic era remained personae non gratae. It is troubling but important to ask why, in the age when the academy was retrieving and embracing the prose of Virginia Woolf in England and Kate Chopin in America, in the age when the gothic fiction of both Mary Shelley and Ann Radcliffe were being seriously explored, even revisionist histories of literature failed to acknowledge the women poets of the Romantic era. Why, for example, did the first edition of *The Norton Anthology of Literature by Women* simply skip over them as if they had never existed?

I do not pretend to have simple answers to these questions. But several personal recollections from that era leave me uneasy. Unlike most others teaching "Romanticism" courses in the 1970s, I knew of the poetry of Letitia Elizabeth Landon and Felicia Hemans, for they had been published, along with Mary Shelley, in the literary annuals, a publishing phenomenon that I had researched. But I never considered teaching Landon and Hemans, for they seemed mere historical curiosities, unlike Mary Shelley, whose fiction I did teach. Partly, of course, I believed what was widely held—that Hemans and Landon were mere popular hacks. Who has time to question every truism? But I distinctly remember a day, sometime in the seventies, when I looked into a volume of Landon's collected works, reading a few poems at random, and confirmed for myself that they were, in fact, unimpressive. It never occurred to me to consider that such an experiment, conducted using a book of, say, William Wordsworth's collected poems (which even his staunchest supporters concede is uneven) and assuming a similar ignorance of the whole corpus of his work, would most likely yield a similar result. I had tested Letitia Landon, and she had, in my view, failed.

This judgment remained unexamined until the late 1980s, when an un-

dergraduate student in my "Romanticism" class asked why we were only read-
ing Mary Shelley and Dorothy Wordsworth, both prose writers. Weren't there
any women poets? Yes, of course, I assured her, there were some women poets,
but they were not very important or very interesting. Though I let my "answer"
stand, it caught in my throat. On returning home, I pulled Landon's poetry off
the shelf, this time giving the volume a fuller, closer reading. And I found
poems that resonated for me: "Marius at the Ruins of Carthage," "The Oak,"
"The Unknown Grave," "Home," and "Lines of Life," among others. Later, I
looked into Hemans, whose work I had noticed in annuals but never seriously
read. I was struck by the power of such poems as "Arabella Stuart," "The Wings
of a Dove," "The Coronation of Inez de Castro," "The Painter's Last Work—
A Scene," "Bring Flowers," and "The Dreamer." The next year I taught an
honors seminar entitled "Women Romantic Poets," with a motley set of bound
photocopies as our "textbook."

So began my work on *British Women Poets of the Romantic Era,* a book an
old friend assured me with a smile would by its very nature "have to be short."
But I was enthralled by the sonnets, odes, elegies, satires, songs, pastorals,
antipastorals, love lyrics, epistles, long narrative poems, ballads, riddles, and
even epics by women poets, by their diversity and innovation and range. The
book grew and grew, eventually including not only works by sixty-two poets
but also descriptions of their contexts—accounts of their lives, poetic careers,
and literary reputations. It occupied eight years of my professional life and is,
in an odd way, an expiation for my complicity, my collaboration with the col-
lective forgetting of our time.

Notes

1. The volumes sold for as little as three shillings sixpence in cloth but could be
bound in more expensive leather for as much as twelve shillings. In the 1880s the
publishing firm of Thomas Y. Crowell, of New York, also issued volumes of Shelley
and Hemans that appear identical on the shelf and were part of a matching set. (Though
I have chosen Shelley for these comparisons with Hemans, matching volumes of sev-
eral other poets of the Romantic period, including Coleridge and Wordsworth, can
also be found.)

2. I have also seen an 1854 edition published in Edinburgh by William Blackwood
and awarded at Dublin College to Arthur Foot in 1858; a New York edition dating
from the 1880s published by Thomas Y. Crowell that reads on the front free endpaper:
"Mark Baldwin, Catlin Greek Prize 1891"; the Hemans volume in the Lansdowne
Poets series published by Frederick Warne in 1897 and awarded at a school in France
in 1898; an edition published by W.P. Nimmo, Hay, and Mitchell of Edinburgh in
1902 and given as a prize for the 1903-04 school session; and another in a prize bind-
ing by the Edinburgh publisher Gall and Inglis, dating from the late 1870s. This last is
in a private collection.

3. For a detailed discussion of Hemans and the reviewers, see Albergotti, "Byron, Hemans, and the Reviewers."

4. Hemans sold at least 18,000 copies of various books in her lifetime. For a detailed inventory of the sales of her books, see my article "The Poet and the Profits." Based upon archival research, William St. Clair estimates the following book production figures for other writers: Wordsworth, 13,000; Austen, 10,000; Coleridge, 8,000; Shelley, 3,000; Keats, 1,500; Blake, 200; Scott, more than 130,000; Byron, more than 207,000 (see William St. Clair, appendix 4, untitled book manuscript).

5. New York publishers included: C.S. Francis; D. Appleton; James C. Derby; Leavitt (later Leavitt and Allen); W.I. Pooley; Mason, Baker and Pratt; World Publishing House; John Wurtele Lovell; Thomas Y. Crowell; Belford, Clarke; A.L. Burt; John B. Alden; Hurst; R. Worthington; The American News Company; The American Home Library Company; The Co-Operative Publication Society; P.F. Collier and Son; and Scribner, Welford, and Armstrong. Reprints of Hemans were published in Philadelphia by: Thomas T. Ash; John Grigg (later Grigg and Elliott); Porter and Coates; Henry F. Anners; Sorin and Ball; Lippincott, Grambo; J.B. Lippincott; E.H. Butler; Claxton, Remsen and Haffelfinger; Burlock; The Keystone Publishing Company. Boston publishers of Hemans included: Hilliard, Gray, Little and Wilkins; Phillips and Sampson; Lee and Shephard; Crosby, Nichols, Lee; and Ira Bradley. In Britain, Willaim Blackwood and his successors controlled the Hemans market for most of the century, but the following publishers also brought out editions: H.G. Bohn; E. Moxon, Son; Gall and Inglis; Frederick Warne; Ward, Lock; Ward, Lock and Bowden; Yardley and Hanscomb; Eyre and Spottiswoode; George Routledge and Sons; Griffith and Farran; Henry G. Clarke; Oxford University Press; Siegle, Hill; Maclaren; William P. Nimmo and his successor W.P. Nimmo, Hay, and Mitchell.

6. The selection of these anthologies was not done by any scientific process; I examined those available for inspection at the Library of Congress and at the Thomas Cooper Library of the University of South Carolina, and those on my own bookshelves. Thirty-three of the anthologies were published in Britain, twenty-five in the United States, and two elsewhere. Though inclusion in anthologies may not necessarily be a measure of academic respectability, it is, it seems to me, one of the best measures of the extent to which a poet's works are remembered and valued by the reading public.

7. See, for example, Wilmott, *Poets of the Nineteenth Century;* Thornbury, *Two Centuries of Song; Choice Poems and Lyrics;* Trench, *Household Book of English Poetry;* Mackay, *Gems of English Poetry;* Bryant, *New Library of Poetry and Song.*

8. See, for example, Lang, *The Blue Poetry Book;* Crowell, *Red Letter Poems;* Inglis, *Gleanings from the English Poets;* Gibbon, *The Casquet of Literature;* Beeton, *Beeton's Great Book of Poetry; Cambridge Book of Poetry and Song;* Fields and Whipple, *Family Library of British Poetry.*

9. See Bethune, *The British Female Poets* (originally published in 1848 but frequently reprinted into the 1860s); Coppée, *English and American Women Famous in Song;* Rowton, *Female Poets of Great Britain* (originally published in 1848 but reprinted in later decades).

10. See the introduction to Feldman and Kelley, *Romantic Women Writers,* 3.

PART ONE

Questioning Reception

The Gap That Is Not a Gap

British Poetry by Women, 1802–1812

Stephen C. Behrendt

Should we have been surprised? Probably not, but the fallacy propagated by much of twentieth-century literary history when it comes to British Romantic writing was neither exposed nor punctured without considerable rethinking. As we are graphically reminded by J.R. de J. Jackson's remarkable bibliography of poetry by women in the years spanning what we customarily think of as an expanded "Romantic period" (1770-1835), what orthodox masculinist literary history used to regard as a considerable hiatus in British poetry during the last three decades of the eighteenth century was no fallow field at all. Rather it was an enlarged site of literary production by increasing numbers of women writers as well as men, including deliberately "networked" writing communities like—but not restricted to—the Bluestocking circle and the Della Cruscans.[1] I say "not restricted to" because the expanded literary activity by women included far more than the privileged and the intellectual elite; noteworthy numbers of working-class women poets began to appear in this period also,[2] along with others whose physical or economic status (disease, blindness, or other permanent incapacity in the former case, and most often indigence in the latter) might be presented to the reader as particularly compelling reasons for that reader's notice and support. In short, what traditionalist literary history long viewed as a hiatus, a missing link, recent revisionary scholarship has revealed to have been a remarkably active and productive literary milieu.

I shall argue that it is equally misleading to see in English Romantic poetry a second "gap" that has resulted from the traditional literary-historical division of the canonical Romantic authors into "first generation" poets (epitomized in Blake, Wordsworth, and Coleridge) and "second generation" ones (associated with Byron, P.B. Shelley, and Keats). For the works of the active women poets of the first fifteen or so years of the nineteenth century reveal a significant thematic and aesthetic continuity that bridges the illusory gap between the two generations. Moreover, closer examination reveals that they frequently exerted a real—if historically unacknowledged—shaping influence upon the work we typically associate with the second-generation male writers. We see their influence particularly in the reformulation of gothic sensationalism, in the development of the alienated hero(ine) and the "modern" individual for whom he (she) stands, and in the establishment of the contestatory stance we associate with much of Regency poetry, with Byron's in particular. If reassessing women's poetic activity in the earlier years of the Romantic period requires us to revamp our views about what was going on in those years, so too does a reconsideration of the period stretching roughly from the Peace of Amiens (1802) to the early Regency and the publication of the first two cantos of *Childe Harold's Pilgrimage* (1812) yield a rather different view of things. Indeed, the aspect of the period is surprisingly altered when we consider the *entire* literary scene and not just the male one.

This period, of course, witnessed the publication of Wordsworth's *Poems, in Two Volumes* (1807), Scott's *Marmion* (1808), and Southey's *Curse of Kehama* (1810). But in 1804 appeared Jane and Ann Taylor's *Original Poems, for Infant Minds* (which had reached twenty-nine English editions alone by 1832). In 1806 came their *Rhymes for the Nursery* (which numbered twenty-seven editions by 1835).[3] These numbers become more meaningful when we remember that as late as 1814 some 230 copies of the original 1,000 of Wordsworth's 1807 collection remained unsold.[4] During the same period, Amelia Opie's *Poems* (1802) had by 1811 reached a sixth edition, Mary Tighe's *Psyche, with Other Poems* (1811) had seen four editions in two years, and Anne Grant's *The Highlanders, and Other Poems* (1803) was by 1810 in its third edition.[5] Even Charlotte Richardson's *Poems Written on Different Occasions* (1806), published originally by subscription, sold six hundred copies beyond the subscription and thus required a second edition in 1806.[6] When Charlotte Smith's *Beachy Head: With Other Poems* (1807) appeared in the year following her death, her extraordinarily successful *Elegiac Sonnets, and Other Poems* had already been published in one form or another many times since they first came out in 1784.[7] Soon to come on the scene were perhaps the most prolific and widely sold of all the women poets, Felicia Browne Hemans (whose *England and Spain; or, Valour and Patriotism* appeared in 1808, as had her earliest collection, *Poems*) and Letitia Elizabeth Landon (who first was noticed in 1821 with *The Fate of Adelaide, a Swiss Romantic Tale; and Other Poems*).

Some years ago A.D. Harvey suggested that although the change in the popular taste in poetry in Britain during the volatile first decade and a half of the nineteenth century might be attributed to the English culture's susceptibility at that historical moment to radical changes in cultural fashion, it might stem equally from the distinctive features of the new poetry that was evolving.[8]

Not surprisingly, Harvey offers the personality and charisma of Byron as "the most potent single element in the new poetry," arguing that Byron's life and circumstances held particularly strong appeal for a public in search of sensationalism. But when we consider the work being published by women poets during these years, we may formulate this change somewhat differently. For some of the elements in Byron's work that many readers then—and since—have regarded as uniquely and characteristically Byronic were already in place in the work of some of the poets whose publications preceded his. Many of those poets were women.

True enough, it was Byron who in 1818 voiced the watchword of Regency consciousness when he wrote in *Don Juan*, "I want a hero." But we should look at what the rest of that first stanza tells us about the context of Byron's announcement. It is not a dearth of heroes that motivates his search, after all. Quite the reverse, "every year and month sends forth a new one" already, although in a short time "the age discovers he is not the true one." But already in 1816, nearly two years earlier, Elizabeth Appleton had written in the "Proem" that opens her ambitious (but mediocre) novel, *Edgar: A National Tale* (1816) that England had "for ages immemorial" had "a tear for every misery, *a hero for every exploit,* a heart for every sentiment" (my emphasis).[9] Perhaps, we might conclude about the plethora of heroes, the fault lies not with any individual hero but rather with the public gaze, which wanders everywhere in search of the new and the novel. And it surely lies, too, with the universal scrutiny by means of which each new hero is relentlessly atomized in the press ("the gazettes") by critics (professional and otherwise) whose opinions are frequently nothing more than cloying—or worse, doggedly and offensively partisan—cant.

Where were all these new heroes coming from? One thinks of course about Southey's Madoc and Thalaba, and about Scott's indigenous heroes, and about the burgeoning interest generally in Romantic orientalism and the exotic. These tastes are reflected also in titles of *earlier* poems such as "The Prophetess of the Oracle of Seam," "The Murcian Cavalier," and "The Prophecy of Merlin," which appear in Anne Bannerman's *Tales of Superstition and Chivalry* (1802).[10] But we need to think about other popular literary forms like the novel, where the exotic could appear at somewhat less remove in figures of "outlanders" like Sydney Owenson's *Wild Irish Girl* (1806), from the novel of the same title that saw seven editions in only two years. We ought to consider too the migration of the gothic hero and the cast of characters associated with that hero—or heroine—from the theater into print materials like the novel and poetry. The French Revolution and the Terror that followed had in many respects been gothic theater in themselves, and they were not infrequently portrayed in the press and on the contemporary stage in precisely those terms. Indeed, the gothicization of historical events offered a convenient means for circumventing censorship of one sort or another and literally "staging" revolutionary politics in public, as Jeffrey Cox in particular has shown.[11] Less commonly recognized is the fact that, particularly for women, the gothic world, in which virtue and innocence—indeed "civilization" (or civility)—are continually jeopardized by brutal, often irrational patriarchal institutions and the codes of behavior they sanction, provided a compelling analogue for the actual, historical situation in which many women found themselves. Hence, at least in part, the heavy involvement of women in writing and reading gothic fiction, in which genre their work was the most prominent and frequently the most lucrative.[12] At the same time that women were expanding and diversifying the range of gothic character and situation types, new stage acting styles were developing as a consequence of the physical demands imposed by the much larger theaters, such as Covent Garden and Drury Lane, which required the proportionally broader stylization, grander gestures, and more dynamic vocalization epitomized on the Regency stage in the athletic, passionate acting of Edmund Kean and, briefly, Eliza O'Neill. These developments in theater practice could not but exert a powerful formative influence on the way character and action were conceived and represented in all the arts. That we encounter them in widely popular poetry by women and men alike therefore should not surprise us.

Given the insufficiently appreciated pervasiveness of the sensationalism that formed so much of the attraction of the gothic, we ought to look with fresh eyes at the collection of poems called *Hours of Solitude* that Charlotte Dacre, author of the widely read gothic novel *Zofloya; or, The Moor* (1806), published early in 1806, the year before Byron published his own tellingly titled *Hours of Idleness*.[13] Moreover, we should consider the implications in the present context of Donald Reiman's accurate assessment of the poems in this collection as "overly dramatic and sensationalized in their expression of emotion" and distinctly free of the learned classical tradition of poetry.[14] This absence of classical veneer may be one reason why the reviewer for the *British Critic* dismissed Dacre's volume scornfully, lumping it with the work of "*Della Crusca, Anna Maria,* or any of that swarm of insect poets, which the Baviad put to flight."[15] Despite the reviewer's disdain (which, though atypical in its severity, echoed the unenthusiastic critical response generally), volumes like Dacre's indicate how the poetry written by women contributed to the shift in literary production—and in popular consciousness—that takes shape in what has typically been portrayed as a transitional gap in the literary output of the male authors delineated by the terms "first generation" and "second generation" Romantics and roughly bracketed by the Peace of Amiens and Waterloo.

As Reiman observed already in 1978, the noticeable parallels in subjects, language, and tone between Dacre's verse and the early work of Byron and Shelley suggests that regardless of their education or social status, male and female poets alike were beginning to respond to the presence of a new and expanding readership that was "not steeped in the classics."[16] This readership not only included very substantial numbers of women; it had been shaped in significant measure by the writing of women, who had begun to apply to British literature generally the democratization of the arts that had been signaled in the 1790s by the work of poets like William Wordsworth and Elizabeth Moody, Jacobin novelists like William Godwin and Mary Hays, and gothic novelists like Ann Radcliffe and Matthew Lewis.[17] In the work of women writers in the first decade and a half of the nineteenth century, we begin to see clearly the conflation of the learned, academic tradition of "high" art with the comparatively unschooled, populist tradition of popular culture. The ground that the "second generation" male poets were to till with increasing success in the years after 1810, then, was in fact already being cultivated in the previous decade by women like Dacre and Amelia Opie, whose works have customarily been dismissed in the last century and a half as unimportant specifically because they fail to conform to the paradigms furnished by the work of the canonical male poets—and the learned tradition that that work represents—who preceded, accompanied, and followed them.

This is not to say that male and female poets were proceeding along precisely the same paths, for as Isobel Armstrong reminds us, the interests of the women poets "do not follow the same intertextual relations as those of the male poets, nor does the trajectory of their intellectual debates parallel that of male writers." Marlon Ross ultimately agrees (while ostensibly disagreeing) when he claims that "the female poets who publish so successfully in the early nineteenth century necessarily wrestle with similar conflicts as their male counterparts, but their gender is so crucial a factor in their cultural and literary experience that it alters the effect of shared social conditions and turns these writers into a distinct class, with its own ideological patterning, rather than merely a species of the overarching class of romantic poets." More recently, Anne K. Mellor has argued eloquently that especially when it came to criticism—aesthetic criticism in particular—the principal women critics insisted that literature's cultural role is "to educate even more than to delight, to educate by teaching readers to take delight in the triumph of moral benevolence, sexual self-control, and rational intelligence."[18] This formulation has the benefit of differentiating among women's literary, critical, intellectual, and social (or familial) experiences and, further, of refusing to impose upon them yet another gendered stereotype in the guise of claiming to liberate them from the tyranny of stereotyping. Certainly there is an element of historical accuracy about the poetic hierarchy Ross describes, which positions "the virile male poet at the top, the effeminate male and proper female poet in the middle, and the bluestocking at the bottom," nor is it unreasonable to argue, as Ross does, that the widespread public awareness of this hierarchy served at once to keep women "hemmed in by masculine demands" and to create a new space in poetry "in which they can experiment, excel, and express the uniqueness of their own desire."[19] Nevertheless, the broader landscape of Romantic poetry inscribed by the presence and activity of men and women alike does not break down quite so neatly along gender lines, nor does it entirely support any critical insistence on an inevitable and essentialist separation and segregation of female poets from male (or male from female, to put it somewhat differently). To insist on such an uncompromising split is to at once misrepresent and oversimplify a complicated historical, social, political, economic, intellectual, and literary setting.

For there was in fact greater coherence and parallelism among members of the Romantic writing community over its entire extent than is perhaps at first apparent from a cursory glance at the works of the principal luminaries, male and female. Much of the poetry written by men and women alike during the 1790s, for instance, was especially preoccupied with themes whose common thread was essentially sociopolitical in nature: poems about impoverishment, societal displacement, the effects on families and communities of warmaking. Running parallel to these themes, and often informing them, was a mixture of compassion and outrage that was activated by a humanitarian impulse and by what the eighteenth century had come to think of as "sympathy," by which mental *and emotional* imaginative response individuals were understood to be able to relate to the joys and the sufferings of others by quite literally experiencing those feelings themselves. This is how David Hume understood the concept of "sympathy" in his *Treatise on Human Nature* (1739) and how it was articulated further by followers like Adam Smith in his *Theory of Moral Sentiments* (1759) and by countless poets (and others) throughout the eighteenth century who delineated the phenomenon that would be called sensibility. Thus the preoccupation in this poetry with community reflects the growing public realization that it was in fact community that was being placed most in jeopardy by the inhumanity whose most telling symptom was the enormously costly (in economic and especially human terms) war being waged against fundamental republican principles epitomized in the French Revolution. This poetry often places the blame squarely upon the reactionary political and economic establishment whose interests were seen to be best served by the extirpation of all such republican initiatives.

The oppositional uses of the rhetoric of sentiment, which continue virtually unabated throughout most of the Regency, are especially evident in antiwar poetry of the period by women and men alike, much of it reflecting the insubordinate posture characteristic of popular Radicalism.[20] Betty T. Bennett and, more recently, Michael Scrivener have collected examples that reveal the connections among several themes in the poetry of social protest in the 1790s and after: the catastrophic effects upon the family (and by implication the nation) of war, the growth of unhealthy callousness to the suffering of others that the conditions of war produce, and the breakdown of human (and humane) community that is the inevitable consequence of these activities.[21] The war poetry in particular traces back to war-making the economic impoverishment of individuals and families when (as is most typical) the male breadwinner is killed or incapacitated in battle. But there is moral impoverishment, too, in the slaughter on both sides and in the jingoistic nationalism that attempts to justify such barbarism according to questionable political criteria. Radical writing's particular contribution to this strain of oppositional discourse is the direct link it forges between the exploitation and destruction of "the people" generally and the selfishness of the opportunistic elite who profit from that dehumanizing activity.

The war dragged on, of course, and in 1802 the doomed Peace of Amiens was celebrated with joy and with plain relief, at least by some. That the peace was at best a mixed blessing for many is apparent from Amelia Opie's "Lines written at Norwich on the First News of Peace" (1802). The beneficial effects for the overstressed poor are immediate:

> Of those poor babes that on your knees
> Imploring food have vainly hung,
> You'll soon each craving want appease,
> . . . .
> For Plenty comes with Peace along.[22]

For the general populace whose families have been disrupted, the effect is no less dramatic:

> And you, fond parents, faithful wives,
> Who've long for sons and husbands feared,
> Peace now shall save their precious lives;
> They come by danger more endeared. [83]

But the joy is not universal, for amid Opie's joyous scene is one "poor mourner" who grieves because "'Peace comes for me too late, ... / For my brave boy in Egypt died'" (84). Most telling, however, is the remarkable first line Opie assigns this woman: "'Talk not of Peace, ... the sound I hate'" (84). Her bitter and inconsolable grief anticipates both the subject matter and the tone that characterizes so much of the poetry of the two decades that followed, as we see for instance in later works like Mary Leadbeater's 1808 "The Widow" and Dorothea Primrose Campbell's 1816 "The Distracted Mother" (a comparable lament for a son killed in battle) or "The Soldier's Widow, at the Grave of Her Only Child" (which records a double loss).[23]

When hostilities inevitably resumed, the national consciousness altered, perhaps because that resumption of bloodshed made manifest what had previously been latent though not entirely unperceived: that the world had entered what today we think of as a state of profound alienation, personal, social, societal, and spiritual. This alienation manifested itself in the political arena, paradoxically, in the jingoistic fervor of anti-Gallic writing that accompanied the renewed alarmist fears of an invasion, especially in 1803. In the process, the traditional English values around which countless writers invited their readers to rally were metamorphosed—without particular subtlety—from the familiar ones of liberty, individual prerogative, community, and sympathy to more immediately antisocial ones of self-justification, intolerance, militarism, and neoimperialist domination.[24] In such an altered world, isolation—physical and psychological—becomes the norm, community is destroyed, and gestures of outreach are spurned. It is a death-in-life state. The flight of the "visionary gleam," of "the glory and the dream," that Wordsworth bemoans in the Intimations ode and Coleridge laments in his Dejection ode marks the absence of this animating, restorative human community, both externally, in society generally, and internally, within the individual consciousness. In its wake come only emotional dysfunction, physical debility, and finally death. Death is, of course, the recurrent theme of a great deal of the poetry written by women like Robinson and Smith, both of whom capitalized on the theme's natural tendency toward hyperbole to dramatize the physical and psychological states of their narrators and protagonists even as they plumbed the depths of the death wish to intensify the affectional appeal of their poems by engaging in apparent authorial self-dramatization. A close examination of Romantic poetry—at least when we include the women in the picture—in fact bears out the accuracy of Stuart Curran's apt remark that, contrary to what we might ordinarily expect, "the unhappy ending is the norm of women writers of the Romantic period."[25]

Alienation and exclusion, the prototypical hallmarks of community disrupted, typify the consciousness that governs much of the poetry written by women during this period.[26] We see it even at the level of titles, where over and over poems are called "The Exile" (Robinson has one in her *Lyrical Tales* [1800], for instance, and Dacre has one in her *Hours of Solitude*). Moreover, social outcasts are everywhere, from vagrants to (more commonly) widows and otherwise abandoned women (most often mothers with languishing, dying children whose passing drives the mothers to despair, madness, and death). There are also slaves (with whose powerlessness women of course found much to sympathize) and others whose racial, religious, ethnic, economic, or even mental status casts them as outsiders for whom the English social and political establishment provides neither haven nor hope. In the latter category we can number countless American Indians, Hindus and other Asian subcontinent natives (like Opie's "Hindustani Girl"), blacks (like Dacre's "The Poor Negro Sadi" or Leadbeater's "The Negro," addressed to Edmund Burke), orphans (Opie's "Fatherless Fanny" and "The Orphan Boy's Tale" or E. Horwood's "The Twins" or Charlotte Caroline Richardson's "The Orphan"), and so forth, as well as the central figure of Amelia Bristow's remarkable 1810 poem, *The Maniac*.[27]

When male poets like Byron turned to themes of exile and exclusion, whether they externalized the trauma of exclusion and alienation in the adventures of passionate characters like the Giaour or internalized the torments of self-exile in the tortured consciousnesses of the protagonists of dramatic poems like *Manfred* or, later, *Cain*—and of course *Childe Harold's Pilgrimage*—they were merely carrying to their next logical stage the sort of preoccupations that are evident already in poems by women from the first decade of the nineteenth century. Curran has remarked that, especially when we factor in the prose fiction written by women, it may at first appear that "women are abused and expire in such ingenious ways and with such inexhaustible plentitude" that all this emphasis on female suffering is "simply macabre." But as he observes further, this theme "takes on other dimensions" within the historical context of the Romantic period.[28] For however productive they might have been in verse or in prose (fiction or otherwise), women writers ultimately carried little immediate public authority, especially when they presumed to address "serious" intellectual, political, social, economic, moral, or spiritual issues. It is not unreasonable, therefore, to regard the countless deaths in these poems as in some respects displaced images of their authors' own suffocation.

Silenced to a considerable extent by both the conventions of formal print discourse and the intellectual and social expectations that undergirded those conventions, women authors often tended out of plain necessity to turn to those forms of discourse that *were* allowed them. Principally, this meant children's verse like that produced in great quantity by the prolific Jane and Ann Taylor, for instance, or like Sarah Richardson's *Original Poems, Intended for the Use of Young Persons* (1808), or Elizabeth Turner's *The Daisy* (1807), which had reached a sixth edition by 1816 and a tenth by 1823. It also included devotional verse like Alice Flowerdew's *Poems, on Moral and Religious Subjects* (1803), Mary Sewell's *Poems* (1803), and Letitia Parsons's *Verses, Hymns and Poems, on Various Subjects* (1806). Frequently it combined these two in poetry that yoked moral/spiritual authority to social control, as in Mary Stockdale's *Family Book; or, Children's Journal* (1798) or Adelaide O'Keeffe's *Original Poems; Calculated to Improve the Mind of Youth, and Allure It to Virtue* (1808), or as in Jane West's long didactic effort, *The Mother*.[29]

Facts—and numbers—like these thus complicate what we may conclude about the silencing of the voices of Romantic women poets in their own time, even leaving aside their misrepresentation, marginalization, and even erasure in the following decades. This is why the hostility to Anna Letitia Barbauld's radical *Eighteen Hundred and Eleven* (1812) is, as we shall see, so instructive. There was no question about women's public acceptability as poets when they confined themselves, as Felicia Hemans did in her first major volume, to "domestic affections," which included not only household affairs and family life but also the education (moral and otherwise) of children: thus the astonishing success of efforts like those of Ann and Jane Taylor in this latter area, to which I alluded earlier. Another interesting case is that of Jane West, whose *The Mother: A Poem, in Five Books* (1809) saw a second edition the following year.[30] West, who had published her *Miscellaneous Poetry* already in 1786,[31] was staunchly Tory and Church of England in principle and in practice, as might be inferred from the pseudonym of "Prudentia Homespun" that she occasionally adopted. Her long five-part poem on mothers, motherhood, and mothering, a work overlaid with broad didacticism, won approving comments even when her poetic skills themselves were candidly deprecated in the press. The *British Critic* is typical in this respect: "Strong sense, maternal, patriotic, and, above all, Christian feeling, without cant, without a tincture of fanaticism, are the characteristics of this poem; which, though it may be slighted by the fastidiousness of false criticism, will be ever the delight of those who are formed or trained to feel as man should feel, whether as relative to his fellow men, or as a candidate for that life where painful feelings will have ceased." This is a poem grounded in sensibility and the Humean complex of sympathy associated with it, in other words, and addressed *to* the sensibilities of its readers, as the end of the sentence indicates, a poem that draws a clear line from the domestic circle to the storing up of virtue that points to an eternal reward. In this respect, contemporary criticism of the poem makes clear, this is very much the sort of poem a woman "should" write and is expected to write. Indeed, in the concluding paragraph the *British Critic*'s reviewer pointedly reminds us of the female author's exclusion from classical education and hence from the thorough and accurate vocabulary of classical reference and allusion that the critic obviously would expect of her male contemporaries: "If the stern critic should note a few classical names or unusual words not quite correctly given, (and they are *very* few) we should say, without hesitation, that the mind which, unassisted by classical refinement, could produce such a poem as this, must deserve only the higher admiration for its own internal strength; and that all the blemishes which even malice could find in it might be removed by the labour of less than half an hour."[32] Left unspoken is the painfully obvious implied answer to the question of who then could remove all these blemishes from a poem of nearly 250 pages in only half an hour: presumably it is the male poet/critic/reader.

West's poem attracted considerable attention from the periodical press: it was reviewed at length in the *British Critic*, the *Critical Review*, the *Eclectic*

Review, the *Gentleman's Magazine,* the *Universal Magazine,* and the *Literary Panorama,* in addition to receiving brief notices elsewhere. It also attracted the notice of the reactionary Tory *Satirist,* whose March 1809 number (one of the earliest responses in the periodical press, always a point of pride with the *Satirist*) anticipates the response a modern reader is likely to have to a didact like West. Citing her two conduct books, *Letters to a Young Man* (1810) and *Letters to a Young Lady* (1806) and her earlier moral exemplum, *The Advantages of Education* (1793), the *Satirist* observes with the pointed ambiguity of its best ironic prose:

> They exhibit in a very respectable manner, much propriety of thought, real tenderness of sentiment, rigid purity of morals, devout and sound principles of religion; and each of those pleasing treatises are calculated, in a limited degree, to promote glory to God and good will towards men. We hesitate not to place her—to use a familiar Cambridge term—*in the first bracket,* among the Hamiltons, the Mores, the Trimmers, &c. &c. &c. the most illustrious female *wranglers* of our day. We speak the conviction of soberness and sincerity; and the lady may rest assured, that neither have we lightly formed our opinion of her merit as a sensible prose writer, nor shall we in the sportive spirit of wantonness, attempt to ridicule her humbler effort, now before us, to improve her partial readers, by a didactic poem in tolerable blank verse.[33]

In an interesting deviation from the *Satirist's* customarily savage negative reviews,[34] the author here calls attention to the review's uncharacteristic forbearance, which serves to make its critical ambivalence the more slippery for the reader. Indeed, the criticism seldom warms beyond the concluding observation that since "an undescribable monotony reigns throughout the treatise," the reviewer would much prefer that West dispense with the uncomfortable imposition of poetic form and simply recast the work in the form of "an essay, 'On the Maternal Character, and its Important Duties.'"[35]

The singling out of Jane West's apparent lack of intimacy with the classical system helps us better to appreciate the observations of the *British Review* in 1820 on Felicia Hemans's *The Restoration of the Works of Art to Italy* and *The Sceptic.* Anticipating by nearly two centuries (though for different reasons) some of the gender-specific assumptions I have already discussed, the reviewer observes that "it is not to disparage either sex to say that as they usually live in different worlds, so they must naturally write in different styles." Hence this critic's apparent delight at finding in Hemans's poems the unexpected: the "elaborate finish" that "does not usually fall to the lot of female writers," whose minds are "not usually favourable to that deep-toned emotion which constitutes the very essence of the higher kinds of poetry," and which women writers are unable to achieve precisely because they *feel* their experiences too acutely and are therefore unable to achieve the detachment necessary for the creation of "really first-rate versification."[36] That the reviewer goes on to praise Hemans's poems with real warmth is therefore all the more remarkable.

But that praise, and the manner in which it is couched and extended, nevertheless reinforces a gendered stereotype. Moreover, it denigrates that poetry whose objective and aesthetic differ from those that characterize the work of the dominant poetic patriarchy represented in the educated, leisure-class male poet, whether he be an enduring talent like Scott or Byron or a lesser one like the earnest Thomas Campbell (*The Pleasures of Hope*, 1799), the engaging and popular country person Robert Bloomfield (*The Farmer's Boy*, 1800), or the astonishingly ambitious Charles Hoyle (*Exodus; An Epic Poem*, 1807). Already by the middle of the first decade of the nineteenth century, we are beginning to see more clearly in the emerging bourgeois culture the division of expectations about the *new* male and female writers. Marlon Ross observes, for instance, that the female writer was viewed as "a sort of freelancing handmaiden who has indirectly a socio-moral obligation to the state because she writes to civilize, moderate, and chasten an increasingly factionalized and fractious citizenry," unlike the male poet who aims to "establish the self-fathering strength of his own voice over culture." Or as Anne Mellor has succinctly said of the woman artist as critic: "[T]he critic is a mother, educating her children."[37] Though the formulation as Ross states it is not entirely accurate when we factor in male poets of the period who were *not* preoccupied with exercises in the sublime or the anticommunitarian as well as women poets whose agendas were not what Ross describes, it nevertheless characterizes at least some of the gendered assumptions visible in much of the published criticism of the period. For in the opinion of the *Quarterly Review* in 1820, for instance, what is still regarded as the appropriate territory for women writers is obvious:

[D]elicacy of feeling has long been, *and long may it be,* the fair and valued boast of our countrywomen; but we have had too frequent reason of late to lament, both in female writers and readers, the display of qualities very opposite in their nature. Their tastes, at least, have not escaped the infection of that pretended liberality, but real licentiousness of thought, the plague and the fearful sign of the times. Under its influence they lose their relish for what is *simple and sober, gentle or dignified,* and require the stimulus of excessive or bitter passion, of sedition, of audacious profaneness.[38]

These remarks reveal how the *Quarterly's* familiar conservatism melded social politics with gender politics and pointed toward the sort of smug security with which Frederic Rowton could some thirty years later tick off "the delicacy, the softness, the pureness, the quick observant vision, the ready sensibility, the devotedness, the faith of woman's nature" as those qualities that in his opinion find "their ultra representative" in Hemans, whose works he characterizes as "a perfect embodiment of woman's soul."[39] But already by 1820 Hemans was becoming well-attuned to her audiences and their tastes and predispositions; however we may regret choices she subsequently made about theme, subject matter, style, and—apparently—ideology, simply to lament these choices as either conscious capitulation or unconscious "falling off" does an injustice to a poet whose very considerable intellectual and artistic skills were virtually from the start appreciated and praised—however surprised or grudging that acknowledgment may have been—by the critical (and therefore the high-cultural) establishment. At the same time, Rowton's list of "feminine" characteristics instructively prepares us for the compelling arguments of modern scholars such as Margaret Homans, Susan Wolfson, and Anne Mellor, who have shown us how these same pigments were employed by antagonistic reviewers to paint Keats, for instance, as a "feminine" and therefore an inferior poet.[40]

But the *Quarterly*'s remarks also raise the question about what is meant by the unholy alliance signaled by what its reviewer calls passion, sedition, and profaneness, a point that returns us to the general literary milieu we have been considering. This particular combination, which unsuccessfully attempts to hide the political between two terms more readily applicable to aesthetics or "taste," signals the resistance of Regency thinking to women's attempts to function as players on the public stage of social, political, and economic discourse. It helps, too, to explain how and why the strong negative response to Barbauld's *Eighteen Hundred and Eleven* should surprise us no more than it should have surprised the poet, who was sufficiently chastened that she refrained from further publication of her poetry. Not only was the press virtually unanimous in finding that poem "subversive of national morale," as William McCarthy and Elizabeth Kraft succinctly put it, but "its excellence as poetry, when admitted, was treated as an aggravation of the crime."[41]

McCarthy and Kraft's metaphorical allusion to the criminality of Barbauld's effort is of course both shrewdly insightful and historically accurate. This politically oppositional poem represented just the sort of "sedition" against which the *Quarterly* and other like-minded Tory organs railed. Its proleptic vision of an England whose greatness lay in the past and whose status was therefore at once that of sacred relic and of secular ruin could not hope to find favor with a public increasingly fed with nationalistic jingoism as a seemingly endless war dragged on ever longer. Or could it? After all, that poem which had been so lavishly praised for its sentiments (even when the praise for its *poetry* was lukewarm at best), Jane West's *The Mother*, had two years earlier issued no less dire warnings about England's fate:

> O menac'd Isle!
> Last refuge of integrity and worth,
> To which religion, liberty, and peace

Have flown as to an ark, riding secure
Amid a world of waters; must thou too
Sink in the deluge that hath overwhelm'd
Order and law, and from their base pluck'd up
Empires and states, the elder born of time.
. . . .
   And, native Albion, must thou too become
Thus lost, thus nameless, in the vortex vast
Of universal rule ingulph'd, while all
Thy monuments of glory pass away
Like a poor maniac's dreams; thy sons' renown,
The virtue of thy daughters? The sad Muse
Bends on her harp, and silent bodes a change
Vast, dolorous, fatal to her lofty song.
[book 1; p. 37]

Couched within a long poem celebrating mothers, motherhood, and mother-ing, it appears, such forebodings are acceptable, even if momentarily trouble-some; no contemporary reviewer even hinted that such sentiments, when they are expressed in this context by a safely Tory writer, constitute sedition. As usual, context reveals much.

That being so, we should consider that remarkable and inexplicably ne-glected poem by Barbauld's niece Lucy Aikin, *Epistles on Women*, in which the author traces the history of the world from its very beginnings and credits women with all the significant advances in the human condition that have transpired up through the middle of the eighteenth century (at which point the poem modestly concludes).[42] This ambitious discursive poem—which looks back to Mary Hays's *Female Biography* (1802) and Mary Matilda Betham's *Biographical Dictionary of Celebrated Women of Every Age and Country* (1808) and ahead to Hemans's *Records of Woman* (1828)—is a frankly contestatory poem that explicitly engages the entire history of humankind and radically realigns along gender lines both its accomplishments and its disasters. More than has been appreciated, poems like *Epistles on Women* helped lay the ground-work for more familiar contestatory poems like *Childe Harold's Pilgrimage* and *Don Juan*, whose irreverence is only a dramatically different version of Aikin's own subversion of cultural assumptions and expectations about the nature of heroism.

Given the context of the times, it is interesting to observe the *Critical Review*'s generally positive review in 1811 of Aikin's poem, a review that be-gins by explicitly foregrounding the issue of gender: "[W]e are happy to see a woman asserting the proper dignity of her sex, and evincing by her own ex-ample that female pretensions are well founded. It is quite time that the doc-trine of the natural inequality of the sexes should be exploded: indeed we imagine that most *sensible* people are of this opinion, especially when they recollect, among many others, the names of [Anna] Seward, [Joanna] Bailey [*sic*], [Maria] Edgworth [*sic*], Barbauld, Opie, and [Lady Anne] Hamilton."[43] The reference to "most sensible people," and therefore to that Humean sympathy that operates outside the bounds of strictly rational, intellectual response, as well as to the more modern connotation of logical and rational, cannot have been merely coincidental, nor can its ultimate ambiguity (wavering uneasily between sensibility and "sense," to take up Austen's dualism) be accidental either. Lady Anne Hamilton's inclusion in this list is interesting, incidentally, since her presence presumably reflects the wide visibility of her 1807 poem, *The Epics of the Ton; or, The Glories of the Great World*, which appears to have exerted significant influence on Byron's *English Bards and Scotch Reviewers* of 1809.[44] Here, incidentally, is another instance in which, as we have seen earlier in considering Dacre's *Hours of Solitude*, the ostensible idiosyncrasy of Byron's work looks somewhat different when measured against the literary context of his times, which reveals greater consistency and continuity among a broad range of authors than has been apparent from the limited (and limiting) perspective of most twentieth-century views of British Romantic writing.

The contemporary reviews of Aikin's *Epistles* are generally warm and surprisingly complimentary, even when (in a familiar subterfuge of the reviewing trade generally) they praise the poem and then reprint passages that the reviewer finds inelegant, inartistic, or otherwise objectionable. The *Poetical Register*'s brief notice gives a third of its space to unreserved praise, exclaiming, for example, "We have received great pleasure from the perusal of these epistles. They are, in no common degree, pointed, polished, and energetic. The versification, too, is of the best kind. It is flowing, without being insipid; and varied, without being harsh."[45] The *Monthly Review* had already demonstrated its sensitivity to contemporary women's issues and particularly to women's intellectual pursuits in warmly praising Elizabeth Smith's *Fragments in Prose and Verse* (1808), a posthumous volume by an unusually well-educated and articulate woman who had died at an early age. It was similarly supportive of the cause that lay behind Aikin's project:

We are anxious to assist the present fair writer in . . . convincing man how 'impossible it is for him to degrade his companion without degrading himself; or to elevate her without receiving a proportional accession of dignity and happiness;'—and moreover, we know not one feminine attraction or accomplishment which may not co-exist with the greatest cultivation of the female mind; nor one duty, peculiarly belonging to the softer sex, of which the fulfilment will not be farther secured by such cultivation. If we remove but the fear of neglecting the Graces by a closer worship of the Muses, we shall have removed the chief impediment in the way of an enlarged and more liberal education of our females.[46]

Despite its ostensible egalitarianism, though, the *Monthly Review*'s comments continue to privilege male status by regarding women's accomplishments as ultimately a credit to the men who permit, tolerate, and even encourage those accomplishments. This way of arguing the case, which Mary Wollstonecraft and others had already attempted and to which John Stuart Mill would revert in *The Subjection of Women* (1869), exemplifies the practical rhetorical device of making an objectionable proposition palatable by portraying its consequences as flattering to those whose consent is sought. Women's advances are here characterized in terms of how well they might serve and reflect upon the interests of men. The inherently reactionary appeal to chivalry interwoven in such an argument is revealed by the customary references to women as "fair" and "soft," and by the explicit concern that women *not* neglect the Graces.

To call poems like *Eighteen Hundred and Eleven* and *Epistles on Women* oppositional or contestatory to the prevailing British cultural mind-set of their times is of course to state the obvious. But to see that by the early period of the Regency the voices of their authors were being acknowledged—however partially or grudgingly—in the reviewing press is to recognize how far the women poets had come in a relatively short period. Moreover, that the charges of moral or political incorrectness directed against them by their critics resemble in so many ways the charges leveled against their male contemporaries by like-minded critics tells us that these women authors had in fact achieved both the presence and at least a measure of the viability and seeming parity to which their predecessors had seldom been party.

Still, as I indicated earlier, we shall need for some time to come to examine more closely the expansion during this period of the range of subject matter and poetic forms with which the women poets worked and its relationship to the changes in the trends of male poetic production that become most dramatically evident with Byron's advent and to a lesser extent Percy Shelley's. Despite its epistolary framework, for instance, *Epistles on Women* is in many respects epic in nature, owing in part to its historical sweep and in part to the elevated nature of its subject matter. A much inferior poem, *The Mother* also aspires to the broad sweep of the epic, as does Tighe's much finer *Psyche* and an odd, long "Poem in Six Books" by Eleanor Porden called *The Veils; or the Triumph of Constancy* (1815), which uneasily mixes narrative, science, and Rosicrucian doctrine.[47]

At the same time, the poetry written and published by women during this period traces the growing presence of that ominous modern phenomenon of alienation, which appears in the many poems whose protagonists, subjects, or speakers are socially, economically, religiously, racially, or otherwise rendered as ostracized Others. Excluded from the dominant social, political, and economic community—and even, often, from its principal subgroups—these figures embody the increasing emotional and psychological displacement, the sense not only of exclusion but of a fundamental *inability to belong*, that characterizes so much of the modern condition. We can trace in the poetry written by women in the first decade or so of the nineteenth century much of the escapist impulse that becomes associated with English writing generally during the Regency and afterward. Here it is instructive to note the *Critical Review*'s dismissive tally of seemingly escapist subjects—subjects that repudiate the quotidian world of women and men alike (but of women especially)—that predominate in the admittedly slight volume, *The Test of Virtue and Other Poems*, published after the death of its author, P. Barrell. According to the reviewer, "these poems consist of little tales and simple ballads, of forsaken maidens and perjured knights, with red mantles and white plumes of feathers riding on prancing steeds."[48] That the poems are of poor quality is without question; that they share with increasing numbers of poems by contemporaries of both sexes an increasing interest in places remote in both time and place is, on the other hand, noteworthy. Like many citizens at this crucial moment in English cultural history who were coming to the inescapable conclusion that they no longer "belonged" in their own time and place, nor in the lives they were leading in those quotidian locales, many of the women poets entered enthusiastically into the cult of the exotic, the foreign, the "oriental" whose prominence may be suggested by Thomas Phillips's famous portrait of Byron in his Albanian costume[49] but whose greatest flowering is almost certainly embodied in the remarkable quantity of work Letitia Landon would subsequently devote to this subject.

My point must by now be abundantly clear. Romantic writing, whether poetry specifically or written discourse generally, emerged from and participated in a *dialogue* in print. That dialogue transpired among writers who were engaged in complicated intellectual and imaginative transactions with audiences who were themselves often surprisingly well read and whose knowledge of the works and lives of the members of the contemporary writing community was frequently very extensive indeed. Not only in the *works* of female and male poets but also in the public *reception* of those works, the period covering roughly the first twelve to fifteen years of the nineteenth century reveals a surprising continuity in the nature, substance, and direction of British poetic production. When we finally read the poetry of this period with historically and culturally attuned eyes, we will better appreciate that the old line of demarcation inscribed by traditional literary history between "first generation" and "second generation" Romantics is—and always has been—both misleading and inhospitable to the actual facts of the Romantic literary scene. Recognizing how clearly the poetry written by women in this period both foreshadows and shapes the poetry later published by their traditionally more famous male contemporaries and successors helps us to see what was long concealed: the centrality of women's contributions to the development of both the substance and the increasingly modern intellectual and psychological orientation of later Romantic poetry.

Notes

1. Jackson, *Romantic Poetry by Women.*
2. See Landry, *The Muses of Resistance.*
3. Jackson, *Romantic Poetry by Women,* 324-32.
4. Jones, *Wordsworth's Poems of 1807,* xxi.
5. Jackson, *Romantic Poetry by Women,* 247, 349, 137-38, 365. Tighe's poem first appeared in 1805 as *Psyche; or, the Legend of Love.* The first edition of *Psyche, with Other Poems* was published by Longman et al. in 1811.
6. Jackson, *Romantic Poetry by Women,* 268-69.
7. Smith, *Beachy Head.* For a partial history of the publication of *Elegiac Sonnets,* see Jackson, *Romantic Poetry by Women,* 299-302.
8. Harvey, *English Poetry,* 132-36.
9. Appleton, *Edgar.* In calling this novel ambitious, I simply echo the author, who set out, she tells us, to write something "worthy of a higher rank in literature than that of a *Novel,*" something lying "between poetry and prose." She even coined a term for such a work, *epicast,* a term derived from Greek and Latin roots and meaning "chaste narration" (1:vi-vii).
10. Bannerman, *Tales of Superstition and Chivalry.*
11. Cox, *Seven Gothic Dramas.* Cox's introductory essay offers a particularly insightful reading of the ways in which historical events are gradually mythologized as their literary and theatrical presentations proceed in time from the moment at which they actually transpired.
12. There was, of course, substantial profit to be made in this highly popular genre, and numbers of women, many of them with little other recourse available to them, managed to support themselves and their dependents by catering to the market for the gothic.
13. Although the title page of Dacre's *Hours of Solitude* is dated 1805, Donald Reiman indicates that actual publication took place in early 1806. See Reiman's introduction to the 1978 facsimile edition (v).
14. Reiman, introduction to Dacre, *Hours of Solitude,* xi.
15. *British Critic* (April 1806): 428-29.
16. Reiman, introduction to Dacre, *Hours of Solitude,* xi.
17. In a quite different context Anne Mellor likewise stresses the democratizing of poetic language in women's poetry that was one consequence of women's exclusion from the classical education to which men (at least the privileged ones) routinely had access. See Mellor, "The Female Poet and the Poetess."
18. I. Armstrong, "The Gush of the Feminine," 16. M.B. Ross, *The Contours of*

Masculine Desire, 6. Mellor, "A Criticism of Their Own," 45. See also Mellor's comments in her *Romanticism and Gender.*

19. M.B. Ross, *The Contours of Masculine Desire,* 189-90.

20. I have discussed women's role in this radical response in Behrendt, "British Women Poets."

21. Bennett, *British War Poetry;* Scrivener, *Poetry and Reform.*

22. Opie, *Poems by Mrs. Opie,* 83.

23. Leadbeater, *Poems;* D.P. Campbell, *Poems.*

24. A good example among the canonical male poets is furnished by Wordsworth, whose political sonnets of the period trace many of the key features of this shift in nature and substance; for a discussion see Behrendt, "Placing the Places in Wordsworth's 1802 Sonnets."

25. Curran, "Romantic Poetry: The 'I' Altered," 203. Not all women poets followed this pattern, however. Catherine Ann Dorset, a talented poet equally at home with carefully rendered natural history and with sparkling wit (see her *The Peacock at Home,* in both its juvenile [1807; much reprinted] and its "adult" [1809] forms), whose poetry had appeared along with Charlotte Smith's in the latter's *Conversations Introducing Poetry . . . For the Use of Young Persons* (1804), has a poem called "Written in Southhampton in 1806" that turns in its penultimate stanza to blasted hopes and longings for death: "Far happier they, whose struggles o'er, / Have reach'd the port on death's safe shore, / And clos'd their troubl'ous day." But the final stanza finds the poet rescued from her dark thoughts by Fortitude, Patience, and Hope, while "Faith entrusts to mortal hands, / Her compass for their guide." [Dorset], *The Peacock at Home; and Other Poems,* 95-96.

26. Curran notes for instance that the "accent on the dispossessed and marginalized" we find in Robinson's poetry and fiction in the 1790s and Smith's (before her death in 1806) was "widely replicated by the voices of other women." "Women Readers, Women Writers," 187. This comes through not just in the poems and tales but, often more pointedly still, in the prefatory materials in which the authors speak in their own voices of their cruel circumstances. A good example is furnished by the little-known Elizabeth Sarah Gooch in the dedication and preface to her *Sherwood Forest,* v-xii.

27. Horwood, *Instructive Amusements for Young Minds.* This collection is, as the author freely admits, styled after the Taylors' *Original Poems for Infant Minds.* C.C. Richardson, *Harvest.* Bristow, *The Maniac, a Tale.*

28. Curran, "Women Readers, Women Writers," 187.

29. S. Richardson, *Original Poems;* E. Turner, *The Daisy.* Flowerdew, *Poems, on Moral and Religious Subjects* (1803); a second edition appeared in 1804, and an enlarged third edition was published in 1811 by the larger firm of Sherwood, Neely, and Jones. Sewell, *Poems.* Parsons, *Verses, Hymns and Poems.* Stockdale, *The Family Book;* see also her *Mirror of the Mind.* O'Keeffe, *Original Poems;* O'Keeffe contributed to some of the collections assembled by the Taylor sisters, where her contributions are identified by the name "Adelaide." West, *The Mother.*

30. [Browne], *The Domestic Affections.* West, *The Mother.*

31. West, *Miscellaneous Poetry.*

32. *British Critic* (June 1809): 618, 623.

33. *Satirist,* 273. Hannah More and Sarah Trimmer are immediately identifiable, but the third woman is much less familiar. Alyson Bardsley has suggested to me that the reviewer is referring here to Elizabeth Hamilton, author of such works as *Memoirs of Modern Philosophers* and *The Cottagers of Glenburnie.* Her works share much with both the substance and the spirit of the sort of didactic and children's works composed by Maria Edgeworth; her presence here with More and Trimmer, who cultivated similar ground, is therefore not surprising.

34. See Sullivan, *British Literary Magazines,* 385.

35. *Satirist,* Mar. 1809, 276.

36. Hemans, *Restoration of the Works of Art to Italy;* Hemans, *The Sceptic.* See the *British Review* (Jan. 1820): 299-300.

37. Campbell's most popular work appeared in 1799 and had seen twelve further editions by the time of Waterloo; Bloomfield's *Farmer's Boy* saw three editions in its first year (1800), and twelve more by that same point; Hoyle's poem, happily, appeared in only one edition. This four-hundred-page recasting of Exodus in thirteen books comprises some ninety-five hundred lines of blank verse. Hoyle, *Exodus.* M.B. Ross, *The Contours of Masculine Desire,* 192. Mellor, "A Criticism of Their Own," 35.

38. *Quarterly Review* (Oct. 1820): 131, emphasis mine.

39. Rowton, *Female Poets of Great Britain* (1981), 386.

40. See Mellor, *Romanticism and Gender,* esp. 171-86. See also two important earlier discussions of this matter: Homans, "Keats Reading Women"; Wolfson, "Feminizing Keats."

41. Barbauld, *The Poems of Anna Letitia Barbauld,* 310.

42. L. Aikin, *Epistles on Women.* The only substantial modern discussion of this poem is in Mellor, "The Female Poet and the Poetess."

43. *Critical Review* (Aug. 1811): 419, my emphasis.

44. See Jackson, *Romantic Poetry by Women,* 143. [A. Hamilton], *The Epics of the Ton;* by the end of 1807 a third edition, "with considerable Additions" had been issued by the same publisher. The Hamilton-Byron connection is immediately suggested by passages like this:

> Should'st thou, my lay, shine splendid as thy theme,
> Like rushlights to thy sun, all bards should seem:
> Then still might Southey sing his crazy Joan,
> Or feign a Welshman o'er th' Atlantic flown,
> Or tell of Thalaba the wondrous matter,
> Or with clown Wordsworth chatter, chatter, chatter;
> Still Rogers bland his imitations twine,
> And strain his Memory for another line;
> Good-natured Scott rehearse in well-paid Lays
> The marv'lous chiefs and elves of other days;
> Or lazy Campbell spin his golden strains,
> And have the Hope he nurtures, for his pains—
> [A. Hamilton, "The Female Book," lines 29-40]

45. *Poetical Register* (1810-11): 553.
46. *Monthly Review* (Apr. 1811): 380-81.
47. Porden, *The Veils.*
48. *Critical Review* (Nov. 1812): 554. Barrell, *The Test of Virtue.*
49. Thomas Phillips, Byron (1813), National Portrait Gallery, London.

The Subject of Violence

Mary Lamb, Femme Fatale

Adriana Craciun

Would a woman be able to hold us (or, as they say, "enthrall" us) if we did not consider it quite possible that under certain circumstances she could wield a dagger (any kind of dagger) against us?

Nietzsche, The Gay Science

Mary Lamb's career as a writer may not have been possible had she not murdered her mother in 1796.[1] This possibility presents an intriguing problem for any gender-complementary model of writing, and of Romantic period writing in particular, that would align violence and mastery exclusively with masculinity. Gender-complementary models of Romanticism such as Margaret Homans's in *Women Writers and Poetic Identity* and *Bearing the Word* and Anne Mellor's in *Romanticism and Gender* differentiate between women's uses of language and men's and in many respects offer a welcome correction to earlier ungendered (read androcentric) comprehensive models of Romanticism and poetic identity.[2] Yet such gender-complementary models, though valuable for their gender specificity, often reinscribe the rigid gender boundaries that many women and men of the Romantic period defied. Violence, both rhetorical and physical, presents the greatest challenge to such gender-complementary feminist poetics, in part because it seems so clearly attributable to men and masculine interests.

Central to feminist literary criticism on nineteenth-century British women writers in general is the usually unspoken aim to demonstrate that women as a class (that is, a sex outside of class) eschew violence, destructiveness, and cruelty, except in self-defense or rebellion, as does Gilbert and Gubar's imprisoned madwoman in the attic.[3] This faith in women's inherent benevolence, for it is a foundational belief of many modern feminisms, has its origins in the rise of the bourgeois order itself, which enshrined the maternal, nurturing middle-class woman as the protected, private moral center of this new socioeconomic order. I want to insist on this connection between contemporary feminist re-evaluations of the Romantic period and the normative (though not hegemonic) ideology of gender and sexual difference of that period, because I think current scholarship too often replicates this gendered Romantic ideology unthinkingly, and often unproductively.

Rescuing women writers and their female protagonists from charges of wanton cruelty and capitulation to "masculinist" behavior such as objectifica-tion and exploitation seems to be a primary goal of gender-complementary approaches to women writers; this strategy is dangerous (all strategies are) be-cause it leaves unquestioned the "repressive hypothesis" of power, in Foucault's famous formulation, and pursues an ideal of the autonomous female deep sub-ject outside masculine power and violence, an ideal that is itself power's most productive effect. Gilbert and Gubar's landmark *The Madwoman in the Attic* (1979) most famously established this reading of nineteenth-century British women writers as engaged in a struggle to release the repressed female self from the grip of male power; *Jane Eyre* is the central text in their reading of repressed female rage and rebellion, as it gives their book its title, and Brontë's novel remains central to much feminist literary criticism of the nineteenth century because it so wonderfully illustrates middle-class women's struggle for intellectual, economic, and emotional independence. Michelle Massé has more recently located in *Jane Eyre* Women's triumphant transcendence of the vio-lence central to the "Gothic economy" of patriarchy: "[S]he will not be an accomplice to unjust authority. Jane's testimony as spectator identifies what might overturn the Gothic economy: not eroticizing aggression against one's self and becoming beaten, not repeating the cycle of violence by oppressing others as beater or accomplice, but rather persisting in the search for love *and* independence."[4] Jane Eyre continues to represent liberal feminism's dream of female love and independence outside power and history; yet as the compel-ling critiques of Gayatri Chakravorty Spivak and Nancy Armstrong have shown, this traditional reading of *Jane Eyre* fails to examine its own class and cultural interests in its celebration of the autonomous female subject. Armstrong and Leonard Tennenhouse, in the volume *The Violence of Representation* (1989), have argued that in *Jane Eyre* we can trace the shift from the earlier order of spectacular violence to the modern order of violence as representation, of the repressive hypothesis, where Jane's oppositional discourse of self and other pro-duces the deep female subject at the expense of Others, such as Blanche Ingram and Mrs. Reed. "So attached to the novel's heroine," Armstrong and Tennenhouse write, "we neglect to see how her descriptive power becomes a mode of violence in its own right."[5] Jane claims a "position of powerlessness" as her source of authority and authenticity, and as such "[s]he is the progenitrix of a new gender, class, and race of selves in relation to whom all others are deficient."[6] Gender-complementary readings of Romanticism and nineteenth-century women's literature in general celebrate and duplicate Jane's claim of "powerlessness" and attempt to speak from and for this place outside power when they banish violence to the domains of masculinity and the male.

The subject of violence that I will discuss in this essay is not, therefore, the elusive autonomous female subject that erupts in rebellious rage against the repressive constraints of male power, as Gilbert and Gubar's monstrous women do, for example. Mary Lamb's writings certainly are rife with images of repressed violence and rage, and her repeated incarcerations in private asylums following violent outbursts throughout her life make it clear that the repression (and production) of her violence was itself a process of actual, not just rhetorical, violence against her self and her body. It is significant, however, that Mary Lamb's rage, murderous rebellion, and legal status as madwoman did not warrant her inclusion in *Madwoman in the Attic*. Mary Lamb's rebellion and rage cannot safely be assimilated in the literary humanist feminism of Gilbert and Gubar, nor in subsequent gender-complementary scholarship, precisely because her violence, her lack of provocation, and her female object render the feminist use value of her violence low and its destabilizing potential high.[7] The rage and rebellion of the female subject are welcome as long as the violence is that of representation, as is Jane Eyre's, or is a metaphorical rebellion and self-defense, as is Bertha's. The subject of violence itself remains masculine when it is aggressive (not defensive), physical (not metaphorical), sadistic, and/or sexual. Mary Lamb stabbed her mother without immediate provocation after attacking her assistant; her violence therefore exceeds the functions of rebellion and rage and demonstrates the precariousness of women's status as reservoirs of bourgeois benevolence and sympathy, qualities necessary to the new social order's claim to moral progress.

"The subject of violence is always masculine," though its object may be either feminine or masculine, argues Teresa de Lauretis in her important feminist response to Derrida's "The Violence of the Letter," because violence is engendered through representation.[8] Violence cannot escape gender or the historical power imbalances between men and women: men are responsible for most violent acts, and the victims of their violence are most often women. De Lauretis's critique of Derrida's dangerous eliding of the gendering of violence is persuasive and important; yet what, if anything, can we say of the subject of violence who is also a woman? Must the subject of violence be masculine (even if not male)? I suggest that the answer is no and that, even while we keep in mind de Lauretis's crucial gendering of violence as masculine, we must continue to examine how Lamb's writings explored the possibilities of a female subject of violence.

Subsequent treatments (or lack thereof) of Lamb's violence reveal the inability and unwillingness of gender-complementary criticism to account for violence when it does not fit the model of female metaphorical rebellion or resistance against male domination. Mary Lamb's violence tends to disappear in new critical work on her writing, or it is neatly and quickly dismissed as an effect of "mental illness" (as if this explains anything); such acts of exclusion are themselves acts of rhetorical violence, for they displace violence onto an external, perhaps unnatural, source instead of acknowledging (feminist) criticism's and women's participation in violence.

In order to demonstrate why Lamb's work invites us to revise our assumptions about women, violence, and language, I will first briefly examine Margaret Homans's influential argument regarding women's violent exclusion from the male symbolic order in *Bearing the Word.* I argue that women are necessarily subjects both of language and of violence and that one reason the Lacanian symbolic order is always gendered masculine in such valuable feminist revisions of psychoanalysis as Homans's is precisely in order to distance women from what Derrida termed the "arche-violence" preceding the violence of writing. Just as we cannot "safeguard the exteriority of writing to speech," as Derrida argued in "The Violence of the Letter," so we cannot safeguard the exteriority of violence to women.[9] Focusing on Lamb's first tale from *Mrs. Leicester's School,* "Elizabeth Villiers: The Sailor Uncle," as well as on her poetry, I go on to argue that Mary Lamb's writing demonstrates women's undeniable participation in the violence of the letter as well as in empirical violence and that modern accounts that overlook this violence ironically do violence to her work; by extension they also do violence to Romantic-period women's writing because they impose onto it a teleological model of the moral progress of female (and feminist) benevolence.

Mary Lamb and the Violence of the Letter

Death strolls between letters.
   Derrida, *"Edmond Jabès and the Question of the Book"*

Mary Lamb presents an intriguing set of problems for feminist scholarship because she embodies irreconcilable qualities of violence and gentleness, assertiveness and self-effacement and because these irreconcilable differences she embodies are directly related to writing. To a significant degree, Lamb exemplifies the "feminine Romantic" subject as Mellor described in *Romanticism and Gender:* she did not publish under her own name; she was lauded by her friends for being self-effacing, gentle, reasonable, and domestic; she worked in professions typical for women of her time, being a seamstress and later a private tutor; she wrote almost exclusively for children. Wordsworth's well-known description of Lamb is typical: "the meek, / The self-restraining, and the ever-kind."[10] And yet these "feminine" qualities represent only one dimension of Mary Lamb's life and writing, as they represent only one dimension of women's participation in Romanticism. For Lamb was also capable of murderous violence and rage, not only in her actions but in her writing. It may seem odd for me to order the previous sentence as I did, implying that our greater concern may be not with one violent incident when she murdered her mother but with the violence that remained a part of her and her work long after the deed was done. But it is precisely the "violence of the letter," as Derrida termed it, that interests me here, because the violence of the murder is typically and unsatisfactorily explained away as a result of "mental illness," often anachronistically and retroactively diagnosed as manic-depressive disorder. I want therefore to focus a consciously feminist inquiry specifically on the Romantic-period woman subject and author, in this case Mary Lamb, in order to question the limits we ourselves place on female subjectivity and authorship and to reintroduce the transgressive potential of typically "masculine" actions and desires that many Romantic-period women in fact exercised.

Jane Aaron, in *A Double Singleness: Gender and the Writings of Charles and Mary Lamb*, writes of how difficult it was for Lamb to incorporate her violence into her concept of self and how throughout her life she distanced her "sane" feminine self from her aggressive "insane" self; Charles Lamb likewise could not reconcile Mary's gender with her behavior and, as Aaron writes, "appears to have seen the deed as having been committed by a dominant masculine madness, satanic or divine, which had taken possession of his sister. . . . Nurturative female values, embodied very consistently from all contemporary accounts by Mary during her periods of sanity, are thus seen as endangered by aggressive masculine drives."[11] Mary's violence was so disturbing in a woman that it needed to be displaced onto an inhuman and unfemale source. Her recurring bouts of madness and rage were thus experienced by her brother as possession by masculinity, and she was repeatedly removed from their home to the care of professionals during such periods.

Yet we must be careful not to duplicate this gesture of suppression in our reevaluation of women's position as Romantic subjects and authors. To reduce women such as Lamb to "male-identified," masculinist, or "mentally ill" subjects would be to rely on and reinscribe a circular argument that attributes violence and mastery solely to masculinity. The subject of violence has the power to destabilize such concepts of complementary female subjectivity both in the Romantic period and in our own. Thus, rather than emphasize the virtues of women's exclusion from power and the masculinist symbolic order, I will examine the feminist possibilities of what I would argue is women's undeniable participation in a symbolic and political order that is admittedly grounded in violence.

In *Bearing the Word,* Margaret Homans, drawing on the work of Nancy Chodorow, locates the origin of the Lacanian symbolic order in the murder and subsequent idealization of the mother by the poet/son: "The symbolic order is founded, not merely on the regrettable loss of the mother, but rather on her active and overt murder. Thus a feminist critique begins by indicating the situation in which women are placed by a myth of language that assumes the speaker to be masculine."[12] Women are indeed placed in the position of object, listener, or amanuensis of male language; yet I would argue that feminist revisions of Lacanian psychoanalysis highlight and critique this positioning of women as object in part because of the originating violence of the symbolic order and their desire to deny women as subject of this violence. Mary Lamb's murder of her mother is in fact inseparable from her position as author, and this association between writing and death is a prevalent theme in her works. Thus, in this feminist critique I begin, like Homans, by indicating that in Mary Lamb's myth of language the object of violence and language is indeed female, but as we shall see, so is the subject.

The most striking connection between women as subject of violence and of writing in Mary Lamb's work occurs in the first story from *Mrs. Leicester's School,* "Elizabeth Villiers: The Sailor Uncle." *Mrs. Leicester's School,* published anonymously in 1809, contains a series of narratives in which young girls tell their life stories to their fellow inmates at a boarding school. Elizabeth Villiers, the heroine of the first tale, tells of learning to read at her mother's grave (see fig. 1):

The first thing I can remember was my father teaching me the alphabet from the letters on a tombstone that stood at the head of my mother's grave. I used to tap at my father's study door; I think now I hear him say, "Who is there?—What do you want, little girl? "Go and see mamma. Go and learn pretty letters." Many times in the day would my father lay aside his books and his papers to lead me to this spot, and make me point to the letters, and then set me to spell syllables and words: in this matter, the epitaph on my mother's tomb being my primer and my spelling-book, I learned to read.[13]

The father not only authorizes but also encourages the girl to read of her mother's death, literally to read her death sentence, thus reiterating her absence and exclusion. Because the girl and the mother share the same name, Elizabeth Villiers, the girl is in fact reiterating her own death. She is initiated into the symbolic order by putting into practice the violent exclusion of the lost referent (the mother, or the female). Thus, Elizabeth's coming to writing is in many respects an ideal example of Homans's persuasive critique of the symbolic order and its sacrifice of the female.

Yet what is curious about this opening scene of instruction is that the subject who is initiated is female. The previous reading might deny the girl

W. Hopwood. del.   J. Hopwood. sculp

*In this manner, the epitaph on my mother's
tomb being my primer and my spelling-book,
I learned to read.* — Page 9.

Fig. 1. Frontispiece and inscription from the first edition of Mary Lamb's
Mrs. Leicester's School. The frontispiece illustrates and quotes from Mary
Lamb's story "Elizabeth Villiers: Or the Sailor Uncle." Courtesy of the
Department of Special Collections, UCLA Library.

agency in the Lacanian symbolic order because she was instructed by the father to read of the death of her mother, suggesting that the symbolic is ordered by the Law of the Father; and the girl is also absolved of any blame for the mother's death, the violence that sets in motion this order, for this same reason. But we could instead say that one is authorized as a subject only within a system of power that precedes one's existence. Likewise, the subject of language is not an autonomous agent outside that language, but only emerges as a possibility within it. Thus, the construction of Elizabeth as female subject of discourse and action is, I would argue, neither the product of a proper external agent (the father, or "power"), nor is it a freely chosen action of the preexisting self (one who teaches herself to read in a gesture of self-empowerment and self-creation). As Judith Butler explains in *Bodies That Matter,* the construction of a subject "is neither a subject nor its act, but a process of reiteration by which both 'subjects' and 'acts' come to appear at all. There is no power that acts, but only a reiterating acting that is power in its persistence and instability." Thus, we see Elizabeth instructed to read by the father, and yet, when her uncle asks who taught her to read, she answers, "'Mamma,' . . . for I had an idea that the words on the tombstone were somehow a part of mamma, and that she had taught me. 'And who is mamma,' asked my uncle. 'Elizabeth Villiers,' I replied."[14] The origin of Elizabeth's language is thus not unmediated nature, nor the authority of the Father, but the repetition of signs. "Elizabeth Villiers" names both mother and daughter of language, the simultaneously self-authorizing and externally authorized female subject.

Derrida, in *Writing and Difference,* articulates the model of language as absence, of which Mary Lamb's text is an "ideal" example: "The first book, . . . the eve prior to all repetition, has lived on the deception that the center was sheltered from play: the irreplaceable, . . . a kind of *invariable first name* that could be invoked but not repeated. The center of the first book should not have been repeatable in its own representation. Once it lends itself a single time to such a representation—that is to say, once it is written—when one can read a book in the book, an origin in the origin, . . . it is the abyss, it is the bottomlessness of infinite redoubling."[15] The repetition of this invariable first name, Elizabeth Villiers, in Lamb's text effectively replaces the center of original presence, which some theorists claim for women's language, with the abyss of endless deferral. Both mother and daughter in the text, "Elizabeth" was also mother and daughter in Lamb's life, being the name of her murdered mother as well as of two dead sisters. The death of the first Elizabeth predated Lamb's own birth, her origin, so that her own act of murdering "Elizabeth" is not, literally speaking, original: it repeats an act of exclusion and returns as an echo of an earlier lost "Elizabeth."

Far from being an unmediated female presence, nature for Elizabeth Villiers is mediated by language, and both are imbued with death: "the words on the tombstone were somehow a part of mamma." When reflecting on her image of her mamma, the young Elizabeth evokes the pleasure she gains from nature's presence, yet this living, green presence is within the grave: "I used to wish I was sleeping in the grave with papa and mamma; and in my childish dreams I used to fancy myself there; and it was a place within the ground, all smooth, and soft and green. I never made out any figure of mamma, but still it was the tombstone, and papa, and the smooth green grass."[16] Life and death are here indistinguishable; nature becomes the impossible living green space within the grave, and her living father and dead mother share this liminal state. The child cannot experience mother or nature as presence; rather, the maternal is dispersed throughout her world and is experienced through signs (a place within the ground, the tombstone, the grass).

Percy Bysshe Shelley's account of the poet's desire for mother nature in *Alastor* bears a striking resemblance to Mary Lamb's, and yet it is precisely Shelley's exclusion and idealization of the mother that Homans, quite rightly I think, uses to exemplify the violence of the dominant Western myth of language:

> Mother of this unfathomable world!
> Favour my solemn song, for I have loved
> Thee ever, and thee only; . . .
> . . . .
> . . . I have made my bed
> In charnels and on coffins, where black death
> Keeps record of the trophies won from thee.[17]

Homans writes that Shelley's hero's ideal female figure in the above quotation "is a figurative substitute for a mother that has been killed . . . in order to set the poem's chain of signifiers in motion"; "the narrator . . . makes it clear that it is her association with death—and therefore I would suggest her death itself— that motivates and makes possible his song."[18] But we must acknowledge that Mary Lamb's "song" in *Mrs. Leicester's School* is also set in motion by her own murder of her mother Elizabeth and is repeated in the motherlessness of her female characters.[19]

Jean Marsden has recently also argued that in Lamb's works "learning to read via the mother becomes a complex nexus of death, education, and loss that each child presents as the defining moment of her life." Lamb's allegories "suggest a traumatic induction into a Lacanian symbolic order,"[20] as I have argued, yet it is crucial to insist on the writer's (always limited) agency in this "death" and "loss" at the heart of her language. The mother is not merely lost; she is killed, much as Virginia Woolf argued that women must kill the angel in the house in order to write. If we celebrate Woolf's feminist rage, must we not also, at the very least, accept Mary Lamb's violence, instead of continually attempting to exorcise it?

The poem "Memory" from Mary and Charles Lamb's *Poetry for Children* (1809) (Mary's authorship of which is uncertain, as will be discussed shortly) celebrates this power of language over nature and history. A "young forgetful" girl desires heightened Memory and would "travel for her through the earth"; "a female figure came to her," writes Lamb, and advised her,

> "The only substitute for me
> Was ever found, is call'd a pen;
> The frequent use of that will be
> The way to make me come again."[21]

Mary Lamb understood language's radical separation from nature and valued it precisely for this reason, since it allowed her to rewrite her own history and her memory of her mother.[22] Both Aaron and Leslie Friedman examine in great detail the striking correspondences between the deprivations of Lamb's female characters and those of her own life; Friedman notes in particular that the efficient manner in which "unwanted family members can be whisked out of sight in her stories" is characteristic of Lamb's use of writing as mastery: "The power of words and wishes is great, and believing in that power, Mary is able to enact bloodless aggression in the stories." Anne Mellor cites the possibility that "the masculine mind can receive pleasure from the silencing of the female" as one of the most troubling characteristics of masculine Romanticism; yet Mary Lamb seems to have derived a similar pleasure from the power of writing as aggression. Mellor herself warns that to assume that "male Romantic writers constructed one kind of self and female Romantic writers another"[23] is to oversimplify and essentialize. However, gender-complementary models still associate masculinity with violence and mastery through selective readings, because, I would argue, the consolations of female pacifism and benevolence are still appealing and therefore are reinscribed. Contrasting Dorothy Wordsworth's building of "refuges" through language with the dominant model of language as violent exclusion of the referent (and the female), as Margaret Homans does, is important, but equally important is questioning why the subject of language's violence is *necessarily* masculine.

Like her female characters who were "unhappy, angry and quarrelsome,"[24] Mary Lamb was far from being a meek and self-effacing woman. Her essay "On Needlework,"[25] a powerful protest against the destructive effects of women's unpaid labor on their intellect and status, is signed "Sempronia," which I believe refers to the classical Sempronia, best known through the Latin historian Sallust, whom the Lambs mention by name in another poem.[26] Sallust's

Sempronia participated in the Catilinarian conspiracy, and he describes her as "a woman who had committed many crimes that showed her to have the reckless daring of a man"; however, he says, despite her sexual promiscuity and recklessness, "her abilities were not to be despised. She could write poetry, crack a joke, and converse at will with decorum, tender feeling, or wantonness; she was in fact a woman of ready wit and considerable charm."[27] Mary Lamb's decision to name herself after such a controversial female figure, especially one known for criminal activity and radical politics, reveals a degree of defiance and assertiveness on her part that did not end with her act of murder.

Mary Lamb and *Poetry for Children* (1809)

The authorship of the individual poems in Mary and Charles Lamb's *Poetry for Children*, published in 1809 "by the author of Mrs. Leicester's School," remains largely inconclusive and unreliable. We know from Charles Lamb's letters that Mary wrote two thirds of the seventy-three poems, yet because the book was published anonymously, the authorship of only a few of the poems (which were later published elsewhere or claimed in letters) is clear. I want to examine briefly the authorship dispute, which I believe unresolvable given current knowledge, because I will be discussing several poems whose authorship is in dispute and also, and more interestingly, because the editorial criteria used for attributing authorship is uneasily influenced by Mary's violence. Thus, not only is Mary Lamb's critical reception as a Romantic-period poet in significant part determined by our reactions to her violence, but so to a certain extent is the very body of her work bound up in and circumscribed by this violence.

Lucas's authoritative edition of the works of Charles and Mary Lamb, published in 1903, supplants earlier editions of their work, such as H. Carew Hazlitt's, and offers different, and speculative, attributions. In his notes to *Poetry for Children*, Lucas writes: "I have placed against the poems . . . the authorship—brother's or sister's—which seems to me the more probable. But I hope it will be understood that I do this at a venture, and, except in a few cases, with no exact knowledge."[28] Of the seventy-three poems, Lucas attributes definitive authorship to only six; for the remaining poems he offers conjectural arguments for authorship for a few, but for the majority of the poems we are given a suggested author with no support. We must be wary of accepting these attributions as "most probable," however, not because Lucas may be wrong (he may very well be right), but because I think his criteria are necessarily informed by a desire to account for and exorcise Mary's violence from the poetry (just as mine would, possibly, be informed by an opposed desire).

More recently, Cyril Hussey suggested a method for assigning authorship based on textual scholarship, internal evidence (Mary's "faulty rhymes"), and most importantly for my purposes, "the gentle morality one associates with Mary Lamb."[29] Hussey thus articulated the central, unspoken dilemma of most Mary Lamb scholarship—how best to redeem her gentleness in the face of her violence. For example, Hussey clinches Mary's authorship of "A Birthday Wish" by finally comparing "the nature of the poem itself" (4) (i.e., peaceful) to the nature of Mary Lamb: "It could be argued that having been through the terrible period of mania when she killed her mother, then the prayer of gratitude to God which the poem embodies, could not have been written by the same person. This does not take into account the gentle and trusting nature of Mary Lamb" (4). Hussey then goes on to quote at length Gilchrist's account of the murder, and here, significantly, Hussey makes the same move as do virtually all who write on Mary Lamb.

Gilchrist's account in *Mary Lamb,* like the account in the *Morning Chronicle* on which it is based, downplays Mary's agency as murderer not just by repeatedly emphasizing her "frenzy," "insanity," "nervous misery," but by eliding the scene of violence itself:

[S]eized with a sudden attack of frenzy, she snatched a knife from the table and pursued the young apprentice round the room, and when her mother interposing, received a fatal stab and died instantly.
Mary was totally inconscious [*sic*] of what she had done.[30]

It is Mary who is "seized" by madness, and her mother who interposes and receives a fatal stab—Mary the murderer is nowhere to be found, so that we as readers, perhaps because we desire to, remain as unconscious as Mary is said to have been.

I find it surprising, and disturbing, that virtually all work on Mary Lamb repeats this same violent exclusion of Mary's violence by relying on the accounts of Charles Lamb and the *Morning Chronicle* unquestioningly, to the point of echoing their language and certainly their (sympathetic) refusal to hold Mary responsible for her actions. The *Morning Chronicle* report offers us only the "menacing" Mary Lamb who "approaches" her parent, and the postmurder discovery: "the dreadful scene presented to him [the landlord] the mother lifeless, pierced to the heart, on a chair, her daughter yet wildly standing over her with the fatal knife."[31] As if inducing in us Mary's unconsciousness, this oft-repeated account reinforces woman's violence as impossible and unrepresentable by violently excising it—simultaneously, of course, making this same violence central.

Charles's letter to S.T. Coleridge five days after the murder provides the second oft-repeated strategy of dealing with it: "My poor dear dearest sister in a fit of insanity has been the death of her own mother." Jane Aaron's excellent study of the Lambs, even while it goes into great depth examining the complex political, social, and personal forces Mary Lamb had to contend with, still echoes Charles's words and their gesture of displacement, abstracting Mary's act of murder to a bringing about of death: "Mary Lamb, in a sudden outbreak of violent mania, brought about the death of her mother." Pamela Woof's diction in her recent article on Lamb and Dorothy Wordsworth transforms the murder into an even more ambiguous affair: "If through some notion of saving Mary pain, her friends never mentioned the catastrophe of her mother's murder." If one did not already know otherwise, one might imagine from this sentence that someone else had murdered Elizabeth Lamb, not her daughter. Gilchrist's, Ross's, and Ashton and Davies's studies of Mary Lamb, as well as recent articles such as Marsden's, similarly cushion the impact of her violence by inserting mental illness, insanity, madness as the true agent of the deed.[32] I am not arguing that Lamb's violence was an indication of her "free will," her intentional and transgressive agency as an "autonomous" subject. But neither can I accept modern diagnoses that emphasize her lack of responsibility (the most popular being bipolar or manic-depressive disorder), for they represent our current medical and often anestheticizing approach to such disturbing behavior and cannot in my opinion be offered (as they now are) as helpful explanations; like the explanations of possession, or unreason, or moral failure, they reveal little about Mary Lamb and much about the current dominant construction of "mental illness" and its ideological interests.

Certainly such sidestepping and medicalization of Mary Lamb's violence is done today, as it was in her lifetime, "through some intention of saving Mary pain."[33] I have great respect for this sympathetic intention, and my insistence on attending to Lamb's violence is not motivated by a contrasting desire to cause pain. I want to insist that our accounts of this writer accept the violence in her life and writing because her physical, matricidal violence is the most shocking example not of one woman's illness and unconscious actions, but of all women's complex involvement in political, linguistic, and cultural systems that rely on violence. It is precisely because our accounts of Mary's "illness" mirror (with updated diagnoses) those of two hundred years ago so closely (of a possessing, masculine demonic madness, as Charles saw it) that we need to be suspicious of them. Why, we need to ask, is women's violence so dangerous to us? What is so worth preserving that one woman's violence more than two hundred years ago must be expelled from our writings and hers? The answer I want to suggest to these questions is the "woman writer": across race, class, historical, and cultural lines, the woman writer shares an ideal prepatriarchal, nurturing, benevolent, nonviolent human potential, culturally designated as feminine, which her unjustifiable violence would destroy, or so many accounts of nineteenth-century British women's literature suggest. In our historical moment, as we reexamine Romantic poetics and their complex indebtedness to misogynist practices, the desire to establish a complementary Romanticism, or a female Gothic, seems widespread and sincerely desired and is in many respects a valuable feminist project. Even today, however, Mary Lamb remains a danger to expectations of a complementary feminine subject, and for this reason all accounts of her murder repeat almost verbatim either the newspaper or Charles's account, interposing a dismissive mental derangement between Mary Lamb and her violence or obliterating the violence altogether.

Yet Mary Lamb's violence remained a part of her writing, as violence remains a necessary part of all symbolic systems. Jane Aaron, among others, has nicely demonstrated how Mary's painful, excessive self-restraint was but an extreme version of the self-restraint expected of all proper women of her time. In Mary Lamb's oft-quoted letter to Sarah Stoddart in 1805, for example, she admonishes herself for the trace of anger in a previous letter: "I wrote under a forcible impulse which I could not at that time resist, but I have fretted so much about it since, that I think it is the last time I will ever let my pen run away with me."[34] This is one of many incidents in Lamb's letters in which she shrinks from expressing any anger or protest, as Aaron and others have noted; yet it is more than a retraction of her anger. Lamb specifically admonishes herself for being overcome by a "forcible impulse" and expressing anger in a specific way—*while writing*. Her pen runs away with her much as the "fatal knife" had run away with her in 1796, leaving Lamb at once the victim of a demonic power (either of "mental illness" or of language) and a dangerously aggressive writer *and* murderer, who recognizes the dangerous affinity between pen and knife. We cannot separate the writer of children's verse from the murderer, precisely because Mary Lamb tried to do just that for fifty years, and as in the above letter, found that she could not.

I turn now to several poems from the Lambs' *Poetry for Children* (1809), the definitive authorship of which remains in dispute, as stated earlier. It is important to note, however, that although it is generally assumed that the poets' identities remained unknown for some time, some of the Lambs' contemporaries considered Mary Lamb as the sole author of the poems; the reviewer for the *Monthly Review*, for example, made the following startling comment: "We hear that [the poems] are the production of Miss Lambe [*sic*], whose brother published 'Tales from Shakespeare,' and we think that this lady will be entitled to the gratitude of every mother whose children obtain her compositions." The most interesting of the poems in my opinion is "The Beasts in the Tower," which Hazlitt attributed to Mary and Lucas to Charles.[35] Regardless of authorship, this poem clearly engages the problem of Mary's violence through an allegory of ferocious beasts caged in a tower menagerie (perhaps the Tower of London, which served as a menagerie for such beasts for centuries). In the poem, the narrator warns a young boy about life's destructive forces; the ferocious beasts are described in detail, focusing on their power and beauty while emphasizing their strict confinement: "Within the precincts of this yard, / Each [is] in his narrow confines barr'd."[36] The panther in particular exemplifies the beasts in their deadly beauty: "the fairest beast /. . . / He underneath a fair outside / Does cruelty and treach'ry hide" (408). The narrator details the killing methods of each beast, warning the child that though the tiger "with ease / upon the tallest man could seize . . . and into a thousand pieces tear him," not the smallest infant need fear, for the beast is "cabin'd so securely here." Yet the narrator's sympathy is with the caged beasts: deprived of their "wild haunts" and placed in servitude, "Enslaved by man, they suffer here!" (407).

The precarious nature of the beasts' confinement is emphasized throughout, and on one level it is clearly symbolic of the confinement of women to domestic spaces where rage is restrained beneath beauty, yet also exacerbated because of its repression: "Yet here within appointed lines / How small a grate his rage confines!"[37] Women's diminutive or fair outside, the poem suggests, can never wholly contain rage and violence. Lamb's own periodic breakdowns attest that the "unrelenting restraint"[38] she imposed upon herself was only temporary. The poem's closing moral echoes the Lambs' rationalization of their mother's murder as providential:

> This place, me thinks, resembleth well
> The world itself in which we dwell.
> Perils and snares on every ground,
> Like these wild beasts, beset us round.
> But Providence their rage restrains,
> Our heavenly Keeper sets them chains;
> His goodness saveth every hour
> His darlings from the lion's power.[39]

Both Mary and Charles (and subsequent scholars) absolved Mary of responsibility for the murder, Charles writing to Coleridge that Mary was "the unhappy and unconscious instrument of the Almighty's judgements on our house."[40] A few days after the murder, Mary was "calm and serene," says Charles, and she herself wrote from the asylum where she was confined, "I have no fear. The spirit of my mother seems to descend and smile upon me, and bid me to live and enjoy the life and reason which the Almighty has given me. I shall see her again in heaven."[41] If Providence and its chains alone restrain destructive violence, as Lamb's poem states, then its release is also divinely ordained.

When her murder was attributed to "lunacy" and she was spared execution or incarceration, Mary Lamb effectively surrendered the right to her own rage and violence by placing them in divine hands. She likewise surrendered her public position as author by not publishing under her own name because that name was notorious.[42] And yet her crime was liberatory in two senses—it freed her from the excessive burden of caring for her sick mother (who appears to have been both cruel and neglectful), and it marked the beginning of her career as writer, since as far as we know she did not write before the murder. Her dual positions as author of the deed of murder and author of texts are thus inextricably bound. Unlike Foucault's Pierre Rivière, who, later in the century, gained notoriety as author both of a murder and of its narrative, Mary Lamb withdrew from public literary attention precisely because her murder in 1796 did not fit into a "historical field" of murder/narratives by women.[43] As I have tried to argue, however, this rage and violence remained a part of her work and life. And to an important extent, her position as murderer made possible her position as author, despite the fact that publicly she wanted to claim neither position.

Mary Lamb, Femme Fatale

High-born Helen, round your dwelling
  These twenty years I've paced in vain:
Haughty beauty, thy lover's duty
  Hath been to glory in his pain.
    Mary Lamb, "Helen"

We do have one context in which her position as subject of violence would not be anomalous—the French Revolution and its accounts and allegories of women's aggression. This revolutionary context for Lamb's violence is suggested by Fuseli's sketch of a Bacchante, inscribed "Mary Anne" and "Maria [illegible] 179[?]" by an unknown hand and generally thought to refer to Mary Anne Lamb. Lamb's murder on 22 September 1796 occurred in a context of great English anxiety about revolutionary changes in France and at home. The women's march on Versailles during the October Days of 1789 and other acts of violence committed by women such as Charlotte Corday throughout the Revolution shocked the British no matter their political inclinations. Following the Terror in France and its accompanying images of female violence, which remain with us to this day, Lamb murdered her mother one day after the fourth anniversary of the Republic.[44]

As Madelyn Gutwirth has shown in *The Twilight of the Goddesses: Women and Representation in the French Revolutionary Era,* the image of woman as deadly Maenad or Bacchante came to represent, with ultimately deleterious effects for women, the destructive potential unleashed by the Revolution as a whole. Yet all such persuasive accounts of female allegory in the French Revolution examine largely the works or representations of men, and we have much work to do in recovering women's own uses of such images. Even the male-authored allegories of women as Bacchantes or Liberty served as dangerous examples of real female militancy, as Gutwirth, Hunt, and others have shown, and for this reason were replaced by male allegorical figures such as Hercules. We should not, therefore, accept too easily that such allegories of women's violence are misogynist. Instead, as Donna Landry has recently argued regarding the revolutionary Amazon, we must continue to analyze the complex functions of "the Amazon spectrally haunting the figure of the domestic woman" so that we may read "against the grain of much late-eighteenth-century English discourse on womanhood and of many current Anglo-U.S. academic accounts of that discourse."[45]

Reading against the grain, then, I would argue that Henry Fuseli's portrait of a Bacchante inscribed "Mary Anne" and "Maria [illegible] 179[?]" is a rare celebration and elevation of Mary Lamb's aggression into political allegory (see fig. 2). Philip Martin, in *Mad Women in Romantic Writing*, cites this sketch as an unusual "breach of Romantic decorum" because it portrays the mad woman, Mary Lamb, not as a casualty, but as dangerous.[46] Shown wielding a knife and bedecked with a headdress of grapes to signify her allegiance to Dionysus, god of wine and excess, the woman smiles menacingly at us, holding the leg of what may be a sacrificial lamb or buck and a knife, Lamb's murder weapon. Like the tiger in "The Beast in the Tower" who could "into thousand pieces tear" any man, the Bacchante represents women's allegiance with darkness and excess and the threat this allegiance poses to male culture, exemplified in the poet Orpheus, who was torn apart by the Bacchantes.

Though this image of woman as Bacchante was used by men during this period, as Gutwirth and Lynn Hunt have argued, to justify restricting women's rights even further, the image of Mary Lamb as destructive Bacchante can also serve women's interests. The head of the astonished man to the right of the Bacchante is faintly drawn (and inscribed "Fuseli") and seems to vanish before the fierce gaze of the Bacchante, so that her face, her subjectivity, seems to emerge as his recedes in terror. Most importantly, the Bacchante's association with the French Revolution contextualizes Mary Lamb's violence within a larger arena of women's violent struggle. No longer an isolated incident of one woman's tragic madness, which contemporary scholars continue to subsume "in a fit of insanity," her violence in the revolutionary context Fuseli's sketch provides gains collective strength while maintaining our sympathy.

Though Mary Lamb certainly never celebrated her murderous violence as liberation from the constraints of domesticity as Bacchantes traditionally do, Elizabeth Villiers in *Mrs. Leicester's School* does delight in her freedom at her mother's grave: "I might say anything, and be as frolicsome as I pleased here; all was chearfulness [*sic*] and good-humour in our visits to mamma."[47] Elizabeth's sailor Uncle proceeds to cultivate in young Elizabeth the "awe and reverence" she should have felt at her mother's grave. The dead mother provides an edu-

Fig. 2. This drawing by Henry Fuseli, known as *Woman with a Stiletto, Man's Head with a Startled Expression* (1810-20), bears three inscriptions by an unknown contemporary hand, the first two along the upper edge: "Mary Anne" and "Maria [illegible] 179[?]"; the third, "Fuseli," can be seen beneath the man's head. The word after "Maria" appears either smudged or erased. The "179" is a date, though the final digit has been cut off by the edge of the paper. These inscriptions and the incomplete date (possibly 1796, the year Lamb murdered her mother) are generally thought to refer to Mary Anne Lamb. Courtesy of the Ashmolean Museum, Oxford.

cation both inadequate and dangerous, as Marsden has argued, yet the corrective emotional education Elizabeth receives from her uncle, who teaches her to see her dead mother as "a real mamma, which before seemed an ideal something" (281), is also dangerous, precisely because it teaches her "to behave like mamma" and acquire the graces of "womanly character":

And he told me that the ladies from the Manor-House, who sate in the best pew in the church, were not so graceful, and the best women in the village were not so good, as was my sweet mamma; and that if she had lived, I should not have been forced to pick up a little knowledge from him, a rough sailor, or to learn to knit and sew of Susan, but that she would have taught me all lady-like fine works and delicate behaviour and perfect manners, and would have selected for me proper books, such as were most fit to instruct my mind.

[281]

This fantasy of proper bourgeois motherhood bore no resemblance to Mary Lamb's own experience with her mother; rather, it resembles precisely the model of middle-class domestic maternal education found in the writings of Mary Wollstonecraft, Maria Edgeworth, and Hannah More, a model that, as Jean Marsden and others have argued, Mary Lamb rejects in *Mrs. Leicester's School*. Despite the cultural power of this model of benevolent maternal education, which is often used to contrast the violent symbolic order of the father, we must make room for Mary Lamb's radically different perspective on the mother as educator and of the daughter's coming to writing.

Conclusion: Beauty in Unloveliness

[T]o forsake . . . shelters, to turn away, to unshelter oneself, is . . . one of the major peripeties of knowledge.
                    Maurice Blanchot, The Writing of the Disaster

The title of my essay refers to Mary Lamb as femme fatale both because she was, literally, a fatal woman and, more importantly, because her poetry demonstrated an interest in fatal beauty, that like the beasts in the tower, "underneath a fair outside / Does cruelty and treachery hide." Romantic femmes fatales are commonly thought to originate in and appeal to solely the male imagination, being as Mary Ann Doane succinctly put it, "not the subject of feminism but a symptom of male fears about feminism."[48] A discussion of Romantic-period women writers' contributions to the femme fatale traditions, which in no way limit themselves to a critique of the femme fatale's supposed inherent misogyny, is beyond the scope of this essay. I want to introduce Mary Lamb's use of the femme fatale by way of a conclusion, however, in order to make a case for more adventurous reexaminations of Romantic-period women writers.

One of Mary Lamb's poems (which is indisputably hers), "Salome," focuses on the representation of the traditional femme fatale, the beautiful woman who destroys men with her dangerous sexuality. In Mary Lamb's "Salome" (published in Charles Lamb's *Works* [1818]), Salome demands the death of the rather unsympathetic, "most severely good" John the Baptist, who "preached penitence and tears."[49] Lamb's poem concludes with a meditation on painters' depictions of Salome's "beauty in unloveliness," so that her meditation on the biblical femme fatale becomes a self-referential meditation on her own representation of Salome, and on how her writing continues the ambiguous celebration of the fatal woman at the expense of the "saint" sacrificed for such art:

> When painters would by art express
> Beauty in unloveliness,
> Thee, Herodias' daughter, thee,
> They fittest subject take to be.
> They give thy form and features grace;
> But ever in thy beauteous face
> They show a steadfast cruel gaze,
> An eye unpitying; and amaze
> In all beholders deep they mark,
> That thou betrayest not one spark
> Of feeling for the ruthless deed,
> That did thy praiseful dance succeed.
> For on the head they make you look,
> As if a sullen joy you took,
> A cruel triumph, a wicked pride,
> That for your sport a saint had died.
> [35-36]

Lamb referred to her own mother as a "saint," and in this poem we can draw a close connection between her writing and the violence with which it was inextricably intertwined. Lamb questions her own and others' representations of the fatal woman, leaving the woman's true "feeling" about her act unreadable. Salome feels neither remorse, nor pity, nor wicked pride, nor sullen joy—these are all the feelings we as readers and writers of the femme fatale "would by art express," and Lamb leaves her "beholders" with no stable meaning, no tidy moral to take away after gazing on the face of the fatal woman. The impossibility of the female subject of violence is precisely what Lamb examines in "Salome": although the poet herself was literally such a subject of violence, her poem is concerned with the construction and representation of this subject, or rather with the limits of its representation. Salome in Lamb's poem represents one instance (of many throughout the Romantic period) of a femme fatale figure in part serving women's interests, and exceeding any misogynist intentions it may have in male-authored texts and their "fear of feminism" or of women.

In contrast, Bernard Barton in his poem about Salome, "The Daughter of Herodias" (1828) offers an unambiguous account of Salome's sadistic cruelty, and quotes Mary Lamb's poem in the process:

> More revolting was *thy* part,
> Blending cruelty with art;—
> Girl-hood's grace without its heart,
> Hateful makes the fairest.
>
> Bard or painter, who would dress,
> "Beauty in unloveliness,"
> Draw from thee: and thus express
> All thy charms have brought thee;—[50]

Barton's "Daughter of Herodias" does not pose any questions about how women's cruelty and beauty are represented by painters and "bards," such as Lamb; his Salome is a perfect example of a heartless and hateful beauty, not an example, as she is in Lamb's poem, of how artists *represent* this fatal woman as heartless and hateful. In Barton's "Fireside Quatrains, to Charles Lamb," published in the same volume as "Herodias," he offers a portrait of Mary Lamb that reinscribes an unambiguous definition of "Girl-hood's grace" as both beautiful and loving, in direct contrast with his negative example of Salome. For Barton, Mary Lamb epitomizes "womanhood in all its grace" (line 37), plying "Her sempstress [*sic*] labours," and he notes "The mute expression of her downcast eyes" (line 32). The mute, meek, and feminine seamstress, not the published author (not to mention murderer), is Barton's ideal of womanhood; his ironic quotation from Lamb's conflicted portrait of beauty in unloveliness makes her efforts to explore the possibility of femininity and cruelty coexisting appear even more remarkable.

Nietzsche's question about the enchanting woman, which served as this essay's epigraph, illuminates the dangerous affinity between the femme fatale and the violent woman: "Would a woman be able to hold us (or, as they say, "enthrall" us) if we did not consider it quite possible that under certain circumstances she could wield a dagger (any kind of dagger) *against us*?"[51] By "us," of course, Nietzsche means men, the enthralled male lovers of the cruel Belle Dame sans Merci. Yet Lamb's "Salome" is more interested, as was the poem "The Beasts in the Tower," in the "cruel gaze" and "sullen joy" a woman (or "the fairest beast") can take in committing a ruthless deed, the murder of a saint. Lamb emphasizes that it is the painters themselves who "make [Salome] look / As if a sullen joy [she] took" in murder—thus we are left wondering if Salome (and Mary Lamb) did indeed find a sullen joy, a "cruel triumph," in murder. The poem's ironic tone and its shift at the end to question artists' representations of the murderous woman, suggest the answer "no"; yet, by asking the question and then suggestively leaving it unanswered, she also leaves the answer "yes" as an unspoken and disturbing possibility. Mary Lamb never discusses her murder openly in any surviving records, and I am not suggesting that this poem, or any other, contains her "true intentions" or "private" thoughts or that she took pleasure in the murder of her mother. I simply want to point out that she did ask the most difficult of questions about women's capacity for cruelty and violence, and hence about the existence of "woman" outside her representations.

Lamb's "Salome" remains a portrait of "beauty in unloveliness" and as such echoes Fuseli's drawing of a knife-wielding Bacchante inscribed "Mary Anne." Fuseli's representation of the fatal woman, like Mary Lamb's self-representation in "Salome" (as the murderer of a saint), both connect traditional Romantic femmes fatales with one woman's violent act of murder; both artists thereby invest the representation of the femme fatale with a serious, dangerous significance for real, historical women and their actual and potential violent deeds.

I turn now to Margaret Homans's final question in her postscript to *Bearing the Word*: "[I]s it, at the very least, possible to stop excluding and killing the mother for the sake of representation's projects? And can the mother and the linguistic practices she and her daughters can share, tainted as they are by the patriarchal culture with which they are intertwined and by which they come into being, be recuperated for gynocentric, perhaps even for feminist projects?"[52] In response to these most important questions, I would like to pose two others: Is it possible to stop overlooking women's killing, violence, and cruelty for the sake of feminist projects? Is it possible to stop seeking the untainted, prepatriarchal feminine, which we imagine as benevolent and just, in our rediscovery of women's writing? I do not believe that it is fully possible, or entirely desirable, but I firmly believe that we as feminists must allow such questions to be asked, in addition to (not instead of) the ones we are now asking. Mary Lamb asked such a question in her explorations of "beauty in unloveliness," and it remains a worthwhile, and unanswered, question.

Notes

For their helpful comments on this essay, I am grateful to John Logan, Seth Schein, Kari Lokke, Harriet Kramer Linkin, and Stephen Behrendt. I presented a shorter version of this paper at the British Association for Romantic Studies international conference in July 1995 at the University of Wales, Bangor.

1. Mary Anne Lamb (1764-1846), sister of Charles Lamb, stabbed her mother to

death in 1796, after years of suffering neglect and overwork while caring for her ill mother. She was spared incarceration and execution because the inquest determined the cause of the murder was "lunacy," and she remained in her brother Charles's care until his death, with periodic incarcerations in private asylums during violent outbreaks.

2. See Homans, *Women Writers and Poetic Identity* and *Bearing the Word;* Mellor, *Romanticism and Gender.*

3. Gilbert and Gubar, *The Madwoman in the Attic.*

4. Foucault, *The History of Sexuality;* Foucault, *Discipline and Punish.* Massé, *In the Name of Love,* 238.

5. Spivak, "Three Women's Texts," 262-80; N. Armstrong, *Desire and Domestic Fiction.* Armstrong and Tennenhouse, "Representing Violence," 7.

6. Armstrong and Tennenhouse, "Representing Violence," 8.

7. My argument regarding the use value of Mary Lamb's violence is informed by Bataille's important essay, "The Use Value of D.A.F. de Sade."

8. De Lauretis, "The Violence of Rhetoric."

9. Derrida, "The Violence of the Letter: From Lévi-Strauss to Rousseau," in *Of Grammatology,* 101-40.

10. W. Wordsworth, "Written after the Death of Charles Lamb," in *The Poetical Works,* 1947, 4:275.

11. Aaron, *A Double Singleness,* 126. Aaron, "A Modern Electra," 10.

12. Homans, *Bearing the Word,* 11.

13. Mary Lamb, *Mrs. Leicester's School; or, the History of Several Young Ladies, related by themselves* (London: Godwin, 1809), in Lamb and Lamb, *Works* (hereafter referred to as Lamb), vol. 3, *Books for Children,* 276.

14. J. Butler, *Bodies That Matter,* 9. Lamb, 3:276.

15. Derrida, "Ellipsis," in *Writing and Difference,* 296.

16. Lamb, 3:277.

17. Shelley, "Alastor; or, The Spirit of Solitude," in *Shelley's Poetry and Prose,* 71.

18. Homans, *Bearing the Word,* 10.

19. Leslie Friedman elaborates on the prevalence of this theme in her dissertation on Lamb: "In each of Mary Lamb's stories in *Mrs Leicester's School,* the little girl who narrates has been abandoned by her parents before being sent to the school," and in all but two of her stories it is "the mother alone who is guilty." "Mary Lamb," 2:427.

20. Marsden, "Letters on a Tombstone," 36, 34.

21. Published in *Poetry for Children* (1809), Lamb, 3:377. Lucas suggests that this poem is Mary's but offers no evidence.

22. In *A Double Singleness* Aaron writes, "In many of her stories for *Mrs. Leicester's School* she appears to be struggling, in covert ways, both to tell the tale of her relation with her mother, and resolve the tensions it created" (125).

23. Friedman, "Mary Lamb," 2:441. Mellor, *Romanticism and Gender,* 19, 168.

24. Friedman, "Mary Lamb," 2:443.

25. "On Needlework," an essay in the form of a letter to the editor, was published in the April 1815 issue of the *British Lady's Magazine,* 257-60. Aaron offers a persuasive reading of the significance of class in Lamb's "On Needlework" in her "'On Needle-

work,'" as well as throughout *A Double Singleness*. Pamela Woof also treats Lamb's essay as a "radical speculation" in "Dorothy Wordsworth and Mary Lamb," parts 1 and 2.

26. Aaron suggests that the name derives from an (unflattering) character in Mary Hays's *Letter and Essays, Moral and Miscellaneous. A Double Singleness*, 51. Sallust is mentioned in the Lambs' poem "The Sister's Expostulation on the Brother's Learning Latin," the authorship of which is in dispute.

27. Sallust, *The Jugurthine War*, 192-93. Sallust's Sempronia was the wife of D. Junius Brutus (consul in 77 B.C.E.). For a second classical Sempronia, one rumored to have been involved in her famous Gracchi brothers' revolutionary conspiracy, see the entry in Lemprière's *Classical Dictionary of Proper Names Mentioned in Ancient Authors*, first published in London in 1788.

28. Lucas in Lamb, 3:491.

29. Hussey, "The Poems of Mary Lamb," 9. Hussey examined early editions of Mylius's *First Book of Poetry* (1810), in which several of the Lambs' poems were re-printed (some with author's initials); he suggests that "The Coffee Slips" and "A Sister's Expostulation on the Brother's Learning Latin" are by Mary, not by Charles as Lucas suggests; Hussey does not discuss "The Beasts in the Tower." I am grateful to Bonnie Woodberry for bringing this article to my attention.

30. Mrs. Gilchrist, quoted in Hussey, "The Poems of Mary Lamb," 5.

31. *Morning Chronicle* (London), 26 Sept. 1796, quoted in full in Lamb and Lamb, *Letters*, 1:45.

32. Charles Lamb to S.T. Coleridge, 27 Sept. 1796, Lamb and Lamb, *Letters*, 1:44. Aaron, *A Double Singleness*, 97. Woof, "Dorothy Wordsworth and Mary Lamb (part 1)," 50. Mrs. Gilchrist's *Mary Lamb*, 23, follows the *Morning Chronicle* and its elision of the murder almost verbatim, as does E. Ross in *The Ordeal of Bridget Elia*, 24, and Ashton and Davies in their *I had a Sister*, 32. Anthony's account in *The Lambs* is the most forthright, though she links Lamb's violence to the "archaic fury" (44) of natural forces such as the storms accompanying the autumnal equinox of 21 September, the day before the murder; Anthony also links Lamb's violence to the fourth anniversary of the French republic, also 21 September (43). More recently, Mary Blanchard Balle, in "Mary Lamb: Her Mental Health Issues," offers the most detailed discussion of Lamb's "diagnosis" of bipolar disorder; she argues that "[m]ost psychiatric authorities agree that Mary suffered from the major affective disorder commonly known as manic-depressive" (8), though she does not cite any; it certainly seems that literary scholars working on Mary Lamb agree on this diagnosis. Meaghan Hanrahan Dobson offers a detailed and valuable feminist examination of Lamb's theory and practice of writing in "(Re)considering Mary Lamb," and an important response to Aaron's *Double Singleness*.

33. Woof, "Dorothy Wordsworth and Mary Lamb (part 1)," 50.

34. Lamb and Lamb, *Letters*, 2:186.

35. Review of *Poetry for Children*, 102. W. Carew Hazlitt lists this poem as one of those written by Mary in *Mary and Charles Lamb;* but Lucas in Lamb, 3:496, suggests that "The Beasts in the Tower" might be one of the few poems in the volume by Charles, because the poem contains an allusion to Blake's "The Tyger," which we know Charles

admired, and according to Lucas that means that Charles must have written it. I do not find this deduction convincing, because we simply do not know Mary Lamb's thoughts on Blake or his poem, and even if we did, that would not be sufficient evidence to make a definitive attribution. Regardless of this poem's authorship, we can see that in this and other works both Mary and Charles tried to rationalize and make sense of Mary's act of murder.

36. Lamb, 3:407.

37. Lamb, 3:409.

38. Aaron, *A Double Singleness*, 111.

39. Lamb, 3:409.

40. 3 Oct. 1796, Lamb and Lamb, *Letters*, 1:47.

41. Quoted in Charles Lamb's letter to S.T. Coleridge, 17 Oct. 1796, ibid., 1:52.

42. Friedman, "Mary Lamb," 2:419.

43. Foucault, "Tales of Murder."

44. Katherine Anthony points out this connection in *The Lambs*, 43.

45. Gutwirth, *The Twilight of the Goddesses;* Lynn Hunt, *Family Romance of the French Revolution.* Landry, "Figures of the Feminine," 108, 107.

46. See the caption to figure 2, Fuseli's *Woman with a Stiletto, Man's Head with a Startled Expression,* for details on the drawing's three inscriptions. The verso of this drawing is also inscribed, again in an unknown hand: "Nothing could afflict Mr. F." See *Earlier British Drawing,* 300-301. I am grateful to Jon Whitely of the Ashmolean Museum for his help with the inscriptions. P.W. Martin, *Mad Women in Romantic Writing,* ix.

47. Lamb, 3:277.

48. Mary Ann Doane, *Femmes Fatales*, 2-3.

49. Lamb, 5:37. Lucas suggests that "Salome" was composed in 1808-9.

50. Barton, "The Daughter of Herodias," 37-44.

51. Nietzsche, *The Gay Science,* (book 2, no. 69, "Capacity for Revenge"), 126. Emphasis in original.

52. Homans, *Bearing the Word,* 287.

"Tales of Truth?"

Amelia Opie's Antislavery Poetics

Roxanne Eberle

Even as a young woman, Amelia Alderson Opie (1769-1853), daughter of a well-to-do Presbyterian doctor and an Anglo-Indian mother, had strong connections to the organized antislavery movement in England. In an autobiographical fragment written late in life, Opie attributes her "early and ever-increasing zeal in the cause of emancipation" to a youthful awareness of "the sad tale of negro wrongs and negro slavery."[1] Indeed, in order to fully understand Opie's antislavery poetics, it is important to note her lifelong association with abolitionist activism. Adolescent friendships with Norwich Quakers, most notably John Joseph Gurney and his sister, Elizabeth Fry, were forged during the early days of antislavery agitation. Through the Gurneys, Opie became acquainted with prominent abolitionist proponents, including Thomas Clarkson and Thomas Fowell Buxton.

Opie's reformist interests were further cultivated in the 1790s by her involvement in a very different community: the politically radical circle surrounding William Godwin, Thomas Holcroft, and Mary Wollstonecraft. During the turbulent final decades of the eighteenth century, Norwich was home to an enthusiastic group of writers, political activists, and philosophers whose commitment to the doctrine of the "rights of Man" included abolition. Indeed, Dr. Alderson and his daughter were enthusiastic supporters of Thomas Hardy, Horne Tooke, and John Thelwell during their trials for treason in 1794.[2] Opie also authored her first literary works at this time, during what she later acknowledged to be "the most interesting period of [her] long life."[3]

Years later, long after her republican enthusiasm had faded and during a revitalized period of antislavery activity in the 1820s, Opie renewed and strengthened her ties to the Norwich Quakers she had known in her youth. In 1825 she was formally accepted into the Society of Friends on the condition that she would abandon her successful career as a novelist. John Joseph Gurney, by then a prominent Quaker evangelist and abolitionist, and Elizabeth Fry, well known for her work reforming the British prison system, were her spiritual mentors. And by the end of her life, Opie was as celebrated for her abolitionist activism as for her writing. She was even prominently represented in Benjamin Haydon's panoramic representation *The Anti-Slavery Convention*, a painting that commemorated the epic 1840 gathering of British and American abolitionists in London. In Opie's own life, then, we can see the direct influence of arguably the two most important forces in the late-eighteenth-century outcry against slavery: outspoken Jacobins and dissenting Quakers.[4]

Between 1790 and the mid-1830s Opie produced seven novels, one play, three volumes of poetry, and seven collections of tales. Although several of her works have Afro-Caribbean or Afro-English characters, most notably the novels *Adeline Mowbray* (1805) and *Valentine's Eve* (1816), in this essay I will discuss two abolitionist poems that frame her writing career. "The Negro Boy's Tale" appeared in the first collection of Opie's poetry in 1802, when she was most closely associated with prominent British radicals. "The Black Man's Lament; or, How to Make Sugar" was published in 1826 as an illustrated pamphlet, just one year after she joined the Society of Friends.

Given Opie's shifting ideological alliances, her forays into abolitionist verse pose quite a challenge for the twentieth-century critic interested in interrogating antislavery poetics. Critical studies by Moira Ferguson, Patrick Brantlinger, and others have addressed the vexed nature of abolitionist texts.[5] Ferguson's *Subject to Others* is of particular relevance to my project because she focuses on the texts of abolitionist women active in Britain and its colonies. Ferguson argues that the "feminist-abolitionist" position allowed white women to represent themselves as reforming "subjects" at the expense of African subjectivity; they accrued "cultural power" as social critics, but they also encouraged "Anglo-Africanism" by implying—often quite explicitly—that black men and women were essentially inferior to white women. But Ferguson also opens a space for less compromised activism. She suggests that the 1790s saw women authoring texts that "created a special context that inveighed against prejudice and promoted liberation and the concept of human rights." According to Ferguson, and Opie's poetry often supports her position, Revolution-era Romantic writers tended to represent African speakers as not unlike British radicals or disenfranchised women; all are intent upon securing their divine as well as their constitutional liberties. And although Ferguson takes care to remind us that even here "Europe speaks for Africa," she privileges "jacobin" rhetoric in suggesting that radical writers "endowed Africans who lived inside and outside their prose with more of a subject than a subjected status."[6]

Other critics, including Deirdre Coleman, Jean Fagen Yellin, Jenny Sharpe, and Karen Sanchez-Eppler, argue that any unproblematized identification of

black slaves with oppressed white women inevitably undermines the abolition-
ist position and diverts attention from the specific horrors of slavery—even
during the 1790s.[7] Deirdre Coleman expresses this position most powerfully.
According to Coleman, white women writers "capitalize upon fashionable anti-
slavery rhetoric for their own political objectives, an effect most evident in
their employment of the emotive but clichéd analogy between their own dis-
enfranchised lot and the plight of enslaved Africans." Although Sanchez-
Eppler's argument finally confirms Coleman's critique in some respects, she
also interrogates our twentieth-century compulsion to graph racism and self-
less philanthropy on a continuum that ranges from the extremes of guilt to
innocence. Sanchez-Eppler's own critical practice remains steadfastly focused
on the ambiguity of narrative and "rests on the double assumption that all
expression is necessarily embedded in politics and that all politics is necessarily
rhetorically structured. Furthermore, in any given instance the social and liter-
ary implications of these interweavings are never fully under authorial control
and may well prove multiple or even contradictory."[8]

    As Sanchez-Eppler makes clear, we cannot hope to read Opie's verse
through the perspective of her contemporaries. Certainly Opie constructed
her verse in order to evoke a specific response; she wanted her readers to take
away from the poem either a newly born or a reinvigorated commitment to
abolition. To that end she reconfigures her personal and political interests—
sometimes submerging the one into the other—into an effective antislavery
poetics. We, as twentieth-century readers, receive and subsequently re-render
her text through our own historical perspective. In this essay I examine Amelia
Opie's abolitionist poetics, as well as her personal biography, through the lens
of literature and history in an attempt to chart the shifting nature of her anti-
slavery politics. We must trace out intersections of unattractive personal inter-
est and culturally approved racism, as well as admirable reformist goals and
often ambiguous antislavery polemic, if we intend to fully engage the troubling
legacy of abolitionist literature. In an always already thwarted attempt to un-
tangle this Gordian knot comprised of both sincere political activism and rac-
ist—as well as racialist—representation, I will be examining several different
elements of Opie's verse. Finally, I hope to avoid the twin pitfalls of uncritically
celebrating Opie as a proponent of unequivocally admirable reform goals and
condemning her for falling far short of our twentieth-century standards of
antiracist discourse.[9] I would like to further avoid celebrating one poem at the
expense of another. Most of Opie's verse has been ignored by twentieth-cen-
tury critics, but those who have approached her antislavery poetry have tended
to play favorites. Moira Ferguson, for example, discusses "The Negro Boy's
Tale" at length but fails to mention "The Black Man's Lament." And Donald
Reiman grudgingly allows that though "The Black Man's Lament" may have

some merit, "The Negro Boy's Tale" is "one of her most ridiculous poems to modern readers . . . [because of] its attempt to represent the speech of a slave." Most recently, Anne Mellor has negotiated the problem of reading Opie's abolitionist writings by contextualizing them not only within the history of English abolition, but also among the work of other women writers, particularly Joanna Baillie and Maria Edgeworth. Mellor's conclusion, that these writings model a "rhetoric of sympathy" even as they privilege a new "'slavery' of assimilation," asserts the importance of approaching antislavery texts with an eye toward their complex politics.[10]

In both "The Negro Boy's Tale" and "The Black Man's Lament" we find Opie grappling with the very dilemma that so vexes her current audience: what is the appropriate role of the white abolitionist when in conversation with the black slave? Opie's interest in this continuing problem evidences itself in the shifting representations of the "abolitionist" and the "slave" over the course of her career. In this essay I hope to trace out those changes by focusing on questions raised within the body of Opie's abolitionist verse, without definitively dismissing either poem. The first set of questions arises from Opie's representation of Afro-Caribbean speech and its relevance to her portrayal of the slave's subjectivity. What does it mean when a white abolitionist "voices" Jamaican Creole? Does it necessarily imply denigration? In its own historical context, can it be employed to signify positive difference? The second set of questions can be seen as related to the first. These questions emerge from Opie's poetic representation of the abolitionist intent upon "telling" the slave's narrative for him. When, and how, does the presence of the sympathetic white woman, possessing both social privilege and jural-political privation, distract from activist polemic? If we assume that her presence invariably signifies either collusion in enslavement or political self-interest—or both—then we miss any value she may have as a "witness" of atrocity.

The abolitionist author's material distance from West Indian slavery further complicates her representation of a dialogue between the black slave and the white woman at the site of enslavement: Amelia Opie never actually "witnessed" scenes of Caribbean slavery. What then is the value of either the "testimony" of the imagined witness—the white narrator of Opie's verse—or that of the author herself? Shoshana Felman has argued that "the specific task of the literary testimony is . . . to open up in that belated witness, which the reader now historically becomes, the imaginative capability of perceiving history— what is happening to others—*in one's own body,* with the power of sight (of insight) usually afforded only by one's own immediate physical involvement."[11] The author as witness, according to Felman, has value because she can represent for the reader the "imaginative act" of constructing history itself.[12] I would suggest that Felman's assertion has a particular resonance in the context of nineteenth-century abolitionist writings precisely because they are produced in order to incite action. The imaginative act of the author, in the case of the British abolitionist far from Jamaica, models the possibility of imagining what the reader does not actually "know." The abolitionist poem compels its readers to "witness" the atrocity in progress, if you will, and then invites them to interject themselves within the scene, thus changing the projected trajectory of history. Opie's verse is riddled with questions posed to the reader by either the abolitionist narrator or the narrating slaves. Such use of the question as the dominant rhetorical mode further summons the reader into the text; readers are asked to grapple with the moral questions raised by slavery and to answer them with the fervent "yes" of the newly converted reformer. The process of reading should transform the reader into an agent of change rather than stasis. I would further argue, however, that at its most subtle Amelia Opie's abolitionist writings also acknowledge that some elements of the "slavery question" remain unanswerable. Many possible answers do not comfortably fit within the confines of the white abolitionist's voice or acceptable imaginings, constrained as they are by the rhetorical tools available to an identity constructed within even the relatively enlightened discourses of Christian Republicanism.

Unlike many British abolitionists, Amelia Alderson Opie appears to have been extraordinarily aware of the African presence in eighteenth-century England. In the autobiographical fragment I alluded to at the beginning of this essay, Opie recalls that as a child she had a great "terror" of black men.[13] Her mother, who held advanced views on the education of girls, forced her to confront that fear by befriending the African manservant of a neighbor; it is unclear from the text whether he was a free man or a slave. Opie writes

[I] was forced to shake hands with the black the next time he approached [me], and thenceforward we were very good friends. Nor did [my parents] fail to make me acquainted with negro history; as soon as I was able to understand, I was shewn on the map where their native country was situated; I was told the sad tale of negro wrongs and negro slavery; and I believe that my early and ever-increasing zeal in the cause of emancipation was founded and fostered by the kindly emotions which I was encouraged to feel for my friend Aboar and all his race.

[Brightwell, 13]

Opie also recalls overcoming her fear of a skeleton found in her physician father's office. Again a racial element figures prominently in her account: "The skeleton of which I was afraid was that of a girl, black, probably, from the preparation it had undergone; be that as it may, I was induced to take it on my lap and examine it, and at last, calling it my black doll, I used to exhibit it to my wondering and alarmed companions. Here was vanity again perhaps" (12-13). As a child, then, Opie saw British Africans doubly and, as I will later demonstrate, both of these possible relationships are found again in her abolitionist verse.

Although the adult Aboar is her "friend" and hence more of her equal, the "black doll" certainly holds a much lower place in her implicit hierarchy. Opie's second anecdote is chilling, and not just in its self-involved "vanity." At least her friendship with Aboar encourages dialogue between the author and the "black man," as well as between Opie and her parents. In the second case, Opie "exhibits" an irrevocably silenced black child to a correspondingly mute "wondering" audience (13). In the later relationship narrative power is securely located in the hands of the author at the expense of both the "subject" and the auditor.

Another family anecdote further illustrates the often vexing subjective referent Opie attached to the cause of abolition. As an orphan, her mother was accompanied to England from India by an East Indian nurse named Savannah. Found among Opie's papers was a letter, dated 1749, in which an uncle discusses her mother's arrival in Norfolk. After commenting upon how easily his niece has adapted to England, he writes: "[T]he black girl, her nurse, is not reconciled to England; and, thinking she never shall be so, she is determined to return to Bengal by the Christmas ships. As my mother will give her entire liberty to be at her own disposal, I believe her design is to enter into service, as other free women do. If it be in your power, you are very much desired by all my niece's friends to prevent Savannah's being bought or sold as a negro."[14] Opie's family appears to have been well aware of the dangers to free people of color on the streets of English cities; as historians point out, dark-skinned East Indians, as well as free Afro-English citizens, were subject to harassment and illegal seizure.[15] Early on, then, Opie's associations with the fate of black slaves, as well as free men and women in the dangerous position of being mistaken for slaves, were closely linked to her memories of childhood and to family mythology. They serve as satisfying reminders that she was always on the "right" side of the slavery debate; her anecdotes consistently provide evidence for either her own tolerance or that of her family.

Although Opie's declaration that her abolitionist commitment "grew with her growth and strengthened with her strength"[16] supports the idea that the "personal is the political," one might argue that in making abolition the measure of her spiritual growth, Opie subsumes the larger issue of antislavery into an often self-interested account of increasing wisdom, tolerance, and piety. In many ways Opie's autobiography is very much a "fiction of self-identity," which, as Jenny Sharpe points out in *Allegories of Empire,* is necessarily complicated by race, class, and nationality in an age of imperial expansion and enthusiastic social reform.[17] Opie's triumphant narrative of her "education" in racism nearly overwhelms the lesson itself. Furthermore, Opie was more than willing to make literary use of the slave figure, at the expense of the actual historical individual. In a verse memorial written many years after Mrs. Alderson's death, Opie figures her mother's arrival in England as follows: "An orphan'd babe, from India's plain / She came, a faithful slave her guide!"[18] Savannah, whose status as a "free woman" is of paramount importance in the letter from Opie's uncle, becomes a "faithful slave" in the author's poetic rendering of her mother's life. Opie enhances the drama of her mother's biography and of her own poem by "selling" Savannah—at least to her readers—as a slave; consequently, she violates the family's laudable desire to keep Savannah free.[19]

As we turn toward Opie's overtly antislavery literary production, we must keep in mind both her sincere commitment to abolition and her seeming willingness to refigure those beliefs as it suited her. Certainly Opie garnered both personal and political power in positioning herself as an abolitionist, even as she contributed to antislavery discourse.

In the 1802 poem, "The Negro Boy's Tale," Opie employs the discourses of revolutionary feminism and sentimental poetry in a denunciation of the "fiend-delighting trade."[20] Although abolitionists continued to fight for the cessation of the slave trade, historians of the period note that the early 1800s were lean years for British antislavery proponents.[21] The conservative backlash following the Terror in France led to a concerted suppression of any agitation aimed at parliamentary reform, including abolition. The gains of the highly visible and well-orchestrated antislavery campaigns of the 1780s and 1790s, when Parliament nearly passed a bill outlawing the slave trade, were in grave danger of being obliterated. Yet prominent reformers like Thomas Clarkson continued to publish abolitionist pamphlets, and women poets, including Amelia Opie and Mary Robinson, proceeded to write antislavery verse.[22] But unlike Hannah More and Ann Yearsley, who had published poems in the 1780s under the auspices of the Anti-Slavery Society, the abolitionist verse of Opie and Robinson appeared in volumes of poetry largely innocent of overt political critique. Opie's "Negro Boy's Tale," for example, was first published among rather conventional Romantic and Sentimental fare. The frontispiece of *Poems by Mrs. Opie* (fig. 3) illustrates the lyric "I once rejoiced, sweet Evening Gale." In the engraving a melancholic young woman, whom we assume to be the speaker of the poem, stands before "Henry's lonely tomb" and mourns lost innocence. For the most part, the volume invites its readers to identify Opie as a lyric poetess, more interested in love than liberty.[23]

"The Negro Boy's Tale" marks a departure not only from other Opie poems, but also from other abolitionist verse. Unlike Hannah More's "Slavery" (1788) or even Thomas Cowper's "The Negro's Complaint" (1778), with which it shares a greater affinity, "The Negro Boy's Tale" attempts to replicate the polyphonic nature of the slavery debate within a single poem.[24] The poem has five characters, although three dominate the verse. There is Trevannion, a British gentleman just departing Jamaica after securing his fortune; Zambo, a young slave who pleads for passage to England; and Anna, Trevannion's daughter and

Fig. 3. Frontispiece to *Poems by Mrs. Opie* (1804). Courtesy of the General Research Division, The New York Public Library, Astor, Lenox and Tilden Foundations.

the auditor of Zambo's story. In addition to these speakers, there is an overtly abolitionist narrator who frames the poem with moralizing commentary and interprets the actions of the characters throughout, as well as a silent overseer who attempts to beat Zambo into submission.

The poem opens with Trevannion's words: "Jamaica, sultry land adieu! / Away! and loitering Anna find! / I long dear England's shores to view" (lines 2-4). But Anna, in spite of the best attempts of her father, remains hidden from his sight. The reader finds her "mute, listening to [Zambo's] prayer" (line 10). Zambo implores Anna to bring him to England, where he can find employment and earn enough as a free man to return to Africa. He sees England in precisely the same way as Trevannion perceives Jamaica; it possesses the resources of liberty and wealth that he needs to secure in order to return home. Although Zambo's words explicitly echo those of Trevannion, the slave's desire is expressed in Jamaican Creole: "Oh! ven no slave, a boat I buy / . . . / And over wave again I fly / Mine own loved negro land to view" (lines 25-28). In *Subject to Others,* Moira Ferguson argues that representations of black speech in the early nineteenth century invariably mark "linguistic difference" between slaves and reformers, as well as between slaves and masters; this "emphasize[s] the 'stupidity' of slaves and reinforces the need for British intervention."[25]

Certainly, Zambo is a somewhat naive speaker who seeks guidance from Anna Trevannion. He imagines England as a "mother" land, a nation where he mistakenly believes that "De helpless Negro slave be free" (line 20). The poem leads us to believe that Zambo has heard about the Mansfield Judgment and like many other slaves has put his faith in the British legal system. As historian Folarin Shyllon points out, however, the Mansfield Judgment was widely misunderstood by both abolitionist and proslavery forces.[26] On the one hand, it did provide British blacks with habeas corpus, thus ensuring that once in England they could not be forcibly taken out of it. On the other hand, it did not emancipate them; nor did it guarantee them the right to keep the wages they earned. The young boy of Opie's poem, however, does not know this; he separates Mother England's desires from that of her slave-trading sons and reluctant magistrates: "Oh! if dat England understand / De negro wrongs, how wrath she be!" (lines 83-84). Zambo envisions England as a crusading and angry woman whose maternal nurturance will ensure a return to his own mother. He tells Anna:

> It is a long time since lass ve meet,
> Ven I was take by bad vite man,
> And moder cry, and kiss his feet,
> And shrieking after Zambo ran.
> [lines 33-36]

Although the apparently motherless Anna sympathizes with Zambo, she acknowledges "Mother England's" true role in the slave trade with a telltale blush. She knows that, in fact, England encourages her slaver sons' economic ambitions and ruthless actions. In this section of the poem we find support for those critics who argue that abolitionist poetry calls attention to the superiority of the white reformer over the naive slave. Anna knows that Zambo will not be free in England and therefore can never return to his mother, but out of a misguided desire to protect his feelings, she chooses not to enlighten him as to actual British policy and practice.

Zambo's naïveté, which can be read through his trust in Mother England and—if we are so inclined—by his use of Jamaican Creole, is undercut by a savvy attempt to negotiate for freedom. Zambo, like many historical slaves, has converted to Christianity. In most cases such conversions were in defiance of plantocratic law because Christian slaves were likelier candidates for emancipation; recent historians have pointed out the ways in which many slaves utilized conversion to secure freedom.[27] Zambo promises piety in exchange for passage; he vows that once in Africa he will teach his mother to say Christian prayers for Anna's soul. He does reveal a streak of skepticism, however, in his added caveat: "Though men who sons from moders tear, / She'll tink, teach goodness never could" (lines 63-64).

Does Zambo's use of Afro-Caribbean dialect detract from his pointed critique of the barbarous practices of a Christian nation? Certainly a white woman's vocalization of Afro-Caribbean makes Opie's twentieth-century readers uncomfortable. Keeping in mind Jenny Sharpe's reminder that "the past is not available as a hidden presence for us to recover," I would like to examine Opie's use of Creole in the context of late-eighteenth-century racial discourse.[28] On the one hand, representations of Afro-Caribbean speech are rampant in the overtly racist caricatures printed in periodical literature; in such cases they serve to distance and dehumanize enslaved Africans for white readers. In proslavery tracts, descriptions of black English and Afro-Caribbean rhetoric further serve this purpose. In his *History of the British Colonies in the West Indies* (1793), for example, Bryan Edwards characterizes the language of slaves as follows: "Among other propensities and qualities of the Negroes must not be omitted their loquaciousness. They are fond of exhibiting set speeches, as orators by profession; but it requires a considerable share of patience to hear them throughout; for they commonly make a long preface before they come to the point; beginning with a tedious enumeration of their past services and hardships."[29] The text of advertisements for the sale of slaves as well as notices of escaped slaves invariably comments upon the linguistic skills of the individual; for example, a 1712 notice in the *Daily Courant* reads "Negro 22 years—run away—middle Size, with English stammering speech." Yet another, published in the *Public*

Ledger in 1761, announces the sale of "A healthy Negro Girl, aged about fifteen years; speaks good English, works at her needle."[30] The antislavery community also demonstrates an awareness of what we might call the politics of language. Most abolitionist editors, although eager for compelling narratives demonstrating the cruelty of slavery, downplay Afro-Caribbean speech by promoting the work of European-educated Africans fluent in English or by rewriting orally delivered slave narratives in "the King's English."[31] On both sides of the political spectrum, then, the acquisition of "correct" English or the use of Afro-Caribbean serves as an identifying marker read for meaning.

If we accept the hypothesis that the late eighteenth century was particularly preoccupied with language use within black communities, what can be said about Opie's representation of Zambo's distinctly Afro-Caribbean English?[32] Opie's reviewers found it to be at best a distraction and at worst aesthetically unconvincing—although for very different reasons from those we might have as twentieth-century readers. The *Critical Review* argues that "'The Negro Boy's Tale' is told in the broken language of the slaves: peculiarities of this kind always excite the reader's attention; but when the language is thus dramatically preserved, the thoughts also should be in character. Zambo is too poetical." The reviewer for the *Edinburgh Review* is even more explicit in his assumptions about the philosophical limitations of those who speak Jamaican Creole: "[Zambo's] argument on the natural equality of the Negro, and his sarcasms against those who practise not what they preach, are more in the character of the poet than of the supposed speaker."[33] It appears, then, that Opie's representation of an intelligent young plantation worker able to employ the radical discourse of inalienable natural rights and to negotiate the religious requirements of the reformer's Christian mission while speaking Jamaican Creole, affronted some readers in its assertion of linguistic difference that did not entirely conform to a racialist understanding of the connection between race, language, and humanity. Although we cannot definitively identify Opie's intentions here, it is important to recognize that other Romantic authors, including Robert Burns and William Wordsworth, were also experimenting with dialect as both an aesthetic and a political tool.

Zambo's Afro-Caribbean voice dominates most of Opie's poem. Except for her telltale blush, Anna remains silent and nearly invisible throughout his narrative. In the twenty-eighth quatrain she breaks that silence only to acknowledge her powerlessness: "'*I* cannot grant thy suit,' she cries; / 'But I, my father's knees will clasp, / Nor will I, till he hears me, rise'" (lines 110–112). Anna's deployment of standard and, one might argue, poetic language does not indicate any actual power at all: Trevannion ignores his daughter's words. Angry at the delay, he insists that she be "mute." Agreeably silent when listening to Zambo's pleas, Anna resists her father's command. She pleads for the slave's passage; her words—and then her "shrieks"—mingle with the sound of Zambo being beaten on the shore. Anna's failure to enact change points to the difficulty for white women abolitionists who attempt reform in the context of their own political invisibility. Although Zambo's mother and Anna are metaphorically identified with their respective "nations," they are unable to control the actions of either the state or the more empowered male citizen. Anna tries to refuse her own passage until Trevannion hears her plea, but he will not engage in dialogue: "Without reply, the pitying maid / Trevannion to the vessel bore" (lines 127-28). Trevannion employs his superior physical power to silence his importuning daughter; he bears her to his ship in a manner not unlike that of Zambo's original captors. In the metaphoric logic of Opie's poem, then, Anna is symbolically linked to both Zambo and his mother. Like Zambo she is carried upon a departing ship against her will, and like his mother she protests the young boy's enslavement. If we go outside the scope of the poem, we might argue that she is further positioned with Zambo because she is part of her father's "property"; she is undoubtedly intended for an advantageous match back in England, where her father's newly acquired colonial wealth will provide a dowry worthy of a highly placed bridegroom possessed of a "name" or "property," or both. And yet, I hesitate to stress a reading that emphasizes the subjectivity of the abolitionist rather than of the slave. Finally, Anna's fate radically differs from that of the slave, and the poem's focus remains steadfastly fixed upon Zambo's actions.

Zambo, "by despair made bold," plunges into the ocean in pursuit of the Trevannions' departing ship (line 145). At this point Anna's father, inexplicably impressed by the young boy's bravery, commands his crew to save him, but it is too late: "the struggling victim sinks, and dies" (line 172). In killing off Zambo, Opie's poem conforms to antislavery rhetoric, which celebrates the slave's escape through death and his or her greater reward in heaven. The abolitionist speaker asks, "Can I his early death deplore?" (line 180). In *Subject to Others* Moira Ferguson lauds the representation of Zambo's death as a subversive suicide because it deprives the slave owner of his property and so undermines the slave system. But Karen Sanchez-Eppler warns twentieth-century readers of the dangers inherent in abolitionist "appropriation" of slave bodies "for the purposes of political and literary discourse"; she contests a vision of liberty that employs "death as a glorious emancipation."[34] And indeed, even as Opie's poem employs the familiar narrative structure of the "dying Negro" for her readers, the narrator refuses to join Trevannion and Anna in their weeping. She turns her attention to those still living in slavery:

> I pity those who live, and groan;
> Columbia countless Zambos sees; . . .

> For swelled with many a wretch's moan
> Is Western India's sultry breeze.
> [lines 181-84]

She concludes by calling upon a vengeful—and, I would argue, revolutionary—personification of Justice:

> Come, Justice, come! in glory drest,
> O come! the woe-worn negro's friend,
> The fiend-delighting trade arrest,
> The negro's chains asunder rend!
> [lines 185-88]

Justice, not mere "Pity," can enact change. The tears of Anna and her father indicate their respective feelings of "virtuous woe" and "keen remorse" (lines 173-74) and so somewhat vindicates them for their failure to "save" Zambo. But finally, the narrator turns away from the mourning Trevannions. Representations of tragic death and subsequent sorrow may be useful if they lead to corresponding feelings in the reader, but even as the poem employs the tools of melodrama, its ultimate lesson is that such stagings of sorrow are ultimately futile unless they lead to "just" action.

I would suggest that the tragic conclusion of "The Negro Boy's Tale" functions not unlike the indeterminate endings of several Jacobin novels written during the 1790s, including Godwin's *Caleb Williams* (1794) and Wollstonecraft's *The Wrongs of Woman* (1798). The weeping Trevannions are literally left midway between Jamaica and England and philosophically between impotent Pity and proactive Justice. Tilottama Rajan, in *The Supplement of Reading,* argues that "reading beyond the ending" of a political text is crucial to enacting the social reform envisioned in the literary work itself. The radical writer wants to "provoke the reader to revolt against the prison of things as they are."[35] "The Negro Boy's Tale," written in a climate of political apathy and conservative backlash, shamelessly evokes sentimental tears and denies its readers a "happy ending" in an attempt to goad them into taking abolitionist action.

After the abolition of the British slave trade in 1807, antislavery activism in England entered a period of relative inactivity; abolitionists seeking gradual emancipation chose to work quietly and through familiar appeals to sympathetic members of Parliament. They believed that by stemming the flow of Africans to the colonies, slavery itself would cease. The 1820s, however, saw a renewed period of agitation, during which activists turned their attention toward constructing aggressive appeals aimed at changing public opinion.[36] Indeed, some abolitionists, frustrated by the fact that slavery still flourished in spite of the 1807 legislature, began to argue for immediate rather than gradual emancipation. In 1824, for example, Elizabeth Heyrick, who, like Opie, was a recently converted Quaker, published an influential pamphlet entitled *Immediate not Gradual Emancipation.*[37] Heyrick exhorts her readers to examine their own complicity in West Indian slavery, asking: "We that hear, and read, and approve, and applaud the powerful appeals, the irrefragable arguments against the Slave Trade, and against slavery,—are we ourselves sincere, or hypocritical? Are *we* the true friends of justice, or do we only cant about it? To which party do *we* really belong?—to the friends of emancipation, or perpetual slavery? The perpetuation of slavery in our West India colonies, is not an abstract question, to be settled between the Government and the Planters,—it is a question in which we are *all* implicated;—we are all guilty."[38] Three million tracts were published by the Anti-Slavery Society between 1823 and 1831 as abolitionists turned toward swaying public opinion on a grand scale,[39] through well-publicized boycotts of slave-produced goods, petitions, and increasingly well-organized provincial societies, many of which were made up of women; Opie herself belonged to the Norwich Ladies Anti-Slavery Auxiliary, and her name headed one petition of eight hundred thousand names.[40]

Opie's first contribution to antislavery polemic in the 1820s was a new edition of "The Negro Boy's Tale." Excerpted from the 1802 volume, repackaged, and newly illustrated, the poem was reissued as one in a series of tales and poems intended for adolescent readers.[41] Instead of the image of the melancholic young poetess found in the 1802 volume, an illustration of Zambo's death introduces the poem in 1824 (fig. 4). In the foreground the drowning slave struggles against the waves; the ship carrying Anna and Trevannion appears in the background. Although Opie made only negligible revisions in the body of the poem, she did add a short "Address to Children."[42] She exhorts her "dear young friends" to complete the reform work begun in the 1780s. She offers up her own poem as one inspired by the "labours of such men as Clarkson, Wilberforce, William Smith, Fowell Buxton, and other philanthropists." Throughout much of the preface Opie describes the horrors of abduction and enforced slavery, acts that she abhors as "contrary to the first principles of liberty, of justice, of the rights of man, and of CHRISTIANITY."[43] Opie's abolitionist position in 1824 hearkens back to the 1790s and her immersion in republican rhetoric, even as it points forward to her increasing commitment to Quaker ideology.

In 1824 Opie had only just applied for membership in the Society of Friends; her private correspondence with Elizabeth Fry indicates that in January of that year, she had expressed doubts about her readiness for conversion.

I think I need not add that with all this going on in my mind, I am not likely to ask for membership. To say the truth, much as I should like to belong to a religious

Fig. 4. Frontispiece to *The Negro Boy's Tale* (1824). Courtesy of the Photographs and Prints Division, Schomburg Center for Research in Black Culture, The New York Public Library, Astor, Lenox and Tilden Foundations.

society, and much as I see, or think I see, the hand of my gracious Lord in leading me, to whom have been given so many ties to a worldly life, in the various gifts bestowed on me, (I mean accomplishments, as they are called,) to communion with a sect which requires the sacrifice of them almost in toto, thereby trying my faith to the uttermost.[44]

As I noted before, Opie's conversion was dependent upon her abandonment of a successful writing career; it was a requirement that Opie was to struggle against even after her formal acceptance into the Society of Friends in August of 1825. One of the ways in which Opie quietly subverted John Joseph Gurney's prohibition against publication was to reposition herself as a Christian moralist rather than a society novelist. "The Black Man's Lament; or, How to Make Sugar," published just one year after her conversion, allowed Opie to return to the public sphere as a published author under the aegis of antislavery activism.[45]

In "The Black Man's Lament" Opie abandons the sentimental discourse of "The Negro Boy's Tale"—along with her attempt to replicate Afro-Caribbean Creole—in order to present a more Anglicized black speaker who eloquently describes the socioeconomic institutions that enslave him. This later poem thoroughly conforms to very specific abolitionist goals of the 1820s, when antislavery advocates were loudly asserting the utility of a free laboring force of black workers. Employing economic arguments in support of their position, they worked at convincing planters as well as Britons who were used to slave-produced luxuries that free labor would result in more profits and cheaper goods. Heyrick herself argues, "It has been abundantly proved that voluntary labour is more productive, more advantageous to the employer than compulsory labour." Recent historians have cast a rather skeptical eye upon such nineteenth-century arguments. David Brion Davis has argued that "[l]iberation from slavery did not mean freedom to live as one chose, but rather freedom to become a diligent, sober, dependable worker who gratefully accepted his position in society."[46] Certainly, Quaker ideology privileged successfully run business nearly as much as pacifism or plain speech.

The enslaved narrator of "The Black Man's Lament" is an eminently knowledgeable worker whose voice overwhelmingly dominates the text; all but five of the poem's forty-three quatrains are attributed to him. As Anne Mellor points out, Opie's verse grants him "social equality and moral authority."[47] It seems apparent that in writing this poem Opie was influenced by the published narratives of such African writers as Olaudah Equiano and Ignatius Sancho, as well as the parliamentary debates, which provided exceptionally detailed accounts of a slave's life from capture until death. Her intent is certainly to provide her readers with an articulate and rational speaker. But the "Black Man" begins speaking only after an abolitionist narrator introduces him to us. In a gesture borrowed from the stage, she presents his narrative under the heading: "Negro speaks."[48]

The Afro-Caribbean narrator then goes on to provide an expository description of the actual processes of planting and processing sugar cane, from the capture of the workers until the conversion of sugar into rum. The "making of sugar" is shown to parallel the making of free men into slaves, even as the speaker explicitly and implicitly asserts his own humanity. The working metaphor of the poem is that in eating sugar and drinking rum, the British people are consuming the flesh and blood of the African slave. Although this is a familiar rhetorical figure for the abolitionist, Opie's use of it is rather subtle.[49] Unlike much verse and prose of the time, her poem merely implies the metaphor through the black man's description of laboring bodies producing sugar, rum, and molasses. Even the abolitionist speaker merely suggests the comparison: "And that they may this *sugar* gain, / The Negro toils, and bleeds, and dies" (lines 11-12).

In the course of his narrative, the black man proves his proficiency as a laborer, as well as his command over logic and the English language. His powerful words are further supported by the brightly colored illustrations that accompany the text; these include rather "inoffensive" images entitled "Clearing Away the Weeds" and "Manuring," for example (fig. 5). But the violence of the system continually interrupts the slave's often dispassionate account of "making sugar." Evocative images entitled "Torn from His Friends" and "The Exhausted Slave Whipped" (fig. 6) appear alongside seemingly innocent depictions of "Sugar-Cane" and "Shipping the Casks." Furthermore, the narrator's commentary often forces the reader to examine an apparently inoffensive image more critically. The rather innocuous representation of "Negroes Holing the Cane-Field" for example, is accompanied by the following lines:

> As holes must all *at once* be made,
> > *Together* we must work or stop;
> Therefore, the whip our strength must aid,
> > And lash us when we pause or drop.
> [lines 49-52]

In describing and illustrating "holing," Opie adds her voice to those of other abolitionists opposed to this particularly brutal method of planting.

Activists working within Parliament described the procedure at length: "[I]t is necessary that every hole or section of the trench should be finished in equal time. . . . The tardy stroke must be quickened, and the languid invigorated [by the drivers]. . . . No breathing time, no pause of languor, to be repaid by brisker exertion on return to work, can be allowed to individuals: all must work, or pause together."[50]

Fig. 5. "Manuring," illustration from *The Black Man's Lament; or, How to Make Sugar* (1826). Courtesy of the Lilly Library, Indiana University, Bloomington, Indiana.

The use of illustrations further marks this poem's allegiance to the organized antislavery campaigns of the 1820s. The success of the Wedgwood antislavery medallion with its depiction of a chained and supplicating slave, as well as popular reprints of Thomas Clarkson's 1808 design of a slave ship, encouraged abolitionists to use the visual medium as part of their message.[51] A cribbed version of Clarkson's *Slave Ship* accompanies the seventh stanza's evocation of the middle passage: "From tender wife, and child to tear; / Then in a darksome ship to place, / Pack'd close, like bales of cotton there" (lines 22-24). And the first image of "The Black Man's Lament" evokes the Wedgwood medallion even as it simultaneously represents that other successful tool of antislavery agitation: the petition (fig. 7).

Nevertheless, in spite of its canny deployment of word and text, there is something rather disturbing about the first part of Opie's poem. On the one hand, the black man's impressive body of knowledge indicates his potential as a worker if he were an emancipated laborer. And yet the quatrains read as a

Fig. 6. "The Exhausted Slave Whipped," illustration from *The Black Man's Lament; or, How to Make Sugar* (1826), courtesy of the Lilly Library, Indiana University, Bloomington, Indiana.

rather disturbing primer for young boys interested in making a colonial fortune. All they need to know about enslaving a population and forcing them to labor can be found embedded within the black man's lament.[52] Furthermore, the detailed descriptions focus with an almost prurient interest on the spectacle of laboring and abused slave bodies. Sanchez-Eppler notes that antislavery stories for adults and children were extremely popular and very profitable; readers were fascinated, she writes, "by the abuses they ostensibly oppose[d]. For despite their clear abolitionist stance, such stories are fueled by the allure of bondage."[53] It is only in the last eighteen stanzas of Opie's poem—which are not illustrated—that we find the black man's musings upon the psychological and spiritual damage done by slavery.

In these final stanzas, the speaker compares his lot to that of the English peasant in an attempt to answer proslavery assertions that a slave's existence mirrors that of the English farmer. The inclusion of proslavery arguments was a very common rhetorical strategy employed by abolitionist writers. And dur-

Fig. 7. "The Petition for Abolishing the Slave-Trade," illustration from *The Black Man's Lament; or, How to Make Sugar* (1826), courtesy of the Lilly Library, Indiana University, Bloomington, Indiana.

ing the 1820s they were particularly preoccupied by proslavery assertions that English peasants and African slaves shared a common lot. Opie's speaker asks:

> Who dares an English peasant flog,
>   Or buy, or sell, or steal away?
> Who sheds his blood? treats him like dog,
>   Or fetters him like beasts of prey?
> [lines 113-116]

In posing such questions, the black man of Opie's poem rehearses arguments also made by Thomas Clarkson and other writers.[54] In turning proslavery rhetoric back upon itself, abolitionists assert that if the English peasantry are "free," then so too should be the slave. Opie further pushes toward a rhetoric of equality by having her speaker experiment with even more incendiary equations of similarity. Her speaker yearns to employ the golden rule—taught to him by

Christian owners—to exact vengeance: ". . .Oh! would I could / Make White men Negroes' miseries feel." (lines 127-128). The black man of Opie's poem overwhelmingly refutes the myth of the "happy" Christian slave:

> There are, I'm told, upon some isles,
> > Masters who gentle deign to be;
> And there, perhaps, the Negro *smiles*,
> > But *smiling* Negros *few* can see.
> [lines 149-152]

In the very last stanzas of the poem he also rejects Christian promises that a greater reward awaits him after death. Although he yearns to believe in a benevolent God who does not distinguish between black and white, or master and slave, he doubts that he will achieve heaven because of the "rage" that "burns" within him (line 167). On the one hand, Opie's representation of the slave as a religious skeptic seems rather unexpected, but Elizabeth Heyrick, in her 1824 pamphlet, had also argued that slaves could not be expected to embrace a faith practiced by those who enslave and torture them. Heyrick and Opie suggest that only emancipated Africans can be true Christians—a goal much desired by their reading audience.

After representing the "Black Man" as an articulate and even angry subject, insistent upon his claims to freedom and justice, Opie turns away from his narrative. The final stanza is again in the white abolitionist's voice:

> He ceas'd; for here his tears would flow,
> > And ne'er resum'd his tale of *ruth*.
> Alas! it rends my heart to know
> > He only told a *tale of truth*.
> [lines 169-172]

It is tempting to read "The Black Man's Lament," as a more sophisticated and even-handed abolitionist poem than "The Negro Boy's Tale." In the later work we find a much more conventionally articulate African speaker, who dominates the entire verse. Furthermore, there is little sentimental rhetoric or excessive literary device; it is a "tale of truth." Yet "The Black Man's Lament," I would argue, is also compromised by its faith in "objective" rhetoric as well as its absolute investment in abolitionist party politics.

Whereas the "The Negro Boy's Tale" ends with a call for "Justice," as well as a promise to free the "wretched" laboring in Columbia (line 183), the black man of Opie's later text will never escape his fate as a laborer in thrall to British landowners. And unlike Zambo—who implies that he will accept Christianity when its proponents "practise what they preach"—the black man yearns to be embraced by the white father of Christianity. Most disturbingly, perhaps, the abolitionist narrator of "The Black Man's Lament" intrusively asserts her ulti-mate authority over the slave's words. She assures her readers that "He only told a tale of truth" (line 172). We do not have to accept the black man's word; the confident voice of the white narrator gives final testimony. I would suggest that here Opie turns toward the rhetorical structure of the abolitionist slave narrative in which the white editor confirms the slave's story. In Opie's poem, the abolitionist narrator's assurances are not unlike the authentication given by Mary Prince's female amanuensis, who verifies the horror of the narrative by tracing its truth in the scars upon Prince's body.[55]

Finally, I would argue that Opie's representation of Anna Trevannion's failure indicates the author's readiness to grapple with the inherent contradic-tions within abolitionist discourse. "The Negro Boy's Tale" explicitly acknowl-edges the rhetorical limitations of even the most dedicated reformer: Anna tries to tell Zambo's story but does not succeed. Her unsuccessful vocalization of his narrative—already experienced by the reader—disappoints: Zambo does best when he tells his own story. "The Black Man's Lament," with its rhetorical stance of objectivity and its discourse of economics, however, seemingly privi-leges the white abolitionist's right to bracket the black man's story. The antisla-very activist of the 1820s is granted more authority; she both "allows" him to be heard and suggests the proper answers to his questions. And yet, even as we acknowledge the poem's sometimes programmatic fidelity to the abolitionist agenda of the mid-1800s, to read Opie's later abolitionist verse as irrevocably mired in antislavery party politics is finally to do it a grave disservice.

There are elements of "The Black Man's Lament," powerfully persuasive and always compelling, that finally escape the poet's—and the narrator's—careful regulation of his voice. Many questions are left unanswered when the "abolitionist speaks." At one point the black man queries,

> "Then, where have we *one* legal right?
>   White men may bind, whip, torture slave.
> But oh! if we but strike one White
>   Who can poor Negro help or save?"
> [lines 145-48]

Because the narrator fails to address the myriad possibilities in the black man's final question, Opie again puts the responsibility for action in the hands of her audience. The question posed by him is a difficult one to answer. If the reader focuses on just the final line, "Who can poor Negro help or save?," the appro-priate answer, of course, would be "me." But the full question is: "if we strike one White / Who can poor Negro help or save?" As in "The Negro Boy's Tale,"

Opie's verse remains indeterminate when it approaches the fatal conclusions ordained by dominant abolitionist discourse. The implications of the complete question are that "if" the reader does not interject himself into history, insurrection will prevail and all will be lost; the white reader cannot "help or save" the black man who turns away from Christian patience and practice. Furthermore, the "rage" that burns within the black man seems far stronger than any of the projected means to contain it.

In both poems, then, Opie offers the promise and solace of Christian redemption and proactive reform: in response to the tragic drowning of Zambo and in response to the implied threat of the black man's rebellion. Finally, however, her verse only points to these possible "happy endings." Questions remain unanswered: Is Zambo a "true" convert? Will the black man practice Christian patience or rebel against his lot? If readers do commit to the cause of antislavery, will they actually succeed in ending such an economically successful practice? In refusing to provide readers with the comfort of "simple" answers, Opie continues to goad them into entering the debate over slavery as active participants. Opie's verse implicitly poses the same question asked by Elizabeth Heyrick in 1824: "Are *we* the true friends of justice, or do we only cant about it?"[56]

Opie's interrogatory verse seems to have found its audience and answers during the period of greatest antislavery activism. She was widely acknowledged as one of the grande dames of British abolition both before and during the British and Foreign Anti-Slavery Society World Convention held in 1840.[57] It was only after abolition's goals prevailed and emancipation became "history" that Opie's reputation lost its luster. Although Edwardian and early twentieth-century biographers usually mention her prominence in abolitionist circles, she is largely seen through the lens of a somewhat indulgent nostalgia for a risqué and slightly ridiculous Regency past.[58] When her writing is mentioned, it is her work as a lyric poet that is most commonly praised, while her overly "moralistic" tendencies are gently mocked.[59] Later twentieth-century readers have tended to interpret nineteenth-century abolitionist writings with an often disciplinary eye; our reading habits lean toward absolute judgment. And, as I hope that I have shown, Opie has alternately been both castigated and praised. At this historical moment we tend to design narratives of interpretation dependent upon "proving" racism or "vindicating" now troubling nineteenth-century reformist goals.[60] History—the history of abolition as well as the history of "reading" Opie—remains elusive, however. In this essay I have tried to follow Opie's own rhetorical lead and leave at least some of the questions raised by her verse open-ended. I think it is important for us to preserve in our own interpretations the tone of ineffable questioning present within the texts themselves. Opie's narratives—her poetry, her "biographical" rendering of her own life, and the narratives generated around Opie by contemporary and current readers—remain multiple. We can only construct "tales of truth" that allow for the manifold possibilities and contradictions inherent both in the text and in our interpretation itself.

Notes

1. Quoted in Brightwell, *Life of Amelia Opie,* 13.

2. David Turley identifies this group as the "Octagon Circle" and notes that it included the highly respected Octagon minister Dr. John Taylor, his daughter (an Opie correspondent) Susannah Taylor, the Opies, the Barbaulds, and the Martineaus; see Turley, *The Culture of English Antislavery,* 85. One of Opie's biographers, Margaret Eliot Macgregor, notes that Robert Southey was also a frequent guest of the Taylors; see Macgregor, *Amelia Alderson Opie,* 10. Certainly William Godwin and Thomas Holcroft were also often found in Norwich.

3. Brightwell, *Life of Amelia Opie,* 52.

4. See Ferguson, *Subject to Others,* 3-4; Turley, *The Culture of English Antislavery,* 18-19.

5. Ferguson, *Subject to Others,* 19. Also see Brantlinger, "Victorians and Africans."

6. Ferguson, *Subject to Others,* 163.

7. See Coleman, "Conspicuous Consumption"; Yellin, *Women and Sisters;* Sharpe, *Allegories of Empire;* Sanchez-Eppler, *Touching Liberty.*

8. Coleman, "Conspicuous Consumption," 341. Sanchez-Eppler, *Touching Liberty,* 13.

9. Devoney Looser, in "Scolding Lady Montagu," poses a similar critical question to feminist scholars tempted to label recently recovered women writers as "feminist" or "anti-feminist." Looser asks us to consider the consequences if we "move away from the 'feminist/not a feminist' or 'progressive/not a progressive' dichotomy[;] . . . are we left with a critical vacuum? Rather than working to castigate or exonerate Montagu more thoroughly, a turn to generic, historical, and disciplinary questions—to difficult matters of historicizing—may prove a way to deal with these either/or feminist options" (54). Looser goes on to conclude: "Rather than scolding or exonerating [Montagu] (or any of our predecessors), we might instead move toward more complex tasks of shifting, local theorizing, and examining complicity as thoroughly as we do resistance" (58).

10. Ferguson, *Subject to Others,* 238-40. Reiman, Introduction to *Poems, by Amelia Opie,* viii. Mellor, "'Am I not a Woman,'" 325-26.

11. Felman, "Narrative as Testimony," 261.

12. The work of Jean-François Lyotard, as well as that of Felman, has been very useful to my argument here. Nonetheless, Lyotard's and Felman's theorizing, in many cases, revolves around the specific historical moment of the Holocaust. Lyotard and Felman are interested in how the testimony of the eyewitnesses of the Holocaust helps to create history after the fact. In the case of Amelia Opie's abolitionist verse, however, we are talking about the framing of history during the historical moment itself, understood from a chronological distance of nearly two hundred years. And, as I acknowl-

edge in the body of the essay, Opie never actually viewed Caribbean slavery at all: hers is an almost entirely imaginative act of testimony. See Lyotard, *The Differend.*

13. Brightwell, *Life of Amelia Opie,* 12.

14. Ibid., 8

15. Fryer, *Staying Power,* 78.

16. Brightwell, *Life of Amelia Opie,* 32.

17. Sharpe, *Allegories of Empire,* 11-12, 32.

18. "In Memory of My Mother," lines 1-2, in *Lays of the Dead.*

19. Another fictional double of Savannah appears in the novel *Adeline Mowbray* (1805). In this earlier work the character of Savanna is an escaped slave who faithfully serves the eponymous heroine as a free woman. She is an outspoken proponent of freedom—for both herself and Adeline—and an unrelenting critic of the status quo. See Eberle, "Amelia Opie's *Adeline Mowbray,*" 142-43.

20. Amelia Opie, "The Negro Boy's Tale," line 187, in *Poems.*

21. Halbersleben, *Women's Participation,* 13.

22. Mary Robinson's "The Negro Girl" appeared in *Lyrical Tales* (1799). Also published by Longman, Hurst, Rees, and Orme, Robinson's volume is advertised at the back of Opie's *Poems.*

23. The only other poems that address "public" politics are "Lines written at Norwich on the first News of Peace," "Lines respectfully inscribed to the Society for the Relief of Persons imprisoned for Small Debts," and "On reading, since the Duke of Bedford's Death, Mr. Burke's Letter reflecting on his Grace."

24. Within the body of Cowper's antislavery verse we do find a variety of voices. "The Negro's Complaint," for example, makes a slight attempt to replicate the slave speaker's Afro-Caribbean English. In "The Morning Dream," the speaker of the poem dreams of a "goddess-like Woman" (line 34) who sings of freeing the slaves and who is later revealed to be "Britannia" herself (line 45). In "Sweet Meat Has Sour Sauce: or, The Slave Trader in the Dumps," the speaker is a slave trader, and in "Pity for Poor Africans" a Briton expresses sympathy for the slave but reveals himself to be a hypocrite unable to give up slave luxuries. See Cowper, *Poems.* Opie's "Negro Boy's Tale" is the only poem I have read that attempts to put such voices in conversation with each other.

25. Ferguson, *Subject to Others,* 103.

26. See Shyllon, *Black People in Britain,* 4-5. Shyllon suggests that the 1772 judgment was meant to counter the Yorke and Talbot Opinion, otherwise known as the "slave owners' Bill of Rights," which stated that "a slave did not become free on coming to England, he did not become free by baptism, and, finally, any owner might compel his slave to return with him to the West Indies or America" (5). But Shyllon and other historians also note that a confusion of opinions tended to dominate rhetoric on both sides of the slavery issue. Douglas Lorimer, for example, argues that even if the Mansfield Judgment did little judiciously, it allowed blacks more authority by which to demand wages and/or their freedom; see Lorimer, "Black Resistance," 65-67.

27. Shyllon, *Black People in Britain,* 17. See also Walvin, *Black and White,* 64.

28. Sharpe, *Allegories of Empire,* 14.

29. Quoted in Walvin, *The Black Presence,* 135.

30. Walvin, *The Black Presence,* 79-80.

31. In the case of prominent black writers like Phillis Wheatley and Olaudah Equiano, it has been argued that their use of standard English allowed them a space in which to oppose racist ideology while positioning themselves within the black community. See Marren, "Between Slavery and Freedom." For a more theoretical examination of the equation made between the acquisition of English and the slave's humanity, see Gates, *Figures in Black.*

32. J.R. Oldfield notes that during the 1780s and 1790s British playwrights also began representing their entirely admirable Afro-English characters as speakers of dialect. See "The 'Ties of soft Humanity,'" 11.

33. Review of *Poems, 1802, Critical Review,* 36. Review of *Poems, 1802, Edinburgh Review,* 120.

34. Ferguson, *Subject to Others,* 239. Sanchez-Eppler, *Touching Liberty,* 9.

35. Rajan, *The Supplement of Reading,* 173.

36. Turley, *The Culture of English Antislavery,* 55.

37. Heyrick's pamphlet is really quite radical. In *Immediate, Not Gradual Abolition,* she insists that freedom is an inalienable "right" and that slavery is a crime (5). She steadfastly turns the matter over to her reader's conscience, proclaiming that everyone is an "active supporter" or "active opposer" of slavery with no "neutral ground" available (4). She calls upon her readers to boycott West Indian sugar, thus ruining the planters economically. Overall, she has absolutely no interest in appeasing the proslavery forces on economic grounds and suggests that there should be "compensation" for slaves rather than for their masters (16). Although I have found no direct evidence linking Heyrick and Opie, they certainly circulated within the same society. Like Opie, Heyrick was an intimate of the Gurneys, Buxtons, and Frys; see Fladeland, *Men and Brothers,* 178.

38. Heyrick, *Immediate, Not Gradual Abolition,* 4.

39. Turley, *The Culture of English Antislavery,* 48,

40. Fladeland, *Men and Brothers,* 220.

41. The publishers, Harvey and Darton, also reissued editions of William Cowper's "The Negro's Complaint," *A Narrative of remarkable Incidents in the Life of Solomon Bayley, formerly a Slave in the State of Delaware,* and several other abolitionist texts accessible to young readers, including "The Black Man's Lament." See Opie, *The Negro Boy's Tale: a poem, addressed to children,* and *The Black Man's Lament.* Indeed, Cowper's poem was accompanied by illustrations like those found in "The Black Man's Lament." The abolitionist poetry of Opie and Cowper appeared together in an 1825 American edition of "The Negro Boy's Tale" and "A Morning Dream": *The Negro Boy's tale: a poem / by Amelia Opie.*

42. Opie deleted a reference to Joanna Baillie's *Count Basil* that compared Anna's feelings for Zambo to Victoria's "adoption" of Mirando. Opie also changed three lines slightly. In the first case, "pity's hand" (*Poems,* 1802, line 115) becomes "Pity's hand" (*The Negro Boy's Tale: a poem, addressed to children,* 1824, line 115). The line "Might (blessed chance!) might now be mine" (*Poems,* 1802, line 132) becomes "Might (blessed thought) might now be mine" (*The Negro Boy's Tale: a poem, addressed to children,* 1824,

line 132), and "Ah! Fate was near" (*Poems*, 1802, line 169) becomes "Ah! Death was near" (*The Negro Boy's Tale: a poem, addressed to children*, 1824, line 169).

43. Opie, *The Negro Boy's Tale: a poem, addressed to children*, iv, v.

44. Amelia Opie to Elizabeth Fry, 19 Jan. 1824, in Opie Papers.

45. Joseph John Gurney expressed his general opinion on the subject of publication in 1838: "I do not approve of ladies speaking in public even in the anti-slavery cause except under the immediate influence of the Holy Spirit. Then and only then all is safe"; see Rose, *Elizabeth Fry*, 185. Although Opie appears to have been very much influenced by Gurney, I might also note that she continued to publish tales after 1825; she just insisted that they were "factual" rather than "fictional." For the most part the distinction was one of rhetoric rather than reality.

46. Heyrick, *Immediate, Not Gradual Abolition*, 5. Davis, "The Quaker Ethic," 64.

47. Mellor, "'Am I not a Woman,'" 324.

48. Opie, *The Black Man's Lament*, line 17.

49. Mary Wollstonecraft's use of this figure in *A Vindication of the Rights of Woman* is perhaps one of the most famous applications of it: "Why subject [the British woman] to propriety—blind propriety, if she be capable of acting from a nobler spring, if she be an heir of immortality? Is sugar always to be produced by vital blood? Is one half of the human species, like the poor African slaves, to be subject to prejudices that brutalize them, when principles would be a surer guard, only to sweeten the cup of man?" (167).

50. *Substance of the Debates in the House of Commons and in the House of Lords*, 194.

51. These are several fine reproductions of the Wedgwood medallion in Yellin's *Women and Sisters*. She also undertakes an extensive discussion of the abolitionist medallion's significance in British and American antislavery campaigning. Yellin, *Women and Sisters*, 7-9; Turley, *The Culture of English Antislavery*, 49-50.

52. Donald Reiman also makes this point in his introduction to a reprint of Opie's *Poems* of 1802. He goes on, however, to dismiss the poem, as well as Opie's commitment to abolition; see Reiman, introduction to *Poems, by Amelia Opie*, viii.

53. Sanchez-Eppler, *Touching Liberty*, 25.

54. Davis, "The Quaker Ethic," 78-79.

55. Prince, *History of Mary Prince*, 119-20. There is a similar move in the first edition of Phillis Wheatley's poems: "We, whose names are underwritten, do assure the World, that the Poems specified in the following Pages were, (as we verily believe) written by Phillis, a young African Girl, who was but a few years since, brought an uncultivated barbarian from Africa, and has ever since been, and now is, under the disadvantage of serving as a slave in a Family in this Town [Boston]. She has been examined by some of the best Judges, and is thought qualified to write them." Quoted in Shyllon, *Black People in Britain*, 195.

56. Heyrick, *Immediate, Not Gradual Abolition*, 4.

57. Fladeland, *Men and Brothers*, 178, 220; Halbersleben, *Women's Participation*, 50.

58. Hall, *A Book of Memories*, 174. Hall recollects: "Mrs. Opie was certainly one of the pillars of the tea-table, laughing and listening (she never could have been so universally popular had she not been a good listener), and being to perfection the elderly

English lady, tinged with the softest *blue,* and vivified by the graceful influence of Parisian society" (174).

59. Opie's entry in the *Dictionary of National Biography* (1895) exemplifies early-twentieth-century renderings of her life: "Mrs. Opie's poems are simple in diction. Two or three of them are deservedly found in every anthology, and one, 'There seems a voice in every gale,' is well known as a hymn. Her novels, which were among the first to treat exclusively of domestic life, possess pathos and some gracefulness of style, but belong essentially to the lachrymose type of fiction, and are all written to point a moral." Both the *DNB* and Hall also note the minor tourism that sprung up around Opie's home in Norwich. Hall reprints engravings of "The Dwelling of Amelia Opie at Norwich" on Opie Street and of "Amelia Opie's Sitting-Room at Norwich" in his volume; see Hall, *A Book of Memories,* 176-77.

60. It should also be noted that the antislavery verse of women writers has suffered from a twofold neglect. The abolitionist writings of British reformers has only just attracted the attention of literary scholars; the reclamation of women authors is an ongoing project begun in the last decade. Although the early-twentieth-century editors of the *Dictionary of National Biography* can confidently state that Opie's poems appear in "every anthology," I cannot make the same claim about contemporary collections.

PART TWO

Anticipating Reception

"Dost thou not know my voice?"

Charlotte Smith and the Lyric's Audience

Sarah M. Zimmerman

O! grief hath chang'd me since you saw me last,
And careful hours with time's deformed hand
Have written strange defeatures in my face:
But tell me yet, dost thou not know my voice?

Shakespeare, The Comedy of Errors

No other grief that ever sighed has worn so much crape and bombazine.

Viscount St. Cyres, "The Sorrows of Mrs. Charlotte Smith"

Two poems addressed to Charlotte Smith appear in the August 1786 edition of the *European Magazine,* one submitted by a "constant Reader." The poems respond to the author of *Elegiac Sonnets,* a collection that had been "universally admired" (in Anna Letitia Barbauld's words) when it appeared two years earlier.[1] One of the poems, a twelve-line sonnet, begins by admitting that propriety recommends against the intensely autobiographical quality of Smith's lyric poems: "'Tis said, and I myself have so believ'd / 'Fiction's the properest field for Poesy.'" Yet it is the quality protested that arouses a response:

> For sure than thine more sweet no strains can flow,
> Than thine no tenderer plaints the heart can move,
> More rouse the soul to sympathetic love;
> And yet—sad source! they spring from REAL WOE.[2]

Despite the reader's qualms, it is Smith's "REAL WOE" that is engaging. Many critics proved no more immune than a "constant Reader" to the spectacle of Smith's autobiographical speaker lamenting her plight in natural settings. And like this reader, they responded to the sonnets' forging of high emotion and believability. Readers and critics often reacted with "sympathy," their responses similarly personal in tone. According to Richard Phillips's *British Public Characters 1800-1801,* "an elevation of sentiment, a refinement of taste, a feeling, and a delicacy breathe through her productions, which, by moving the affections and engaging the sympathy of the reader, excite a lively and permanent interest."[3]

Smith had practical reasons for needing to generate an "interest" both "lively" and durable. *Elegiac Sonnets* was published for her family's support after her husband's imprisonment at the King's Bench for debt in December 1783. Smith had been born into far different circumstances: her father owned estates in Sussex and Surrey and a townhouse in London. She experienced a social fall into economic instability only after her marriage at age fifteen proved emotionally and financially disastrous. Benjamin Smith, second son of a West Indian merchant and a director of the East India Company, plunged the family into debt. Her father-in-law's death might have alleviated the family's precarious situation, but their circumstances were actually worsened by Richard Smith's intricate will, which was, ironically, crafted to protect Charlotte and the children from Benjamin's unreliability. When her husband was sent to debtor's prison, Smith turned to publication as a way to maintain the family's social standing until the estate was settled and her children could be educated as she desired. But the will generated legal entanglements that remained unresolved throughout her career; the Chancery suit was not finally settled until after her death. As a result, Smith's temporary venture into the literary marketplace lasted twenty-two years.

Elegiac Sonnets succeeded—both in providing financial respite and in establishing Smith as a popular poet who would supply her family's primary income after the couple separated in 1787. This essay is an account of how she found her audience with an unlikely vehicle: quiet, reflective sonnets featuring a solitary speaker lost in private sorrow. Rather than reaching out directly to the readers she needed so urgently, Smith turned away from them, performing the gesture that Northrop Frye describes as characteristic of the lyric poet, who "turns his back on his audience."[4] Smith made an important discovery about the mode, which counters prevailing views of it: she found that a lyric speaker could win readers and hold their attention precisely by appearing to ignore them, by seeming absorbed in thought and oblivious to her surroundings. She became aware, in other words, of the impact that her poet could have on an audience to whom she turns her back in only the most literal sense. Her strong popular appeal illuminates the relationship between lyric poet and reading audience as a dynamic exchange, a different account from predominant paradigms, which generally characterize the lyric's auditor as passive and silent. The availability of a wealth of contemporary responses to Smith's lyric poet by critics and readers illuminates a neglected aspect of the period's lyric poetry. The mode's rhetorical capacities have been eclipsed by a conventional focus on psychological and emotional subtlty.

The discrepancy between Smith's immediate popularity and her virtual disappearance in the later arena of twentieth-century critical reception recommends a return to her contemporaneous readers and critics. The contrast between their eager responses and her subsequent obscurity in literary history is telling. Smith's case provides an excellent occasion to rethink canonical paradigms of Romantic lyricism. We learn that qualities now generally deemed antithetical to the mode did not appear so to her readers: her sonnets combine self-consciousness with sincerity, introspection with rhetorical power. Popular success is not necessarily precluded in canonical models (although Byron's exclusion from M.H. Abrams's account of the "greater Romantic lyric" is suggestive), but a focus on the poet's subjectivity has discouraged consideration of readers' responses to lyric poems and lyric poems' responsiveness to their environments.[5] Smith's poems suggest a methodology for reading the period's lyric poems within the specific circumstances of their production and consumption and within the trajectories of the poets' careers. Smith's readers included those who have defined canonical Romanticism—William Wordsworth, Samuel Taylor Coleridge, Lord Byron, Leigh Hunt, and John Keats. Together, Smith and her reading audiences bring into focus the mode's potential for a more dynamic relationship to its social contexts than we have come to expect.

Smith's sonnets are an important measure of how the Romantic canon was shaped according to one particular version of Romantic lyricism, a model based largely on the poems and critical prose of two of her successors, Coleridge and Wordsworth. Wordsworth's debts to Smith are political and poetic: he visited her in Brighton on his way to France in 1791, and he was given letters of introduction to her acquaintances, including Helen Maria Williams (who had left Orléans by the time he arrived). His literary debts to her begin at Hawkshead, where he read *Elegiac Sonnets,* and are formally acknowledged in a lavish 1835 explanatory note, expanded in 1837, to "Stanzas Suggested in a Steam-boat Off St. Bees' Heads."[6] He describes Smith as "a lady to whom English verse is under greater obligations than are likely to be either acknowledged or remembered": "She wrote little, and that little unambitiously, but with true feeling for rural nature, at a time when nature was not much regarded by English Poets; for in point of time her earlier writings preceded, I believe, those of Cowper and Burns."[7] Coleridge's admiration of William Lisle Bowles is critical commonplace, and Bowles was, as Stuart Curran observes, one of Smith's "followers." Yet the connection between Coleridge and Smith is even more direct: in his "Introduction to the Sonnets" (1796), Coleridge cites Smith and Bowles as the poets who "first made the Sonnet popular among the present English," and he feels "justified" in "deducing its laws" from their works. According to their examples, the sonnet is a "small poem, in which some lonely feeling is developed," preferably "deduced from, and associated with, the Scenery of Nature."[8]

The qualities responsible for Smith's appeal to Wordsworth and Coleridge—solitariness, an attraction to natural scenes, an emphasis on feeling—are recognizable in foundational accounts of Romantic lyricism, including Abrams's influential definition of the "greater Romantic lyric." Abrams bases his paradigm largely on Coleridge's and Wordsworth's early poems, written in the period in which Smith's influence on them was keenest. It is not surprising, then, that the qualities that Coleridge and Wordsworth exclude in their laudatory portraits of Smith were also qualities subsequently deemed antithetical to canonical Romantic lyricism: a proven rhetorical ability and popular success. What was lost to canonical paradigms in Smith's example was an understanding of the form's potential for engaging readers and responding to social concerns. Her poetry is especially provocative for the task of revising critical expectations of the period's lyric poems because her work resembles Wordsworthian poetics in important ways and yet manifests marked differences, which cluster around the issue of her popular success. Thus, Smith helps to blur the lines between popular and canonical lyricism.

Yet, why return to the paradigms of Abrams and Frye, when their models have been thoroughly critiqued by feminist and new historicist critics? Feminist critics have elaborated the gendered politics of Romantic lyricism: how a masculine poetic subjectivity is often defined against a feminized natural environment.[9] Romantic new historicism has, in turn, found in the mode's emphasis on interiority a desire to turn away from, or repress recognition of, the historical contexts of the wars with France and intense socioeconomic unrest at home. I would argue, however, that one important condition of these critiques has been the tacit acceptance of the mode's conventional association with transcendence of its natural and social environments. Neither canonical accounts of Romantic lyricism nor these critiques of them have fully acknowledged the mode's rhetorical capacity. They have thereby de-emphasized its potential for complexity (both psychological and ideological) and for contradiction.

Feminist and new historical critics have elaborated the ideological construction of canonical paradigms, yet the inclusion in the field of women poets and others, such as John Clare, presents another critical dilemma: how to handle the period's range of lyrical practices. One solution has been to define alternative paradigms to account for noncanonical poetics. My reluctance about this strategy is that, although it promises great subtlety in defining various lyricisms, it tends to define lesser-known writers according to their divergences from canonical practices. Thus, canonical poems remain monolithic, unquestioned even when their new juxtaposition with lesser-known poems invites their reconsideration. Lesser-known writers, in return, remain "alternative" and hence excluded from centers of definitional power. Smith's example helps us to revise the paradigms that have contributed to keeping the period's canon small by implying that Romantic lyricism's interest in subjectivity leads only inward and upward—into the psyche and beyond the material contexts—but not outward, to actual readers and to sociohistorical events.[10]

Smith's most important challenge to conventional assumptions about Romantic lyricism is her success in winning readers by seeming oblivious to them. Her example restores the significance of an overlooked corollary to Frye's famous description of the poet turning away from an audience: an acknowledgment that the audience, despite being ignored, remains on the scene. Frye cites an anecdote from William Butler Yeats's *Autobiography* as exemplary of the lyric's audience. Engaged in a debate with an acquaintance, Yeats recalls, "I would say, quoting Mill, 'Oratory is heard, poetry is overheard.'" His interlocutor would "answer, his voice full of contempt, that there was always an audience; and yet, in his moments of lofty speech, he himself was alone no matter what the crowd."[11] Smith's poet often appears to have reached that state for which Yeats's acquaintance strived, when the presence of listeners is forgotten. Yet she knows that by seeming to forget her readers she gives them the pleasure of "overhearing"; she employs the rhetorical allure of eavesdropping. Smith makes shrewd use of what is perhaps lyricism's most appealing quality, that of intimacy. She understands that the actor's gesture of turning away from an audience only encourages its members to lean closer to listen.

Like Wordsworth, Smith finds in lyricism a vehicle for foregrounding the reflections and feelings of the poet. And like him, her intense introspectiveness drew charges of "egotism."[12] This focus on interiority has been crucial to canonical definitions of Romantic lyricism as a mode that turns away—inward—from contemporary social scenes. In Abrams's "Spirit of the Age," a paradigm-making essay closely related to his articulation of the "greater Romantic lyric," Wordsworth's and Coleridge's early optimism about political change is supplanted, in the aftermath of the Terror and war with France, by hopes for internal, aesthetic renovation. The retreat from social to interior arenas is marked formally by the emergence of Romantic lyricism: "The great Romantic poems were written not in the mood of revolutionary exaltation but in the later mood of revolutionary disillusionment or despair." This social history of poetic forms is confirmed by Alan Liu, although to different critical ends. Liu finds in Wordsworthian lyricism, particularly the lyrical autobiography of *The Prelude*, history's effacement by selfhood. Liu locates in book 8 of *The Prelude* "the transformation of the French Revolution—and, at last, empire—into lyrical autobiography": lyricism breaks the narrative ties of social history and strives for the atemporal, aesthetic realm of the imagination.[13]

Smith's sonnets demonstrate that the lyric's focus on subjectivity could serve social ends: in her hands, an emphasis on the autobiographical engaged readers in concerns both private and public. Her lyric poetry drew readers to her and elicited responses that matched her own in intensity. Sir William Jones's comments on her sonnets exemplify the reaction that Smith desired. En route to India to assume a judgeship, Jones undertook a course of reading that included *Elegiac Sonnets*. In a letter, he thanks the friend who had given him "the tender strains of the unfortunate Charlotte, which have given us pleasure and pain." He reserves special praise for her most autobiographical poems: "the sonnets which relate to herself are incomparably the best." The *Gentleman's Magazine* concurs in its notice of the third edition (1786) of *Elegiac Sonnets*, judging that the "pieces . . . which are the genuine offspring of her own fancy, are by far the most interesting in her whole collection."[14] Although, from the first edition, the collection included both poems other than sonnets and translations of others' sonnets (Goethe, Petrarch, and Metastasio), the autobiographical sonnets that Jones admired established Smith's reputation.[15]

In her sonnets, an emphasis on interiority, which would also define the poetics of her canonical successors, turns a focus on the personal into a cult of personality. Smith's focus on the personal in *Elegiac Sonnets* is underlined by its frontispiece portrait (fig. 8), which appeared in the first edition and in some subsequent editions: an engraving from a crayon drawing by George Romney, under which she places the first three lines cited in my epigraph, from *The Comedy of Errors* (lines that she slightly misquotes).[16] She omits the fourth line that I cite, but that is the line which, I would argue, underlies her poetic strategies: "But tell me yet, dost thou not know my voice?" Because Smith articulates private sorrows in the sonnets, readers came to feel as if they knew her, and so might respond to her as a familiar face in future volumes. A reviewer for the *British Critic* describes Smith's appeal to readers and includes a quotation from her: "So exquisite are the charms of Mrs. Smith's poetry, that it would indicate the utmost degree of insensibility not to be affected by her 'tale of tender woe, her sweet sorrow, her mournful melody.'"[17] Critics and readers not only associated the sonnet speaker with the poet herself, but they also often addressed her as someone personally known, in reviews and in letters and poems submitted to periodicals (such as the sonnet by a "constant Reader").

The sonnets themselves aim to present the poet with the vividness of a portrait. Smith allows readers ample opportunity to observe her, since she articulates her reflections and feelings while wandering through natural scenes. Readers respond because nothing, apparently, is demanded of them. "To the moon" (sonnet 4) is an especially apt example because it is accompanied, in some editions, by an engraving featuring a solitary female figure, one hand on her heart, the other extended before her as she gazes on the moon (fig. 9). The engraving visualizes, in the upward tilt of her head and the expressive position of her arms, the stylized verbal gestures of Smith's poetry, an unsurprising con-

Fig. 8. Engraving of Charlotte Smith, after a portrait by George Romney. Frontispiece to volume 2 of *Elegiac Sonnets*, second edition. Courtesy of Princeton University Library.

gruence given that she was closely involved with the production of her volumes and provided instructions for the plates commissioned for *Elegiac Sonnets*.[18] The first half of line one appears underneath the engraving:

> Queen of the silver bow!—by thy pale beam,
> Alone and pensive, I delight to stray,
> And watch thy shadow trembling in the stream,
> Or mark the floating clouds that cross thy way.
> And while I gaze, thy mild and placid light

Fig. 9. Engraving for "To the Moon" (sonnet 4), frontispiece to volume 1 of *Elegiac Sonnets*, eighth edition. Courtesy of Princeton University Library.

Sheds a soft calm upon my troubled breast;
And oft I think—fair planet of the night,
That in thy orb, the wretched may have rest:
The sufferers of the earth perhaps may go,
Released by death—to thy benignant sphere;
And the sad children of Despair and Woe
Forget, in thee, their cup of sorrow here.
Oh! that I soon may reach thy world serene,
Poor wearied pilgrim—in this toiling scene![19]

Smith's speaker is characteristically occupied in observing her natural surround-
ings and pursuing the thoughts they prompt, leaving the reader free to observe
her. In poem and engraving, she looks away from an audience (in the portrait
by Romney, Smith's gaze is averted, too. Addressing her thoughts not to the
reader but to the moon, she turns to the "fair planet" and imagines transcen-
dence. Not only does the poet fail to notice auditors, but she also imagines
leaving the quotidian arena they share, for another "benignant sphere." She
wants to "forget," and like Yeats's interlocutor, she succeeds in losing sight of
an audience and her environment. In the final couplet, the intensely personal
nature of her meditations becomes apparent, with her confession that she is
one of the "wretched" of whom she has spoken. The poem ends with a sharp
focus on the poet herself, a "[p]oor wearied pilgrim."

Yet how do we account for the voyeuristic pleasure that Smith's sonnets
provided a popular audience? What is its mechanism? Michael Fried makes a
relevant argument in his treatment of French painting in the second half of the
eighteenth century. He describes the powerful effect on the viewer of watching
a human figure who is absorbed, either in thought or in an event taking place.
This air of distraction can create a "supreme fiction": that of the beholder's
absence. The illusion of being ignored has an unexpected side effect—the be-
holder may experience the sensation of entering the picture, precisely because
he or she is not made self-conscious in the act of watching, an awareness that
can produce resistance. Smith's sonnets achieve a similar effect, via the poet's
apparent obliviousness to an audience. What seems to be a desire on her part
to turn away from social scenes as she wanders, "alone and pensive," proves
captivating. Fried describes a "paradoxical relationship between painting and
beholder": the painter seeks "to neutralize or negate the beholder's presence, to
establish the fiction that no one is standing before the canvas." Yet "only if this
is done can the beholder be stopped and held precisely there."[20] Fried's para-
digm helps make explicit what is implicit in *Elegiac Sonnets:* just as on the
stage, the social world is not excluded by the gesture of turning one's back to an
audience. Like a member of a theater audience or the beholder of a painting,
the reader of a lyric poem must lose the self-consciousness of spectatorship,

must feel forgotten in order to forget himself or herself and make the necessary leap of identification.

Fried's argument is particularly relevant to Smith's sonnets because the poems resemble small *tableaux* in the volume's layout, one poem per page; their intensely autobiographical quality renders them miniature, verbal self-portraits. Thus the reader is also a viewer, or spectator. The sonnets' copious natural images emphasize their pictorial quality, and the engravings that accompany several sonnets visualize the scenes that the poems describe, sometimes elaborately framing those scenes. An ornate border for the oval engraving of "To the moon" features thick foliage and an owl—presumably Athena's—atop a book. The speaker addresses Diana, "Queen of the Silver Bow," whose unstrung bow and quiver frame the bird, as if the god has turned aside from the hunt to other topics. The engraving significantly supplements the act of reading the poem, for readers can "see" the poet as they read her words, and these emblems further characterize her: she is associated with wisdom and purity, and female strength. Readers can also "hear" her: working within the conventions of sensibility, Smith's liberal use of exclamations, sighs, and pauses strives to approximate the cadences of spoken language.

The emphasis on the visual in *Elegiac Sonnets* contributes to a theatrical dynamic that structures the poet's relationship to her audiences. It might seem that the dramatic cast of Smith's sorrows could alienate potentially distrustful readers. Early in her career, before she had made explicit the biographical sources of her elegiac tenor, a critic ventured to hope that her sorrows were fictitious: the *Gentleman's Magazine* could not "forbear expressing a hope that the misfortunes she so often hints at, are all imaginary," since "[w]e must have perused her very tender and exquisite effusions with diminished pleasure, could we have supposed her sorrows to be real."[21] Yet, as David Marshall explains, presenting oneself sympathetically, as Smith urgently needed to do, demands a measure of theatricality. Drawing on Adam Smith, Marshall argues that "since we cannot know the experience or sentiments of another person, we must represent in our imagination copies of the sentiments that we ourselves feel as we imagine ourselves in someone else's place and person." This means that "acts of sympathy are structured by theatrical dynamics that (because of the impossibility of really knowing or entering into someone else's sentiments) depend on people's ability to represent themselves as tableaux, spectacles, and texts before others."[22]

Smith uses all available verbal and visual means to create a fullness of presence which might captivate readers. The theatrical aspect of *Elegiac Sonnets* is rendered explicit in the frontispiece portrait, which depicts Smith as a Shakespearean character. The sonnets demonstrate a theatrical dynamic in the lyric's often overlooked relationship between poet and auditor: her poems make clearer the implications of Frye's representation of the poet turning his back to an audience. What seems to be pure un-selfconsciousness on the poet's part, and passive reception by the reader, actually operates more dynamically: the poet presents herself frankly by expressing her reflections and emotions, as in a soliloquy. The reader's ideal response is the going-out-of-oneself that Coleridge describes as readerly or sympathetic identification. Smith learned what Marshall, quoting Diderot, claims that good actors know: that it is "more important for the spectator to *feel* forgotten rather than literally *be* forgotten."[23]

In his account of the sonnet's "laws" derived from Smith and Bowles, Coleridge suggests that the reader's role involves an act of identification. He describes a mode of consumption that encourages a sense of intimacy: "Easily remembered from their briefness, and interesting alike to the eye and the affections, these are the poems which we can 'lay up in our heart and our soul,' and repeat them 'when we walk by the way, and when we lie down, and when we rise up.'" The reader identifies so strongly with the poet's "moral Sentiments, Affections, or Feelings" that they seem to be his or her own, and "hence they domesticate with the heart, and become, as it were, a part of our identity."[24] In a letter to Smith, William Cowper exemplifies the kind of response that Coleridge describes: "I was much struck by an expression in your letter to Hayley, where you say that 'you will endeavor to take an interest in green leaves again.' This seems the sound of my own voice reflected to me from a distance, I have so often had the same thought and desire."[25] Smith's poems and her letter to Hayley operate similarly: she succeeds in convincing others that they can understand her sorrows. In reading her words, Cowper mistakes her voice for his own and equates his thoughts and desires with hers. In Cowper's case, Smith won not only sympathy but the practical assistance it inspires: he allowed her to dedicate *The Emigrants* (1793), her first long poem, to him. According to Marshall, when an act of sympathy is successful, the viewer may be moved to respond not just emotionally, but materially. He describes "the more specific response to a scene of tragedy, danger, or suffering that not only leaves one *affligé* but calls upon one to come to the assistance of someone in distress." Thus, Cowper reacts appropriately when he writes to William Hayley, who had himself accepted the dedication of the first edition of *Elegiac Sonnets:* "I never want riches except when I hear of such distress."[26]

Accounts of Romantic lyricism have traditionally emphasized the poet's sympathetic imagination, which forges a bond between poet and natural environment: according to Coleridge, when the poet's feelings respond to nature, the result is "a sweet and indissoluble union between the intellectual and the material world."[27] Smith's sonnets highlight another, less noticed structure of identification—between poet and reader. It is not that the reader has been entirely forgotten in paradigms of Romantic lyricism, but that figure is generally considered tangential to the genre's main concerns: the identifications and understandings of the poet. The intense identificatory relationship between poet and reader is, however, a primary site of the mode's rhetorical salience. The theatrical dynamic that informs Smith's lyric poems recommends a revision of paradigms that emphasize a standard of sincerity without attention to how it operates rhetorically. As the period's "poetic norm," the lyric has seemingly embodied its premium on sincerity, a quality traditionally associated with a naturalness of emotion and an emphasis on expressivity.[28] As a result, the theatrical dynamic established by the lyric scenario of "overhearing" articulated emotion has been neglected. Smith's sonnets foreground one of the mode's key complexities: the unexpected complementarity of sincerity and theatricality for contemporaneous readers, an issue to which I will return.

First, however, I want to address more specifically how *Elegiac Sonnets* won a popular audience. Smith's shrewd attention to the framing of her sonnets in the collection recommends a strategy for analyzing the rhetorical capacity of lyric poems: by situating them in the context of the volumes in which they appear. This approach assumes that "a lyric's location determines its significance"; it requires, as Paul Magnuson puts it, awareness of the poem's contemporaneous contexts, including the "public" poet and the "public location of the poem." Smith is an excellent candidate for this kind of analysis because she reinforced the appealing self-portrait of the sonnets by carefully surrounding them with prefaces, explanatory notes, and engravings. The publication history of *Elegiac Sonnets* suggests that Smith understood the nature of her readers' receptivity to her solitary poet. She took an active role in what Judith Phillips Stanton calls, quoting the poet, her "'literary business,'" and this included crafting the volume to capitalize on the popularity of her melancholy speaker.[29] Although Smith had a succession of patrons and relied upon the assistance of various publishers, she involved herself closely in the processes of her literary production. After the collection's initial success, she expanded the prose sections, which grew in number and length as *Elegiac Sonnets* grew (between 1784 and 1800) to two volumes and ninety-two sonnets. The prefaces and explanatory notes operate variously, but primarily they heighten the collection's autobiographical claims. In her first preface she explains the sonnets' origins: "Some very melancholy moments have been beguiled by expressing in verse the sensations those moments brought." The prefaces and notes, with their conversational, quotidian prose, exaggerate qualities conventionally associated with Romantic lyricism by casting into bolder relief the poems' emphases on solitude, introspection, and a desire for transcendence.

In the sonnets themselves, Smith provides her audience with the pleasure of watching a poet removed from all that is mundane by the very language in which she spoke. Despite some experimentation with English and Italian forms, the poems follow strict rhyme schemes and use formal diction, a strategy that heightens the effect of the poet's detachment from daily experience. Thus, in addition to their strong focus on subjectivity, Smith's sonnets conform to another of the main ways in which lyricism is often assumed to distance itself from social contexts, by a specialization of language that removes the poem from "the ordinary circuit of communication," in Jonathan Culler's terms.[30] In "Written at the close of spring" (sonnet 2), an explanatory note provides a measure of the poem's apparent distance from the quotidian, by marking its linguistic difference from "ordinary" speech. It begins by describing how

> [t]he garlands fade that Spring so lately wove,
> Each simple flower which she had nursed in dew,
> Anemonies, that spangled every grove,
> The primrose wan, and hare-bell mildly blue.

A brief explanatory note consists of two alternate names for the anemone: "*Anemony Nemeroso*," and "[t]he wood Anemony." Smith's gloss of "anemone" seems to translate the rarefied language of poetry into material terms, the language of science and of the vernacular. In the process the flower is transformed from poetic prop into an object from the reader's environment. In the poem the anemone is significant only as one natural detail, which reminds the poet of her own lack of rejuvenation. In the explanatory note, the focus shifts to the flower as a natural object in the reader's environment. The effect is to distinguish between poet's and readers' worlds, separating the poet's experience from the everyday.

The sense of the poet's remove from the ordinary is augmented by the establishment of a different temporality in the sonnets: within the volume the poet is held in a moment of perpetual sorrow that contrasts with a world of process in the prefaces and notes. "Written at the close of spring" thematizes the atemporality of the poet's world by juxtaposing the progress of the seasons with her unchanging state. The closing couplet asks, "[a]nother May new buds and flowers shall bring; / Ah! why has happiness—no second Spring?" Sharon Cameron has made an influential case for lyric poetry's impulse to disrupt the temporality of everyday life, which leads, inevitably, to death.[31] The lyric, associated with a desire for immortality and transcendence, seeks to wrest itself out of the cause and effect of social history, an impulse which has been foundational for new historicism's critique of the Romantic ideology. "Written in the church-yard at Middleton in Sussex" (sonnet 44) and its accompanying note exemplify how Smith's sonnets seem to register fleeting moments detached from their narrative contexts:

> Press'd by the Moon, mute arbitress of tides,
> While the loud equinox its power combines,

The sea no more its swelling surge confines,
But o'er the shrinking land sublimely rides.
The wild blast, rising from the Western cave,
Drives the huge billows from their heaving bed;
Tears from their grassy tombs the village dead,
And breaks the silent sabbath of the grave!
With shells and sea-weed mingled, on the shore
Lo! their bones whiten in the frequent wave;
But vain to them the winds and waters rave;
They hear the warring elements no more:
While I am doom'd—by life's long storm opprest,
To gaze with envy on their gloomy rest.

The sonnet records an almost gothic moment: the sea, driven by the moon, washes on shore in a wave that removes dirt from the village cemetery, uncovering the dead. By using the present tense, Smith emphasizes the transitoriness both of the poet's view of the white bones and of her flash of recognition: that unlike herself, the dead can no longer be "opprest" by "life's long storm." Natural event and psychological revelation occur instantaneously. The reader who turns to the back of the volume to read the accompanying note finds, in contrast, a world of gradual but inexorable change: "Middleton is a village on the margin of the sea, in Sussex, containing only two or three houses. There were formerly several acres of ground between its small church and the sea, which now, by its continual encroachments, approaches within a few feet of this half-ruined and humble edifice. The wall, which once surrounded the church-yard, is entirely swept away, many of the graves broken up, and the remains of bodies interred washed into the sea; whence human bones are found among the sand and shingles on the shore." This note contains the prehistory and the results of the sonnet's moment—its context. It reads as if the viewer has pulled back to a place from which the human and natural consequences of a transformative lyric instant could be surveyed. Smith's notes to the sonnets document a world of myriad change, embodied here in the erosion altering the landscape and the villagers' lives, while the speaker remains in an unalterable state of melancholy.

The sonnets' sense of timelessness is so pronounced that Smith eventually found it necessary to publicly defend her lingering sorrow. She addresses the issue in the preface to the sixth edition (1792), by reporting an exchange with a friend, who had recommended that she try "a more cheerful style of composition." The person who made what St. Cyres describes as this "highly unfortunate suggestion" receives in response a pointed justification: an account of continued misery. Recalling her early sonnets, she explains, "I wrote mournfully because I was unhappy—And I have unfortunately no reason yet, though nine years have since elapsed, to *change my tone.*" Smith's poet continues to hold her melancholy pose: it is as if she has been caught in one repeated moment of intense sorrow. Her sonnets seem to epitomize Cameron's description of how lyric poems "fight temporality with a vengeance," although Smith suggests that her stasis is involuntary.[32] Yet St. Cyres cannily points to the rhetorical effect of this sense of lyric timelessness: "Having chosen to come forward as a Laureate of the Lachrymose, she thought herself bound in honour to live consistently up to her part, and treat whatever subject happened to engross her pen in terms of undiluted lachrymosity." Variety, she intuited, was not what her readers wanted. St. Cyres speculates that "quite an appreciable proportion of her tears was due to purely literary requirements," reminding us that she "was the servant of the public, and her many-headed master called for a melancholy tune."[33] His ironic commentary on Smith's career recognizes the rhetorical salience of a turn away from quotidian temporality and into an interior realm of the emotions, which have a chronology of their own.

I have been arguing that Smith's sonnets win readers with the demonstration of her oblivion to their presence, a pose enhanced by her formal language and what Cameron calls "lyric time." Yet her success depended equally upon her believability: the reader had to have the sensation of witnessing "real woe" in order to respond with the sympathy and loyalty she required, publishing on average one work per year. The sonnets' success required both extreme emotions and a perception of their authenticity, a combination of exaggeration and actuality, theatricality and sincerity, that contemporary readers did not find contradictory. Leigh Hunt confirms her success at combining these qualities in her sonnets, testifying that several of them "are popular for their truth alone": "everybody likes the sonnets because nobody doubts their being in earnest, and because they furnish a gentle voice to feelings that are universal." One of Smith's readers acts upon a similar conviction of the sonnets' "truth" in submitting to the *Universal Magazine* a sonnet "To Mrs. Smith, on reading her Sonnets lately published." The reader protests Smith's personal suffering, declaring that although it was appropriate that she should mourn for others, she should never have to suffer such despair herself:

> [o]h! cou'd or fame, or friendship, aught impart
> To cure the cruel wounds thy peace has known;
> For others sorrows still thy tender heart
> Should softly melt, but never for thine own.[34]

That most of Smith's readers seemed persuaded of the sonnets' truthfulness is especially remarkable given their self-consciously theatrical tenor. Moreover, as Adela Pinch points out, Smith's habitual use of literary allusions raises epistemological questions about the sources of her sorrow, since she borrows so many phrases to express it. How are her readers, or even the poet herself, to be sure that the despair she voices is her own? Yet by the time the first edition of the sonnets appeared in 1784, Smith's potential readers were schooled in the conventions of sensibility, a tradition that collapsed the ostensible boundaries between life and art by presenting codes of behavior to be followed by poets, novel characters, and readers alike. As Janet Todd explains, "[i]n all forms of sentimental literature, there is an assumption that life and literature are directly linked, not through any notion of a mimetic depiction of reality but through the belief that the literary experience can intimately affect the living one."[35] Thus, Smith's readers would not necessarily question the authenticity of her poet's lamentations, even though her responses to loss were modeled on literary figures who had experienced a similar despair. The symbiotic relationship between art and life that sensibility prescribed would have encouraged Smith to borrow from other poets, even as her readers would feel encouraged to model their own expressions of grief on her poet—as various contemporaneous sonnets addressed to or about Smith in periodicals suggest that many did.

Smith's success in winning her readers' belief in her sorrow required, however, careful attention to the details of the sonnets' publication. The poems' autobiographical truthfulness is enhanced, for instance, by the section of "Quotations, Notes, and Explanations," which identifies the sources of Smith's literary allusions and provides information on flowers, animals, and places mentioned in the poems. The notes contribute to the volume's intensely autobiographical tenor by grounding the poems in Smith's extensive reading and in her very public biography. A note to "Written in Farm Wood, South Downs, in May 1784" (sonnet 31), glosses a reference to "Alpine flowers": "An infinite variety of plants are found on these hills, particularly about this spot: many sorts of Orchis and Cistus of singular beauty, with several others." The note contextualizes the poem autobiographically: the sonnet was written on walks in her native Sussex, where "Alpine flowers" grew. Sir Walter Scott, who preferred her novels to her poetry, comments: "It may be remarked, that Mrs. Smith not only preserves in her landscapes the truth and precision of a painter, but that they sometimes evince marks of her own favourite pursuits and studies."[36]

The notes' attention to natural historical detail provides an authenticity to the volume that lends credence to her emotional claims: her poet's extreme sorrow is more believable because Smith situates her in a carefully documented environment. Thus, although Smith sets up a contrast between the obviously poetic natural imagery of the sonnets and the empirical and vernacular vocabulary of the notes, the notes serve to confirm the poems' truthfulness by showing that her descriptions—of her environment and, by implication, her emotions—are verifiable. Thus the notes reify the timelessness of the speaker's plight even as they verify her sentiments. She is both removed from and made more accessible to readers. John Clare testifies to the effectiveness of what might be termed a rhetoric of empirical evidence in the notes. In a description of "[t]he Fern Owl or Goatsucker or Nightjar or nighthawk" in one of his unpublished Natural History Letters, he alludes to an explanatory note to Smith's "Composed during a walk on the Downs, in November 1787" (sonnet 42). He says of her poems, "I felt much pleasd with them because she wrote more from what she had seen of nature then from what she had read of it there fore those that read her poems find new images which they had not read of before tho they have often felt them & from those assosiations poetry derives the power of pleasing in the happiest manner."[37] Clare echoes Cowper's sense that reading Smith's sonnets is like finding one's own reactions recorded in them. For Clare it is not emotions, but responses to natural scenes that seem familiar yet "new." He testifies to the pleasure of this experience as a reader and incorporates her example into his own poetics, especially his early, richly de-scriptive sonnets. What Clare learns from Smith is that a sense of the sincerity of the poet's responses to a natural environment could be compelling, a lesson he proves himself with his initial success in *Poems Descriptive of Rural Life and Scenery* (1820).

Smith's deft use of the lyric mode in *Elegiac Sonnets* made her a popular poet by drawing readers to her autobiographical lyric speaker. Yet Smith's promi-nence in her own works—in the form of her poems' speakers and her novels' autobiographical characters—had complex consequences for her career. Though Smith's literary practice of self-portraiture kept her readers engaged in her unfolding story over the years, her sheer visibility also rendered her particularly vulnerable to censure along gendered lines, and specifically to charges of im-modesty and impropriety. In the early editions of the sonnets, Smith makes herself a sympathetic figure partly by presenting herself as reserved and soli-tary by nature. She adopts a familiar trope of modesty by confiding that she submits herself to public view only at others' urging: "Some of my friends, with partial indiscretion, have multiplied the copies they procured of several of these attempts, till they found their way into the prints of the day in a mutilated state; which, concurring with other circumstances, determined me to put them into their present form." But in the course of her career, it became clear that she continued to appear in public willingly, if under financial duress.

Smith risked gendered critiques even more directly when she eventually explained the biographical sources of her poet's habitual elegiac tenor. The sixth edition of *Elegiac Sonnets* marks a turning point in the volume's history: for the first time, Smith assigns a material cause to her unhappiness by refer-ring to her legal battle with the trustees of her father-in-law's estate. Critics have noted that in her novels, her anger emerges in her villainization of law-yers, the judicial system, and extravagant and abusive husbands. Her rage also surfaces in her poems and prefaces. In 1792 she elaborates her story in the context of the conversation with the friend who suggested she might venture "a more cheerful style of composition," explaining, "The time is indeed arrived, when I have been promised by 'the Honourable Men' who, *nine years ago,* undertook to see that my family obtained the provision their grandfather designed for them,—that 'all should be well, all should be settled.' But still I am condemned to feel the 'hope delayed that maketh the heart sick.'" What are the implications of Smith's eventual attribution of a precise source of agency to sorrows that in early editions seemed almost existential? In making a more explicit call for sympathy from readers, as she does in this preface, Smith relinquished some of the indirection that had constituted the sonnets' appeal, and in doing so she discovered the rhetorical limits of her popular success as a woman writer.

These restrictions, however, were not formal but social. Critical ambivalence reflected not lyricism's rhetorical incapacity, but rather social restrictions on what a women poet with radical sympathies and a proven ability to move readers could say in a politically turbulent period. For Smith's new specificity about the sources of her sorrow gave her lamentations a political inflection that she increasingly employed not only to argue her own case in the court of public opinion, but also to speak for others whom she considered fellow sufferers. Later editions of the *Sonnets* reflected this shift in Smith's public profile, when she added poems that alluded more explicitly both to the biographical sources of her poet's despair (such as "Written at Bignor Park in Sussex, in August, 1799," sonnet 92), and to social events (such as "The Sea View," sonnet 83, which expresses antiwar sentiments). More strikingly, in the same year that the preface to the sixth edition of the sonnets appeared, Smith published her fourth novel, *Desmond,* which features an English protagonist who travels to revolutionary France and is persuaded by its ideals.

Smith's increasing explicitness about the material conditions of her own melancholy was prompted by her frustration with the Chancery suit and the exhausting pace of her career. She established herself with the sonnets but soon found it necessary to turn to a more remunerative genre, the novel. *Emmeline* appeared four years after the first edition of *Elegiac Sonnets,* which was then in its fourth edition. After the success of this novel, she published nine others between 1788 and 1798. She also entered the burgeoning marketplace for children's literature, beginning with *Rural Walks: in Dialogues; Intended for the Use of Young Persons* (1795). Smith took several breaks from writing (in 1801, 1803, and 1805) in order to devote herself to her campaign to have her father-in-law's estate settled when it seemed that the Chancery suit might be resolved.[38] But persistent legal frustrations, and the continued financial needs of her family, kept her writing until her death in 1806; two works appeared posthumously, *Beachy Head, with Other Poems,* its title poem unfinished, and *The Natural History of Birds, Intended Chiefly for Young Persons,* both in 1807.

Smith also suffered the intermittent returns of her husband, who had legal rights to her earnings despite their separation. A book contract for *Desmond* named Benjamin, rather than Charlotte, as the legal party.[39]

In its notice of volume 2 of *Elegiac Sonnets* (1797), Joseph Johnson's politically liberal *Analytical Review* exemplifies the ideal response to her growing frankness. The reviewer advances Smith's bid for sympathy, and thus attempts to lend her the practical assistance that Cowper also wanted to provide: "We have chosen to extract these passages from the preface of our author, for the purpose of contributing, so far as lies in our power, to the notoriety of her injuries, and of exciting the public attention to the peculiar circumstances of aggravation which attend them." The critic anticipates that, not only would publicizing Smith's cause fan the flames of popular support—it might also shame her adversaries in the Chancery suit into greater benevolence: "As to her oppressors, however they may be dead to honesty and humanity, we can scarcely believe it possible that they should have outlived *all* sensibility to shame: no man is not gratified with the smiles of the world, or is any one so completely hardened, that he would not feel mortified at one universal frown of contempt and indignation." The critic becomes Smith's advocate, publicizing her cause and using the periodical's influence to pressure her "oppressors."[40]

Yet critics from both ends of the political spectrum—including those at the *Analytical Review*—were alarmed when it became clear that Smith understood her influence as a popular cultural figure and that she was willing to use it to address social issues. They recognized that even Smith's habitual practices of self-promotion and self-defense were political gestures, for as Curran notes, many of her works reflect "her recognition that the law is a social code written by men for a male preserve, and that the principal function of women within its boundaries can only be to suffer consequences over which they have no control."[41] Critics have identified various different moments as inaugurating a decline in Smith's popularity and have attributed this decline to various causes, including her prolific output. The government-supported *Anti-jacobin*, a periodical resolutely hostile to Smith's politics, noted with exasperation in 1801 that "she has almost wearied criticism in its attempts to keep pace with her."[42] Yet there is a suggestive consensus among Smith's latter-day critics that this decline began sometime in the years in which her public figure became politicized, with the publication of the sixth edition of *Elegiac Sonnets, Desmond, The Old Manor House* (1793), *The Emigrants* (1793), and *The Banished Man* (1794).[43] In the two latter works, Smith renders sympathetic French *émigrés* from the nobility, aristocracy, and clergy in works that some critics read as a retraction of her support in *Desmond* of revolution abroad and reform at home.

Critical responses to *The Banished Man* by the *British Critic* and the *Analytical Review* testify to a keen contemporaneous recognition of the influence that Smith could exert in treating political topics. The *British Critic*, delighted with Smith's seeming change of heart about the revolution, deems that "she makes full atonement by the virtues of the Banished Man, for the errors of Desmond," and closes its review by "congratulating the lovers of their king and the constitution, in the acquisition of an associate like Mrs. Charlotte Smith." The critic concludes by declaring with evident satisfaction that "[s]uch a convert, gained by fair conviction, is a valuable prize to the commonwealth." The legitimacy of this boast is supported by the simultaneous lamentation of the *Analytical Review* for its perceived loss of Smith as an ally: "As commonly happens to new converts, she is beyond all measure vehement in her exclamations against the late proceedings of the french."[44]

Although critics such as these often directly assailed Smith's politics, others employed a more ingenious strategy by censuring Smith's conduct as a woman writer. She was assailed for the very quality that had initiated her success—her works' intense autobiographical focus—when critics charged her with "egotism," a critique particularly damning for a woman whose literary success was greatly facilitated by her personal appeal. The *European Magazine* focuses on the autobiographical impulse of Smith's works in its review of *The Banished Man*. The critic explains that "the apology she makes for her frequent recurrence to family distresses will have its full weight with us," yet "we would have her rail like a gentlewoman always." Smith is warned that the strong language she uses for her enemies in the legal battle over her father-in-law's estate is reserved for men: "terms of abuse," she is told, have been "appropriated" by the "male sex," and their rights to them are not to be "invaded" by women, with one significant exception, "those resistless nymphs who deal out the scaly treasures of the ocean from a certain part of this metropolis."[45] Smith is warned that her writings are taking her out of the company of respectable women and placing her with the women who sold fish at the Billingsgate Fishmarket and whose colorful and unusually inventive obscenities have earned them a place to this day in encyclopedias of English culture and language.

In the course of her career, Smith discovered that she could only act indirectly, winning readers who might become advocates by turning away from them, asking for nothing. In the lyric, she found a mode in which she could render herself sympathetic by expressing her sorrows, ostensibly to herself, her solitary stance proof against charges that she had designs upon readers. Thus, Smith's averted gaze in the sonnets was both effective and necessary. Readers, including patrons and critics, were often glad to act for her, and Smith received generous assistance from publishers, including her first publisher, Thomas Cadell Sr., and from various patrons throughout her career. But she was reliant upon their continued sympathy and upon the sustained interest of her readers. She similarly lacked the ability to act for herself in the Chancery suit: she could not prod its resolution directly because women could not act as legal agents. The necessity of enlisting the help of others, including Sir George O'Brien Wyndham, third Earl of Egremont, and continually urging them to act eventually cost her patrons, including Egremont and Hayley. In the sonnet "To Dependence" (sonnet 57) Smith's poet laments, "Dependence! heavy, heavy are thy chains." In the poem, Smith alludes to the legal suit in declaring her determination to devote herself to "the Mountain Nymph" (Milton's Liberty in "L'Allegro") even "tho' Pride combine / With Fraud to crush me."

In its final review of her poetry, published after her death, the *British Critic* provides a clear picture of Smith's predicament. The review opens by acknowledging, "We could not, indeed, always accord with her in sentiment." The critic chastises her in gendered terms: "With respect to some subjects beyond her line of experience, reading, and indeed talent, she was unfortunately wayward and preposterous; but her poetic feeling and ability have rarely been surpassed by any individual of her sex." This censure, however, is somewhat countered by the review's close: "We take our leave of this author with unfeigned regret and sympathy." The critic explains why: "Her life was embittered by sorrow and misfortune, this gave an unavoidable tinge to her sentiments, which, from the gay and the vain, and the unfeeling, may excite a sneer of scorn and contempt; but in the bosoms of those who, like Charlotte Smith, with refined feelings, improved by thought and study, and reflection, have been compelled, like her, to tread the thorny paths of adversity, will prompt the generous wish, that fortune had favoured her with more complacency; and will induce the disposition to extenuate such portions of her productions, as sterner judgment is unable to approve."[46] This eulogy of Smith, patronizing and "generous," censorious and admiring, testifies to her precarious position throughout her career: she could win sympathy but could not state her case bluntly without risking her income and her gentlewomanly reputation.

In the lyric, Smith found a formal vehicle of indirection and complexity: by appearing to be lost in mournful reflections she won a popular audience, and in presenting herself as a mother writing only to support her children she gained a public position from which to pressure the trustees of her father-in-law's estate. Her career makes plain that for a woman writer dependent upon her earnings, the lyric offered the necessary guise of modesty, the proper stance of an averted gaze. In the sonnets, then, there is an illuminatingly direct connection between formal features and socioeconomic contexts that is valuable for reconsidering our understanding of Romantic lyricism as a poetics of privacy. Smith's pragmatic view of the form is highly instructive. By continuing to present her readers with more sonnets in the multiplying editions of *Elegiac*

Sonnets, she proved herself wise enough to know that she had found in the genre's "small plot of ground" a rare and viable, yet sharply circumscribed forum for a woman to make public the sorrows of dependence.

Notes

1. Barbauld, "Mrs. Charlotte Smith," iii.

2. "Sonnet to Mrs. Smith."

3. *British Public Characters,* 3:65.

4. Frye, *Anatomy of Criticism,* 271.

5. Abrams, "Structure and Style."

6. Bishop C. Hunt Jr. describes a copy of the fifth edition (1789) that Wordsworth owned at Cambridge and which contains his marginalia. Hunt provides an extensive account of Smith's influence on Wordsworth in "Wordsworth and Charlotte Smith."

7. W. Wordsworth, *The Poetical Works of William Wordsworth,* 1896, 7:351.

8. Curran, *Poetic Form and British Romanticism,* 32. S.T. Coleridge, "Introduction to the Sonnets," 543.

9. Margaret Homans establishes this foundational feminist account of the traditional construction of Romantic subjectivity as masculine in *Women Writers and Poetic Identity.*

10. Frye and Harold Bloom have defined the Romantic "quest" by its direction: not outward, toward a redeemed natural and human world, but "downward and inward, toward a hidden base of identity between man and nature," in Frye's terms. Within this broader paradigm, Romantic lyricism is the formal vehicle of internalization. See Frye, *A Study of English Romanticism,* 33. Bloom, "The Internalization of Quest-Romance."

11. The acquaintance was the barrister and orator John F. Taylor. See Yeats, *Autobiographies,* 97.

12. In her preface to *The Banished Man* (1794), she reports, "In the strictures on a late publication of mine, some Review (I do not now recollect which) objected to the too frequent allusion I made in it to my own circumstances." See *The Banished Man,* 1:viii. Other defenses against charges of egotism are found in the prefaces to *Marchmont* (1796) and to volume 2 of *Elegiac Sonnets* (1797).

13. Abrams, "English Romanticism," 107. Liu, *Wordsworth,* 223.

14. William Jones to J. Shore, Esq., 16 Aug. 1787, in Shore, *Memoirs of Sir William Jones,* 2:139. Unsigned notice of *Elegiac Sonnets,* 3d ed., in *Gentleman's Magazine* 56 (1786): 334.

15. From the first edition, *Elegiac Sonnets* contained poems other than sonnets, but the sonnets continually outnumbered them. These poems, like the sonnets, multiplied with expanding editions. Metastasio is Pietro Trapassi (1698-1782).

16. The lines she puts in her own mouth are Egeon's. The lines under the engraving slightly misquote Shakespeare: "Oh! Time has Changed me since you saw me last, / And heavy Hours with Time's deforming Hand, / Have written strange Defeatures in my Face." Shakespeare's lines are quoted correctly in my epigraph (see *Comedy of Errors* 5.1.298-301).

17. Review of *The Emigrants*, 403.

18. One group of Smith's letters at Princeton University's Firestone Library contains instructions for an engraver about altering the frontispiece portrait and one of the collection's engravings. I quote the letter at length in "Charlotte Smith's Letters and the Practice of Self-Presentation," *Princeton University Library Chronicle* 53 (1991): 50-77.

19. All quotations from Smith's poetry (poems, prefaces and notes) are taken from Smith, *Poems*.

20. Fried, *Absorption and Theatricality*, 108.

21. Review of *Elegiac Sonnets*, 3d ed., 333.

22. Marshall, *The Surprising Effects of Sympathy*, 5.

23. Ibid., 107.

24. S.T. Coleridge, "Introduction to the Sonnets," 543.

25. William Cowper to Charlotte Smith, 26 Oct. 1793, in Cowper, *Correspondence*, 4:462.

26. Marshall, *The Surprising Effects of Sympathy*, 128. Cowper to William Hayley, 29 Jan. 1793, in Cowper, *Correspondence*, 4:363.

27. S.T. Coleridge, "Introduction to the Sonnets," 543.

28. For Abrams's account of the significance of sincerity to Romantic poetry, see *The Mirror and the Lamp*, 317-19. For "the lyric as poetic norm," see 84-88. A number of critics have complicated Romantic accounts of sincerity. See especially Lionel Trilling, *Sincerity and Authenticity* and Judith Pascoe, *Romantic Theatricality*.

29. Magnuson, "Politics of 'Frost at Midnight,'" 3. Stanton, "Charlotte Smith's 'Literary Business.'"

30. Culler follows Frye's claim that in the lyric "we turn away from our ordinary continuous experience in space or time, or rather from a verbal mimesis of it." According to Frye, this detachment requires a rejection of "the kind of language we use in coping with ordinary experience." See Frye, "Approaching the Lyric," 31, 34. Culler, *Structuralist Poetics*, 197.

31. Cameron, *Lyric Time*.

32. Ibid., 203.

33. Northcote, "The Sorrows of Mrs. Charlotte Smith," 686-96.

34. Leigh Hunt, *The Book of the Sonnet*, 1:85. "Sonnet, To Mrs. Smith, on reading her Sonnets."

35. Pinch, *Strange Fits of Passion*. Todd, *Sensibility*, 4.

36. W. Scott, *The Miscellaneous Prose Works*, 2:64.

37. Clare, *The Natural History Prose Writings*, 34.

38. Stanton, "Charlotte Smith's 'Literary Business,'" 393.

39. Ibid., 376-77.

40. Review of *Elegiac Sonnets*, vol. 2, 158.

41. Curran, *Poetic Form and British Romanticism*, xxi.

42. Unsigned review of Smith's *Letters of a Solitary Wanderer*, vols. 1-3, *Anti-jacobin* 10 (1801): 318.

43. Judith Phillips Stanton makes a cogent case that in *The Old Manor House*, "after her first three conventional novels, Smith had begun to test the limits of what a

woman might write." Derek Roper points out that, with the exception of the *Critical Review,* the major periodicals viewed this novel positively. He argues that Smith's decline in popularity began with her next novel, *The Banished Man,* since this and subsequent novels were "of less interest." See Stanton, introduction, ix. Roper, *Reviewing before the Edinburgh,* 130.

44. Review of *The Banished Man, British Critic* 4 (1794): 623. Review of *The Banished Man, Analytical Review* 20 (1794): 254.

45. Review of *The Banished Man, European Magazine* 26 (1794): 276. A reviewer for the *Critical Review* makes a related charge about *Letters of a Solitary Wander.* The critic suggests that "the story of the Hermit speaks to every one's bosom; and the affectionate sensibility of Frank Maynard is equally interesting and pathetic." Yet, the critic goes on to suggest: "To similar tales of domestic life and domestic feelings perhaps Mrs. Smith might, with propriety, confine her exertions." See review of *Letters of a Solitary Wanderer, Critical Review* 32 (1801), 39.

46. Review of *Beachy Head.*

"Be Good!"

Acting, Reader's Theater, and Oratory in Frances Anne Kemble's Writing

Catherine B. Burroughs

So she [Kemble] did dream: a long straight road of clangorous iron sweeping away and away across wet green fields until it dissolved into the distant mist. At the end of the road, mountains? But the mist was obscenely infested; shadow-shapes of rutting Turks, absurd and lurid; not just one sultan, but two, and both silver-haired—all over.

John Arden, "Uses of Iron"

Even though she is better known to late-twentieth-century readers as an actress and a diarist, Frances Anne Kemble is an important figure for considering how female poets sometimes drew upon the cultural position of London actresses to discuss women, gender, and British social theater during the transitional period called late Romantic or early Victorian.[1] Because Kemble's earliest poems date from 1825—first composed at sixteen, when as yet she felt no pressure to join the acting profession that was her legacy—a reading of the lyrics she composed between her teen years and mature adulthood can help us appreciate the crucial role this romantic outlet afforded her as she expressed her affinity with "the sensuous woman," a persona she frequently eschewed onstage and in her nonfictional writings. Poetry was among the first of many genres to claim her heart, and throughout her writing life—especially in her personal narratives—Kemble would return to paradigms delineated by those Romantic lyrics she created before the 1860s in order to chronicle the workings of a dramatic and passionate sensibility seemingly out of sync with her own era.

As John Arden's imaginative reconstruction of Kemble's thought process suggests above, Kemble's anxieties about gender emerged when she indirectly revealed her attraction to the sexual. This was a subject she addressed head on in her lyrics but dealt with obliquely in her journals through animating the opposition—familiar in Romantic theater criticism—between embodiment and reading. Through this closet/stage dichotomy—which she frequently equated with her father, Charles, on the one hand, and Lord Byron on the other— Fanny Kemble gestured toward a fantasy that turns on her vision of an actual space in which she is permitted to read, rather than act, her way into people's hearts. This space would seem to be purged of the performing female body, until one considers how attractively Kemble renders this body in her romantic love lyrics. Likewise, her journals—published between 1835 and 1891—reveal that acting on the stage had a particular charge for her, one that perhaps affected her at a bodily level more profoundly than it affected her female colleagues, who, by the 1830s, could enter theaters with less trepidation, largely because of the decorous performance of femininity given in the previous era by Kemble's aunt, Sarah Siddons. Especially in her early twenties, when she performed in *Romeo and Juliet* and explored the story of a young girl's sexual awakening, Fanny Kemble found herself in the both uncomfortable and disturbingly attractive position of directing her blushes and emotional intensity alternately to actors old enough to be her father, to the actress Ellen Tree (who, in Kemble's view, looked the part of Romeo but violated propriety by playing a man's role) (RG, 2:27),[2] and to her father himself. Although Kemble greatly admired her father's acting style—it cannot be excelled, she wrote, in its "high and noble bearing [or its] gallant, graceful, courteous deportment" (JYA, 57)—the fact that in her view his performance epitomized the gentleman did not minimize the difficulties she encountered in having to passionately perform with him in public view.

This difficulty of publicly performing a sexually active woman was reflected in Kemble's tendency in her prose narratives to pit acting negatively against reading and oration, and it fueled some of her most dramatic writing, especially in her lyric poems in which the speakers counter the poetry's collective obsessiveness with material and psychic loss by dwelling with startling vigor upon the details of physical intimacy. This emphasis on bodily "throbbing" points to one of the many contradictions in Kemble's fascinating and complex biography:[3] though in her journals she celebrates "good-breeding"— the phrase she used to describe her father's acting style (JYA, 57)—and expresses a horror of "public exhibition" as a "business . . . unworthy of a woman" (RG, 2:61), Kemble's verse sometimes revels in the spectacle of female passion dramatically voiced. This contradiction is not in itself remarkable, since, as feminist critics have demonstrated at length, nineteenth-century British women writers frequently produced a fiction at odds with their personal narratives. "Conflicts," observes Alison Booth in reference to Fanny's "multiplicitous" identity and her progress from Miranda to Prospero as she played a variety of roles (both on and off the stage) in relation to her actor-father, "however disturbing and illegible they may have been in the actual life, are what we look for when we focus the lens of biographical interpretation on historical women; we readily dramatize ideological strains as antagonistic motives within the famous woman's personality."[4] But the conflicts *within* Kemble's writing, as she moves among an astonishing variety of genres, and between fiction and nonfiction, are indeed noteworthy for drawing attention to those moments when Kemble unapologetically unleashed a sensual persona that revels in bodily joy.

Gesturing toward many of those conventions we have come to associate with what Anne K. Mellor calls "masculine romanticism,"[5] in her poetry Kemble also confounded expectations for the Romantic lyric by refusing to make loss the index of her creative sensibility. Nor do her speakers find sweet pleasure in intense pain. As Arden has put it, "her romanticism must not forever fling itself about through past ages, a wood-pigeon trapped in a bell-tower."[6] Instead of merely imitating the Romantic lyrics she read as a young girl, Kemble used a familiar Romantic vocabulary to dramatize how horrible it is to wander in spiritual exile from one's beloved. The lyrics' narrow range of vocabulary—as speakers describe their distress—should not suggest that Kemble's verse does not vary in tone or subject, however. In the 1866 collection, which contains more than 175 poems (many written during the late Romantic period), several sonnets composed to the greatness of Shakespeare's and Dante's poetry are scattered among relatively cheerful poems about a laughing maiden, a beautiful sister, Italian cities, and tributes to Thomas Moore and Sarah Siddons. There is at least one attempt at humor, it would seem, in the poem called "Fragment; from an Epistle Written When the Thermometer Stood at 98 in the Shade," in which the speaker exclaims,

> O! in a pond
> Would I were over head and ears!
> (Of a *cold* ducking I've no fears,)
> Or any where, where I am not;
> For, bless the heat! it is too hot!
> [P, 196]

Yet because the major project of Kemble's poetic oeuvre involved acts of crying out against the terrors of emotional homelessness, the sensual lyrics are striking for lodging vital protests against the loss of a physical intimacy, which the persona Kemble created in her journals frequently disdained, and often feared.

For instance, in one sonnet a speaker confesses that

> There's not a fibre in my trembling frame
> That does not vibrate when thy step draws near,

There's not a pulse that throbs not when I hear
Thy voice, thy breathing, nay, thy very name.
[P, 172]

These words are a prelude to the speaker's saying that she or he dreams about the lover's "greeting clasp," that is, a muscular embrace of the kind that also figures in "An Invitation," when the speaker imagines being "clasped in thy upholding arms" (P, 173). In a poem called simply "Song," Kemble describes the memory of sexual intimacy when braids are loosened and kisses are bestowed on the brow of the lover "sleeping on my [the speaker's] breast" (P, 174). By far the most sensual in detail, however, is Kemble's trilogy of poems respectively called "Morning, Noonday, and Evening By the Seaside," in which the body of the lover is pored over and elaborated upon in ways that make more understandable why Kemble would have expressed surprise at some people's offense over Kotzebue's notorious play, *The Stranger,* in which, when a wayward wife is forgiven, the husband clasps her to his chest (RLL, 346-48). This sort of all-encompassing physical embrace, which, in Kemble's poetic portrayals, seems to eradicate every other social concern in a rush of sexual excitement, is alluded to in the morning poem by the speaker's inviting the addressee to "let me lock in mine thy hand." To underscore the importance in Kemble's poetry of such an image, the seaside landscape turns turbid as soon as the request is made: "See, how the swollen ridges of the waves / Curl into crystal caves," the speaker asks us to observe:

> Rising and rounding,
> Rolling and rebounding,
> Echoing, resounding,
> And running into curves of creamy spray.
> [P, 50-51]

The noontime of this passion—its "piercing fervid heat"—is pictured with references to "silver clover," which "like spicy incense quivers the warm air" (P, 52); and while one lover drowses in the sun, the other holds the head of the beloved on her/his breast, drinking in the sight of the "thick rolls of golden hair" and vowing not to let "tumultuous sigh" or the "irregular bound" of a "heart throb" disturb this intimate nesting fostered by the kisses bestowed on "[f]air fringed lids" (P, 54).

Evening brings a progressively melting ecstasy, played against the backdrop of roaring waves, which—despite their roughness—cannot disturb the speaker's faith in sensual experience, even as they move the soul profoundly. In the opening lines of the evening poem are heard the echoes of Puck's dark epithalamium at the end of *A Midsummer Night's Dream*—"Now the hungry lion roars / And the wolf behowls the moon" (5.1.378-79)—as if Kemble's verse challenges the legitimacy of conventional matrimony through the celebration of an unspecified, perhaps unsanctioned, love relationship:

> The monsters of the deep do roar,
> And their huge manes upon the shore
> Plunge headlong, with a thundering sound
> That shakes the hollow-hearted ground.
> [P, 55]

Yet the speaker finds comfort in the turbulent landscape by focusing on the physical details of the beloved, and the result is a radiant vision:

> And yet, amidst this din I hear
> Thy gentle voice close at my ear,
> Whispering sweet words of love, that shake
> My soul with the soft wound they make.
>
> The cup of Heaven o'erflows with light,
> The sea's broad shield is burnished bright,
> And the whole earth doth glow and shine
> Like a red, radiant, evening shrine.
>
> And in this splendor, all I see
> Are thy dear eyes beholding me,
> With such a tender, stedfast gaze,
> My life seems melting in their ray.
> [P, 55]

In these lyrics, the issue of maintaining control over the voice and the body—the central concern for Kemble whether she performs as actor or reader—recedes in importance to the act of being able to transform the impassioned sadness of a bruised soul into the comforting sensualism of a heart unfettered and unleashed.

This brief discussion of some of Kemble's love lyrics is a prelude to my suggestion that they can be positioned as significant expressions of late Romanticism's ambivalence about the idea of the performing woman, a point I hope to clarify by contextualizing the poems with passages from Kemble's writing, especially her "theory of theatre." As I have elsewhere argued,[7] the theater theory produced through the ages by those who have written for and about what have traditionally been called public and private stages is an important context for appreciating how playwrights and actors—particularly women—have figured their conflicts with social performance. Those conflicts, in turn, can be used to provide an invaluable context for studying the performed contradictions that structure dramaturgical features of an author's body of writing, whether fictional or nonfictional texts. Kemble's writing about acting, reader's theater, and oration is no exception. Profoundly affected by the problem of how to perform the socially viable female, in her theater theory Kemble offers historians and literary critics some of the best examples of how the struggle to say something about the theater arts often dramatizes the social struggle of the theorizing performer.[8] In the context of this volume on Romantic women poets, Kemble's stage theory reminds us of the degree to which "romantic theatricality" permeated the literary productions of early-nineteenth-century writers to the point where an investigation of the material conditions of theatrical performers seems increasingly an indispensable part of our understanding of how Romantic poetry by women disseminated, and reflected, early-nineteenth-century cultural values.[9]

Though she characterized herself as the "worst reasoner, analyser, metaphysician that ever was born" (RG, 2:103), Kemble's comments about acting resulted in what George Arliss has assessed as "perhaps the most careful analysis of the actor in juxtaposition with his art that one is likely to find in dramatic literature."[10] Ironically, however, Kemble's theory was the by-product of her frequent disgust with what she called "my most impotent and unpoetical craft!" (JYA, 109). Trying to come to terms with what made performing so "curious" and "complicated" for her (RG, 2:104), Kemble alternately emphasized the absurdity and the fascination of professional acting. Her journals tell of one incident after another in which actors—especially those with whom she worked in America—forget lines, perform stage business antithetical to the text, wear implausible costumes, paw the female actors (he "clung to me, cramped me, crumpled me—dreadful!" [JYA, 39]), misplace props, and literally knock Kemble over in their zeal to embrace her.

Because acting combined "elements at once so congenial and so antagonistic to my nature" (RG, 2:18-19)—which Kemble described as "irregular," "passionate" and full of "vehemence" (RG, 2:58)—she seems to have both relished and feared onstage performances as the means by which her ever-lurking sensuality could hijack the decorous aims of the socially self-conscious woman. Arden beautifully recreates Kemble's conflicted relationship to acting when imaging how she—from the time of her stage debut in 1829—"stood for her cue in the wings of the Theatre Royal, and yet again cleared her mind for the night's work by reckless release of metaphorical fantasy—" "[S]he was a Christian captive of virtuous habit but, alas, libidinous nature, compelled as an odalisque into the seraglio of the Grand Turk—drastic tearing of her spirit between outrage and exaltation, horror and sleek pride—who could say which emotions would in the long run prove stronger?"[11] Less studied than inspired

(Kemble received only three weeks' rehearsal before she made her stage debut), Kemble's acting resulted in moments when the character she was playing seemed to overtake her body so profoundly that she lost sight of that "double process" that, as she described in the journal she published in 1878 (*Records of a Girlhood*), is necessary to any actor, "a sort of vigilant presence of mind . . . which constantly looks after and avoids or removes the petty obstacles that are destroying the imaginary illusion, and reminding one in one's own despite that one is not really Juliet or Belvidera" (RG, 2:103).

According to that same journal, especially in the early stages of her career in the 1830s, Kemble sometimes surprised and frightened herself with the wealth of emotion that issued forth from her person, as if she were a conduit for someone else's expressive history. Not having rehearsed the moment in Otway's *Venice Preserved* when Belvidera is to "utter a piercing scream," Kemble discovered in the first performances of that role that she "uttered shriek after shriek without stopping, and rushing off the stage ran all round the back of the scenes, and was pursuing [her] way, down the stairs that led out into the street, when [she] was captured and brought back to [her] dressing-room and [her] senses" (RG, 2:86-87). Losing herself to a pleasurable physiology, which she nevertheless portrays as a kind of madness, Kemble writes that she experienced a similar moment when first performing Juliet publicly in the balcony scene, the spirit of which, she wrote in her critical analysis of Shakespeare's plays (published in 1882), "is that of joyful tenderness, and something of a sort of sweet surprise at the fervid girl-passion which suddenly wraps [Romeo] round, and carries him as with wings of fire towards the level of its own intensity."[12] The "passion I was uttering [was] sending hot waves of blushes all over my neck and shoulders," she recalled in *Records of a Girlhood*, "while the poetry sounded like music to me as I spoke it, with no consciousness of anything before me, utterly transported into the imaginary existence of the play. After this, I did not return into myself till all was over" (RG, 2:60). These kinds of experiences—and her remembrances of them—prompted Kemble to publish a journal in which she confessed that she never "presented [her]self before an audience, without a shrinking feeling of reluctance, or withdrawn from their presence without thinking the excitement I had undergone unhealthy, and the personal exhibition odious" (RG, 2:61).

Yet she was frequently less amused then angered by her profession. In the diary of her first years as a professional actress and of her tour to America in the early 1830s, Kemble compared acting unfavorably to other creative modes of expression, especially the writing of poetry, even as she showed that she cared deeply about trying to excel in acting.[13] In fact, it was the poetic element, rather than the theatrical, in Shakespeare's plays that elicited her greatest enthusiasm and praise throughout her life. In *Records of Later Life* (1882), Kemble writes that she envisioned her reader's theater—in which she spoke Shakespearian scenes from behind a desk in the 1850s—as a poetic form in which "dramatic effect, which of course suffers in the mere delivery from a reading desk would, I hoped, be in some measure compensated for by the possibility of retaining the whole beauty of the plays *as poetical compositions*" (RLL, 632, my emphasis).

Nina Auerbach has observed that the "fear of performance that pervades nineteenth-century humanism finds its epitome in the immobility of the Victorian Shakespeare";[14] Kemble expressed this fear not only by reading Shakespeare in public performance but also by reviving in her own theater commentary the closet/stage dichotomy common to early-nineteenth-century theater criticism. Comparing stage embodiment unfavorably to poetry in *Records of Later Life,* she wrote that acting's "most miserable deficiency . . . is most apparent" in the fact that it can only endure "in the dim memories of some few of [actors'] surviving spectators"; acting "lacks . . . the grand faculty which all other arts possess—creation"; it "originates nothing" (RLL, 125). Thus, while Kemble "constantly asserts the primacy of the real life that takes place off-stage—the life in which she is an ordinary middle-class daughter—over the fictions of the public theater, where her participation in a disreputable display threatens her sense of identity,"[15] she struggled at length to get a perspective on those disturbing and uplifting experiences she had on stage.

Because Fanny's fears about acting are tied to her concern about how the female body could be employed on stage to betray the acting woman's desire for social acceptability, they are complicated by the fact of her father's having initiated her into the theatrical arena. This initiation seems to have had lasting effects on her, some positive, others not. It is important to realize that, because he urged her to take the stage in ingenue roles, Kemble's male parent directly and indirectly tutored her in how to emit a sexual expressiveness for performance in a socially sanctioned context. But by encouraging her to embrace the role of professional actor, Charles Kemble also ensured that Fanny would take up a position with which she would inevitably call her culture's attention to the specific contours of female psychic life.[16] The language Fanny uses in her journals to qualify her praise for her father's style of performing suggests that this situation was not without problems for her. In addition to telling us that it was "difficult!" to act Juliet to her father's Romeo (JYA, 61), in the journal that Kemble kept about their tour to America (1832-34) she locates the drawbacks of Charles Kemble's performance style in "the very minute accuracy and refinement" of his "workmanship," which "renders it unfit for the frame in which it is exhibited" (JYA, 55).

Whether we read this last comment as critical or admiring, Kemble's suggestion that Charles Kemble's acting is better fitted for closet than stage evokes the antitheatrical bent of Romantic critics such as Lord Byron and Charles Lamb, whose views Fanny essentialized in *Records of a Girlhood* with the assertion that the "*happiness* of reading Shakespeare's heavenly imaginations is so far beyond all the excitement of acting them." "While I can sit obliviously curled up in an armchair," Kemble wrote, "and read what he says till my eyes are full of delicious, quiet tears, and my heart of blessed, good, quiet thoughts and feelings, I shall not crave that which falls so far short of any real enjoyment" (RG, 2:105).

Because Kemble preferred to channel her acting talent into forums in which she could peruse rather than embody Shakespeare, one can speculate that she may have wanted to put distance between herself and that performing parent who evoked in her such mighty emotion. By publicly reading plays aloud instead of acting in them—as in the 1850s, when she turned to reader's theater[17]—Kemble could present her body in a controlled and decorous posture, in contrast to the sensuous performance of Juliet she gave when acting with her father. Her embrace of the act of reading Shakespeare suggests that she believed she could inspire others to curb their own threateningly expressive bodiliness.

As a result of her disastrous marriage to the American plantation owner Pierce Butler in 1834, Kemble ironically seems to have come closest to inhabiting the kind of utopian performance space she associated with feminine propriety and bodily control when suddenly she found herself the unwilling mistress of slaves on a sea island in Georgia. On several Sundays in 1839, she gave a series of prayer readings to the slaves as if to atone for her participation in their suffering. What interests me about those readings is the fact that, in Kemble's account of them in her well-known *Journal of a Residence on a Georgia Plantation* (1838-39), she focuses less on the slaves than on the effects her orations supposedly had in bringing the slaves to civilized heel—an expression of her belief that reading could exert a moral influence on the bodily excesses of others—as well on her own experience of performing: "[I]t was encouraging to see the very decided efforts at cleanliness and decorum of attire which they had all made," she writes of the black bodies who filled the little plantation church. But then she turns quickly to discuss her own responses: "I was very much affected and impressed myself by what I was doing, and I suppose I must have communicated some of my own feeling to those who heard me" (JR, 262).

Since throughout her journals the act of oration is portrayed as a safe and acceptable outlet for passionate expression, Kemble portrays herself as untroubled by relishing the intensity of what Booth characterizes as her abolitionist and pedagogical mode.[18] She recalls that:

there was something in relation to the poor people by whom I was surrounded that touched me so deeply while thus attempting to share with them the best of my possessions, that I found it difficult to command my voice, and had to stop several times in order to do so. When I had done, they all with one accord uttered the simple words: "we thank you, missis," and instead of overwhelming me as usual with petitions and complaints, they rose silently and quietly, in a manner that would have become the most orderly of Christian congregations accustomed to all the impressive decorum of civilized church privileges. Poor people! They are said to have what a very irreligious young clergyman once informed me I had—a "*turn* for religion." They seem to me to have a "turn" for instinctive good manners too; and certainly their mode of withdrawing from my room after our prayers bespoke either a strong feeling of their own, or a keen appreciation of mine.

[JR, 262-63]

Imagining herself an instrument of decorous and civilized behavior, Kemble finds herself moved by the experience of using her reading voice to render "orderly" the African Americans whom she describes throughout her journal as constantly pressing upon her for relief from bodily injury.

Notably, it is in these moments of frustration with her own positionality—with her seeming powerlessness to do anything to help others trapped within patriarchal and racist systems—that Kemble often employed her theatrical training as a strategy for unburdening her heart. At one point in the Georgia journal—upset by the broken female bodies she saw all around her on the plantation—she bursts into a brief prose poem in which she draws on her intimate knowledge of Shakespeare to emit a voice not unlike some of the Byronic lyrics that fill her poetry collection: "Beat, beat, the crumbling banks and sliding shores, wild waves of the Atlantic and the Altamaha! Sweep down and carry hence this evil earth and these homes of tyranny, and roll above the soil of slavery, and wash my soul and the souls of those I love clean from the blood of our kind!" (JR, 233).

There is also the incident of the "tall, emaciated-looking negress" who "unfolded to me a most distressing history . . . ," who told of being "the mother of a very large family, and complained to me that, what with childbearing and hard field labor, her back was almost broken in two" (JR, 67). Unable to change the woman's condition, Kemble nevertheless tries to evoke empathy for her suffering by painting the woman as a tragic heroine, using the language of the stage[19] to record her "almost savage vehemence of gesticulation" at the moment when the woman "suddenly tore up her scanty clothing, and exhibited a spectacle with which I was inconceivably shocked and sickened" (JR, 67).

These outbursts appear consistently in her diaries from the early years. In the journal she kept of her stage tour of America in 1832-34—the years leading up to her marriage and brief residence in Georgia—Kemble assumes Byronic postures in the process of divulging several scenes to her reading audience in which excessive emotion and histrionicism take center stage.[20] For instance, when a bottle containing a letter that Kemble is sending back to England misses a passing ship, Kemble confesses that she "screamed as the black sea closed over my poor letter. Came down to my cabin and cried like a wretch" (JYA, 8). And when the captain of the ship tries to comfort her by giving her a land-swallow, she describes its death soon after in language that portrays her as the overly sensitive heroine of the novel of sensibility or the hyperexpressive female lead in early Victorian melodrama: "My poor little bird is dead. Poor little creature! I wish it had not died—I would have borne it tenderly and carefully to shore, and given it back to the air again" (JYA, 8).

Through exaggerated gestures and vocal pyrotechnics, these passages show Kemble indirectly challenging what would come to be recognized as the early Victorian ideal of the silent and self-effacing woman. Often employing "the voice of passionate expostulation and importunate pleading against wrongs" (JR, 210), throughout her journals Kemble paints pictures of herself as a robust woman—of an "Amazon" (JR, 218)—who was perfectly capable of dealing with the many emotional and physical challenges thrown her way. Yet this sense of confidence wavered. In *Records of Later Life* (1882), for example, Kemble includes entries from the time of her marriage when she occasionally voiced the desire to be "a man!" (RLL, 42), forecasting Daisy Buchanan's famous lament in *The Great Gatsby* by confessing in 1835 on the birth of her baby girl: "I was at first a little disappointed that my baby was not a man-child, for the lot of woman is seldom happy, owing principally, I think, to many serious mistakes which have obtained universal sway in female education" (RLL, 25). Kemble regarded this education—against which her feminist foremothers in the 1790s had protested for forcing women to acquire decorative rather than intellectual skills—as having made her unfit for devising practical ways to respond, for instance, to the plight of an epileptic slave. "How much I wished," she writes in the Georgia journal, "that, instead of music, and dancing, and such stuff, I had learned something of sickness and health, of the conditions and liabilities of the human body, that I might have known how to assist this poor creature, and to direct her ignorant and helpless nurses!" (JR, 75).

But when she focused on the act of reading (as opposed to embodiment), Kemble seems to have perceived herself as moving closer to emulating her feminine ideal, Portia from *The Merchant of Venice*, whose carefully modulated performance of femininity struck Kemble as superior to Juliet's sensual passion. "Juliet," she recalled in *Records of a Girlhood*, "I act; but I feel as if I *were* Portia—and how I wish I were!" (RG, 2:108). By assessing the role of Portia as not "generally much liked by actresses, or one that excites much enthusiasm in the public," Kemble suggests that it is Portia's unactorly quality—the play's lyrical rather than dramatic element—that attracted her to playing a role that she seems to have regarded as more suitable for the woman in real life than for the romantic actor on stage:

[T]here are no violent situations with which to (what is called) "bring the house down." Even the climax of the piece, the trial scene, I should call, as far as Portia is concerned, rather grand and impressive than strikingly or startlingly effective; and with the exception of that, the whole character is so delicate, so nicely blended, so true, and so free from all exaggeration, that it seems to me hardly fit for a theatre, much less one of our immense houses, which require acting almost as *splashy* and coarse in colour and outline as the scene-painting of the stage is obliged to be. [RG, 2:108]

Significantly, Kemble's emphasis on Portia's "delicacy" and unfitness for theatrical performance evokes the language she often used to describe her father's acting. Praising her father's "[p]olished and refined tastes," his "acute sense of the beauty of harmonious proportions, and a native grace, gentleness and refinement of mind and manner" (JYA, 57), Kemble mused at the age of twenty-three: " 'Tis curious . . . when I see him act I have none of the absolute feeling of contempt for the profession that I have when I am acting myself. What *he* does appears indeed like the work of an artist. I certainly respect acting more while I am seeing him act, than at any other time" (JYA, 158, my emphasis). As long as she could direct her passionate feelings to her father, Fanny required little imagination to produce Juliet's emotions, and she praised her father's performances of Romeo by describing her pleasurable response: "[W]ith all other Romeos, though they were much younger men, I have had to do double work; first to get rid of the material obstacle staring me in the face, and then to substitute some more congenial representative of the sweetest vision of youth and love" (JYA, 61).

Kemble's longing for closet space—the site for which her father's acting was apparently best suited—directs us to consider the extent to which this longing may have registered Kemble's protest against performing in the theater as a dutifully passionate daughter. Indeed, it is the close alliance in Kemble's rhetoric between oratory, reading, and decorum that sets in relief Kemble's attraction to and attempted rejection of the passionate postures she associated with both her gentlemanly father and the licentious Byron of her youth.

Throughout Kemble's journals, references to Lord Byron and his estranged wife, the former Annabella Milbanke, highlight Kemble's struggle to find an acceptable outlet for the passionate expressiveness she displayed in her Romantic lyrics yet which she disdained as a publicly performing actor. In *Records of a Girlhood*—the journal that describes the events of her life from her birth in

1809 to her marriage in 1834—Kemble refers to the conflict she had with her actress-mother, Marie Therese De Camp, over how to read Thomas Moore's edition of Byron's letters and journals (1830). Forecasting the disagreements about slavery that Kemble would have with her own daughter, Frances Butler Leigh, Kemble told her friend Harriet St. Leger that this difference of opinion about Byron—her mother romanticized Byron as "absolute perfection" and "hate[d] . . .his wife"—was so upsetting to the two women that they could no longer discuss the issue (RG, 2:245).

Linking Byron's verse with danger and impropriety, Kemble tells us in *Records of a Girlhood* that, in her early twenties, she gave up reading Byron's poetry because "I was quite convinced of its injurious effect upon me" (RG, 1:270). Yet it had not been easy to do so. To "forego" Byron in fact required a "great effort and a very great sacrifice, for the delight I found in [his poetry] was intense." "[N]obody was ever a more fanatical worshipper of his poetry than I was," Kemble confessed: "time was that I devoured his verses (poison as they were to me) like 'raspberry tarts'" (RG, 270). Despite confessing that Byron's closet plays like *Manfred* and *Cain* "stirred my whole being with a tempest of excitement that left me in state of mental perturbation impossible to describe, for a long time after reading them," Fanny expressed her belief that her happiness was at stake through her aggressive attempt to wean herself from "the infection of the potent, proud, desponding bitterness of his writing" (RG, 1:270).

This sense that Byron's verse had the power to infect her is significant, since, in contrast to Byron—whom Kemble characterized in *Records of a Girlhood* as having "done more mischief than one would like to be answerable for" (RG, 2:246)—Kemble cast Lady Byron as an upright heroine in an effort to underscore her own commitment to proper behavior. Yet by including in her journal an anecdote of the evening when Lady Byron expressed envy of Kemble's role as an orator of Shakespeare, Kemble revealed that her fondness for propriety—indicated perhaps most dramatically by her seeming preference for reader's theater—required her to excise important parts of herself, to cut off a whole range of sexual, romantic, and feminist feelings that the act of embodying characters on public stage encouraged her to display.

According to Kemble, one night in the midcentury as they were proceeding to one of her Shakespearean readings, Lady Byron exclaimed: "'What would I not give to be in your place! . . . Not to read Shakespeare [before hundreds of people], but to have all that mass of people under your control, subject to your influence, and receiving your impressions'" (RG, 1:212). Lady Byron "then went on to say," Kemble tells us, "she would give anything to lecture upon subjects which interested her deeply, and that she should like to advocate with every power she possessed" (RG, 1:212).

Kemble's response is worth noting in light of the fact that, for her, reading represented respectability and restraint, even though she writes that her Shakespearean readings "oftener appeared to me to justify my own regret than the envy of others." Kemble tells us she made Lady Byron laugh by confessing to her that more than once, when looking from my reading-desk over the sea of faces uplifted towards me,"

a sudden feeling seized me that I must say something *from myself* to all those human beings whose attention I felt at that moment entirely at my command, and between whom and myself a sense of sympathy thrilled powerfully and strangely through my heart, as I looked steadfastly at them before opening my lips; but that, on wondering afterwards *what* I might, could, would, or should have said to them from myself, I never could think of anything but two words: "Be good!" which as a preface to the reading of one of Shakespeare's plays . . . might have startled them. Often and strongly as the temptation recurred to me, I never could think of anything better worth saying to my audience.
[RG, 1:212-13]

It may strike us as paradoxical that Kemble portrays herself in this passage as an almost speechless orator, in the sense that the only directive she can think to impart to her audience "from myself" evokes the injunction to women in late-eighteenth- and early-nineteenth-century conduct books to be pleasantly benign. But the fact that the meager phrase "Be good!"—recalling Princess Victoria's statement to Baroness Louise Lehzen concerning her commitment to public service, "I will be good"[21]—is the only spontaneous utterance this popular speaker can imagine emerging from her mouth precisely underscores the difficulty Kemble experienced in allowing her passionate heart to guide her public performances. Indeed, because a number of her lyrical poems work against this imperative to others to behave well, they contradict a reading that would portray Kemble's struggle to find a creative outlet for her sensuous longing as dampened by her insistence on elevating reading over acting.

So do other of her fictional writings. Especially when read in the context of Kemble's sensual lyrics from her 1866 collection of poetry, the rhetoric of familial exclusivity (or sexual stinginess) in Kemble's drama, *An English Tragedy* (1863), resonates with particular poignancy in reference to Kemble's biography. Judge Winthrop's lines—"My wife is little more than half my years; / She might have been my daughter"[22]—suggest eerie parallels with Kemble's own life, as does Anne Winthrop's suicidal monologue in 3.3, which Kemble tells us in a prefatory note to the play was inspired by an "anecdote of real life, which I heard my father relate."

In fact, a number of passages from *An English Tragedy* evoke the language of Kemble's poems, in which she often used a suicidal persona to express her real-life depression over the final breakdown of her marriage to Pierce Butler in 1845 when she returned to England without her children. For instance, starting with the first line of Kemble's first poem—"The Year's Progress"—in which the speaker sighs, "I look upon the dusty dreary way" (P, 1), to the poem in the volume's last third entitled "Departing"—which bids farewell to the household gods in process of urging the addressee to "Gird up the loins, and let us now depart" (P, 285)—the 1866 volume presents us with a shockingly anticommunal spectacle. The speakers of many of these poems—separated from children, lovers, family—wander solitarily in dejected postures through unpeopled and autumnal landscapes. Similarly, in *An English Tragedy*, Kemble portrays Anne Winthrop deep in the fantasy of drowning herself at the disappointment over having to "think of him whom I did love so madly, / Whom now I fear and loathe so utterly!":

> No more fear; no more to think and suffer;
> No more to know; no more to recollect.
> O blessed fate! no more to recollect!
> I'll do it: it grows night—no one will see me;
> And far, far, when the cruel morning breaks,
> My body will go tumbling on the waters
> To the great sea–
> [3.3, p. 102]

But what makes *An English Tragedy* so interesting from a late-twentieth-century feminist perspective is not only its focus on the psychic pain of Anne, who has an extramarital affair and compounds her guilt about betraying her older husband by borrowing money from him to pay her lover's gambling debts. In addition, emotional and sexual incest drives the play's action, especially during moments like the following, when Judge Winthrop chastises his sister Mary for her apparent refusal to put her hand in his in order that he may then transfer it to James, as he reluctantly consents to their betrothal: "Why what's the matter?" he asks her with all the quickness and vivid imagination of the jealous paranoid: "did he [James] hold you / So tight, you could not get your hand away?" (2.3, p. 66).

Earlier in the drama, when asked by James to give his consent for his sister to marry, Winthrop responds in oddly tormented language: "Sir, I cannot give that child away! / You might as well ask me for half my heart! / *I cannot want her*—I can't live without her" (2.3, p. 61, my emphasis). A few lines later, he tries to explain his refusal by saying that Mary "oft has sworn to me, she never / Should love a man, to have him for her husband" (2.3, p. 62), and, in response to James's suggestion that "Mistress Mary heeds my suit" (2.3, p. 62), Winthrop reveals more fully the character of his ties to his sister:

> O heaven! this is the way! a whole dear life
> They [sisters] live upon our knees, and in our arms,
> The darlings of our very souls—and lo!
> A stranger, passing by, but beckons them,
> And straight they turn their back upon their homes,
> And make their lodging in a new-found heart.
> Oh! I had dreamt of this—but it is bitter,
> Now that 't is come to pass!
> [2.3, p. 62]

Moaning that a "husband is a wall that builds itself / Between a woman and all other things" (2.3, p. 63), Winthrop displaces his frustrated desire for his wife onto Mary by portraying her future marriage as not only depopulating his household but also doing so through a seeming act of ingratitude and even betrayal. He compares Mary to "the young bird, in our hedge elm trees here, / Warmed in the nest" who nevertheless "drives thence / The ancient brood, who made their proper home there" (2.3, p. 63) and calls her potential marriage "her burial," in the sense that he "scarce could feel [it] more sadly" (2.3, p. 65).

Winthrop's fantasy of preserving his family line by keeping his sister at home is realized at the play's end when the deaths of both Anne and Mary's fiancé allow Winthrop to indulge his desire to invite Mary to remain within his domestic space, and his speech that begins with the line, "Come and live with me, here, until I die" (5.4, p. 192), underscores the play's argument that marriage is antithetical to personal fulfillment. Yet it also suggests that—in Winthrop's case—Mary's potential marriage has posed a challenge to a domestic ideology founded on patriarchal rituals in which fathers school daughters in a form of bodily control that permits the male parent, often begrudgingly, to hand over a young woman docilely to a father substitute in marriage. Through the enshrinement of an insularity that encourages, if not advocates, boundary-crossing between parent and child, this domestic ideology promotes the likelihood of an incestuous experience before marriage that Western culture is not prepared to condone.

Although Kemble did not experience this kind of docile upbringing—in 1829, instead of being prepared for matrimony, she found herself being groomed by her father to become his stage partner—I want to suggest that this unusual situation of playing her father's lover onstage at an age when other women were wedding husbands could have contributed to Fanny's association of acting with inappropriate, even scandalous, behavior as well as to her sense of relief, in middle age, at turning to the solo mode of reading with which she performed Shakespeare for public view. By marrying Pierce Butler shortly after her acting career had begun and while on tour with her father to perform in American theaters, Kemble actually participated in a kind of rebellion, embracing the very institution most threatening to the bourgeois family structure, since it removed young women from a situation in which many, having assumed a fiercely identificatory relationship to the father, had also temporarily apprenticed themselves to the father's power. In Fanny's case, she transferred her allegiance from a father who was also an acting partner to a husband to whom she could legitimately direct her sexual longings, even though sex seems not to have been her focus. Instead, as a five-month bride in 1834, Kemble described her vision of matrimony in a letter to Anna Jameson (included in her *Records of Later Life*) in terms that resemble her Shakespearian readings: she portrays marriage as one long independent study. Having "pictured no fairy-land of enchantments within the mysterious precincts of matrimony," Kemble tells her friend that she expected from it instead, *"rest, quiet, leisure to study,* to think, and to work" in addition to "legitimate channels for the affections of my nature" (RLL, 1, my emphasis). Rather than romantic mutuality in which the physical life throbs—as it does in a number of her poems and in those onstage performances that troubled her so greatly—Kemble regarded marriage as legitimately directing her "affections" toward a legally sanctioned love object. That she perceived herself as moving from her father's tutelage in sexual expression to an offstage venue in which marriage would allow her to study quietly suggests why the subject of acting arouses her passions and shows Kemble the writer actively trying to come to terms with her rejection of, and attraction to, public embodiment.

Because Kemble kept releasing into her range of writing what has traditionally been called "romantic" expression, all the while wrestling with how to restrain herself, a study of her poetry in the context of her prose reveals how perfectly (yet uncomfortably) she was positioned on the cusp of an era in which the female actress would begin to enjoy an increasing measure of respectability while still feeling keenly the indignity of being ogled by the public eye. In this sense, then, Kemble's discourse about acting, reading, and oratory—her theory of performance, if you will—enriches our understanding of those theatrical contexts that shaped female social performance prior to 1850. Conversely, her fictional and nonfictional writing directs us to look more closely at how Kemble's "theory of theatre" was forged through deeply personal responses to the movement she charted for herself as a social actor trying decorously to navigate between closet and public stage.

Notes

In addition to the editors' helpful comments, I gratefully acknowledge Alison Booth's responses to this essay.

1. See Carlson's discussion of antitheatricality and gender in *In the Theatre of Ro-*

manticism. In reference to Kemble's "exposure of cultural hierarchies," Alison Booth writes that Kemble "can seem uncannily postmodern." "From Miranda to Prospero," 228. Jacky Bratton observes that Kemble's "internalizing of the ideological struggle that was going on all around her . . . made her personally a battleground over which the redefinition of the role of the middle-class woman was fought out." "Working in the Margin," 130.

2. The following abbreviations are used in the text and the notes for citations of Kemble's works:

JR:*Journal of a Residence on a Georgia Plantation in 1838-39, by Frances Anne Kemble*
JYA:*Fanny Kemble: Journal of a Young Actress*
    Poems
RG:*Records of a Girlhood*
RLL:*Records of Later Life*

3. In his editor's introduction, John A. Scott observed that the *Journal of a Residence on a Georgia Plantation* is "written by one of the most gifted women that the nineteenth century produced, and it affords insight into the life and mind of a great artist" (x). Scott also praises Kemble as "one of the grandest and most articulate Victorian women of letters" (xi).

4. Booth, "From Miranda to Prospero," 247.

5. See Mellor, *Romanticism and Gender.*

6. Arden, "Uses of Iron," 221.

7. See chapter 2 of C. Burroughs, *Closet Stages.*

8. Booth, exploring how Kemble drew upon her partiality for *The Tempest* to reflect "an ambivalence between filial loyalties and a demand for liberty and justice" ("From Miranda to Prospero," 232), as well as to show how "the slave, the actress, and the middle-class wife were alike condemned to strategic mimicry rather than agency" (233), has suggested that Fanny's attitude toward public performance—about which she tells us in her journals she was never "able to come to any decided opinion" (RG, 2:61)—sheds light upon her offstage acting, especially her relationships with her father and her American husband.

9. For a study of this phenomenon, see Pascoe, *Romantic Theatricality.*

10. Arliss, introduction, 1.

11. Arden, "Uses of Iron," 212.

12. Kemble, *Notes Upon Shakespeare's Plays,* 166.

13. See Kemble, JYA, 108-9.

14. Auerbach, *Private Theatricals,* 4.

15. Corbett, *Representing Femininity,* 114.

16. Jacky Bratton, "Working in the Margin," offers a tantalizingly brief comment that animates the intriguing subject of Kemble's relationship to her parents, sexuality, and the theater when she observes: "It is interesting that, when writing of this [her rejection of the theater and "breaking away from parental attitudes"] much later in life, she suddenly switches, for no obvious reason, to describing an acquaintance of this time of her life, 'that exceedingly coarse, disagreeable, clever, and witty man, Mr. Theodore Hook': her revulsion from the sexual challenge posed by the unregenerate,

corrupt man of the theatre is palpable" (130). The most suggestive discussion I have seen of the fraught character of Fanny's relationship with her father appears in John Arden's story, "Uses of Iron," which includes the line, "[T]he thought of *his Romeo* [Charles Kemble's] had distressed her so irrationally . . ." (220, my emphasis).

17. For more information on Kemble's Shakespearian readings, see Kahan, "Fanny Kemble Reads Shakespeare."

18. Booth, "From Miranda to Prospero," 242.

19. Booth makes a similar observation in reference to Kemble and the slaves: "Often she seems to observe herself and the slaves in a kind of musical drama in which she is leading lady—a reinterpretation, perhaps, of the relationship of Miranda and Caliban." Ibid., 240.

20. Fox-Genovese, foreword to *Fanny Kemble,* in writing about the *Journal of a Young Actress* as a text that "steadfastly eschews the confessional mode" (xii) and is crafted as a "subtle and refined self-promotion" (xiii), overstates Kemble's resistance to "wanton exhibitionism" (xiii).

21. This statement is cited in Weintraub's *Victoria,* 66.

22. Kemble, *An English Tragedy,* act 4, scene 2, p. 137. Citations to this play appear in the text by reference to act, scene, and page number.

Recuperating Romanticism in Mary Tighe's *Psyche*

Harriet Kramer Linkin

That Mary Tighe still requires reclamation at this stage of our recovery of the literature produced by women during the British Romantic period seems surprising, given the general acclamation she received for her magnificent long poem *Psyche; or, The Legend of Love.*[1] Although there is considerably more to know about Tighe than her authorship of *Psyche,* her reputation rests on this singular achievement, which was celebrated by its first reviewers as a poem of "extraordinary merits" (the *Eclectic Review*), cited for elegant design, exquisite telling, fine feeling, superior style, excellent versification, intellectual richness, and superb execution in the *Quarterly Review,* the *British Review,* the *New Annual Register,* the *Gentleman's Magazine,* and elsewhere. Indeed the *Monthly Review* predicted, "[O]ur poetess has composed a work which is calculated to endure the judgment of posterity, long after the possessors of an ephemeral popularity shall have faded away into a well-merited oblivion."[2] If the *Monthly Review* proved wrong on several counts, what *Psyche* continues to offer posterity is a linguistically sophisticated analysis and revisioning of the masculinist Romantic aesthetic that objectifies or silences the female in its figuration of the beautiful.[3] Tighe adapts the formal properties of Spenserian allegory as she challenges the gendered assumptions that underlie that aesthetic, to create an alternative transcendent poetics that situates the female poet as visionary. Part cultural critique, part aesthetic reformation, *Psyche* opens up a space within traditional Romanticism for the female to commune with the muse in powerfully shaped verse. As Jonathan Wordsworth recently observed, "*Psyche* is a serious and impressive poem. It needs reading more than once, and reading with attention. . . . By virtue of its length and seriousness of purpose, its clear and at times subtle handling of allegory, its excellent craftsmanship, *Psyche* has to be the most impressive single work by a woman poet of the Romantic period."[4] Reading *Psyche* with such attention not only enables a firmer appreciation of Tighe's contribution to Romanticism but may also prompt further thinking about the paradigms that inform our current understanding of women's literary history.

There is no question that Tighe was an influential and highly regarded poet or poetess in her own time. *Psyche* was so admired by contemporaries such as Thomas Moore and Sydney Owenson that James Mackintosh described it in 1812 as "beyond doubt the most faultless series of verses ever produced by a woman" and discussed her work in connection with Virgil, Racine, and Gray as well as Madame de Staël and Joanna Baillie. In 1819 the *Noctes Ambrosianae* identified Tighe as one of the three premier national women poets of the day, proclaiming that "Scotland has her Baillie—Ireland her Tighe—England her Hemans." The next year, William Gifford commenced discussion of Felicia Hemans for the *Quarterly Review* by stipulating that "no judicious critic will speak without respect of the tragedies of Miss Baillie, or the Psyche of Mrs. Tighe; and, unless we deceive ourselves greatly, the author of the poems before us requires only to be more generally known and read to have her place assigned at no great distance from that of the two distinguished individuals just mentioned."[5] Tighe sustained comparable critical approbation throughout the nineteenth century, prompting unusual praise from George Bethune in 1848, who observed, "The prominent fault of female poetical writers is an unwillingness to apply the pruning-knife and the pumice-stone. . . . With the exception of Joanna Baillie and Mrs. Tighe, scarcely any of them seem to have inverted their pen." He commented further that Tighe "is not equalled in classical elegance by any English female, and not excelled (in that particular) by any male English poet. She has the rare quality for a poetess of not sparing the *pumice-stone,* her verses being sedulously polished to the highest degree." Jane Williams pointed to *Psyche* in 1861 as "unquestionably one of the finest poems ever written by a woman; full of imaginative power, passion, and melody," counterposing Tighe to Baillie and Hemans in her concluding overview of *The Literary Women of England:* "Two poetesses superior to them Great Britain has never yet produced. If a third, within the century, be admitted as nearly entitled to a seat beside them, it is Mrs. Tighe." In 1871 E. Owens Blackburne called *Psyche* "one of the most marvellous poems that has ever been written by any woman in any age, Elizabeth Barrett Browning alone excepted. It stands alone in the literature of Ireland—pure, polished, sublime—the outpouring of a trammelled soul yearning to be freed"; for Blackburne, Tighe was comparable not only to Hemans for "having so successfully wooed the Muse" but also to Spenser for her "magnificent outburst of poetry, which for sublimity of sentiment, graceful diction, and true poetic strength, is only second to the 'Faery Queen.'"[6]

Although there is no question that Tighe achieved great acclaim in the nineteenth century, often named in conjunction with Baillie and Hemans as a national woman poet, there is also no question that neither Tighe nor Baillie nor Hemans retained the seats in literary history that Williams sought to reserve for them once the century turned. By 1904 C.J. Hamilton noted that "hardly anything is known in Ireland about Mrs. Tighe, and yet she is doubly interesting from her wonderful beauty, as well as from her poem of 'Psyche,' which won the highest praise from competent critics."[7] In fact the history of Tighe's literary reception from her time to ours is marked by the increasingly familiar trajectory of discovery, dismissal, and recovery that outlines the recuperation of numerous Romantic women poets, including Baillie and Hemans, who achieved a certain kind of fame in the nineteenth century, only to be passed over by the early-twentieth-century critics whose theoretical positions shaped so many of the institutions that constitute the academy. As these critics initiated the processes that eventually resulted in the canonization of six male Romantic poets, Tighe and others were largely forgotten until the work of feminists and new historians came to pressure our learned assumptions and valuations in the last quarter of the twentieth century, to suggest that it might have been the women poets who were the historically unacknowledged legislators of the word if not the world.[8] Because Tighe's most significant claim to fame for those first canonizers was her connection with John Keats, who celebrated "the blessings of Tighe" in his 1815 lyric "To Some Ladies," Keats's anxious rejection of her influence provided a touchstone for subsequent evaluations of her purview: "Mrs. Tighe and Beattie once delighted me—now I see through them and can find nothing in them—or weakness—and yet how many they still delight!"[9] Although Keats certainly indicated resentment of Tighe's audience as much as his new resistance to her poetry in this infamous comment, critics seem only to have heard an aesthetic rejection and applied that rejection in their own commentaries.

One of the first to conflate Tighe with Keats rather than with Baillie or Hemans was Henry Beers, who described Tighe in his 1901 *History of Romanticism in the Nineteenth Century* as "one of the latest and best of the professed imitators of Spenser. There is a beauty of a kind in her languidly melodious verse and over-profuse imagery, but it is not the passionate and quintessential beauty of Keats. She is quite incapable of such choice and pregnant word effects as abound in every stanza of 'St. Agnes.'" Despite the relatively gracious evaluation Beers offered, what stands out in his brief discussion is the gratuitous comparison of Tighe and Keats. Considerably less gracious is Claude Lee Finney in 1936, who dispensed with Mary Tighe as "a plaintive Irish poetess, whose poems drip with the sensibility of the eighteenth century" in his lauded *The Evolution of Keats's Poetry*.[10] Precisely why the recognition of Keats's greatness required the disparagement of a poet like Tighe is a psychological and sociological aspect of criticism well worth investigating; nevertheless, Keats's elevation to canonical status not coincidentally correlates with Tighe's demotion to a footnote in literary history. Tighe and Keats evidence one of many such gendered critical pairings throughout literary history, as unsettling to trace as the lingering effects of Byron's satiric reference to Hemans as "Mrs. Hewoman" in establishing canonical valuations.[11]

This essay's efforts to examine Mary Tighe's reception seeks after more than a simple restitution or the seeming righting of old wrongs through restoration. What I want to assert about the particular contribution Tighe makes to Romanticism has not yet been seen, even during this moment that theoretically welcomes recuperation: Tighe's studied attention as a woman poet to the very issues that consume mainstream male canonical Romantic poets, and how such attention productively troubles both nineteenth- and twentieth-century critical conceptions of the poetess and the woman poet. An argument that insists on the necessity of looking at Tighe's poetry in conjunction with mainstream male Romantic thought necessarily probes a tension within current critical formulations of Romanticism, a tension that derives from the choice we face as critics self-consciously constructing our own historical version of Romanticism and the Romantic period. Do we maintain the former definition of the canonical Romantic movement intact and posit separate movements beyond Romanticism that allow for the inclusion of the other, especially the women but also the men of differing positions defined by nationality, or ethnicity, or sexuality, or class, who work in more genres than the exclusive pale of poetry? Or do we expand the borders of Romanticism itself to include the excluded other, those or that once determined minor or noncanonical, to reconstitute or reconstruct canonical Romanticism?

The crux of canonicity versus the noncanonical is the basic defining issue that informs every effort to reclaim the work of women writing during the Romantic period, sometimes deliberately but elsewhere implicitly. To date critics engaged in theorizing the recovery of Romantic women writers—especially Curran, Ross, Mellor, and Jerome McGann—have preserved our definitions of canonical Romanticism nearly intact to examine women's poetry, in particular, as a separate phenomenon that emerges out of primarily female (or feminine) and occasionally feminist (or protofeminist) concerns and cultural experiences.[12] As feminist theory rightly insists, such separation proves essential to an initial exploration and revaluation of women's work, insofar as it enables the distinctive language of the muted group to emerge without the restraining influence of the dominant male culture.[13] The virtue of separatism lies in its opening up the possibility of hearing the different voices of women writers who have been inaccurately or inconsistently assessed on scales designed to measure the male body, the male voice, and the male mind. The danger of separatism, though, lies in its potential for reinforcing a form of segregation that maintains the nonessentiality of women's contributions to

Romanticism, to position women writers as noncanonical addenda to the Romantic period. In its harshest manifestation, separatism can result in a ghettoization that establishes yet another set of barriers that prevents us from seeing women working in the same theater as men, or from recognizing the value of women writers who do work in the same theater as men. Because Mary Tighe directly engages the precepts of canonical Romanticism from an intrinsically female perspective, revaluing her work requires an expansion of our current critical paradigms so that we begin thinking about the women who write from within rather than without Romanticism; as such the project of recuperation shifts from the separation model to a mode of integration that might sustain the individual as well as gendered identities of a comprehensive community we know as Romanticism.

If we read Mary Tighe's poetry as participating within the comprehensive community we know as Romanticism, what do we gain? As I argue elsewhere, I believe Tighe makes an important contribution to the development of high Romantic thought because she speculates on the specularization of the female to locate a potent source for women's poetry. Indeed she transgresses the gender ideology promoted in her own time and ours in positing the artist's gaze as a source for a feminine as well as a masculine Romantic aesthetic. That she challenges the purview of a purely masculinist gaze is especially interesting from a biographical perspective, insofar as she inhabits the socially constructed identity of a beautiful woman and experiences firsthand the dilemma the masculinist Romantic aesthetic arguably poses for the aspiring female artist. It is no accident that Tighe's great long poem takes up the story of a mortal whose beauty proves the source of conflict: Psyche's story is Tighe's story. Journals that describe the circumstances of Tighe's marriage to her cousin Henry and her uneasy relations with her mother-in-law, Sarah, suggest that the plot of *Psyche* offers a place for Tighe to puzzle through her own relationships.[14] The poem's allegorical framework enables her to couch an introspective statement that exalts Wordsworthian withdrawal from society, even as her style and content anticipate the younger generation of Romantics, whose treatment of the myth Marilyn Butler locates as central to their exploration of sexuality and human love.[15] Tighe's *Psyche* bridges the seemingly disparate generations of male Romantic poets, like the works of the women poets Curran identifies as the "missing link[s]" who "impel the history of poetry" at the end of the eighteenth century, very much within the "gap" Stephen Behrendt fills elsewhere in this volume.[16] Yet to categorize Tighe's *Psyche* as emblematic of a transitional poetics reinscribes aspects of the canonical history this essay queries; we can only wonder what would happen if we rewrote literary history entirely via the voices of women poets like Tighe, who usefully trouble our gendered definitions of the Romantic period.

That Tighe was intimately aware of the dynamics of specularization seems clear from testimony that speaks to the cultural role she fulfilled in her lifetime as the not-so-obscure object of desire among the members of her social circle, for whom she embodies the beautiful in every way. What she might anticipate but could never know is how much her beauty would become the object of her posthumous reception. Blackburne pointedly begins her memoir of Tighe with an extended description of the oil portrait by Romney, which depicts her "rich flowing, dark-brown hair, a few tendrils of which stray upon her smooth, intellectual forehead. The eyes are of a deep blue: large and pellucid, with a wonderful wistful look in them: the lower part of the face is exquisitely formed, the chiselled round chin and rather small, full, soft mouth indicating, in a remarkable degree, sensitiveness and sensuousness—the latter an essential of the poetic temperament—without the slightest trace of sensuality."[17] Throughout the memoir Blackburne highlights Tighe's physical and intellectual beauty as a magnetic "centre of attraction in the brilliant vice-regal Court of Dublin before the Union. . . . that brilliant assemblage of which she became speedily so bright an ornament." Similarly, when C.H. Crookshank commemorates Tighe's mother, Theodosia Blachford, for her early promulgation of Methodism, he observes how the daughter was "remarkable for the loveliness of her person, the fascination of her manners, and her high mental culture" and, notably, "composed beautiful poems." Even the Reverend Pierce remarks on Tighe's compelling beauty to his wife when he visits the family in 1796; in a manuscript letter William Howitt reproduces, Pierce describes her as "young, lovely, and of sweet manners, united with as sweet a form. She entered the room, soon after I came to Rosanna, with a chaplet of roses about her head. 'Where,' I thought, 'were the beauties of the garden and the parlour so united before?'"[18]

When Howitt reports his own fascination with Tighe as writer, he speaks to the bewitching nature of her seductive appeal, but ensconces any untoward desire in the certain knowledge of her death, presenting her as an actual angel in the house:

The poem of Psyche was one which charmed me intensely at an early age. There was a tone of deep and tender feeling pervading it, which touched the youthful heart, and took possession of every sensibility. There was a tone of melancholy music in it, which seemed the regretful expression of the consciousness of a not-far-off death. It was now well-known that the young and beautiful poetess *was* dead. . . . She came before the imagination in the combined witchery of brilliant genius, and the pure loveliness of a seraph, which had but touched upon the earth on some celestial mission, and was gone for ever.[19]

In Howitt's bald Victorian predication, "Mrs. Tighe was an angel." But so too Tickler's Romantic vision in the *Noctes Ambrosianae*, "And was not Tighe an angel, if ever there was one on earth, beautiful, airy, and evanescent, as her own immortal Psyche?"[20] These angelic figurations exemplify contemporary reviews of the posthumous publication of *Psyche,* many of which irresistibly advert to the portrait Tighe's brother-in-law William includes in the first edition.[21] The typical response to Tighe's beauty during her lifetime becomes the archetypal image perpetuated after her death, well represented by Leigh Hunt's conflation of poem and person: "The *Psyche* of Mrs. Tighe has a languid beauty, probably resembling that of her person. . . . The face prefixed to the volume containing her poem is very handsome." Even the staid *Dictionary of National Biography* notes she "was a very beautiful woman."[22]

As famous for her beauty in life as in death, as account after account reports, Tighe records her struggles with the problematic nature of an admiration whose seductive appeal continually tempts her away from the precious time and space she sets aside for writing. She is a woman who knows all too well what it means to be the silenced object of admiration, and more, what it means to want to be the object of admiration. An early lyric, "Verses Written in Solitude, April 1792," details the dilemma admiration poses to the formation or rather loss of poetic identity, when the lesser but more immediate pleasures of flattering attention make her desire to be the romanticized subject:

> To fix the attention of admiring eyes,
> To move with elegance and talk with ease,
> To be the object of the practised sigh,
> To attract the notice, and the ear to please.[23]

When the lyric describes her return, at last, to the solitude that enables communion with the muse, she deplores the way her own desire to be desired casts obstacles in the path of connection, even prevents her ability to compose:

> Lost in a crowd of folly and of noise,
> With vain delights my bosom learnt to beat,
> . . . .
> Yet these had charms which now I blush to own,
> Powers, which I then believed not they possess'd.
> The Muse to banish from her humble throne,
> Where she so oft had fired my glowing breast.
> [lines 9-10, 25-28]

Marriage exacerbates rather than eases the problem of admiration for Tighe, not because of the usual spousal sequestering thought to inhibit so many women writers but because Henry Tighe evidently enjoys displaying his prized wife to the admiring throng. Blackburne portrays him assuming "the *rôle* of a London man of fashion. His wife's beauty and her many other superior attractions were powerful influences to gather around them a large circle of all those in the Metropolis famed for the graces of mind or person."[24] Since so many of Henry Tighe's acquaintances were "idle young lawyers who associated with him to discuss literary subjects and admire his pretty wife," marriage provides neither respite from the crowd nor release from its temptations.[25] As Tighe herself confesses in a 1796 diary entry, "Very unhappy in my mind—Yet I find it impossible to resist the flattering temptation of being admired, & showing the world that I am so. My conscience this day has been disturbed—I feel uneasy at the vanity, the folly, the dissipation in which I am engaged, yet without the power to wish myself disengaged from it."[26]

Given Tighe's status as a beauty, then, her decision to write an extended poem that remythologizes Psyche indicates potent material for self-reflection, a position that contrasts with the still-current critical devaluation of her poem as non-Romantic allegory.[27] Indeed the Mary Blachford Tighe so subject to the psychologically disabling effects of admiration in her social environment is the poet who makes the issue of beauty and admiration the subject of *Psyche*, where she locates a powerful means to reconstruct the specularized image of the female in poetry. What better place for such reconstruction than a myth that foregrounds the issue of transgression when woman looks at rather than away? Tighe's *Psyche* presents a remarkable revision of Apuleius's story of Cupid and Psyche in six cantos (372 Spenserian stanzas in all) that explore the nature of culturally conditioned identity for women like Tighe in the context of the psychological and moral components of familial, romantic, and marital relations. In terms of plot, the poem more or less follows Apuleius in relating the myth of Cupid and Psyche up to the moment when Psyche looks and Cupid leaves; once Psyche starts her quest to fulfill Venus's commands, Tighe takes her characters through very different terrain. Perhaps the most radical revision entails Tighe's provision of a companion for Psyche, a knight who turns out to be Cupid, notably not convalescing at his mother's house but in stride for his own educational journey. The quest itself has nearly nothing to do with completing Venus's tasks, and everything to do with Psyche and Cupid's confronting ambiguous situations in which they must locate a path that leads to greater psychological, emotional, and ethical development.

Tighe's feminist revision of the myth pointedly insists that men and women must act in concert to secure satisfying relations; and such attention to relationships certainly positions her within the critical category of feminine Romanticism. At the same time Tighe examines her own position as poet within the poem, making overtly self-reflexive gestures that denote her participation in an egotistical sublime of a piece with masculine Romanticism's focus on the formation of poetic selfhood.[28] Most significantly, however, she employs a linguistically rich, poetically complex, and ultimately strategic syntax throughout the poem, which encodes a sharp critique and reformulation of masculinist Romantic aesthetics. For Tighe, an aesthetic that objectifies the female actually effects a reciprocity between admirer and admired. Just as the female is spelled into silence by the admiring male gaze, the male is spellbound by the object of his admiration. When the poem's narrator suggests that Psyche's troubles emanate from the masculinist objectification of her beauty, the verse ambiguously states, "[M]en her wondrous beauty deified" (canto 1, *W* 12). Neither "men deified her wondrous beauty" nor "her wondrous beauty deified men," the line allows both possibilities to operate at once in a syntactic formulation that blurs the grammatical distinction between the subject and object of deification. If the masculinist Romantic aesthetic teaches us to see how men deify and thereby objectify the female, Tighe's syntax demonstrates how the Romantic aesthetic similarly deifies and objectifies the male. Syntax enables a complex representation of the romanticized female situated as object, whose image absorbs the vision of the enchanted observer. That same syntactic reciprocity evidences itself when Venus commands her son to punish Psyche for her beauty with a poisoned arrow: "Deep let her heart thy sharpest arrow sting" (canto 1, *W* 16). Even as Cupid's arrow stings Psyche's heart, so will her heart sting him in turn. Tighe is not the only Romantic poet to recognize the reciprocity of aesthetic objectification, but her analysis occurs before the second generation of masculinist Romantic poets anxiously examine comparable issues (particularly Keats, so directly influenced by her, but also Byron and Shelley). That Tighe offers such analysis as a woman poet looking at looking is central to the larger reappraisal at hand.

Tighe's analysis of the masculinist Romantic aesthetic as a process that establishes what I term "reciprocal objectification" is manifest in her depiction of the initial encounter between Cupid and Psyche, which illustrates how the male gaze redirects itself from object back to gazer. Cupid effectively becomes what he beholds when he views Psyche because the gaze that freezes her into an aesthetic object seals his subjectivity as her admirer:

> Lightly, as fall the dews upon the rose,
> Upon the coral gates of that sweet cell
> The fatal drops he pours; nor yet he knows,
> Nor, though a God, can he presaging tell
> How he himself shall mourn the ills of that sad spell!

> Nor yet content, he from his quiver drew,
> Sharpened with skill divine, a shining dart:
> No need had he for bow, since thus too true
> His hand might wound her all-exposed heart;

> Yet her fair side he touched with gentlest art,
> And half relenting on her beauties gazed;
> Just then awaking with a sudden start
> Her opening eye in humid lustre blazed,
> Unseen he still remained, enchanted and amazed.
>
> The dart which in his hand now trembling stood,
> As o'er the couch he bent with ravished eye,
> Drew with its daring point celestial blood
> From his smooth neck's unblemished ivory.
> [canto 1, *W* 22-23]

Even as Cupid fulfills his mother's command by piercing Psyche with a poisoned dart, that dart tellingly pricks him in turn, in Tighe's revision of Apuleius. She reconceives Cupid as the artist whose eye is ravished by the ravished subject, who is stilled into silent invisibility by his own silencing gaze: "Unseen he still remained, enchanted and amazed." Moreover, if the scene positions Cupid as active and Psyche as passive, the syntax of the lines undermines linguistic representation of Cupid's causal force by displacing connections between agent and act. Although Tighe apologizes in her preface for any undue contortions in the language necessitated by her adherence to Spenserian form, the rhyme scheme does not require inversion when she writes "Lightly, . . . / . . . / The fatal drops he pours" or "No need had he for bow." Such language play blurs the distinctions between actor and acted-upon, between gazer and gazed-upon, to insinuate a shifting of subjectivities that places Cupid in the position usually reserved for the romanticized female. Such shifting subjectivities could produce an interestingly interdependent renegotiation of male and female selfhood. But Tighe knows too well the gendered inequities that underlie the process of reciprocal objectification. In this instance, and most others, Cupid initiates the reciprocal exchange that compels Psyche's participation. When Psyche takes it upon herself to look first, she is not only characterized as overstepping the boundaries that constitute her cultural and psychological positioning as gazed-upon, but her gaze actually precipitates the dissolution of their marriage, so that "ruin's hideous crash bursts o'er the affrighted walls" (canto 2, *W* 58).

Tighe figures Psyche as an innocent so devoid of egocentric pride that her character can prove frustrating to modern readers, but her timidity exemplifies the culturally acceptable behavior that ensures her survival:

> timid as the wintry flower,
> That, whiter than the snow it blooms among,
> Droops its fair head submissive to the power
> Of every angry blast which sweeps along

Sparing the lovely trembler, while the strong
Majestic tenants of the leafless wood
It levels low.
[canto 1, *W* 13]

To meet power with power inevitably results in loss, but to submit means to survive, and, for some, to locate avenues that allow for subversion. Psyche's best path is submission, as Venus insists when she excoriates the inappropriate competition Psyche's beauty effects: "'With me the world's devotion to contest / Behold a mortal dares'" (canto 1, *W* 15). With syntax so heavily contorted, the sentence is turned inside out, compared to the more straightforward "Behold a mortal dares to contest the world's devotion with me." Tighe's language thereby mimes the social disorder overt agonistic behavior among women produces. Psyche's strategic submissiveness makes her particularly viable for Tighe's readers, the "young ladies" Jackson envisions reading a "cautionary tale," who can safely point to the status of this unthreatening heroine as a fit model even as she actively pursues her quest.[29]

The cultural constraints Tighe resolutely observes in sketching Psyche do not apply to her representation of herself as female poet, however. Whereas Psyche decorously averts her eyes in conformity with the teachings of culture and myth, Tighe gazes with bold abandon. Her rejection of any limitation on poetic vision is evidenced in her distinctly sensual portraits of Cupid and Psyche. Hindered by neither psychology nor decorum in turning her gaze on the male or female, Tighe offers a more lushly sensual and detailed description of Cupid, at first, than of Psyche. While Cupid's "quiver sparkling bright with gems and gold, / From his fair plumed shoulder graceful hung" (canto 1, *W* 21) as Zephyrs waft "the fragrance which his tresses flung: / While odours dropped from every ringlet bright, / And from his blue eyes beamed ineffable delight" (canto 1, *W* 21), Psyche lies upon a purple couch,

Her radiant eyes a downy slumber sealed;
In light transparent veil alone arrayed,
Her bosom's opening charms were half revealed,
And scarce the lucid folds her polished limbs concealed.
[canto 1, *W* 21]

Even more tellingly, the ruin that comes crashing down for Psyche when she dares to look first at Cupid in her moment of transgression sharply contrasts with Tighe's invocation of a "daring Muse!" to enable her unqualified description of the vision Psyche sees when she bends over Cupid with lamp and dagger in hand:

Oh, daring Muse! wilt thou indeed essay
To paint the wonders which that lamp could shew?

And canst thou hope in living words to say
The dazzling glories of that heavenly view?
Ah! well I ween, that if with pencil true
That splendid vision could be well exprest,
The fearful awe imprudent Psyche knew
Would seize with rapture every wondering breast,
When Love's all potent charms divinely stood confest.
[canto 2, *W* 56]

Although Tighe leaves the evaluation of her sensual portrait of Cupid to her readers, who may or may not be enraptured by the effects of her pencil, she does not leave the portrait itself to the imagination of her readers, but rather indulges her gaze over the next four stanzas with all the fervent detail the Romantic aesthetic allows, to report how

. . . o'er his guileless front the ringlets bright
Their rays of sunny lustre seem to throw,
That front than polished ivory more white!
His blooming cheeks with deeper blushes glow
Than roses scattered o'er a bed of snow:
While on his lips . . .
. . . .
Still hangs a rosy charm that never vainly sues.
[canto 2, *W* 57]

When Psyche sees what Tighe describes, she becomes "Speechless with awe" (canto 2, *W* 58) in a scene that replays almost exactly the reciprocal objectification that occurs in canto 1 as Cupid hovers over Psyche with dart in hand, but not so Tighe, whose status as poet exempts her from specularization. She defiantly positions herself as gazer, periodically interjecting her voice at key moments to wrest the poem's focus from Psyche's submissive victimization to the poet's self-empowerment, insisting on essential differences between Psyche as culturally conditioned character and herself as controlling woman poet who invokes the muse when and where she likes. She effectively appropriates the masculinist gaze to redefine it as the artist's gaze: culture may dictate that women in society demurely cast down their eyes and voices, but art demonstrates that women can gaze as powerfully as men. Indeed Tighe more than analyzes the reciprocal objectification Romantic aesthetics effects; she declares her desire to engage in ravishing communion with the muse, asserting her right to participate in a relation purportedly forbidden to her as female poet and female reader:[30]

Delightful visions of my lonely hours!
Charm of my life and solace of my care!

Oh! would the muse but lend proportioned powers,
And give me language, equal to declare
The wonders which she bids my fancy share,
When rapt in her to other worlds I fly,
See angel forms unutterably fair,
And hear the inexpressive harmony
That seems to float on air, and warble through the sky.

Might I the swiftly glancing scenes recal!
Bright as the roseate clouds of summer's eve,
The dreams which hold my soul in willing thrall,
And half my visionary days deceive,
Communicable shape might then receive,
And other hearts be ravished with the strain:
But scarce I seek the airy threads to weave,
When quick confusion mocks the fruitless pain,
And all the fairy forms are vanished from my brain.
[canto 5, *W* 145-46]

Tighe's self-conscious recognition that the writing of poetry offers a path to female empowerment resists segregation in the domestic sphere; at the same time Tighe carefully points out that women poets need not replicate the pattern that operates for male poets. Indeed she takes note of gendered expectations to argue that reciprocal objectification is more empowering for female poets than for male poets because male poets become lost in solipsistic fantasies that remove them from the active world they should inhabit, or want to so lose themselves, as Sonia Hofkosh suggests.[31] But female poets who might be lost to the dangers of public admiration safely remove to a superior world of retirement:

For none have vainly e'er the Muse pursued,
And those whom she delights, regret no more
The social, joyous hours, while rapt they soar
To worlds unknown, and live in fancy's dream:
Oh, Muse divine! thee only I implore,
Shed on my soul thy sweet inspiring beams,
And pleasure's gayest scene insipid folly seems!
[canto 1, *W* 37]

Thus reciprocal objectification for Tighe the poet supplies a solution to the problematic temptation admiration effects for Tighe as cultural object of desire. When the female poet gazes, she establishes a communion with the muse that results in the speech that is stilled when woman is gazed upon in culture.

Tighe's solution in *Psyche* to the spectacular problem of admiration firmly situates her as a high Romantic poet who empowers herself as visionary by drawing important distinctions between the fixed woman she analyzes in her poetry and the position she inhabits as narrating woman poet who offers such analysis. Indeed, the careful difference she marks between the culturally conditioned station of the romanticized female and her location of herself as a poet dedicated to the muse demonstrates—via her engagement with the gaze—how a woman poet can confront the masculinist aesthetic to work within an expanded Romantic aesthetics as well as voice a feminine aesthetic that values the domestic or the affectional. As such Tighe occupies a place in literary history not much visited in current critical efforts to restore women poets to the Romantic literary scene. That place is not named but certainly is recognized by her contemporary admirers such as Keats and Hemans or Landon, who further her project in their own efforts to identify the reciprocity of the gaze in Romantic poetics. When Tighe reclaims the gaze for women's poetry through her representation of reciprocal objectification, she reshapes masculinist issues in feminist terms. If she projects the image of the silenced female in her poetry, she does so to rewrite Romanticism, to insist on the silenced female as an image constructed by a social reality that need not prevail in the Romantic aesthetic; indeed she argues for a Romantic aesthetic that points to the significance of the artist's gaze for poetry by men and women.

But despite Tighe's insistence upon the equality of men and women as they experience the sublime in their production of poetry, the conclusion of *Psyche* underscores an essential difference, when Tighe describes the devastating aftermath of visionary experience for herself:

> Dreams of Delight farewel! your charms no more
> Shall gild the hours of solitary gloom!
> The page remains—but can the page restore
> The vanished bowers which Fancy taught to bloom?
> Ah, no! her smiles no longer can illume
> The path my Psyche treads no more for me;
> Consigned to dark oblivion's silent tomb
> The visionary scenes no more I see,
> Fast from the fading lines the vivid colours flee!
> [canto 6, *W* 209]

Just as the penultimate stanza tellingly completes Psyche's epic adventures by describing how she is thoroughly reabsorbed by Cupid's admiring gaze—"His fairy train their rosy garlands bring, / Or round their mistress sport on halcyon wing; / While she enraptured lives in his dear eye" (canto 6, *W* 208)—the very last lines of the poem indicate a comparable fate for Tighe as woman Romantic poet who returns from that sublime realm of visionary experience to a quotidian reality she conflates with "dark oblivion's silent tomb." The compensations that male Romantic poets proffer as they lament the loss of visionary experience offer no compensation here: whereas Wordsworth's "Ode" ("Intimations of Immortality") locates

> Strength in what remains behind,
> In the primal sympathy
> Which having been must ever be,
> In the soothing thoughts that spring
> Out of human suffering,
> In the faith that looks through death,
> In years that bring the philosophic mind.
> [lines 183-89]

Tighe never looks to the philosophic mind, much less to memory, as a means of soothing loss.[32] So, for instance, when Psyche first realizes that she has lost Cupid through her transgression, she takes no comfort in her memory of him but rather begs to hear his voice once more and die (canto 2, *W*60-61); nor does Psyche find relief in poeticizing the loss of Cupid, as Wordsworth's narrator does in the Lucy poems via the operation of lyric memory:

> How soon my Lucy's race was run!
> She died and left to me
> This heath, this calm and quiet scene,
> The memory of what has been,
> And never more will be.
> ["Three Years She Grew in Sun and Shower," lines 38-42]

For Tighe the sublimity of the sublime inheres in the actual moment of communion with the muse, rather than in the mastering recollection of that moment in a tranquility that may not be available to her, given the exigencies of her life.

Although Tighe works effectively throughout *Psyche* to represent herself as the visionary woman poet who participates in Romanticism's dominant aesthetic, it is, finally, that last stanza's depiction of her as doomed to oblivion's tomb that comes to bear the weight of her subsequent reception, perhaps because the poem only reaches a general audience when Tighe is dead. The posthumous publication of *Psyche, with Other Poems. By the Late Mrs. Henry Tighe* seemed to make impossible an appreciation of Tighe's remarkable poetic achievement that was not inflected with a morbid awareness of her early death, a death made more poignant via repeated references to her great beauty for a public oddly fascinated, then as now, with dead beauties. Thus Tighe's efforts to critique the Romantic aesthetic as well as demonstrate her engagement with the Romantic sublime underscore the great irony of her place in literary history, which almost immediately consigned her to the category of the beautiful. And even those influenced by her, who surely had a more sophisticated understanding of what Tighe attempted in *Psyche,* failed to articulate her value or position in poetic tradition. Thus, it is instructive to bear in mind the difference between Percy Shelley's work in "Adonais: An Elegy on the Death of John Keats," which carefully situates Keats in a poetic tradition that includes Homer, Dante, and Milton, and Felicia Hemans's complex tribute to Tighe as the unnamed dead body in "The Grave of a Poetess," which, importantly, concludes *Records of Woman.* Hemans pointedly notes a shift in her response to the dead poetess as she initially mourns the death of the "woman's mind," which makes it impossible for Tighe to enjoy the natural beauty of the area in which she is buried, to her sudden awareness that death finally brings peace, because Tighe no longer needs to experience the "dim fear" (line 39) or "haunting dream" (line 40) of her "vain love to passing flowers" (line 41):

> Where couldst thou fix on mortal ground
>   Thy tender thoughts and high?—
> Now peace the woman's heart hath found,
>   And joy the poet's eye.
> [lines 49-52][33]

Hemans's reading of Tighe is far more complicated than I am going to suggest here, where I simply want to observe that the poem never names Tighe as subject, much less as participant in poetic tradition, but it does subtly reinscribe Tighe's visionary poetry within the feminine sphere and equate her success with her death. That equation is one her first editor, William Tighe, seeks to prevent even as he brings her work before the public in the 1811 edition, which identifies her as the late Mrs. Henry Tighe and contains the Romney print engraved by Caroline Watson:

To possess strong feelings and amiable affections, and to express them with a nice discrimination, has been the attribute of many female writers; some of whom have also participated with the author of Psyche in the unhappy lot of a suffering frame and a premature death. Had the publication of her poems served only as the fleeting record of such a destiny, and as a monument of private regret, her friends would not have thought themselves justified in displaying them to the world. But when a writer intimately acquainted with classical literature, and guided by a taste for real excellence, has delivered in polished language such sentiments as can tend only to encourage and improve the best sensations of the human heart, then it becomes a sort of duty in surviving friends no longer to withhold from the public such precious relics.
["To the Reader," *W* iii-iv]

That duty still exists. As we continue to recuperate the writings of women poets such as Tighe, we need to continue thinking about the ways their work invites us to expand our critical understanding of the Romantic period and women's literary history.

Notes

1. *Psyche; or, The Legend of Love* was originally published in a private edition in 1805 and distributed to family and friends; the first public edition was published post-humously and included a selection of Mary Tighe's lyrics and sonnets in a volume edited by her cousin and brother-in-law, William Tighe: *Psyche, with Other Poems*. I quote from the facsimile reprint edited by Jonathan Wordsworth.

2. See reviews in *Eclectic Review* 9 (1813): 217-29 (esp. 217); *Quarterly Review* 5, no. 10 (1811): 471-85; *British Review* 1 (June 1811): 277-98; *New Annual Register, or, General Repository of History, Politics, and Literature* 32 (1811): 364-72; *Gentleman's Magazine* 82 (1812): 464-67. William S. Ward lists ten reviews of *Psyche, with Other Poems* in volume 2 of his *Literary Reviews in British Periodicals. Monthly Review* 66 (1811): 139.

3. Important articulations of this view of Romantic aesthetics may be located in Homans, *Women Writers and Poetic Identity*; Homans, *Bearing the Word*; Hoeveler, *Romantic Androgyny*.

4. J. Wordsworth, "Ann Yearsley to Caroline Norton," 121.

5. Mackintosh, *Memoirs*, 1:195. J. Wilson, Maginn, Lockhart, and Hogg, *Noctes Ambrosianae*, 1:75. Gifford, "Mrs. Hemans's Poems," 130. Hemans herself acknowledged the importance of Tighe's work in several poems of telling psychological complexity, including the significantly placed final lyric of the 1828 volume *Records of Woman*, "The Grave of a Poetess."

6. Bethune, *The British Female Poets*, vi, 102-3. Williams, *The Literary Women of England*, 256, 554-55. Blackburne, *Illustrious Irishwomen*, 2:56-57, 2:108, 2:56.

7. C.J. Hamilton, *Notable Irishwomen*, 103.

8. Stuart Curran concludes his essay "Romantic Poetry: The 'I' Altered" by observing of women poets that "Poets, they might well have told us, even if confined to the domestic circle, are still the unacknowledged legislators of the world" (206).

9. Keats to George and Georgiana Keats, 31 Dec. 1818, *The Letters of John Keats*.

10. Beers, *A History of Romanticism*, 121. Finney, *The Evolution of Keats's Poetry*, 1:66.

11. Byron, *Letters and Journals*. See Marlon Ross's useful discussion of Byron in connection with Hemans in *The Contours of Masculine Desire*.

12. See Curran, "Romantic Poetry: The 'I' Altered"; Curran, "Women Readers, Women Writers"; Curran, "Romantic Poetry: Why and Wherefore?"; Ross, *The Contours of Masculine Desire*; Mellor, *Romanticism and Feminism*; Mellor, *Romanticism and Gender*; [McGann] et al., "Literary History"; McGann, "Poetry, 1785-1832"; McGann, *Poetics of Sensibility*.

13. Cheris Kramerae's application of muted group theory to gender and language studies in *Women and Men Speaking* works equally well to describe canonical valuation.

14. See Linkin, "Romanticism and Mary Tighe's *Psyche*"; Linkin, "Romantic Aesthetics." Tighe's journals were selectively preserved by her cousin Caroline Hamilton, along with journals written by her mother and family histories written by Caroline Hamilton. MS 4810 at the National Library of Ireland, Dublin.

15. The omission of Tighe's *Psyche* notwithstanding, Butler offers an excellent overview of the significance of the Cupid and Psyche myth for various groupings of Romantic poets in M. Butler, *Romantics, Rebels and Reactionaries*. She also differentiates Wordsworth's Romanticism, "reflective, autobiographical, exalting privacy and withdrawal from society" (123), from that of the younger Romantics, "extrovert not introvert, and pagan not Christian. They prefer objective forms, such as narrative and drama, to the confessional forms like autobiography" (124).

16. Curran, in "Romantic Poetry: The 'I' Altered," names Anna Barbauld, Hannah More, Anna Seward, Charlotte Smith, Helen Maria Williams, and Mary Robinson as the six important women poets who fill the seeming gap at the end of the eighteenth century (187-88); Behrendt names many more as he outlines the productivity of women poets between 1802 and 1812 in "The Gap That Is Not a Gap," this volume.

17. Blackburne, *Illustrious Irishwomen*, 52-53.

18. Ibid., 53, 55. Crookshank, *Memorable Women of Irish Methodism*, 144. Howitt, "Mrs. Tighe," 290.

19. Howitt, "Mrs. Tighe," 282.

20. Ibid., 286. J. Wilson, Maginn, Lockhart, and Hogg, *Noctes Ambrosianae*, 2:103.

21. The *British Review* 1 (June 1811) observes that "there is a characteristic delicacy, a 'trew feminitée,' about this publication, which is exceedingly attractive" (297), as is the portrait of Tighe herself: "Expressive as it appears to be of the mind which pervades every part of her poetry, we are credibly informed that it falls short of the beauty and sentiment which illuminated the countenance of the fair original" (298). Indeed six of the ten reviews Ward lists for *Psyche* make some reference to her beauty, such as the review in the *Gentleman's Magazine*, which begins with an allusion to her physical person, a "fair Authoress [who] did not live to witness the approbation her compositions have excited in the publick at large" (vol. 82 [1812]: 464) and ends with a reference to her portrait (467). Both the *Monthly Review* and the *New Annual Register* call her "The fair writer" (*Monthly Review* 66 [1811]: 139; *New Annual Register* 32 [1811]: 364), whereas the *British Critic* 38 (1811) laments "The fair author is, alas, no more" (631). The *Critical Review* 4 (1812) carefully describes how "Mrs. Tighe's poems are a mirror of herself," whose image is "beautiful" in reflecting a "moral portrait" (606).

22. Leigh Hunt, "Specimens of British Poetesses," 1891 ed., 277. *Dictionary of National Biography*, 1898 ed., s.v. "Tighe, Mary," 389.

23. "Verses Written in Solitude, April 1792," lines 17-20, in *Mary, a Series of Reflections*.

24. Blackburne, *Illustrious Irishwomen*, 56.

25. Henchy, *The Works of Mary Tighe*, 6.

26. Entry of 25 Mar. 1796, in Tighe, journals and family histories.

27. Jackson, in *Poetry of the Romantic Period*, remarks, "Mary Tighe excused the wooden allegorizing of her *Psyche; or, the Legend of Love* (1805) by claiming *The Faerie Queene* as her precedent, but she too was writing a cautionary tale for young ladies," as

a prelude to his discussion of the ways Blake, Shelley, and Byron more importantly renew allegorical form for political commentary (218).

28. Insofar as I see Tighe representing herself with self-consciousness in *Psyche*, I disagree with Ross's sense that "her poetry refuses to bring attention to itself. It appears satisfied to be as ephemeral as a moment of delightful sadness felt briefly, briefly remembered, a fleeting response to a particular, quotidian contingency." *The Contours of Masculine Desire*, 158.

29. Jackson, *Poetry of the Romantic Period*, 218. Greg Kucich argues more positively for the "active sojourn that enables Psyche" in his "Gender Crossings," 38.

30. Andrew Ashfield points to the gendered difference that informs eighteenth-century views of reading as ravishment and transport: a male reader could "emerge from ravishment refined with new moral prospects before him. . . . When women experience ravishment and transport, waking dreams and 'ideal presences,' these are viewed as acts of adulterous imagination." Introduction, xiii-xiv.

31. See Hofkosh, "The Writer's Ravishment."

32. W. Wordsworth, "Ode: Intimations of Immortality," in *William Wordsworth*, 183-89.

33. Hemans, "The Grave of a Poetess," in *Records of Woman*.

PART THREE

Reconstructing Reception

A "High-Minded Christian Lady"

The Posthumous Reception of Anna Letitia Barbauld

William McCarthy

When Anna Letitia Barbauld died, obituaries competed in paying tribute to her. In the *Newcastle Magazine* William Turner called her "unquestionably the first [i.e., best] of our female poets, and one of the most eloquent and powerful of our prose writers." "Her various publications," the *Christian Reformer* agreed, "have gained for her a lasting name amongst the best English writers." A memoir of Barbauld in the *Imperial Magazine* delivered the grandest pronouncement: "[S]o long as letters shall be cultivated in Britain, or wherever the English language shall be known, so long will the name of this lady be respected."[1]

The publication of Barbauld's *Works*, edited with a memoir by her niece Lucy Aikin, and of a volume of Barbauld pieces called *A Legacy for Young Ladies*, evoked further assessments of her achievement. The *Monthly Review* could think of "none who, in her line, deserves to rank higher" than Barbauld, and it admired the "masculine . . . powers" and "unbounded . . . grasp" of her mind. The *Monthly Repository,* on its side, declared Barbauld "in the best sense of the word . . . a *popular* writer. She is not known to all readers, but she is unknown to none that have any pretensions to taste and refinement." Because in her "Memoir" Lucy Aikin likened Barbauld's genius to Joseph Addison's, reviewers debated Barbauld's affiliations with leading male writers. Some agreed with Aikin, but with reservations in Barbauld's favor: "[T]he style of Addison," declared the *Eclectic Review,* "is less perfect than hers." The American William B.O. Peabody thought her more intense than Addison because more honest: "He throws out his essays with the easy air of a wellbred gentleman, seldom appearing to pour out his heart in his writings. . . . Her thoughts, on the contrary, evidently flow from the soul . . . and in every appeal to the feelings, sincerity is power." The *Monthly Repository* refused the comparison absolutely, likening her instead to Samuel Johnson: her prose exhibits "Johnson's stateliness and strength chastened by the liveliness and grace of her sex."[2]

That Barbauld could be discussed in this way, by thoughtful comparisons with male writers regarded as classic or becoming-classic, testifies to the seriousness with which she was taken by literary men and women in 1825 on both sides of the Atlantic. "Sound sense, fervent piety, and strong argumentative powers, aided by an irresistible eloquence, with genius to create, taste to modify, and fancy to adorn; . . . all these, and even more, [are] the attributes of Mrs. Barbauld." This encomium by Rachel Lazarus, American educationist, is matched by the praise of other qualified judges far into the nineteenth century: Leigh Hunt, who splendidly perceived that Barbauld had "intellect and passion enough to match a spirit heroical"; Walter Savage Landor, who once challenged guests at a dinner party to "show me anything finer in the English Language" than her poem, "A Summer Evening's Meditation"; and Harriet Martineau, a severe critic of most of her Unitarian coreligionists and by no means disposed to kindly judgments, to whom, nevertheless, Barbauld remained "still . . . one of the first of writers in our language." Even fifty years after her death, it is possible to find Barbauld extolled in terms customarily reserved for preeminent male writers—for instance, by the American feminist Grace Ellis in 1874: "Mrs. Barbauld was one of the great minds which belong to all time for their catholic spirit, their enlightened faith, their love of freedom, their hope for humanity, their communion with nature, and their appreciation of truth and beauty in human life and the great possibilities for the future of the world." From the reviews, the notices, and the comments of fellow writers, it would appear that in 1825 and for some decades thereafter no one would seriously have questioned the *Monthly Repository's* judgment that Barbauld was "the first of English female authors; and we should find it difficult to name more than two or three modern authors of the other sex who can stand a comparison with her in both verse and prose."[3]

A century later, Barbauld's reputation had shriveled. "Her title to fame rests in these days mainly on the poem ["Life"] which [Francis] PALGRAVE included . . . in his Golden Treasury; her other poetical pieces, except perhaps for a hymn or two, and her prose writings hardly survive." This sentence from a 1925 memorial piece in the *Times* all too accurately described Barbauld's standing at the centennial of her death. Forty years after that, most who knew of her at all knew only a caricature: "Mrs. Bar-*bald* " (after a wisecrack by Charles Lamb about "the two Bald Women"—the other woman being the dramatist Elizabeth Inchbald), "a devout Presbyterian, much given to pious, humorless moralizing," who wrote "good simple books for children and dreary poetry for adults." She was "the literal-minded lady" whose sole remembered literary judgment stood as evidence of her obtuseness: that she saw no moral in "The Rime of the Ancient Mariner." Although she could still be found in anthologies—represented almost always by part of one poem, "Life"—her other works had been out of print so long that their very titles could probably not have been named even by historically minded readers.[4]

How could a writer whose importance seemed so self-evident at her death be thus transformed into a stuffed owl? The process by which, over a hundred years, Barbauld became a figure of farce was a synecdoche of a bigger complex, a knot of issues that were played out during the nineteenth and twentieth centuries. Broadly, those issues had to do with vicissitudes of class and gender politics not unknown to historians: the fate of middle-class liberalism, changes in the stance of "serious" writers toward the middle-class public, contested ideas of "woman" and "her place." These and other causes impinged on Barbauld's reputation in mutually reinforcing ways, creating a downward spiral of disesteem and neglect that eventuated in her almost literal obliteration. To attempt to retell them all would be a work of cultural history requiring a book. This essay settles for trying to sketch the course of that downward spiral as it appears to me.

There was, to begin with, a politics in the eulogies of Barbauld—and in the absence of them in other quarters—in 1825. Barbauld was a Protestant Dissenter loosely affiliated with Unitarianism and a spokeswoman for liberal causes. The writers who extolled her were also spokespersons for liberalism and Dissent. The *Monthly Repository,* the *Christian Reformer,* and the American *Christian Examiner* (Peabody's pulpit) were Unitarian journals; to the first Barbauld herself had contributed, and its founding editor, Robert Aspland, greatly admired her. For the *Monthly Review* also Barbauld had written, and it too was liberal by tradition. The Reverend William Turner was a Unitarian, had been a pupil of Barbauld's father at Warrington Academy, and had even, when a lad, been praised by her in a poem. The *Imperial Magazine* was pro-Dissent, pro-Reform, and antislavery; it addressed a lower-middle-class readership, and it also delivered the most unreserved prophecy of Barbauld's lasting fame. On the other side, two journals that literary historians today perceive as having "dominat[ed]" their age, the *Edinburgh Review* and the *Quarterly Review,* did not condescend to notice Barbauld's death or her *Works;* and two middle-aged poetical gentlemen who had once been youthful radicals kept their views on the occasion to themselves. Samuel Taylor Coleridge, in his Unitarian days an admirer of Barbauld, had begun to disparage her when he began receding from liberal politics; by 1825 he had been verbally abusing her—as "Mistress Bare and Bald" and the like—for many years. William Wordsworth, who detested

Barbauld personally although he sometimes acknowledged respect for her abilities, declared that her adherence to Dissent had "spoiled" her as a poet.[5] But the *Edinburgh,* although a Whig journal, had been notorious since its founding for caprice and irritability, and the *Quarterly* for rabid Toryism (it had outrageously mistreated Barbauld's last major publication, the poem *Eighteen Hundred and Eleven*); and by 1825 Coleridge and Wordsworth had long entrenched themselves in hostility to liberalism and Dissent. Theirs were Establishment views (Wordsworth was, after all, to be named Poet Laureate), and by that very token, in 1825 they were intellectually backward.

Thus, Charles Beard, writing on Barbauld in 1874, was not wrong in opining that she "belonged too much to a religious and literary coterie to be fairly judged in her life-time, either by foes or friends." By the 1960s, when a retrospective rewriting of history had long made it appear that Wordsworth and Coleridge were (like the *Edinburgh* and the *Quarterly*) the "dominating" minds of their time, it was inevitable that a commentator on Barbauld, even when trying to express interest in her, could only reconfirm her insignificance by describing her as a mouthpiece of liberal Protestant Dissent, for by then British Dissent had come to appear, even to American students of literature, strictly marginal and sectarian.[6] In 1825, however, liberal Dissent, although the conservative Establishment undoubtedly wished to regard it as a mere sect, and although it was always numerically a fraction of the population, in fact embodied much of the intellectual and political vanguard of Great Britain. In 1825 liberal Dissent was marginal in the sense that it still did not enjoy full civil rights, but this was an insurgent marginality, like that of other groups whose consciousness of being wronged makes them vigilant on behalf of the wronged. In 1825 all the causes that liberal Dissent had championed during fifty years were yet to be won: repeal of the two laws that technically disenfranchised it (1828), Catholic Emancipation (1829), reform of Parliament (1832), the abolition of slavery in Britain's colonies (1833). But it knew itself destined to win them and felt certain of being on the side of moral progress. The liberal sense of being poised on the leading edge of a wave of reform presides over the *Monthly Review*'s review of Barbauld's *Works:* "In our days," the reviewer begins, with a confidence that may be envied in ours, "when right notions are prevalent, and the benefits of rational education have become, or are becoming, obvious to all,—when the mechanics have their institutions,—when it is, moreover, proposed that London shall have its university . . ."[7]

Forty-four years later, after these causes had indeed been won, friends of the journalist and literary lioniser Henry Crabb Robinson commissioned a mural in memory of him for University Hall in Gordon Square, London (then home to Manchester New College, a descendant of Warrington Academy). The mural was to represent all the luminaries with whom Robinson, himself a

Protestant Dissenter by birth, had associated during a long lifetime. It is a varied group, including Wordsworth, Coleridge, Robert Southey, Charles and Mary Lamb, William Blake, and Goethe in one wing and, in another, William Hazlitt, William Godwin, Thomas Clarkson, Landor, Gilbert Wakefield, Friedrich Schlegel, Madame de Staël, and Barbauld. It was titled *The Vanguard of the Age.*[8] Oddly mingled though its personages are—or rather, because they are oddly mingled—the mural is a fair representation of early-nineteenth-century British middle-class literary-political culture, a culture in which Dissent and Barbauld figured alongside names now exclusively canonical, and figured not as a sect but as part of "the vanguard of the age" (see fig. 10).

Liberal Dissent won its political battles and went from being insurgent to being, in some parts of England, politically and economically ascendant. But it was made to pay for its victories by cultural humiliation. In England liberal Dissent always drew its numbers from the "middling" classes; in Barbauld's time it was proud of being middle-class. By the end of the nineteenth century, however, "middle-class" had become synonymous with "philistine." Having attained to political power, at least in big industrial centers such as Manchester, Dissenting businessmen and mill owners whose grandfathers had been graduates and sponsors of eighteenth-century Dissenting academies—centers of intellectual activity, in sharp contrast to then-torpid Oxford and Cambridge—found themselves pilloried as cultural illiterates from right and left alike. Thus, from the right Matthew Arnold, professor of poetry at Oxford, skewers middle-class liberalism in the person of John Arthur Roebuck, M.P. for Sheffield, whose grandfather, an inventor, chemist, physician, and Warrington Academy trustee, had recommended Barbauld's father to a Warrington tutorship.[9] From the left, Karl Marx heaps scorn on mill owners as "crude and half-educated parvenus." True, middle-class liberals did much to earn these attacks. Liberalism's creation of appalling industrial conditions and the selfish resistance of mill owners to legislation alleviating the sufferings of factory workers amounted to reneging on the classic liberal promise of "universal" human rights and went far to discredit the moral pretensions of liberal Dissent. And mid-Victorian Dissent, deeply tinctured by the outlook of Evangelical Christianity, did much to deserve accusations of cultural philistinism. Partly by their own fault, the cultures of liberalism and Dissent came to appear less and less worthy of respect, especially among those intellectuals who were in charge of literary opinion. Partly in protest, nineteenth-century novelists figure Dissenters as Bounderbys and Bulstrodes, and Liberals as Gradgrinds.[10]

In doing so, however, the novelists seldom trouble to discriminate among the many varieties of Dissent, tending to lump Unitarians, Methodists, and Baptists all under a general, pejorative notion of "Chapel"—in contradistinction to "Church," that is, to "respectable" society.[11] As this fact suggests, the

ARMITAGE'S FRESCO IN UNIVERSITY HALL (NOW DR. WILLIAMS'S LIBRARY), LONDON

Flaxman
Blake
Wordsworth
Southey
Lamb
Mary Lamb
Coleridge
Henry Crabb Robinson
Wieland
Herder
Schiller
Arndt
Goethe
Tieck
von Knebel

von Bunsen
Paynter
Dr. Arnold
Rev. F. W. Robertson
Lady Byron
Talfourd
Lord Cranworth
Quillinan
Rogers
Edward Irving
Savigny
Princess Amalie
Mme. de Staël
Schlegel
Wakefield
Landor
Mrs. Barbauld
Clarkson
Godwin
Hazlitt

Fig. 10. Edward Armitage, *The Vanguard of the Age* (1870), reproduced from Edith J. Morley, *The Life and Times of Henry Crabb Robinson*. Reproduced by permission of J.M. Dent.

cultural prejudice against Dissent among Anglicans ran deep and ran long; it cannot be attributed only to honest indignation at the evil consequences of free trade. It is far likelier to go back to Dissent's seventeenth-century offenses against royalism. One way of diminishing Barbauld, when the subject is her children's books, has been to quote Samuel Johnson's ridicule of them:

Miss [Aikin] was an instance of early cultivation, but in what did it terminate? In marrying a little Presbyterian parson, who keeps an infant boarding-school, so that all her employment now is,
    "To suckle fools, and chronicle small-beer."
She tells the children, "This is a cat, and that is a dog, with four legs and a tail; see there! you are much better than a cat or a dog, for you can speak." If I had bestowed such an education on a daughter, and had discovered that she thought of marrying such a fellow, I would have sent her to the *Congress.*

Note the word "Presbyterian" in conjunction with Johnson's ridicule of schoolkeeping. Johnson's remark on Barbauld parallels his disparagement of John Milton's schoolkeeping in his "Life of Milton" (1779): there also Johnson calls attention to a seeming diminishment, and there also his subject is a Dissenter—for Johnson the arch-Dissenter, the man who justified the murder of his king.[12]

Johnson's distaste for Dissenters as a class and his vehement opposition to American independence—a cause favored by most Dissenters, as he well knew (hence his jab about sending Barbauld "to the *Congress*")—are familiar. Wordsworth's hostility to Dissent, less known, was probably more virulent. "For myself," he wrote of an 1834 campaign to absolve Dissenting degree-takers at Cambridge University from the oath of allegiance to the Anglican Church, "I would oppose tooth and nail the petition . . . because it is hypocritical—and if granted will inevitably lead to a demand for Degrees, which will give Votes—open to them the emoluments and offices of the University and make them a part of the governing Body. An event which for innumerable reasons—and not the least for its tendency to overthrow the Est[ablished] Ch[urch] I earnestly deprecate." "Hypocritical," Valentine Cunningham notes, was a favorite Establishment epithet for Dissent in the nineteenth century. One notices also the hysterical, "domino-theory" character of Wordsworth's tirade. The rhetoric had been threadbare even in 1790. Barbauld herself had noticed its triteness in her *Address to the Opposers of the Repeal of the Corporation and Test Acts:* faced with the prospect that the two acts that imposed second-class citizenship on Dissenters might be repealed, conservatives had raised "the old cry of, *the Church is in danger.*"[13]

Wordsworth's disciple, Matthew Arnold, with more finesse but equal spite-fulness kept up an incessant campaign against Dissent ("Hebraism," he called it in his most fastidious moment, in contrast to the "sweetness and light" of "Hellenism"). On one occasion Arnold catalogued "the hindrances" with which "religion in this country . . . has to contend": "beer-shops, Dissent, Ritualism, the Salvation Army, and the rest of the long and sad list."[14] Nor, if an anecdote from my own experience may testify, has Anglican prejudice entirely abated even today. The priest at a City church in London in 1988 greeted me kindly after service, asking what brought me to England. When I said I was there to research the life of a Dissenting writer, the good man grew defensive: eighteenth-century Dissenters, he assured me, did not suffer serious legal disabilities, and their grievances were much exaggerated.

I suggest that the critical practice of slurring Barbauld was to be partly rooted in a habit of resenting the culture of Dissent. This habit was—perhaps still is—native to the British Establishment and the British class structure. (When indulged in by Americans, it is therefore necessarily an imported product—and one that runs counter to American political ideology. But if American political ideology owes its origins to British Dissenting politics, American cultural anxiety has always hankered after the style of British aristocratic-gentry culture.) The fact that I illustrate British resentment of Dissent from three writers now firmly canonical—and could illustrate it further, as Valentine Cunningham argues, from other firmly canonical writers such as Charles Dickens—suggests the extent to which British literary "high culture" came to be defined as an anti-Dissenting culture. As further illustration, this time negative, one might cite the polymath (and Barbauld's friend) Joseph Priestley. Priestley, whose collected nonscientific writings fill some twenty-five volumes, so offended the Church and the government by his radical theology and politics that the local authorities in Birmingham condoned—or even encouraged—riots against him; he was ultimately driven into exile. Only thirty years after Priestley's death, Harriet Martineau "was extremely surprised by being asked by Lady Durham who Dr. Priestley was, and all that I could tell her about him. . . . I found that she, the daughter of the Prime Minister, had never heard of the Birmingham riots! I was struck," Martineau reflects, "by this evidence of what fearful things may take place in a country, unknown to the families of the chief men in it." Just as he was forgotten by a political Establishment to which he had presented only trouble, so Priestley was forgotten as well by literary high culture. Anthologies of eighteenth-century texts that offer bits of Bernard Mandeville, Hume, Burke, and even "Junius" and Tom Paine—all writers in one way or another comparable to Priestley—print nothing of Priestley. In the literary history constructed by Anglo-American high culture, he does not exist.[15]

Matthew Arnold was well situated to institutionalize that literary history. As professor of poetry at Oxford, as schools inspector, and of course as a leading propagandist for "high culture," he campaigned zealously for a poetic canon in which Wordsworth would hold honors and from which Dissenting writers would be banished (Milton alone excepted). As embodied in "The Study of Poetry" (1880), the Arnold canon is notoriously a club with very few members: almost the entire eighteenth century was refused entrance, ostensibly because its concern with "freedom" and "reason" led it to dwell too much in prose,[16] but perhaps more truly because those concerns smacked too much of liberal Dissent. True, Arnold's canon was not his own invention; much of it encapsulated existing revaluative tendencies. As the nineteenth century advanced, respect for eighteenth-century writers in general declined. In commentary on Barbauld from the last third of the century, one can trace the wilting of her reputation in tandem with that of her birth century and the countervailing rise of Wordsworth's.[17]

These motions were accelerated in her case by the publication in 1869 of the diary of Henry Crabb Robinson. A generation younger than Barbauld, Robinson had devoted his energies to "collecting" his literary contemporaries, especially Wordsworth (for whom his admiration verged on toadyism) and Coleridge. Although Barbauld was one of the writers whom Robinson collected, his published diary only helped to fix her in Wordsworth's shade. It was Robinson who gave the world a stick with which Barbauld was to be beaten for many years, Wordsworth's singling out her poem "Life" as, by implication, her one durable poem. Robinson had sent a copy of "Life" (first published in Barbauld's *Works*) to Dorothy Wordsworth in 1826, recommending it—and particularly its last stanza, beginning "Life! we've been long together"—in servile terms to her brother's attention. Years afterward, Wordsworth (so Robinson's story goes) asked him to "'repeat me that stanza by Mrs. Barbauld.' I did so. . . . He was at the time walking in his sitting-room at Rydal with his hands behind him; and I heard him utter to himself: 'I am not in the habit of grudging people their good things, but I wish I had written those lines.'"[18] Even when told with the motive of honoring Barbauld, this story created a perspective trick by which she, the senior writer, was made to appear a minor disciple of Wordsworth, the junior. Here is Charles Beard again: "Such a revolt against the past as Wordsworth and Coleridge began in the 'Lyrical Ballads' requires first a singular vigour of imagination. . . . There are brief hints, fugitive touches, in Mrs. Barbauld's verse, which make us wonder what she might have been if she had been brought up at the feet of Wordsworth and Coleridge and Shelley. She certainly suffers from having found her ideal in the degenerate successors of Pope."[19] But Beard is happy to be able to report (or rather, repeat) that Wordsworth approved of "Life." That poem rapidly became the single "brief hint" or "fugitive touch" by which Barbauld the poet was remembered.

So prevalent was the assumption that an eighteenth-century poet must be shallow by comparison with the "Great Romantics" that by 1883 even a writer who sincerely and perceptively admired Barbauld could find no language of admiration that was not compromised. Anne Thackeray Ritchie's *Book of Sybils* (essays on Barbauld, Maria Edgeworth, Jane Austen, and Amelia Opie) was conceived as a feminist enterprise. Yet, in her essay on Barbauld Ritchie replays gestures that belittle and displace her subject once again. Thus Ritchie strives to assert Barbauld's literary credentials by describing Hampstead, where she lived for some time, as a scene of writing; but the terms of Ritchie's description thrust Barbauld into the chorus line for a cast of male Romantics: "Here Wordsworth trod; here sang Keats's nightingale; here mused Coleridge; and here came Carlyle, only yesterday. . . . Here, too, stood kind Walter Scott. . . . Besides all these, were a whole company of lesser stars following and surrounding the brighter planets—muses, memoirs, critics, poets, nymphs, authoresses."[20] Barbauld disappears into the last noun on the list. Claiming (not unjustly) that Barbauld became a better writer as she aged, Ritchie interprets this to mean that "even at eighty [she] was ready to learn to submit to accept the new gospel that Wordsworth and his disciples had given to the world, and to shake off the stiffness of early training" (22). The evidence of Barbauld's poetic improvement, of course, is "Life," which counts as evidence precisely because Wordsworth approved of it (47); like Beard's, this argument displays its author's inability to think of the category *poet* apart from the category *(male) Romantic*. So complete is the hegemony of Wordsworth in literary discourse that Ritchie, feminist though she is, can imagine no affirmation of Barbauld's poetry other than his. At the close she yields her position entirely, confessing "the great progress which people have made since Mrs. Barbauld's day in the practice of writing prose and poetry. . . . [T]he modest performances of the ladies of Mrs. Barbauld's time would scarcely meet with the attention now, which they then received" (50). When even commentators who were drawn to Barbauld could imagine no other way to justify their interest than by appending her to a name presumed far greater, her reputation was doomed.

By 1925 Wordsworth's stock itself had declined; but that of Coleridge was to rise steadily, especially among the Anglo-American New Critics of the 1930s through the 1950s, for whom almost every word of Coleridge was as Sacred Writ. It is not by accident that two of the quotations cited above to witness the nadir of Barbauld's reputation by the 1960s come from Coleridgian sources. Much as Matthew Arnold had enshrined Wordsworth as the sacred incarnation of Poetry, the New Critics made Coleridge into a high priest of Criticism. They also (and perhaps especially William Wimsatt) did much to rehabilitate Samuel Johnson—establishing, with these two points, a line of what might be called "critical Toryism." Barbauld suffered twice at Wimsatt's hands, once for each of his heroes. In *The Prose Style of Samuel Johnson* (1941), Wimsatt savaged one of the few titles still, by then, associated with her name, an essay "On Romances" written in imitation of Johnson's manner and considered by Johnson himself a good imitation. But not by Wimsatt: "altogether humorless" and "flat-footed," he declares it, in a move that seems willfully intended to knock out one of the few remaining props of Barbauld's reputation, that Johnson had approved of one thing she wrote. In their 755-page *Literary Criticism: A Short History* (1957), Wimsatt and Cleanth Brooks allot Barbauld, who had played a substantial part in the canonization of Samuel Richardson and the English novel generally but who wrote no novels herself, a single, inaccurate sentence: she is "an elderly female novelist [who] complained to Coleridge that [the "Ancient Mariner"] did not have any moral."[21] By 1957 it was no longer necessary to get right even the gross facts about Barbauld.

The supervention of an elitist literary culture bore particularly hard on writers regarded as "popular." Through her children's books Barbauld was widely read, in one form or another, from 1778 until after 1900; Grace Ellis, her American admirer, noted in 1874 that "her name . . . still live[s] in the hearts of the people, and it is as 'familiar as household words' in many homes."[22] Writers whose works, like hers, circulated throughout the middle classes came to be considered by exponents of Arnoldian "high seriousness" as panderers to philistines who therefore must be philistines themselves—if not charlatans: "Charlatanism," declared Arnold, "is for confusing or obliterating the distinctions between excellent and inferior, sound and unsound or only half-sound, true and untrue or only half-true. . . . And in poetry, more than anywhere else, it is unpermissible to confuse or obliterate them." This ultramontane sanctifying of poetry not only decimated the numbers of "genuine" poems, but it also implied that other genres might be more or less contaminated by charlatanism and therefore base. The same work that Arnold was doing on his side of the Atlantic—the promulgation of a moralized, masculinist, discriminatory aestheticism—was being carried out on the American side by the newly founded *Atlantic Monthly* and *Nation*. The internationally respected, enormously best-selling Harriet Beecher Stowe found herself in career trouble at their hands. Henry James, who reviewed for the *Nation*, deplored books written for "that extensive public, so respectable in everything but its literary taste, which patronizes what is called 'Sunday reading'"; such books, he knew, were written "mostly by ladies, and about and for children romping through the ruins of the Language."[23] James's words imply in these writers a childlike indifference to Art that amounts to vandalism of Art. This male-invented aesthetic imputes a special odium to popular "lady" writers; but the stigma of having a wide readership could attach to writers of either sex if they wrote successfully for children, presumably the least discriminating of all audiences. On this ground the reputation of Isaac Watts, who wrote far more widely than the few hymns for which he came to be laughingly remembered and whom Donald Davie does not hesitate to call a "genius," fell at least as far as Barbauld's.[24] Watts was, like Barbauld, a Dissenter; both suffered the stigma of being sectarian-philistine and the contradictory stigma of being popular-philistine. They couldn't win for losing.

A different political problem, related partly to memories of 1790s "jacobinism" and partly to fears of "Wollstonecraftianism," must have troubled Lucy Aikin when she sat down to write the first biography of her aunt. She had already faced it in 1823, writing her father's life; for John Aikin had been, in his daughter's words, "a free speculator" in his opinions, and his heterodoxies appeared to her likely to call down wrath upon his memory: "But think of the age we live in!—think of the Quarterly Review, the Saints, the clergy, the tories & the canters, & tell me how we are to be at once safe & honest!" Aunt Barbauld likewise had espoused radical positions in the early days of the French Revolution, in pamphlets shocking to an Establishment that had previously (despite her being a Dissenter) taken her to its bosom. In 1790 Horace Walpole, once her admirer, recoiled in fury from her: "the virago Barbaud," he sputtered after reading her *Address to the Opposers.* In 1798 politically moderate Richard Polwhele, surveying in *The Unsex'd Females* the disturbed state of modern womanhood, had worried over whether to group Barbauld, whose poems he had long loved, with the "alarming" Miss Wollstonecraft; he earnestly hoped that Barbauld was not tainted.[25] Lucy Aikin, then, was surely mindful in 1825 of the dangers attending a full account of her aunt's politics; she wished not to risk anything approaching the scandal created by William Godwin's too-candid memoir of his wife. She worked cautiously, therefore, skipping lightly over Barbauld's activities during the 1790s and giving a strongly conservative spin to Barbauld's views on women. Her most influential move in that way was to print a letter in which Barbauld appeared to deprecate the very idea of equal schooling for women and men; but she also printed a poem, "The Rights of Woman," which appeared to rebuke Wollstonecraftian feminism.[26] In Lucy Aikin's presentation, Barbauld looked a good candidate to become an icon of non- (or even anti-) Wollstonecraftian ideals of womanhood.

Probably this presentation was necessary at a time when women were expected, even by liberals, to stay out of political contentions. (Even the liberal *Monthly Repository* reiterated the importance of not "interfering with political questions beyond the limits that her sex marked out for her.") In any case, Barbauld was rapidly appropriated by early- and mid-Victorian feminism, which as it grew more conservative did make her into an icon of that sweet womanliness that knows its "true nature" and honors its "natural bounds." In 1825 a writer in the *Lady's Magazine* could still recognize Barbauld in terms compatible with those of Wollstonecraft's *Vindication of the Rights of Woman:* "When females . . . fill their allotted stations with dignity, prudence, and propriety, they are entitled to considerable praise; but, when they add to a strong under-standing the possession of literary talents, and, emerging from a private sphere, endeavour with success to entertain and instruct mankind, they become re-spectable public characters, and consequently claim more general notice and commendation." Likewise, the *Literary Gazette* could hail her for "set[ting] a great example to the female talent of her country." An unsigned appreciation known to me only through an 1845 manuscript copy still envisions a Barbauld possessed of "intellectual fire" and pursuing "lofty aims," whose works for adults "Teach how the female heart may warmly glow / With every high-born feeling man's can know."[27] But the idea of Barbauld as a model for "the female talent of her country" soon transmutes into an idea of Barbauld as a model woman, *tout court*. Although Barbauld's contemporaries had been impressed by what they perceived as her literary androgyny—usually figured as her "masculine" head and "feminine" heart—nineteenth-century commentators liked to dwell only on her "womanliness," a ploy indulged even by her American admirer W.B.O. Peabody: "She seems to have been almost a perfect specimen of an English woman, with reserve enough to redeem the national character, but still pos-sessing those active and affectionate feelings, which make one useful and dear in social life." "Femininity" quickly became her *literary* hallmark as well; so that, as a writer, she came to be perceived as a sort of model housewife: "a singular neatness and perspicuity of style and a feminine elegance of mind . . . characterise all the productions of Mrs. Barbauld."[28] In a comment in *Godey's Lady's Book* in 1838 one can see (and shudder at) the future of this strain of rhetoric: "Dear, good Mrs. Barbauld! . . . In the sphere she chose, her taste and observation were correct and delicately nice; and her moral feelings were el-evated and bright with all that is best and holiest in our nature. . . . Few authors have written with more devoted zeal to do good." The good that Barbauld was said to have done came to be identified almost exclusively as her books for children: commentators seldom failed to remember *Hymns in Prose* (which was reprinted throughout the nineteenth century) as, in the words of one, "a part of the pleasures or the tasks of their childhood."[29] Identifying her chiefly as a writer for children played badly in a climate of growing literary elitism; it im-plied that she was less a writer than a sort of national nanny.

This was not, of course, the fate of Barbauld alone among women writers. A literary canon divided on gender lines was promulgated in 1829 by the *Edinburgh Review*, reviewing Felicia Hemans: "Women, we fear, cannot do every thing. . . . They are disqualified by the delicacy of their training and habits, and the still more disabling delicacy which pervades their conceptions and feelings; and from much they are excluded by their actual inexperience of the realities they might wish to describe. . . . Their proper and natural business is the practical regulation of private life, in all its bearings, affections, and concerns." From these postulates the *Edinburgh* deduced an essentialist division of the canon, allotting to women undisputed sovereignty over the genres of domesticity: "No *man*, we will venture to say, could have written the Letters of Madame de Sevigné, or the Novels of Miss Austin, or the Hymns and Early Lessons of Mrs Barbauld, or the Conversations of Mrs Marcet. These performances . . . are not only essentially and intensely feminine, but they are . . . decidedly more perfect than any masculine productions with which they can be brought into comparison."[30] Barbauld's banishment to the nursery was an effect of an intersection of genre with gender ideology.

Yet Victorian feminism, even when conservative, strove to elevate the domestic character to which middle-class women were being confined; embers of Wollstonecraftian "republican motherhood" still gleam in it, and Barbauld herself would not have been wholly unhappy there. Thus the midcentury feminist Clara Balfour gave a chapter to Barbauld in her *Working Women of the last Half Century* (1854), a book intended to "shew how much the mind and character of woman have aided the mental and moral progress of the present century." In Balfour's vision, woman is called to "a wider usefulness and a higher life than that of contributor to her nation's literature. . . . She must be the reformer in society," and she must be so in her special, maternal role as educator of the young: "[I]n her office as teacher of the young, the highest office that a human being can fill, she has it in her power to implant such principles as shall tell favourably upon the world."[31] Although Barbauld was something of a skeptic, in print, on the possibility of improving the world through formal education, she had in fact striven to implant in her pupils at Palgrave School "such principles as shall tell favourably" upon it, her published teaching texts were part of that effort, and she would have warmed to Balfour's ideal. In any case, she figures in Balfour's book—it is a hagiography of women who effected reforms in society by exertions of their "womanly natures"—as a heroine of modern education.

The role went comfortably with a long-standing tendency in Barbauld commentary to praise the "purity" of her aspirations and to figure her as notably devoted to religion (partly on the strength of her poem "An Address to the Deity" and her verse hymns, which, though not numerous, were widely reprinted). "Her muse was consecrated to piety," the *Monthly Repository* had declared, and Peabody had regarded her "as eminently a *christian* writer." The whole picture—the working for good, the domesticity, the religion, the model of "womanliness"—comes together in the issue of *The Lady's Own Paper* for 25 January 1868, which featured Barbauld as its woman of the week, with portrait, potted biography, and appreciation, in these terms:

In the whole range of literature . . . we should seek in vain for a more honoured memory than that of the high-minded Christian lady whose portrait we engrave this week. A quiet and unostentatious worker, she yet left the impress of her true nobility of character alike within the charmed home-circle and on the literature of the age. It is to her that the cause of National Education is so largely indebted, and the children of the present day owe so much. . . . A star amongst noble women, she exerted her power rather by the influence of an untiring benevolence, and honest, steady working, than by any self assertion, and when she passed away, she left a flood of light around her name.[32]

But the same rhetoric persists even in Grace Ellis, a fact that admonishes me to recall again that it could be deployed for feminist purposes. Her Barbauld, besides being one of the great minds that belong to all time, was "a high-toned . . . person" possessed of "womanly virtues and sweetness of character."[33]

   A difficulty with this kind of valuation (as readers will have been only too ready to notice) was that it entirely lacked humor, irony, or wit. In *Writing Women's Literary History*, Margaret Ezell has traced the project of constructing "the female writer" in the nineteenth century as an enterprise, in good part, of narrowing the range of styles and emotions permissible to women; in the process, "wit" was one of the qualities banished. (Again, what happened to Barbauld was typical of larger changes.) In biographies, commentaries, and anthologies, women writers of earlier centuries gradually lost the rough edges of their identities, becoming more and more like "pattern women"; and thus all, to some degree, were made into stuffed owls.[34] Their apparent humorlessness, their seemingly relentless ethereality or (in the case of women who were noted for teaching) their grim loftiness of purpose—everything that came to be meant by the word "schoolmarm"—made these stock figures easy targets for satirists in the antifeminist backlash that set in late in the century. Literary elitists could thus ridicule women writers either for aesthetic ignorance (as Henry James did) or for "absurd solemnity" (Elaine Showalter's phrase). When Oscar Wilde, cataloging bygone "English Poetesses" in an 1888 essay, named "the worthy Mrs Barbauld," his "worthy" carried a freight of tacit satire. And so does the character Miss Prism in *The Importance of Being Earnest:* "a female of repellent aspect, remotely connected with education," who insists on Cecily Cardew's reading political economy. Miss Prism's first name, alas, is Lætitia.[35]

   One of the weapons used against women by male writers at the fin de siècle was adolescent romance—boys' books, such as *Treasure Island*—a genre that Showalter interprets as a form of male bonding in defense against woman-perceived-as-bitch-mother. (In America, *Huckleberry Finn* is the classic instance: Huckleberry even endures female attempts to "sivilize" him by way of Hannah More's "Moses in the Bulrushes.") Barbauld, who as a teacher performed in many of the roles of a mother, was treated with defensive adolescent humor in her own lifetime: that is the real purport, presumably, of Coleridge's "Mistress Bare and Bald." A century later she had been amalgamated entirely into the generic image of that ultimate schoolmarm, the Victorian "High-Toned Old Christian Woman" who is the butt of male literary pranksterism in Wallace Stevens's poem of that title. The poem begins with Arnoldian lecturing: "Poetry is the supreme fiction, madame"; and, as any 1920s litterateur would know, women cannot be supreme in fictions. The poem directs her to build heaven from the moral law (just the sort of activity "high-toned ladies" were deemed good at), then opposes to it and her "our bawdiness," which "squiggl[es] like saxophones" (in the eyes—or ears—of a high-toned lady a most unseemly instrument). The poem ends by imagining "a jovial hullabaloo among the spheres" that "will make widows wince. But fictive things / Wink as they will. Wink most when widows wince."[36] Thus the supreme fictions not only exclude "high-toned" women but also enjoy hurting them. Barbauld is of course never named, and Stevens probably was not thinking of her. He did not need to, nor did the literary modernists who were reading him. When a literary culture in which she had been made to disappear into the Victorian Angel gave way to a literary culture that turned against the Victorian Angel, her actual identity could be of no possible interest. Everyone knew what all "high-toned old Christian women" must have been: they must have been ridiculous.

Barbauld's reputation was not refurbished by new editions of her writings after 1826. There were, indeed, multiple editions of *Hymns in Prose,* and *Lessons for Children* led a utilitarian afterlife in numerous mangled versions, often with other materials inserted and under alien titles; no one regarded it as a work whose integrity mattered. These editions, although they kept Barbauld's name before the public, could only diminish her literary standing, as "literary" was coming to be understood. Her poems continued to figure in anthologies, but, apart from spikes in 1840 and 1874 (attributable to Barbauld collections by Sarah J. Hale and the ever-honorable Grace Ellis), their number gradually dwindled; a sample of anthologies published between 1890 and 1973 offers just eight poems, of which one, "Life," appears twelve times and the others only once each.[37] Barbauld's prose writings for adults simply disappeared.

Canonization studies suggest that canonization requires, for writers as for saints, persistent advocacy. In the nineteenth century the advocates were likely to be the dead writer's family and friends: the Mary Shelleys, the Sarah Coleridges, the Christopher Wordsworths, the John Forsters. Lucy Aikin filled that role for Barbauld in 1825-26, but only partially: she included in Barbauld's *Works* very few of the "considerable number of pieces" Barbauld left unpublished at her death and even omitted many important published pieces, such as the prefaces to *The British Novelists*. During the rest of the century no one in the Aikin family made up these deficiencies, with the effect (among other effects) that Barbauld's achievement as a critic was rapidly forgotten. Lucy Aikin and her brothers Charles and Arthur preserved Barbauld's papers, occasionally dispensing bits of them to visiting admirers such as Edward Everett, American ambassador to England in the 1840s. A selection from her papers was published in 1874 by Barbauld's great-niece, Anna Letitia LeBreton: chiefly Barbauld's letters to Maria Edgeworth, in one of which she deprecated the idea of a journal written exclusively by women, explaining that "there is no bond of union among literary women, any more than among literary men"—a sentence that would be held against Barbauld in after years. By the time LeBreton's daughter, Mary Emma LeBreton Martin, republished some of this material in *Memories of Seventy Years* (1883), the decline in Barbauld's reputation had begun to be felt by her family. Martin's preface to *Memories* is slightly apologetic and thoroughly Wordsworthianized: "Mrs Barbauld's genius, if modest, was undeniable. A poem that Wordsworth has coveted may be admitted to live, and her works for children . . . have an enduring and delicate charm. . . . Much of her writing is obsolete, but the stanzas on 'Life' . . . have the enduring touch of genius." When Martin died, her children sold her portion of the family papers.[38]

Most of Barbauld's papers, however, passed in 1927 to Charles William Brodribb, her great-great-great-nephew. An editor of the *Times* and a man of staunchly traditional literary tastes, Brodribb was proud of his descent from Barbauld's family and had begun to take an interest in her even before he came into her papers. He acquired Barbauld's letters to her lifelong friend Elizabeth Belsham (they had remained in the family of Belsham's husband until at least 1915); and he had thoughts of publishing from his collection.[39] Had Barbauld not been relegated by modernist anti-Victorian reaction to the dustbin of literature, he might have felt encouraged to publish sooner than he did, and on a larger scale; perhaps, also, he might have felt it appropriate to give her papers to a library. In any case, Brodribb published in 1935 an essay on Barbauld's school at Palgrave, using in it school documents from his collection. His work on the *Times* requiring London lodgings, he moved himself and most of the manuscripts into rooms on the top floor of No. 5 Stone Buildings, Lincoln's Inn. The war came, and with it the air raids over London. The Minutes of Lincoln's Inn Council for 30 September 1940 tell the rest: "[At] 1:30 A.M. on 25th September . . . about 60 incendiary bombs were dropped in the Inn. . . . A serious fire was started on the roof of N° 6 Stone Buildings which spread northwards as far as N° 3., the top floors have been burnt out and the rest of the building seriously damaged by water." Between fire and water, most of Brodribb's Barbauld papers perished.[40] This disaster, arguably a by-blow of Barbauld's loss of literary standing, guaranteed that she would not be easy to revive even should interest in her rekindle.

Apparently unknown to him, Brodribb had a distant cousin who, by 1932, when she was only twenty-five, had also decided to research Barbauld's life. Betsy Aikin-Sneath undertook her research in part from interest in family history. An Oxford graduate, she also participated in the revival of interest in the eighteenth century that set in during the 1920s and 1930s; her first book was a study of eighteenth-century German comedy. She was probably actuated as well by the feminism that inspired many university women in the 1920s, in the wake of the success of Women's Suffrage. Having no trove of Barbauld papers of her own to work from, Aikin-Sneath turned to public archives. She was the first to do so. Twenty-six years later, by which time she was Betsy Rodgers, she published *Georgian Chronicle: Mrs. Barbauld and Her Family*. She had cast a wide net and was able to produce from public archives twenty-one new Barbauld letters. Although her book was not explicitly feminist, it treated Barbauld respectfully; there is in it none of the slippage between aim and rhetorical deed that disabled Anne Thackeray Ritchie's effort. But 1958 was an unlucky year in which to publish on Barbauld—or, indeed, on any noncanonical woman writer. The feminist swell of the 20s and 30s had ebbed, and early Cold War conformism was in ascendance; Barbauld no longer had an audience among children and their parents, and therefore no popular base; in academic criticism Wimsatt, the apostle of Johnson and Coleridge, was a reigning influence. Reviewing the book, historian J.H. Plumb saw no reason to change *his* mind about Barbauld: to him, she remained "dull and tiresome . . . a fit subject for Horace Walpole's sneers and Charles Lamb's jokes."[41]

Nor did the next wave of feminism, in the 1970s, lift Barbauld's boat—not initially, at any rate. Margaret Ezell has examined themes of recent feminist historiography of women's writing: a leading theme, she argues, is its insistence that, in order to be taken as authentic—that is, not as a mere tool of male-dominated culture—a woman must be shown to have been "angry." Anger, for latter-day feminist literary historians, has been something like an Arnoldian "touchstone" of—dare we say?—"high seriousness" in a woman writer. Another theme of this historiography, Ezell argues, is insistence that, again in order to be taken as authentic, a woman must be shown to have resisted the gender roles presumed to have been imposed on her. Since the most common such role was imposed domesticity, she must have played, or wanted to play, a public role; if she is a writer, she must have striven to publish. A third requirement has been that a woman express solidarity with her "sisters": to be feminist, she must support the aspirations of other women. Failure there would amount to treason against her sex.[42]

Without wishing to denigrate women's anger, aspiration to public roles, or solidarity with one another, one may nevertheless observe, as Ezell does, that these concerns of recent feminism may so interpose themselves between today's historians and the older writers whose histories they wish to write that the historians end up only reinscribing on the past the conditions of their own lives—and sometimes, ironically, failing to see the very qualities they seek because those qualities do not appear in familiar form. That, certainly, was what happened when recent feminist literary historians first glanced at Barbauld. Everything Lucy Aikin had done to secure her aunt from Tory rage now exposed Barbauld to attack from the left. Aikin's account of Barbauld's temperament made her look placid, not angry. Aikin's account of Barbauld's reluctance to publish her first book made her look intimidated, not assertive. (Let me emphasize *look*. I am speaking of Lucy Aikin's compromised representation, not of the much more interesting figure whom I—and, at last today, others—perceive in Barbauld.) The centerpiece of Aikin's defense, the letter in which Barbauld appeared to talk down the idea of an academy for young ladies, had been noticed disapprovingly in passing as early as 1905 by advocates of women's education, but now it became the centerpiece of the case against her. Thus, in 1980 Marilyn Williamson trounced Barbauld for this, for the poem "The Rights of Woman," for the letter to Edgeworth declaring that "there is no bond of union among literary women," and for statements in an essay "On Female Studies." "Her attitudes toward the education and intellectual life of her own sex are almost retrograde" (a near-nuclear word in the then feminist lexicon); she illustrates "the refusal of achieving women to acknowledge the claims of feminism, to bond with women as women"; "Barbauld was no feminist."[43] Mary Mahl and Helene Koon, who printed fresh selections from Barbauld in their anthology of English women writers before 1800, *The Female Spectator*, felt obliged to apologize for Barbauld by pleading how much worse she might have been: "[H]er views on the education of girls . . . may appear hopelessly out of date to the modern woman, but they seem almost radical when set in the context of such contemporaries as Hannah More." Finally, just as, in the 1830s, Barbauld's "femininity" came to be read into the fabric of her writing, so, 150 years later, her presumed deficiency in feminism was seen by Marlon Ross as the secret of her supposed deficiency as a poet: "The limits of Barbauld's feminism are also the limits of her poetics. A woman who cannot grant women absolute equal rights with men also cannot grant them the right to write freely from the dictates of their own desire."[44]

Such was the state of commentary on Barbauld when I began research for a new biography of her. Since that time, however, a change of startling dimensions has occurred, with equally startling rapidity, in the academic estimation of her. Quite suddenly, in a 1989 review of Roger Lonsdale's *Eighteenth-Century Women Poets*, Barbauld was declared by Terry Castle "one of the most underrated writers of either sex from the period." And quite suddenly, there has arisen a new growth of commentary on her. The reasons for this efflorescence are concisely given by Theresa Kelley and Paula Feldman in the introduction to their collection of revisionary essays, *Romantic Women Writers:* "[T]he combined influence of increasing numbers of women in the profession, the evolving interest in gender studies, deconstruction, New Historicism, the politics of canon formation, and the popularity of various feminisms all conspired to make us reexamine Romanticism."[45] Barbauld's boat is rising now on the same tide that carries Felicia Hemans and a host of other women writers of that era.

The new commentary is more diverse than the old—a welcome change—and most of it proceeds in a spirit of admiration unlike anything that has appeared in well over a century. Some of it confesses, wisely, that we do not really know yet how Barbauld fits into the academic schemata inherited from an era when only male writers counted: thus John Anderson wonders, in a first-ever "reading" of Barbauld's late poem "The First Fire," whether treating that poem as a version of the "Greater Romantic Lyric" might require us to reimagine that genre; and Isobel Armstrong declares outright, in a first-ever reading of "Inscription for an Ice-House," that we have no hermeneutic for women poets of the Romantic period. Barbauld was not, we must remember, only a poet; her literary criticism also is receiving fresh attention, and her writing for children has evoked a wonderfully percipient essay by Mitzi Myers.[46]

This is all to the good. Yet, at the same time, it is also a bit worrying to see that most current commentators on her are Romanticists by training, whose paradigms derive (inevitably) from discourses to which Wordsworth, Coleridge and the rest are still central; and although their intentions are incomparably more respectful of Barbauld than those of the people who first framed her among the Great Romantics, there remains the danger of reassimilating her to a literary culture that she herself distrusted and which certainly did not treat her kindly. Besides, to reinsert her among the male Romantics would be anachronistic. She was, after all, old enough to be Wordsworth's mother; the boys she taught at Palgrave School belonged to his generation. She was herself a "dominating" presence (if the word must be used) when Coleridge was growing up; her real rival was William Cowper, and her poetic taste was formed on early- and mid–eighteenth-century models—models that a Wordsworthianized criticism was later to treat with contempt.

The Barbauld file is only beginning to be reopened, and there is a great deal still to be learned about her—as well as a great deal that we seem destined never to learn. There exists no edition of her complete published writings. She published in seven journals; not only has her journalism never been collected, but its extent has never been ascertained. Only in 1994 were her known poems collected for the first time; and that edition does not pretend to completeness, if only because I know of poems whose texts I have not found. The extent of her unpublished writing, thanks to Nazi incendiary bombs, will never be known. (How might ideas of her be altered if we had a text of her essay—if it was an essay—viewing "the female part of the creation a century hence on a g[rand or general] revolution of manners which is to take place when Mrs Woolstonecraft has been su[MS torn]"?[47]) Her letters have never been collected, and, thanks to the bombs, at least one supremely important series of letters, those to her life-long friend Elizabeth Belsham, has perished. There is no large collection of Barbauld papers in any public archive; odd bits are scattered over the hemi-spheres. Before 1958 there was no independently researched biography, only various permutations of memoirs authored by family members, all of them more or less reticent about important aspects of her life. (Even *Georgian Chronicle,* although independently researched, depends for most of its length on those family memoirs.) We do not even know the extent of Barbauld's so-cial circle, and we often cannot tell how well she knew a person.

In view of this enormous ignorance, circumspection seems called for. Of course we want to maintain our interest in Barbauld by reading and teaching the texts we do have. But we also need to gather the facts—whatever facts remain to be gathered—and patiently accumulate an empirical understanding of Barbauld and her milieu. We need, in other words, to give her the kind of attention that has traditionally been accorded to—indeed, lavished upon—male writers who became canonical in good part *because* they received such attention. Until a writer exists in editions, in biographies and bibliographies, in all the apparatus of scholarship, she is in danger of vanishing again at the next change in taste or ideology. If it seems unlikely that Barbauld will vanish again, only reflect that few makers of literary opinion in 1825 would have predicted the history that this essay has tried to sketch.

Notes

For information, suggestions, and comments, I am grateful to Paula Feldman, Harriet Linkin, Simon Martyn, Mitzi Myers, Joanna Parker, Rosanne Potter, and Jamie Stanesa, as well as to those people named in the notes below; errors and lapses of judgment are my own. I thank the librarian of Dr. Williams's Library for permission to quote from MS 24.81 (40); the treasurer and Masters of the Bench of Lincoln's Inn for permission to quote from the Minutes of Lincoln's Inn; and the Liverpool Record Office, Liverpool Libraries and Information Services, for permission to quote from MS 920 ROS 67.

1. W. Turner, "Mrs Barbauld," 183; "Mrs. Barbauld," *Christian Reformer,* 141; "Memoir of Mrs. Anna Letitia Barbauld," *Imperial Magazine,* 397.

2. Review of *Works,* by Barbauld, *Monthly Review,* 295; Review of *Works,* by Barbauld, *Monthly Repository,* 484; L. Aikin, "Memoir," xl; Review of *Legacy,* by Barbauld, *Eclectic Review,* 79; [Peabody], Review of *Works,* by Barbauld, 315; Review of *Works,* by Barbauld, *Monthly Repository,* 487.

3. Lazarus, Letter to Maria Edgeworth, 128; Leigh Hunt, "Specimens of British Poetesses," 129; Landor, reported by Murch, *Mrs. Barbauld and Her Contemporaries,* 94; Martineau, *Autobiography,* 302; Ellis, *Memoir,* 338; Review of *Works,* by Barbauld, *Monthly Repository,* 562.

4. "Mrs. Barbauld," *Times* (London), 15e; Gardner, *The Annotated Ancient Mariner,* 187; Plumb, Review of *Georgian Chronicle;* Raysor, "Coleridge's Comment," 89. Lamb's wisecrack first appeared in Coleridge, *Letters, Conversations and Recollections,* 1:203. Barbauld's alleged remark about the "Mariner" comes to us from Coleridge himself (not the best authority) and first reached print in his posthumous *Table Talk* (1835); it appears twice in Carl Woodring's edition, 1:272-73, 2:100. On the anthologizing of Barbauld's "Life," see note 37 below.

5. W. Wordsworth, *Letters,* ed. Hill, vol. 5, part 2: For Turner see Barbauld, *Poems,* 235-36. On the *Imperial,* the *Edinburgh,* and the *Quarterly,* see Sullivan, *British Literary Magazines,* 186-87, 242; for a contemporary view of those periodicals, see James Montgomery, *Lectures on General Literature,* 322-23: although Montgomery admitted to admiring the reviews, he also considered them arbitrary, capricious, and opportunistic. For Coleridge on Barbauld, see *Lectures 1808-1819 on Literature,* 1:118, 159, 220, 407, and *Notebooks,* entries 1848, 2303, 3965, 4035. For Wordsworth's claim to "admire [Barbauld's] genius" (qualified, however, by a claim that "her education [had not] been favourable to imaginative influences"), see C. Wordsworth, *Memoirs of William Wordsworth,* 1:163-64; evidence of his detestation of her appears in two letters (1812) reporting a visit where she was part of the company: in each he calls her an "old snake" (W. Wordsworth, *Letters,* ed. Hill, 8:72, 79).

6. Beard, "Anna Letitia Barbauld," 388. The late-60s commentator is Moore, "The Literary Career": see 2-5, 32-33, 410-11. Moore's treatment of Barbauld is a sad example of the power of a "hegemonic discourse" to thwart even intelligent interest in a subject. In thrall to a post-Wordsworthian notion that the eighteenth century was a "rationalist" wasteland in which no poetry could grow, and persuaded that Barbauld, as a "Rational Dissenter," must have dwelt in the dustiest part of that wasteland, Moore could see no conclusion, after writing a four-hundred-page dissertation on her, other than that Barbauld was deservedly forgotten and not worth revisiting. And yet Moore did a great deal of original research in periodicals and is often acute about details of Barbauld's life and work.

7. Review of *Works,* by Barbauld, *Monthly Review,* 294-95.

8. See Morley, *Henry Crabb Robinson,* 108-09 (from which I reproduce the mural), and Tayler, *Letters,* 2:320-21; title from a lithograph of the mural, Manchester College Library, Oxford. The original was painted over in 1957 (information from Dr. John Creasey, librarian, Dr. Williams's Library, London).

9. On the political success of Dissent, see Cunningham, *Everywhere Spoken Against,* 76-79. For Arnold's treatment of Roebuck, see *Complete Prose Works,* 5:96, 108, 156,

and 3:272-74. It was Arnold who defined the middle class as "philistine," and Roebuck was one of his preferred exemplars, as here:

> At this moment, when the narrow Philistinism, which has long had things its own way in England, is showing its natural fruits, and we are beginning to feel ashamed, and uneasy, and alarmed at it; now, when we are becoming aware that we have sacrificed to Philistinism culture, and insight, and dignity, and acceptance, and weight among the nations, and hold on events that deeply concern us, and control of the future, and yet that it cannot even give us the fool's paradise it promised us, but is apt to break down, and to leave us with Mr. Roebuck's and Mr. Lowe's laudations of our matchless happiness . . . for our only comfort; at such a moment it needs some moderation not to be attacking Philistinism by storm, but to mine it through such gradual means as the slow approaches of culture.
> [*Complete Prose Works*, 3:385-86]

Roebuck's grandfather was John Roebuck (1718-94; see the *Dictionary of National Biography*); his recommendation of the Reverend John Aikin for a Warrington Academy tutorship is recorded in the academy's "Minute-Books," 5 Jan. 1758.

    10. Marx, *Capital*, 1:446. On philistinism in mid-Victorian Dissent, see Davie, *A Gathered Church*, 56-57, 58, 129, 136-38; although sympathetic to Dissent, Davie thinks its intellectual character did deteriorate. For detailed analysis of nineteenth-century fictional treatments of Dissent, see Cunningham, *Everywhere Spoken Against;* he admits that the novelists might have been made "suspicious of every part of the Dissent/industrial-town/millocracy alliance" by their "humane objections to the injustices of the factory system" (88).

    11. Cunningham, *Everywhere Spoken Against*, 23-24.

    12. Boswell, *The Life of Samuel Johnson*, 2:408-09. See Johnson, "Milton," 98: "Let not our veneration for Milton forbid us to look with some degree of merriment on great promises and small performance, on the man who hastens home because his countrymen are contending for their liberty, and, when he reaches the scene of action, vapours away his patriotism in a private boarding-school."

    13. W. Wordsworth, *Letters*, ed. Hill, 5:699; Cunningham, *Everywhere Spoken Against*, 86; Barbauld, *Address*, 5.

    14. Arnold, *Complete Prose Works*, 10:557. For Arnold's linkage of "Hebraism," or "strictness of conscience" invidiously contrasted to "spontaneity of consciousness" (i.e. "Hellenism" [5:165]), with Dissent, see 5:174-75 and chapter 5 of *Culture and Anarchy*. "The persevering vindictiveness of Arnold's polemic against Dissent is not always recognized," remarks Davie (*A Gathered Church*, 141). Certainly it was *felt* by a writer in the Unitarian *Inquirer*, reviewing the Arnold essay quoted in my text: ". . . a gratuitous sneer at his old enemies, the Dissenters. . . . We object to the wholly flippant . . . way in which Mr. Arnold superciliously dismisses a great historical movement which has played a foremost part in the history of this country for nearly two centuries and a half" ("Mr. Matthew Arnold and Isaiah of Jerusalem," 225).

    15. Martineau, *Autobiography*, 254. I have not attempted a survey of eighteenth-century anthologies, but two of the best known and most widely used, *Eighteenth Cen-*

tury Poetry and Prose, edited by Louis I. Bredvold et al., 2d ed. (1956), and *Eighteenth-Century English Literature,* edited by Geoffrey Tillotson et al. (1969), include between them Mandeville, "Junius," Hume, Burke, and Paine.

16. Arnold, *Complete Prose Works,* 9:179-81.

17. "The poems of Mrs. Barbauld . . . resemble most of the poems of [their] day . . . and to us lack the genuine poetical inspiration" (Howitt, *The Northern Heights of London,* 170). ". . . Chiefly written in the elegant pseudo-classical style of the close of the last century. . . . A certain artificiality of manner. . . . Her poetry is without deep thought or passion" (A.M.F. Robinson, "Mrs. Barbauld," 576). "Her poetry belongs to that artificial didactic school of the eighteenth century which is so antipathetic to the present age" (Baker, "Mrs. Barbauld," 308). It was, of course, Wordsworth himself who set this fashion by denouncing, in the preface to *Lyrical Ballads,* the poets of the eighteenth century.

18. This story found its way into the first biography of Wordsworth (C. Wordsworth, *Memoirs,* 2:223 n) but seems to have made its greatest impression when it reappeared in H.C. Robinson's *Diary, Reminiscences, and Correspondence,* 1:119. It was numbingly repeated: see, e.g., Baker, "Mrs. Barbauld," 308; Oliphant, *The Literary History of England,* 2:342; Robertson, *English Poetesses,* 92; "Mrs. Barbauld and the Aikin Family," 162; Ainger, "Mrs. Barbauld," 374; Pryde, "Letitia Barbauld." For Robinson's sending the poem to Dorothy Wordsworth, see Barbauld, *Poems,* 318.

19. Beard, "Anna Letitia Barbauld," 397. This reversal, which makes Wordsworth and Coleridge almost seem chronologically prior to Barbauld, is enacted again in the latest edition (the 6th) of *The Norton Anthology of English Literature.* Pamela Plimpton has noted that in the sequence of its pages "minor" writers follow "major" ones. "Barbauld's placement in the anthology therefore gives the impression that she 'followed' the major poets and had little influence on or association with the literary figures of the day" ("Anna Letitia Barbauld").

20. Ritchie, *A Book of Sybils,* 3.

21. Wimsatt, *Prose Style of Samuel Johnson,* 145; Wimsatt and Brooks, *Literary Criticism,* 43. Johnson commends "On Romances" in Boswell, *The Life of Samuel Johnson,* 3:172. That by "elderly . . . novelist" Wimsatt and Brooks mean Barbauld is clear from their index. Further details of Coleridge's baneful influence on Barbauld's reputation, as mediated through disciples such as John Livingston Lowes, were presented by Vargo, "'Mistress Bare and Bald.'"

22. Ellis, *Memoir,* ix. *Lessons for Children* "still stands unrivalled among children's books" (Hale, *Woman's Record,* 3:197). Hale's entry on Barbauld was reprinted in *Women of Worth* under the title "The Children's Favorite." William Howitt in 1869 opined that Barbauld's prose writings "do not retain their interest like her contributions to one of the most delightful books for children," *Evenings at Home* (*The Northern Heights of London,* 169). "Her little *Lessons* will commend themselves to everybody who loves childhood" (Oliphant, *The Literary History of England,* 2:342).

23. Arnold, *Complete Prose Works,* 9:162; [James], "The Schönberg-Cotta Family," 345; James, *The American Scene,* 242. On Stowe see Hedrick, *Harriet Beecher Stowe,* 288-91, 345-52. James did not, however, confine his antifeminism to "popular" writers;

he went after even George Eliot, using gender against her: "[S]he is eventually [i.e., ultimately] a feminine—a delightfully feminine—writer" (review of *Felix Holt*, quoted in Karl, *George Eliot*, 404). Karl rightly interprets "feminine" to mean "not strong enough," and "delightfully" is of course patronizing. Eliot was perhaps a particularly troubling phenomenon to James: a serious, intellectual woman artist whose books sold awfully well.

24. Davie, *A Gathered Church*, 34.

25. L. Aikin, letter to William Roscoe; Walpole, *Correspondence*, 11:169; [Polwhele], *The Unsex'd Females*, 16-17 n. In 1780 Walpole had been flattered by the belief that Barbauld had imitated *The Castle of Otranto* (*Correspondence*, 41:410; he is thinking of "Sir Bertrand, a Fragment," in her and John Aikin's *Miscellaneous Pieces*).

26. L. Aikin, "Memoir," xvii-xxiv. The poem, apparently never published by Barbauld herself, is poem 90 in *Poems*. Aikin gives just over one page of her sixty-seven-page "Memoir" to the early 90s, one of Barbauld's most active periods. She characterizes the letter on women's education as "a monument of [Barbauld's] acuteness and good sense" (xvi). Her treatment of this letter is so cautious as to verge on fraud: she silently abridges its text and gives the misleading impression that it was sent as a sort of rebuke to Elizabeth Montagu, the Bluestocking feminist. It was not. In its full biographical context, the letter will be seen to bear a rather different meaning from what it appears to say in Lucy Aikin's version.

27. Review of *Works*, by Barbauld, *Monthly Repository* 558; "A Memoir of Mrs. Barbauld," 237; Review of *Works*, by Barbauld, *Literary Gazette*, 611; "Lines to the Memory of Barbauld."

28. [Peabody], Review of *Works*, by Barbauld, 304; Review of *Legacy*, by Barbauld, *Eclectic Review*, 79.

29. "Sketch of Anna Letitia Barbauld"; Review of *Memoir of Barbauld*, by Ellis. Other commentaries emphasizing *Lessons for Children* or *Hymns in Prose* (or both) are Hale, *Woman's Record;* S.A.A., "Notable North Londoners"; and "Mrs. Barbauld, 1743-1825." Two efforts in the 1970s to strike up interest in Barbauld still emphasized *Hymns in Prose*, now as "influence" on the Great Romantics: Zall, "Wordsworth's 'Ode,'" and Pickering, "Mrs. Barbauld's *Hymns in Prose.*"

30. Jeffrey, Review of *Records of Woman*, 32, 33.

31. Balfour, *Working Women*, iii, 4, 6.

32. Review of *Works*, by Barbauld, *Monthly Repository*, 484; [Peabody], Review of *Works*, by Barbauld, 300; "Mrs. Barbauld," *Lady's Own Paper*, 49. Other examples of commentary stressing piety or high-mindedness occur in the headnote to Barbauld's poems in *Select Works of the British Poets*, 3:35 ("[T]he spirit of piety and benevolence that breathes through her works pervaded her life"), and Hale, *Woman's Record*, 197 ("that genuine and practical piety which ever distinguished her character"). On the local level, it persisted into the twentieth century: "A noble character, of high purpose and courage, . . . [Barbauld] passed through life leaving everywhere she went a strong influence for good, an incentive to look always for the best and highest" (Mrs. Ridgway, "An Address").

33. Ellis, "Memoir," 4, 5-6.

34. Ezell, *Writing Women's Literary History*, chaps. 3-4. "Establishing an ideology

190 ~ *William McCarthy*

of the feminine is a key feature of all these texts," whether popular anthologies or biographical encyclopedias (69).

35. Showalter, *Sexual Anarchy*, 76; Wilde, "English Poetesses," 108; Wilde, *The Importance of Being Earnest*, 141, 61, 60. The antifeminist backlash of the 90s is considered in Showalter, *Sexual Anarchy*, chap. 5, "King Romance." Its immediate object, among male writers just coming of age, was George Eliot, whose moral earnestness they perceived as "absurd solemnity . . . the essence of all that was old-fashioned and Victorian" (76). Eliot could thus "represent" the whole congelation of "high-toned" literary womanhood into which Barbauld and others had been rolled.

36. Stevens, *Collected Poems*, 59. Similar high jinks against Victorian womanhood are conducted in E.E. Cummings's sonnet, "the Cambridge ladies who live in furnished souls": "[T]hey believe in Christ and Longfellow, both dead," they do good works such as knitting for Polish refugees, and they gossip about their neighbors. The blinkered creatures see nothing beyond their social routines and "do not care" that "the moon rattles" in the sky "like a fragment of angry candy" (*Complete Poems*, 115). The lines from "the Cambridge ladies who live in furnishd souls," copyright 1923, 1951, (c) 1991 by the Trustees for the E.E. Cummings Trust. Copyright (c) 1976 by George James Firmage, from *Complete Poems: 1904-1962* by E.E. Cummings, edited by George J. Firmage. Reprinted by permission of Liveright Publishing Corporation.

37. Poems by Barbauld have been traced in fifty-four anthologies between 1827 and 1973, but the representation is thin; in later years it consists typically just of "Life" (Watson, "When Flattery Kills").

38. L. Aikin, "Memoir," lx; Barbauld to Maria Edgeworth, in LeBreton, *Memoir of Mrs. Barbauld*, 86; Mrs. H. Martin, Preface, iv. For Arthur Aikin's failure to capitalize on an opportunity to publish a Barbauld anthology in 1848, see Barbauld, *Poems*, xxxiv. Edward Everett acquired an autograph of poem 134, presumably while in London and through family channels (322-23). Martin's share of the family papers included John Aikin's journal of a visit to Holland in 1784 (see *Notes and Queries*) and 137 documents purchased before 1933 by the Scottish artist E.A. Hornel (now MS 15/21, Hornel Library, Kirkcudbright, Scotland). (I have not seen them listed in a sale catalog; provenance is inferred from the presence in MS 15/21 of letters addressed to M.E. Martin and her husband as well as to Martin's mother, A.L. LeBreton.)

39. Information from the late Mr. Conant Brodribb, who generously supplied me with family genealogies; see also "Mr. C. W. Brodribb." Barbauld's letters to Belsham were owned in 1883 by the Reid sisters of Hampstead, great-nieces of Belsham's husband (Ritchie, *A Book of Sybils*, vi, 6; Barbauld, *Poems*, 204). They died in 1914 and 1915 (*Times* [London], 20 Jan. 1915, 3 Feb. 1916). See also note 40 below.

40. Lincoln's Inn, Minutes, 46:340. For the fate of the papers I depend also on Lincoln's Inn, Rent Roll, and on information from Conant Brodribb. In "'Life, I Know Not,'" C.W. Brodribb specifies that the Palgrave School papers and the correspondence with Belsham perished. He mentions other papers and mementos that, housed elsewhere, survived; most of those were sold at auction in 1969 (Barbauld, *Poems*, 204).

Since writing this account, I have learned of another of the catastrophes that may befall books and papers kept only as "family memorabilia." An Aikin heir recently

deceased is said to have had a house full of family artifacts. But the house was ne-
glected, its roof leaked, and when her heirs entered it after her death they found that
the books had been turned to "glue" by rain. One book salvaged from that wreckage
bears Barbauld's autograph on its flyleaf. What we have lost will probably never be
known. For this heartbreaking news I am grateful to Elizabeth Mullard.

41. Information on Aikin-Sneath (the late Lady Rodgers) is from Lady Rodgers,
personal communication, June 1988, and from Aikin-Sneath, "Mrs. Barbauld"; her
first book was *Comedy in Germany in the first half of the Eighteenth Century* (1936). She
acquired Aikin family papers in 1958 (by gift from an Aikin heir) and 1969 (by pur-
chase of surviving Brodribb holdings) and generously permitted me to publish from
them.

42. Ezell, *Writing Women's Literary History*, 25-28, 30-38.

43. Williamson, "Who's Afraid of Mrs. Barbauld?" 91, 98, 90. Lucy Aikin at-
tributes to Barbauld "bashfulness," "extreme humility" in old age, and "reluctance to
appear before the public in the character of an author" ("Memoir," x, liv, xii; I do not say
that these claims are false, but they are selective, and they serve a tendency). The views
in the letter printed by Aikin were deprecated mildly in 1905 by Ainger, "Mrs. Barbauld,"
376, and more severely in 1933 by O'Malley, *Women in Subjection*, 120-21. "On Female
Studies" appeared in Barbauld, *Legacy*, and includes this sentence, singled out by
Williamson: "Men have various departments in active life; women have but one, and
all women have the same. . . . It is, to be a wife, a mother, a mistress of a family" (43).

44. Mahl and Koon, *The Female Spectator*, 260; M. Ross, *The Contours of Masculine
Desire*, 217. Ross offered Barbauld's poem "On a Lady's Writing" as "the best explana-
tion of Barbauld's conception of female poeticizing," which, he found, requires "femi-
nine poeticizing," like "feminine temper," to be "even, steady, easy, correct, and fair"
(217). Ross did, however, take Barbauld's poems more seriously than this equation
would seem to imply; his was the first extended discussion of them since her death.
Recently he has written a more considered essay ("Configurations of Feminine Re-
form") on *Eighteen Hundred and Eleven*.

45. Castle, "Unruly and Unresigned," 1227; Kelley and Feldman, introduction to
Romantic Women Writers, 3.

46. Anderson, "'The First Fire'"; I. Armstrong, "The Gush of the Feminine," 15.
Barbauld's criticism is considered by Rogers, "Anna Barbauld's Criticism of Fiction";
selections from the prefaces to *The British Novelists* appear in Folger Collective, *Women
Critics*. Over the years Myers has produced an exceptional body of essays on Barbauld's
sister writers, most notably Maria Edgeworth. The best essay ever written on Barbauld,
in my opinion, is Myers, "Of Mice and Mothers." Also perceptive is Robbins, *"Lessons
for Children."*

47. C.R. Aikin, Letter to A.L. Barbauld.

"Burst Are the Prison Bars"

Caroline Bowles Southey and
the Vicissitudes of Poetic Reputation

Kathleen Hickok

From her earliest publication, Caroline Bowles (1786-1854) was connected, for better or worse, with Robert Southey (1774-1843), poet laureate of England from 1813 until his death. Southey's effect on Caroline Bowles's poetry, and the cultural influence he exerted on her behalf, culminated with their marriage in 1839, a year and a half after his first wife died. Yet even though Southey's advice and patronage were of enormous benefit to Caroline Bowles during her lifetime, ultimately her association with him proved disastrous for her poetic reputation. When Robert Southey was consigned to critical oblivion after his death, his widow's critical reputation perished as well. Feminist critics of the 1930s (such as Virginia Woolf), who might have recognized and reclaimed poets like Bowles, were too invested in their own aesthetic and cultural differences from the nineteenth century to do so.

Only in the past decade or so has Caroline Bowles been rediscovered. In 1988 Stuart Curran included Bowles in a list of second-generation Romantic women poets who, according to Curran, were "more productive . . . and influential . . . than any male Romantic contemporary, with the exception of Leigh Hunt." In a recent review for the *Times Literary Supplement*, Isobel Armstrong declared Caroline Bowles a "major writer" of the Romantic period.[1] In this essay I will trace the vicissitudes of Caroline Bowles's critical reputation, in order to demonstrate her unique contributions to the redeveloping Romantic canon and in order to shed light on the processes by which a fine woman writer could be excluded for so long. I will illustrate her success with many Romantic genres, techniques, and themes; and I will give a brief overview of her finest work, *The Birthday,* a refreshingly female poetical autobiography published in 1836. Finally, I will indicate the place her poetry now seems destined to fill in the new annals of Romantic literary history: at the nexus of masculine and feminine Romanticisms.

Through a series of personal and professional interactions, which I will detail later, Caroline Bowles's literary reputation became firmly attached to that of Robert Southey. A woman writer's association with a prominent man of letters brings her to the public's attention but also puts her in double jeopardy: first, the critical reception of her work will suffer by implied comparison with his; then, if his literary reputation declines, hers will deteriorate along with it. The cases of Mary Shelley and Dorothy Wordsworth are instructive here. Marlon Ross considers that "their injection in the romantic canon is more a result of their kin relation to male romantics than a result of their 'romantic' tendencies." He continues, "[A]s long as such feminine influence is limited to wives and sisters . . . who write under the glaring eyes of self-professed great men, that influence will always be viewed as secondary and marginal at best," and the women's achievements will be impossible to disentangle from the men's.[2] It is ironic that Caroline Bowles's connection with Robert Southey finally served to obscure rather than highlight her literary work.

For (unfortunately for Bowles) Southey's critical reputation, already in jeopardy in his lifetime, was very much on the wane when he died. Lionel Madden notes in *Robert Southey: The Critical Heritage* (1972), "For serious readers in the first half of the nineteenth century he was an influential figure whose writings demanded critical assessment." But when Southey's ten-volume *Poetical Works* appeared in 1838, it prompted one reviewer to observe, "[I]t often appears to the reader of Southey as if he rather wanted the leisure than the faculty for the development of the finer shades of the poetical character."[3] With the publication of his son Cuthbert's biography in 1849-50, "for a few years Southey was a living subject of critical debate before he again passed into increasing obscurity." Madden recounts how after 1879 Southey's "reputation as a creative writer—and especially as a poet—suffered a severe decline," with the continuing effect that "few critics have sought to interpret Southey's poetry on its own terms."[4]

From this nadir few critics seem interested in retrieving Robert Southey's poetry even now. Why? In 1987 Marilyn Butler described Southey in language similar to that which has recently been applied to women poets of the Romantic period, by Anne K. Mellor and others:

Southey possessed non-canonical qualities—he was contentious rather than reassuring, common rather than genteel, provincial rather than metropolitan, international rather than national. And he was no solitary or recluse, amenable to study out of context, as the more favored Wordsworth and Keats were; he engaged actively with his contemporaries, and they with him. I think it will begin to seem more natural to us in the future to replace the old thin line of national [male] heroes with a richer and more credible notion: that writers represent groups and attitudes within the community, and therefore from time to time come dynamically into contention with one another.[5]

In comparison, Mellor posits a feminine Romanticism "based on a subjectivity constructed in relation to other subjectivities, hence a self that is fluid, absorptive, responsive, with permeable ego boundaries. This self typically located its identity within a larger human nexus, a family or social community." Mellor believes that, as opposed to men's preferred lyrical forms, this feminine ideology "found its appropriate mode of linguistic expression [in the novel,] . . . and in those poetic genres which celebrate the values of the quotidian, of daily domestic and social involvements." Similarly, Meena Alexander writes, "Where the [male] Romantic poets had sought out the clarities of visionary knowledge, women writers, their lives dominated by the bonds of family and the cultural constraints of femininity, altered that knowledge, forcing it to come to terms with the substantial claims of a woman's view of the world." In addition, these women writers "turned their literary powers to a clarification of genius that had to struggle through its enforced marginality, work against images that would deplete it of power."[6] The marginalization of Robert Southey may reflect his lack of conformity to the masculine norms of Romanticism as defined by twentieth-century criticism.

Perhaps the tentative moves toward rehabilitation of Southey's critical reputation prefigure a concurrent restoration of Caroline Bowles's reputation as well. Certainly the obscurity into which Bowles's reputation vanished was much more profound than that of Southey's. A check of the *MLA Bibliography* reveals 160 citations of articles and books about Robert Southey between 1963 and 1996. For Caroline Bowles, such a check reveals absolutely nothing.

The history of Caroline Bowles's critical reception from the 1840s to the present is quite enlightening. Though she was always evaluated as a "poetess" in the nineteenth century, Bowles was initially compared—favorably—with respected male poets. "Mrs. Southey," Hartley Coleridge wrote in 1840, "is the Cowper of our modern poetesses. She has much of that great writer's humour, fondness for rural life, melancholy, pathos, and moral satire." In the 1790s, Robert Southey's poetry had also been compared with William Cowper's, first by Charles Lamb and then by S.T. Coleridge; Cowper, of course, was much admired at that time.[7] Hartley Coleridge compared Bowles's work to George Crabbe's as well, calling "The Widow's Tale" "a beautiful little poem in which Cowper and Crabbe seem united." Like Southey, Hartley Coleridge had no patience with incorrect versification, and it seemed to him that many of the young generation of "modern poetesses" he was reading paid little attention to this important element in a poem; whereas Bowles's poetry he declared "not only generally correct, but in several instances, of very great beauty and perfection."[8]

In 1848 Frederic Rowton included Caroline Southey in *The Female Poets of Great Britain*. Like Coleridge, he approved of the "very perfection" of her verse, and he elevated her over her female peers. His praise is similar to Robert Southey's private commendations of Bowles's work; in a personal letter to Bowles, Southey complimented an early draft of *The Birthday*, saying, "The flow of verse is natural, and the language unconstrained—both as they should be."[9] In comparison, Rowton writes, "It would be difficult, I think, to find among our Female poets, one who in vigour of mind, intensity of feeling, and gracefulness of expression, excels Mrs. Southey. Her poems have a simplicity, a naturalness, which is as pleasing as it is rare . . . whilst at the same time she has the quickness of vision and the sensitiveness of sympathy which characterise her sex."[10]

The *Athenaeum*'s unsigned obituary of Caroline Southey in 1854 begins, "The interest which attaches to the memory of Caroline Southey, not only as the wife of one of the distinguished men of our time, but as an author of no common mark herself, would warrant an extended notice of her life and writings." She never received such a notice, but the *Athenaeum* article compared *The Birthday* with Wordsworth's *Prelude* (1850) and ranked it "among the most graceful and touching efforts of female genius."[11] The bulk of the obituary is a summary of Caroline Bowles's early life, as gleaned from *The Birthday*, and a detailed discussion of her relationship with Robert Southey, including the controversy over their marriage. About forty lines are quoted from *The Birthday* and about sixty from an 1851 letter by Bowles regarding Cuthbert Southey.

Thus far we can observe that Bowles was consistently evaluated by contemporary reviewers as a surprisingly good poet (for a woman) and as the protégée, wife, and widow of the poet laureate. Within twenty-five years, her critical reputation had seriously eroded.

Eric Robertson, writing in 1883 about "English poetesses," notes a serious decline in Bowles's critical reputation, dating back at least to 1867 when "Messrs. Blackwood had the temerity to collect Mrs. Southey's verse, and publish it . . . [though] there was hardly any demand for the book." Praise for Bowles's grace and skill in versification had disappeared; instead Robertson suggests that her work is prosaic: "Mrs. Southey's prose reads much better when it is not snipped up into lengths and called poetry." Edward Dowden, who respected Bowles, nevertheless emphasized her feminine gender. "Her best work," he wrote in 1881, "[though] small in quantity, may rank with the best of its kind that English women have wrought in English verse." Dowden believed her longer poems justified regarding Bowles as "the Crabbe among our modern poetesses," but he went on to qualify that praise significantly: she has become "a Crabbe in whom womanly tenderness [read sentimentality] replaces the hard veracity characteristic of that eminent poet."[12]

In 1892 Alfred H. Miles, in *The Poets and the Poetry of the Century*, also mentions the decline in Bowles's reputation, noting rather sadly that "the writer, who was called 'the Cowper of poetesses,' and declared to be equal to Mrs. Hemans in her own day, is now denied all praise, and treated with but scant courtesy." He sees no prospect of this changing: "Mrs. Southey's verse had a greater charm for her own generation than it can ever have again." Miles connects Bowles with the Lake School and sees her as having followed the lead of Wordsworth poetically. Like Robertson, Miles judges her poetic form as "faulty" though natural, spontaneous, and simple. The best thing he can find to say about her is, "She . . . had a far better idea of the difference between true and false sentiment than most of the women poets of her time."[13] The terms of this judgment illustrate the continuing damage that antisentimental criticism was doing to the reputations of many early- nineteenth-century women poets, including both Bowles and Felicia Hemans. For the next thirty or forty years, Caroline Bowles Southey seems to have disappeared from critical commentary.

In light of the feminism of the 1920s and 1930s, in particular the life and writing of Virginia Woolf, we might have expected Felicia Hemans and Caroline Bowles (and perhaps many other women poets of the Romantic era) to be restored to the canon. But that did not occur. In fact, as Margaret Ezell has pointed out, an uncritical reliance on Virginia Woolf, coupled with an evolutionary theory of women's writing that understands it as culminating in our own times, has misled even contemporary feminist critics so that "in the act of preserving some women writers, we have inadvertently exiled many [others]."[14] That is exactly what Virginia Woolf did, most obviously in the essays collected in *The Common Reader* (1925, 1932), but also in *A Room of One's Own* (1928) and *Orlando* (1928). In *The Common Reader*, Woolf sorts out the "great" women poets of the nineteenth century (Elizabeth Barrett Browning and Christina Rossetti) from the deservedly obscure ones (Jane and Ann Taylor, Mary Russell Mitford, Dorothy Wordsworth). Her tone of condescension to the obscure poets hardly encourages us to search out their poetry and read it for ourselves.

Like most modernists, Woolf clearly prefers the literature of her own day. As she writes in "How It Strikes a Contemporary," despite the glories of the British Romantic period, "[t]here is something about the present which we would not exchange, though we were offered a choice of all past ages to live in. . . . We are sharply cut off from our predecessors. A shift in the scale—the war, the sudden slip of masses held in position for ages—has shaken the fabric from top to bottom, alienated us from the past and made us perhaps too vividly conscious of the present." Even in the great books of the past, Woolf finds an unavoidable dullness. "There is an unabashed tranquility in page after page of Wordsworth and Scott and Miss Austen which is sedative to the verge of somnolence." Their very moral self-assurance annoys her. "They have their judgment of conduct. They know the relations of human beings towards each other and towards the universe. Neither of them probably has a thing to say about the matter outright, but everything depends on it."[15] Woolf's rendition of the moral aesthetic to which Robert Southey and Caroline Bowles subscribed is explicable from a modernist point of view, but it seems unnecessarily contemptuous.

In *A Room of One's Own* Woolf offers many explanations why there have been so few great women writers, yet in so doing she begs the question. In *Orlando*, Woolf ridicules the prolixity and sentimentality of nineteenth-century women's verse as Orlando is overcome with poetic inspiration: "[T]o her astonishment and alarm, the pen began to curve and caracole with the smoothest possible fluency. Her page was written in the neatest sloping Italian hand with the most insipid verse she had ever read in her life." *Orlando* is dedicated to Vita Sackville-West, who shared Woolf's opinion of the verses that appeared in nineteenth-century annuals, as poems by both Caroline Bowles and Robert Southey did. "The scent of the boudoir hangs over all these miniature pages," Sackville-West complained. "They are so exceedingly ladylike." Like Woolf, Sackville-West was very aware of a shift from the traditional style and subject matter of nineteenth-century women poets to those of the moderns: "Far from being prophets, they [the earlier writers] were almost anachronisms. Literature was permitted them as a respectable pursuit, but in the glue and treacle of literary convention they had remained embedded."[16]

This brief account suggests how feminist critics of the 1920s and 1930s, in their rejection of British patriarchy and various Victorian social and aesthetic structures, also rejected women writers whose work we might have expected them to embrace. Feminist critics have long lamented the male modernist establishment's apparent failure to recognize the quality of so many good female writers; as an object lesson, we may want to remember also that female—even feminist—modernists helped establish the principles of critical selectivity that we are now struggling against.

The Adventurous Thirties: A Chapter in the Women's Movement (1933) contains the only rehabilitative feminist scholarship on British Romantic women poets that I could locate from this period. Janet Courtney interprets the 1830s as a period of early feminist activity, citing Harriet Martineau's opinion that "the best advocates of women's rights would be the successful professional women and the 'substantially successful authoresses.'" Yet the women poets of the decade, Courtney concedes, "were of unequal merit. Some of them had no merit at all." Courtney finds Caroline Bowles Southey's life interesting, though it is hard to see how she detects incipient feminism in the poems she quotes ("The Pauper's Deathbed," "To a Dying Infant," and "To the Sweet-Scented Cyclamens.") Ultimately, Courtney is out of sympathy with Bowles's poetry, judging it prosaic, dull, and trivial. She recurs to the poet laureate's influence to explain Bowles's success: "Caroline, like Wordsworth's Lucy, might have bloomed, a violet by a mossy stone, as unknown as she was sweet and fragrant, had not Southey found her out and brought her into the Lakeland garden of poets."[17]

A few years later, Stanley Kunitz and Howard Haycraft assert conclusively in *British Authors of the Nineteenth Century* that the literary reputation of Caroline Bowles Southey was "based primarily upon her intimate association with Southey, under whose influence she wrote." In 1948 Jack Simmons, in his book on Robert Southey, compares Caroline Bowles with Felicia Hemans, whom he obviously does not admire: "Like her contemporary Mrs. Hemans, Caroline Bowles had a slender vein of true poetry in her, thickly overlaid though it was by her didactic purpose and her sentimentality." As for the comparison with Crabbe formerly asserted by both Hartley Coleridge and Edward Dowden, Simmons writes, "The exact antithesis of her poetry is Crabbe's . . . for while hers is weak and imprecise, his is powerful, sombre, accurately observed, and therefore moving." The dismissal is now complete. Bowles has no literary merit and is not at all like Crabbe but opposite to him. As Woolf says in *A Room of One's Own* (quoting the old gentlemen who used to save one so much thinking), "Cats do not go to heaven. Women cannot write the plays of Shakespeare."[18]

Thus dispatched, Caroline Bowles remained extinguished for another thirty years, until I encountered her in my 1984 study *Representations of Women.*[19] The passage that Courtney had quoted disdainfully to illustrate the "infantile dullness" of *The Birthday,* I quoted approvingly as Bowles's complaint about the negative impact of "feminine accomplishments" on women in the early nineteenth century. Then I added, "Caroline Bowles's literary achievements might have been greater had she been able to spend more of her youth in pursuit of mental culture and less in training for future domestic duties." Although I had seen the feminist implications of both the existence and content of *The Birthday,* I think I was misled by prior criticism into an unjustified dismissal of Bowles's aesthetic achievements. After rereading her poems in light of recent critical theories about Romantic women poets and feminine Romanticism, I view Bowles as a particularly effective member of that "group of women writing during the [early] nineteenth century who see themselves and are seen by their contemporaries as a new literary breed," defined by Ross: women writers whose "gender is so crucial a factor in their cultural and literary experience that it alters the effect of shared social conditions and turns these writers into a distinct class, with its own ideological patterning." Nonetheless, I cannot quite agree with Ross that these women poets are not therefore "a species of the overarching class of romantic poets," for I believe Bowles succeeds as a member of this predominantly male class also.[20]

In addition to Mellor and Alexander, Curran and Armstrong are helpful here. Mellor actually follows Curran in emphasizing the importance of the quotidian, a feature particularly evident in the Romantic privileging of "the vernacular, what we are accustomed to call, following Wordsworth, 'the real language of men.'" Curran adds, "It was even more so, with fine irony, the language of women." Curran also points out that "the foundation on which Romanticism was reared" was the cult of sensibility. The later rejection of sensibility as overly sentimental was certainly connected with its continuous use by women writers, as Armstrong's recent explication of the "expressive tradition" of nineteenth-century women poets shows. Armstrong suggests that, at its best, this female tradition "could bring the resources of the affective state to social and political analysis and speculate on the constraints of the definition of feminine subjectivity in an almost innumerable variety of contexts, indirectly and directly."[21] Even a brief review of the work of Caroline Bowles reveals it as an excellent example of feminine Romanticism, sensibility, and the expressive tradition, with *The Birthday* being a particularly fine example but only one among many such poems.

Furthermore, Caroline Bowles deserves to be recognized as a major writer in traditional Romantic terms. She is comparable to Wordsworth in portraying the depth of feeling and the quality of life of common people, especially rural folk. Bowles also shares the Romantic philosophies of transcendence through poetic inspiration and close association with nature in both picturesque and sublime modes. She works successfully in diverse Romantic genres such as the elegy, the ode, the hymn, the lyrical ballad, the sonnet, the meditation, the satire, and the poetic autobiography. Her versification is vigorous and correct, while giving the impression of being natural, free-flowing, and unconstrained. She is equally effective in pathetic and humorous modes. Her social themes include protests against injustices associated with race, class, and gender: she vividly portrays the human costs of enclosure, war, and the factory system. She also works within established women's genres of the period, offering feminist analyses of British culture. Whether we choose to read Robert Southey again or not, we ought to read Caroline Bowles.

For although she worked comfortably within (male) Romantic traditions, she also contributed a feminist sensibility and worldview that we have come to value today and that male writers (even Robert Southey) could not offer. She is uniquely placed to illustrate Ross's premise that "[a]s we recover [women poets'] place in history, we must be sure not to examine them in isolation. Too wary of wedding them erroneously to the romantic movement, we may stray too far in the other direction and forget their complex interrelations with romantic discourse."[22] A survey of Caroline Bowles's career as a poet will, I hope, establish her cultural and literary significance both during the Romantic period and today.

In 1818, in financial distress after the death of her parents, Caroline Bowles dared to send a letter to Laureate Robert Southey, whom she had never met, requesting his help. She asked him to read a long poem she had written and, if he found it worthy, to help her find a publisher. The poem was a metrical tale about a runaway daughter deserted by her husband; the young woman seeks consolation at the moonlit tomb of her mother. (The poet's own mother, a widow, had died in 1816.) To Bowles's great relief, the poet laureate replied with encouragement and specific literary advice. Southey helped Bowles revise her manuscript, and then he sent it to publisher John Murray with his endorsement. Although Murray declined to publish *Ellen Fitzarthur,* Longmans subsequently accepted it and brought it out in 1820. Southey promoted the book in his circle of influence, and he continued to correspond with Caroline Bowles for twenty years.[23] During this time Bowles published four more volumes of verse: *The Widow's Tale* (1822), *Solitary Hours* (1826), *Tales of the Factories* (1833), and *The Birthday* (1836).

The poems in *The Widow's Tale* and *Solitary Hours,* many of them previously published in *Blackwood's Magazine,* clearly show the influence of Southey and the other Lake Poets, particularly Wordsworth. Jean Raimond, in a recent reassessment of Robert Southey's poetic achievement, insists that Southey's early ballads "remain the most living part of Southey's poetical output. . . . 'Pastoral poetry,' Southey wrote in his common place book, 'must be made interesting by story. The characters must be such as are to be found in nature; these must be sought in an age or country of simple manners.' The resemblance to Wordsworth's own theory of poetry is striking," says Raimond. If Southey's most Wordsworthian poetry is what we chiefly value today, the same is also true for Bowles. Introducing a 1996 reprint of *The Widow's Tale,* Jonathan Wordsworth asserts, "Bowles is by instinct a Wordsworthian." In her lyrical ballads, he finds, Bowles "has taken Wordsworth's preoccupation with elemental states of mind on into the world of her own observation," which I would point out is a female world. "It is this Wordsworthian power to imply depth of unvoiced feeling," he continues, "that gives strength to Bowles's . . . narratives."[24] "The Widow's Tale" and "William and Jean" are examples of such poems. Both render the alienation and sorrow of wandering heroes from among the common folk, men who return to scenes of natural and familial devastation in the old rural neighborhoods they abandoned to women and children—rather like the Wanderer coming upon Margaret of the ruined cottage in book 1 of Wordsworth's *Excursion* (1814).

The Widow's Tale also includes the melodramatic sketch "Pride and Passion," which treats sympathetically the theme of sexual and romantic attraction across racial lines—most unusual at a time when, Moira Ferguson reports, "any discourse favoring miscegenation induce[d] massive furor." Even in 1881

Dowden obliquely described this daring piece only as a "passionate and tragic dramatic sketch" that "does not wholly fail of its intention."[25] In "Pride and Passion," Bowles joins the growing cadre of literary women publishing critiques of British racism and cultural imperialism.

Solitary Hours, for which Southey provided the title, likewise includes pathetic narrative poems portraying the lives and emotions of common people, such as "The Broken Bridge," which Hartley Coleridge considered especially fine.[26] It also contains a few prose pieces, both humorous and sentimental, and numerous affecting lyrics of loss and regret, some with overt political implications. For example, "The Mother's Lament," an antiwar poem, is comparable to Southey's "The Battle of Blenheim" (1798). It also anticipates Elizabeth Barrett Browning's "Mother and Poet" (1862), as the maternal speaker contrasts her loss with the nation's gain:

> They told me Vict'ry's laurels wreath'd
>   His youthful temples round—
> That "Vict'ry!" from his lips was breathed,
>   The last exulting sound—
> Cold comfort to a mother's ear,
> That long'd his *living* voice to hear-[27]

"The Mariner's Hymn" and "The Pauper's Deathbed," also from this volume, were among the most popular of Bowles's many poems on mortality. In "The Pauper's Deathbed," the first five stanzas convey the meager life and pitiful death of the pauper; then Bowles makes a classic Romantic move toward transcendence:

> Oh, change! oh wondrous change!
>   Burst are the prison bars:
> This moment *there,* so low,
> So agonised, and now
>   Beyond the stars![28]

The powerful imprisonment and escape image—"Burst are the prison bars"—may also reflect a feminist yearning for freedom from societal constraints. The transformation in status—the elevation of the agonized and lowly soul—likewise suggests the possibility of a posthumous apotheosis, which we can connect with current feminist attempts to reevaluate women writers' achievements and transform the literary canon.

The genre of elegiac verses commemorating the deaths of mothers or children was another type of poem on mortality that Bowles, like so many other women poets of the era, often had occasion to write. When Robert Southey and his wife Edith lost their daughter in 1827, Bowles sent them "To the

Memory of Isabel Southey." Southey was very moved by these verses, which conclude with the following stanza:

> 'Tis ever thus—'tis ever thus, with creatures heavenly fair,
> Too finely framed to 'bide the brunt more earthly natures bear,
> A little while they dwell with us, blest ministers of love,
> Then spread the wings we had not seen, and seek their home above.[29]

Southey wrote to Bowles, "I put them into my wife's hand, and she expressed that sort of pleasure which deep grief is capable of feeling. The pain would have been there in any case: the gratification was so much gain. Thank you, dear friend—thank you, thank you, and God bless you."[30]

Notwithstanding his personal gratitude for this melancholy poem, Southey repeatedly attempted to persuade Caroline Bowles that she should modify the unrelenting pathos of her subject matter. "I do not like such poems," he wrote in 1818, "because I am old enough to avoid all unnecessary pain. Real griefs do not lessen the susceptibility for fictitious ones, but they take away all desire for them." On reading *The Widow's Tale* in 1822, Southey wrote, "[W]hether most to find fault with you for choosing such deeply tragic subjects, or to praise you for the manner in which you have treated them I know not. . . . Give us, I entreat you, a picture in summer and sunshine—a tale that in its progress and termination shall answer to the wishes of the reader." Bowles answered Southey's complaints tactfully: "I entirely agree with you," she wrote: "[W]e need not create to ourself fictitious griefs; life has too many real sorrows; but the mind recently afflicted colours everything with its own sadness." Bowles is probably referring to the loss of her mother. She may also be intending to convey in her verses the tragedy and pathos of women's lives in the early nineteenth century. As I have noted elsewhere, numerous such poems appeared throughout the century reflecting upon "woman's lot" in life; most are melancholy if not tragic in tone. In addition, Bowles explained to Southey that her various editors much preferred her to write sentimental poems: "[S]omehow all the worthies I have ever written for think fit to discourage my comic vein. . . . [T]hey *will* have me 'like Niobe, all tears.'"[31] Bowles had to walk a particularly fine line in addressing the recommendations of her important mentor, Robert Southey, and yet still satisfying the requirements of her publishers, with their sense of the proper tone and subject matter for a poetess. Not until her 1836 volume, *The Birthday*, did she publish a poem of "summer and sunshine."

Instead, Bowles's next volume, *Tales of the Factories* (1833), was an impassioned political protest against inhumane factory conditions, anticipating *A Voice from the Factories* (1836) by Caroline Norton and "The Cry of the Children" (1843) by Elizabeth Barrett Browning. According to Dowden, it was "the actual miseries of English workmen and their children [that] moved Caroline Bowles, in 1833, to write her little volume, *Tales of the Factories*— verses which indignation made. . . . Some of the gaunt misery of the factory life is powerfully expressed in the first of these poems. What is lurid and exaggerated in the remaining pieces is accounted for, if not justified, by the Minutes of Evidence taken before the Committee of the House of Commons." Dowden's condescending description of this book is usefully corrected 115 years later by Jonathan Wordsworth, who finds that *Tales of the Factories* contains "protest-poetry of a very high order . . . [in which] bitter unexpected wit and sudden tenderness show a power one has not known [Bowles] to possess" before she turned her attention to the abuses of the factory system.[32]

Southey read some of these poems in manuscript and encouraged Bowles to publish them. For despite harsh criticisms from Byron and other political liberals, who believed that Southey had abandoned the radical views he espoused as a young man, there was a persistent humanitarian impulse in Southey. As Madden remarks, "Twentieth-century social historians . . . have found much to praise in [Southey's] support for human dignity and individual freedom, his attacks upon the materialism of industrial society, and his agitation for factory reform." "At heart," reflects Dowden, "Southey's poems are in the main the outcome of his moral nature; . . . its breath of life is the moral ardour of a nature strong and generous." About the moral imperative of their work, Southey and Bowles were in agreement, although Southey did not approve of the overt didacticism that sometimes appeared in Bowles's work. Southey's own goal was "to diffuse through my poems a sense of the beautiful and good . . . rather than to aim at the exemplification of any particular moral precept." Still, when he asserts, "The most gratifying reward that an author can receive, is to know that his writings have strengthened the weak, established the wavering, given comfort to the afflicted, and obtained the approbation of the wise and the good," he characterizes the moral intent of Caroline Bowles's poetry as well.[33] As Woolf suggests, the moral convictions of these Romantic poets were strong and deeply held, and the writers confidently expected their readers to share them.

The literary advice that Southey consistently gave to Caroline Bowles was stylistic as well as thematic. He cautioned her against inexact, obscure, and illogical uses of language that he spotted in *Ellen Fitzarthur*, and he showed her exactly how to correct them. He urged her to undertake a philosophical poem in blank verse, situated in her New Forest home in Buckland; in response, she wrote *The Birthday*, which became her life's work, the masterpiece of her mature years. On the other hand, as with his thematic and tonal suggestions, Bowles did not always accept Southey's advice. He was eager to collaborate with her on a narrative about Robin Hood, and he insisted that Bowles could master the complex verse form of Southey's epic *Thalaba the Destroyer* (1801); however, Bowles found it uncongenial at best and impossible at worst. The collaboration never came to pass, though a Robin Hood fragment by Southey was published in a joint edition of poems by Bowles and Southey in 1847, several years after Southey's death.[34]

Most if not all of the pieces Bowles contributed to the Robin Hood volume had been previously published; they include "The Evening Walk" and "The Young Grey Head," pathetic poetic narratives in the Wordsworthian vein similar to those in *The Widow's Tale*, and "The Murder Glen," in which, wrote Dowden, "horror and pity are strangely and powerfully intertwined. The murderer's idiot child . . . pleads, like one of Victor Hugo's piteous human grotesques, for all outcast, despised, downtrodden things." Dowden also noted that Bowles managed the rhymed couplet, a difficult verse form, "with an ease and strength which make one wonder how and where they were acquired."[35] They were acquired from Southey's tutelage of course, and from Caroline Bowles's decades of hard work. But the height of her achievement occurs not in the Robin Hood volume, but in *The Birthday*.

Apparently Bowles began writing the title poem *The Birthday* in 1819; with Southey's encouragement she continued writing it over a period of fifteen years. Southey seems to have recognized *The Birthday* as her potential masterpiece: "[G]o on with it," he told her, "and you will produce something which may hold a permanent place in English literature. . . . Everybody will recognize the truth of the feeling which produces it, and there is a charm in the picture, the imagery, and the expression, which cannot fail to be felt. . . . I am too busy at present to say more; only understand these hurried lines as encouraging you in the strongest and most unequivocal manner to proceed." Armstrong calls *The Birthday* "a gloriously lyrical autobiographical poem," truly comparable with Wordsworth's *The Prelude: or, Growth of a Poet's Mind*. Both poems were written, Armstrong says, "to investigate the deepest ties of [the author's] experience." Indeed, as she notes, *The Birthday* could easily adapt a subtitle from the *Prelude:* "the growth of a *woman* poet's mind." In this lengthy but highly readable blank verse poem, Bowles recounts her earliest memories of belonging to a loving family, receiving a girl's education, discovering literature, communing with nature, and, as she matures, becoming more and more aware of cultural injustices. The innocence of her girlhood is rendered nostalgically and ultimately contrasted with an adult woman's recognition of deprivation and loss. Dowden "regretted that the poetical autobiography goes no farther than her childhood."[36] *The Birthday* is complete enough, though; in it Bowles reveals her mature philosophy of life even as she recounts its development from early experiences.

An only child, Bowles was cherished and indulged by her parents, her grandmother, her great-grandmother, and her faithful nurse. Because he had no sons, her father often took her hiking and fishing with him, and she remembers with great pleasure the country locales they frequented. For youthful companionship she turned to animals, investing a succession of pets with both sentimental and practical interest. Childhood scenes and stories are portrayed in all of their particulars, with the "moral" understated. The episode of the pet lamb, recounted in part 3, is characteristic. On a cold and snowy night, an orphaned lamb is presented to young Caroline by a local farmer. She nurses it, romps with it, and after the lamb, nearly grown, wreaks havoc in the house and garden, she is persuaded to allow it to rejoin the flock. Not until many years later does the adult Caroline realize the probable fate of the beloved lamb in that year's market. She accepts both the loss of innocence and the mortality of all beloved creatures with philosophical grace and even humor:

> I thought not (witless!) of the butcher's cart,
> Nor transmutation fell, by murderous sleight
> Of sheep to mutton. To thy manes peace,
> Offending fav'rite! wheresoever thy grave.[37]

Wordsworth's "Pet Lamb" (1800) seems distanced and artificial by comparison with Bowles's first-person treatment of the same theme.

As a history of a spirited nineteenth-century girl's upbringing, the poem contains many implicitly feminist passages about the disparate education and social expectations for girls and for boys, the tediousness of required feminine accomplishments like needlework, the frustration of being discouraged from adventurous play:

> Then there were dismal outcries—shrill complaints—
> From angry Jane, of frocks and petticoats
> All grim with muddy stains and ghastly rents;—
> " 'Twas all in vain," the indignant damsel vowed,
> " 'Twas all in vain to toil for such a child—
> For such a Tom-boy! Climbing up great trees—
> Scrambling through brake and bush, and hedge and ditch,
> For paltry wild-flowers. Always without gloves
> Grubbing the earth up like a little pig
> With her own nails, and (just as bad as *he*)
> Racing and romping with that dirty beast."
> Then followed serious,—"But the time will come
> You'll be ashamed, Miss, of such vulgar ways :
> You a young lady!—Not much like one now."
> [2:70]

Humorous passages such as this alternate with serious and abstract treatments of philosophic themes, such as nature, art, and poetry.

Bowles remembers how her fond parents encouraged her earliest efforts to write: "For ardently I longed to scrawl at will / The teeming fancies of a busy brain" (1:21). Her poetic inspiration, as she explains it, is Romantic in its sensitivity and responsiveness to Nature:

> Nature in me hath still her worshipper,
> And in my soul her mighty spirit still
> Awakes sweet music, tones, and symphonies,
> Struck by the master-hand from every chord.
> But prodigal of feeling, she withholds
> The glorious power to pour its fulness out;
> And in mid-song I falter, faint at heart,
> With consciousness that every feeble note
> But yields to the awakening harmony
> A weak response—a trembling echo still.
> [1:23]

The self-effacing aspect of this description of poetic power illustrates not only a typical Romantic lamentation, but a requisite feminine modesty as well. Bowles explicitly rejects the idea of herself as extraordinary:

> Alas, dear friends!
> No heaven-born genius, as ye simply deemed,
> Stirred in my childish heart the love of song;
> 'Twas feeling, finely organised perhaps
> To keen perception of the beautiful,
> The great in art or nature, sight or sound,
> The working of a restless spirit, long
> For every pastime cast upon itself—
> [1:22]

Besides the feminist consciousness throughout the poem, there is also the "subtle critique of middle class values" which Armstrong rightly identifies[38]— and some not-so-subtle criticism of British cynicism and greed, as well. For example, in the midst of describing her favorite childhood toys, Bowles writes:

> His hand is eagerly stretch'd out on whom
> Fortune bestows a sceptre; his no less
> To whom she gives the baton of command,
> The marshal's truncheon; and she smiles herself
> At his more solemn transport, from beneath
> The penthouse of enormous wig, who eyes
> The seals of office dangling in his reach.
> And bearded infants—babies six feet high,
> Scramble for glitt'ring baubles; ribbons, stars,

And garters, that she jingles on a pole
For prizes to the foremost in the race,
Or who leaps highest, or with supplest joints
Who twists, and turns, and creeps, and wriggles best.
[2:95]

This Swiftian satirical passage contrasts the innocent delights of children with the cynical manipulations of grasping adults—and contrasts these yet again with the wholesome and productive life of Ephraim, the Bowles family's gardener, who hand-fashioned miniature wooden toys for little Caroline.

The breadth and quality of *The Birthday* can only be suggested by these few excerpts; Bowles rarely falters throughout the whole. But readers of Wordsworth's *Prelude* will find in comparison that *The Birthday* offers an absorbing exploration of the development and fate of "Shakespeare's sister" during the Romantic era (to borrow Virginia Woolf's designation for the gifted woman writer of the Renaissance). An entire essay could easily be devoted to the Romantic similarities with Wordsworth's poem and the feminine differences of view that *The Birthday* simultaneously sustains. The *Athenaeum* obituary of 1854 was certainly correct in placing Bowles's text alongside Wordsworth's, even though the obituary writer treated Bowles's poem as an enlightening source of biography rather than an important work of art. In fact, like *The Prelude, The Birthday* was both.

In addition to the title poem, *The Birthday* contains many other mature pieces, for example, "The Churchyard," a Romantic odal hymn challenging both Keats's "Ode to a Nightingale" (1819) and Shelley's "To a Skylark" (1820). "The Churchyard" expresses the Romantic longing for freedom and transcendence through nature and through poetic inspiration. The first seven stanzas are reminiscent of the "Graveyard School" of poetry and also draw upon Bowles's popular prose tales and meditations called "Chapters on Churchyards," which were published in the 1820s in *Blackwood's Magazine*. The last three stanzas of "The Churchyard" obviously constitute a response to Shelley:

And upward toward the heavenly portal sprang
A skylark, scattering off the feathery rain—
Up from my very feet;—
And oh! how clear and sweet
Rang through the fields of air his mounting strain.

Blithe, blessed creature! take me there with thee—
I cried in spirit—passionately cried—
But higher still and higher
Rang out that living Lyre,
As if the Bird disdained me in his pride.

And I was left below, but now no more
Plunged in the doleful realms of Death and Night—
Up with the skylark's lay,
My soul had winged her way
To the supernal source of Life and Light.[39]

Bowles's skylark is "blithe" like Shelley's. Also like Shelley's, Bowles's bird flies "Higher still and higher," singing all the while, as the speaker yearns to accompany the bird to glory. In Keats's poem also, the speaker follows the flight and song of the bird beyond his own limitations. Despite some critics' attempts to make the final "Forlorn" stanza of the Nightingale ode register a net gain instead of a loss,[40] the ode's speaker returns in the end, as does Shelley's, to his own "sole self," uncertain of the meaning of his experience, uncertain even of his own state of consciousness: "[D]o I wake or sleep?"

Keats's poem is marked with imagery of death and decay; in this regard, too, "The Churchyard" resembles "Ode to a Nightingale." Keats writes, "I have been half in love with easeful Death / . . . / Now more than ever seems it rich to die, / To cease upon the midnight with no pain." In stanza 4 of "The Churchyard," Bowles writes:

Death—death was in my heart. Methought I felt
A heavy hand, that pressed me down below;
And some resistless power
Made me, in that dark hour,
Half long *to be*, where I abhorred to go.

Keats's speaker imagines himself dying while the song of the nightingale rings in his ears; in contrast, while she half wishes for death, Bowles's speaker has not yet encountered her skylark. When she does, the energy of the poem changes sharply. The bird is announced cosmically, by a breaking of the oppressive weather—a breeze high in the trees, a flash of lightning, a thunder-peal, cool raindrops, blue sky. The bird springs heavenward to join with these forces, and the speaker is carried aloft with his song, "now no more / Plunged in the doleful realms of Death and Night." Bowles suspends the reader in midflight toward a universal glory. Perhaps Bowles's speaker is still not fully satisfied, but unlike Keats's and Shelley's she seems genuinely to have drawn inspiration and comfort from this flight of the spirit. She has solved the problem; she has "burst the prison bars," as the other two have not.

With this consolatory conclusion, "The Churchyard" is far more conventionally "hymnlike," and more characteristically female, than either "Ode to a Nightingale" or "To a Skylark." "The Churchyard" is an excellent illustration of the way Bowles characteristically merges "high" Romantic philosophy and form with emerging feminine traditions—in this case, the churchyard meditation, the hymn, and the consolatory elegy. Like Keats's and Shelley's poems, "The Churchyard" expresses the Romantic desire to escape human limitations on the wings of poetry. Bowles uses the same form, the same imagery, to address the same question. But her poem is not therefore derivative; rather, it offers a woman's answer to the question raised by the men, an affirmation in response to the confusion and doubt (as so many women writers would also do in the Victorian period). In this way, Bowles's work enriches the conventional Romantic canon at the same time as it enlarges the nineteenth-century feminine tradition, of which Bowles is an establishing member. This type of blending, which occurs throughout her work, is what prompts me to locate Bowles's poetry uniquely at the nexus of masculine and feminine Romanticisms.

Other poems in *The Birthday* range from meditations on age like "Once Upon a Time" and "The Old House Clock" to humorous pieces like "The Hedgehog" (concerning the management of prickly husbands) to complex poems on "Oriental" themes like "The Legend of Santarem" and "The Last Journey." Certainly, *The Birthday* ought to be the next volume by Caroline Bowles to be reprinted, for it contains her most mature and most accomplished work.

When Caroline Bowles married Robert Southey in June 1839 after the death of his first wife in November 1837, many considered it a very fitting union between two similar people. William Jerdan viewed Bowles's marriage as consummating a "long cherished admiration for her poetic father." Southey at sixty-five was past his prime; the breakdown leading to his death would begin on his honeymoon, but this catastrophe could not have been foreseen. The bride, too, was considered past her prime, being about fifty-three years old. A few months before the wedding, Southey wrote to his friend Walter Savage Landor, "There is just such a disparity of age as is fitting; we have been well acquainted with each other for more than twenty years, and a more perfect conformity of disposition could not exist."[41] This representation of their marriage has persisted. As late as 1977, a Southey biographer explained that during twenty years of correspondence Southey had "communed with his soulmate, the spinster and sentimental poetess Caroline Anne Bowles, who for many years provided an inspiration that Mrs. Southey, for all her wifely devotion, could not give. . . . They [Southey and Bowles] resembled each other remarkably."[42]

In October 1838 Southey assured his grown children that his marriage to Caroline Bowles meant no disrespect to their dead mother; he wrote Bertha that he hoped she and Kate would "understand how suited to each other we are in all respects."[43] Unfortunately, most of Southey's adult children refused to accept their stepmother, and when Southey died in 1843, Caroline Bowles Southey returned to Buckland.[44] She had forfeited a comfortable annuity to marry Southey, and she received substantially less from his estate. Two years before her death she was awarded a Civil List pension of two hundred pounds.

Evidently Caroline Bowles wrote little after her husband's breakdown, a circumstance that, along with the collaborative volume of 1847, helped to establish in the public mind the idea of her literary dependence upon Southey, which in turn strengthened the linking of her critical reputation with his. Their moral and domestic poems, though differently gendered, were so similar in intent and in publication venue, that the public did not sustain a strong sense of the distinctions between Bowles's verses and Southey's. After Caroline Bowles married Southey in 1839, her literary publications, including reprintings and new editions, generally appeared under the name of either "Caroline Southey" or "Mrs. Southey."[45] Unlike Robert Browning and Elizabeth Barrett Browning, who married in 1846, Robert Southey and Caroline Bowles Southey did not experience in their marriage an enhancement of their literary endeavors.

The disparity between Robert Browning's and Robert Southey's attitudes toward women writers may partly account for this difference. In 1837, Southey wrote to Charlotte Brontë, who had sent him an unsolicited poetry manuscript to review, just as Caroline Bowles had done eighteen years earlier: "Literature cannot be the business of a woman's life, and it ought not to be. The more she is engaged in her proper duties, the less leisure will she have for it, even as an accomplishment and a recreation. To those duties you have not yet been called, and when you are you will be less eager for celebrity. You will not seek in imagination for excitement, of which the vicissitudes of this life . . . will bring with them but too much."[46] This sentiment, expressed by Southey just two years before he married Caroline Bowles, illustrates the power of the conventional ideas about marital duty and womanhood that would dominate the Victorian era. Indeed, it is painful to observe how quickly Southey shifted Caroline Bowles in his mind from literary protégée to supportive, duty-bound wife.

To me, the history of Caroline Bowles Southey's reputation stands as a cautionary tale about the perils of judging nineteenth-century women poets by the commentaries that have been written about them. In *The Birthday* Caroline Bowles rendered a Romantic poet's life as a woman, an achievement that ought to have pleased the author of *Orlando* a century later. But by then Virginia Woolf apparently saw no reason to be reading Caroline Bowles Southey. We need not make the same mistake today; instead, we should remember that, over time, literary historians have a way of reversing their critical judgments about a writer. Rather than assume that all the fine Romantic poets have already been identified, we should read more deeply in the literature of the period. When we do, we discover that not only *The Birthday,* but many other poems as well by Caroline Bowles and other Romantic women writers, deserve to be read alongside the enduring poems of the male Romantic poets. Therefore, we should approach the poetry of Romantic women writers with our faculties of judgment strengthened by contemporary theory and not preempted by the vicissitudes of poetic reputation. If we can do so, then truly "Burst are the prison bars" that have confined Romantic women poets in the dungeons of literary history for so long.

Notes

1. Curran, "Romantic Poetry: The 'I' Altered," 188. I. Armstrong, "Caterpillar on the Skin." The other reprints reviewed are *Eighteen Hundred and Eleven* (1812) by Anna Laetitia Barbauld, *Sonnets and Metrical Tales* (1815) by Mary Bryan, and *The Lay of Marie* (1816) by Matilda Betham.

2. M. Ross, *The Contours of Masculine Desire*, 4-5.

3. L. Madden, *Robert Southey*, 1. [Merivale], review of *Poetical Works* (in L. Madden, *Robert Southey*, 401).

4. L. Madden, *Robert Southey*, 27, 30-31.

5. Butler, "Revising the Canon," 1359.

6. Mellor, *Romanticism and Gender*, 209, 210. Alexander, *Women in Romanticism*, 2-3.

7. Lamb and Coleridge quoted in Wu, *Romanticism*, 602.

8. [H.N. Coleridge], "Modern Poetesses," 402, 400-401.

9. Dowden, *Correspondence of Southey with Bowles*, letter 7 (21 May 1819), 17.

10. Rowton, *Female Poets of Great Britain*, 1848 ed., 374.

11. "Caroline Southey," 969. The *Dictionary of National Biography* attributes this obituary to T.K. Hervey.

12. Robertson, *English Poetesses*, 251. Dowden, *Correspondence of Southey with Bowles*, xiii, xxviii-xxix.

13. Miles, "Caroline (Bowles) Southey," 40-42.

14. Ezell, *Writing Women's Literary History*, 163.

15. Woolf, *The Common Reader*, 241-43.

16. Woolf, *Orlando*, 238. Sackville-West, introduction to *The Annual*, v. Sackville-West, "Women Poets of the Seventies," 121. Although Sackville-West is speaking about women poets of the 1870s rather than the 1830s, her point remains the same.

17. Courtney, *The Adventurous Thirties*, 1, 4, 43.

18. Kunitz and Haycraft, *British Authors*, 575. Simmons, *Southey*, 178. Woolf, *A Room of One's Own*, 48.

19. I am not alone in my efforts to resurrect Bowles. In the 1990s Caroline Bowles has been included in several biographical dictionaries and new anthologies of Romantic poetry. See, e.g., Blain et al., *Feminist Companion to Literature;* Shattock, *British Women Writers;* Wu, *Romanticism;* Ashfield, *Romantic Women Poets.* Wu includes a few stanzas from *Ellen Fitzarthur* and "There is a Tongue in Every Leaf" from *Blackwood's Magazine.* Ashfield prints a few short excerpts from *The Birthday.* Blain's useful text, *Caroline Bowles Southey* (1998), forthcoming as my essay went to press, is a cross between an anthology and a critical biography; Blain reprints the title poem of *The Birth-*

day in its entirety, along with various short poems and extracts from longer ones published between 1820 and 1847.

20. Hickok, *Representations of Women*, 38. M. Ross, *The Contours of Masculine Desire*, 6.

21. Curran, "Romantic Poetry: The 'I' Altered," 195, 197. I. Armstrong, "'A Music of Thine Own,'" 377. See also I. Armstrong, "The Gush of the Feminine."

22. M. Ross, *The Contours of Masculine Desire*, 6.

23. About half of their letters were published by Dowden in *Correspondence of Southey with Bowles*. In letters 11 (13 Feb. 1821) and 15 (7 July 1822), 20-21, 26-27, Southey describes his efforts to promote *Ellen Fitzarthur* among his friends.

24. Raimond, "Robert Southey," 263. Geoffrey Grigson, *A Choice of Southey's Verse*, has likewise suggested that Southey's best poetry was written in 1798 and 1799. J. Wordsworth, introduction to *The Widow's Tale*, v-vii.

25. Ferguson, *Subject to Others*, 246. Dowden, *Correspondence of Southey with Bowles*, xx.

26. Dowden, *Correspondence of Southey with Bowles*, 99. [H.N. Coleridge], "Modern Poetesses," 404.

27. Bowles, *Solitary Hours*, 1839 ed., 152.

28. C.B. Southey, *Solitary Hours*, 103. Hartley Coleridge reproduces "The Pauper's Deathbed" and "The Mariner's Hymn" in his *Quarterly Review* essay.

29. C.B. Southey, *Poetical Works*, 164. The poem was originally published by Alaric Watts in the *Standard* in 1827.

30. Dowden, *Correspondence of Southey with Bowles*, letter 74 (Oct. 1827), 129-30.

31. Hickok, *Representations of Women*, 27. Dowden, *Correspondence of Southey with Bowles*, letters 2 (28 May 1818) and 4 (17 June 1818), 6, 24-25; letters 3 (3 June 1818) and 87 (22 Dec. 1828), 8, 149.

32. Dowden, *Correspondence of Southey with Bowles*, xxvi. J. Wordsworth, introduction to *The Widow's Tale*, viii. *Tales from the Factories* is also available in a Woodstock reprint.

33. L. Madden, *Robert Southey*, 29. For a more recent consideration of Southey's ambivalent class politics, see Heinzelman, "The Uneducated Imagination," 110-22. Dowden, *Southey* (in L. Madden, *Robert Southey*, 476-78). Quoted in Morgan, "Southey on Poetry," 80-81. Morgan is quoting in the first instance from C.C. Southey, *Life and Correspondence of Southey*, 3:351, and in the second instance from the *Quarterly Review*, 41 (1829): 295.

34. Jonathan Wordsworth erroneously gives the date of this volume as 1874.

35. Dowden, *Correspondence of Southey with Bowles*, xxx.

36. Ibid., xxx, xxviii-xxix, and letter 7 (21 May 1819), 16-17. I. Armstrong, "Caterpillar on the Skin," 27. Dowden, *Correspondence of Southey with Bowles*, xxvii.

37. Bowles, *The Birthday and Other Poems*, 3:142-43. Further documentation from books 2 and 3 of *The Birthday* are from this edition. Citations of book 1 of *The Birthday* are from C.B. Southey, *Poetical Works*.

38. I. Armstrong, "Caterpillar on the Skin," 27.

39. C.B. Southey, *Poetical Works,* 238-39. *Chapters on Churchyards* was collected and published by Blackwood in 1829, with a new edition in 1841.

40. See, e.g., Swingle, "The Romantic Emergence."

41. William Jerdan reported in 1866 that Southey had suffered some kind of fit of raving and disorientation in Caroline Bowles's presence several days before their wedding. She evidently consulted the friend who would give her away and there was considerable discussion, "but matters had been carried so far that the die was cast, and it was decided to abide the result." Jerdan, *Men I Have Known,* 413, 419. Dennis, *Robert Southey,* 441-42. Dennis adds, "The sympathy between the two poets was one of heart as well as intellect" (442).

42. Bernhardt-Kabisch, *Robert Southey,* 179, 187.

43. Curry, *New Letters of Robert Southey,* 2:479 (15 Oct. 1838).

44. As Curry reports, Kate Southey and Caroline Bowles Southey quarreled; the Wordsworths sided with Kate, while Walter Savage Landor and others took Caroline's part. Cuthbert Southey's biography gave short shrift to Caroline Bowles. So does Mark Storey's 1997 biography of Southey, *Robert Southey: A Life.* Once he even erroneously calls her "Charlotte" Bowles (295).

45. These included *Chapters on Churchyards, Autumn Flowers and Other Poems,* and *Select Literary Works,* as well as *Poetical Works.*

46. Quoted in Gaskell, *The Life of Charlotte Brontë,* 173. Southey wrote this letter from Buckland, where he and his ailing wife were visiting Caroline Bowles.

Felicia Hemans and the Revolving Doors of Reception

Susan Wolfson

The New Hemans

The 1993 bicentennial of Felicia Hemans's birth passed without the parade of conferences, exhibits, special issues of journals, and collections of retrospective and prospective essays that have marked and will continue to mark other Romantic-era bicentennials of the 1980s and 1990s. This is partly because Hemans, one of the most prolific, popular poets of her day, in both England and America, did not come back into view until about ten years ago, and publications reflecting this attention, with a couple of prescient exceptions (notably, Marlon Ross and Norma Clarke), were just getting drafted in 1993.[1] The current revival of interest is confirmed and further assisted by her representation in anthologies: a section of her poetry in the second edition of David Perkins's classroom veteran, *English Romantic Writers;* a substantial unit (almost seventy pages of poems, letters, and a play) in Anne Mellor and Richard Matlak's new rival, *British Literature 1780-1830;* a brief but interesting selection in Duncan Wu's *Romanticism: An Anthology;* a seemingly odd, but tellingly inaugural place, with twenty pages, in Angela Leighton and Margaret Reynolds's *Victorian Women Poets;* featured status in *Longman's Anthology of British Literature,* and over one hundred pages in Wu's *Romantic Women Poets: An Anthology.*[2]

Yet, if Hemans is back, she is so with a difference. Nineteenth-century readers identified her, for better or worse, as the epitome of the "feminine," or more essentially, "female"; her poetry was a primer in the sphere of the domestic affections, religious piety, and patriotic passion, and of the female (more particularly, maternal) responsibility for binding these sensibilities together. In an age in recoil from the polemics for women's rights, Hemans seemed, blessedly, to idealize the "essentially feminine" as essentially "domestic" and "self-sacrificing." Although readers at the end of the twentieth century have not contested the basis for this identification, they have been questioning its total containment—both of the multivalent range of Hemans's poetry beyond the anthology favorites, and of the wavering, sometimes strained commitments of particular poems (even the anthology favorites) whatever the overt ideological signal.[3] Tracing this shift in Hemans's cultural register—from her celebrity in the 1820s and for several decades after, to her near effacement from anthologies and literary histories a century later, to her reemergence in the recent assessments of the Romantic-era writing—illuminates the forces of reception that come into play in different historic moments for the professional female poet. Amplified in Hemans's story, moreover, is the dependency of her reception on what her poetry was heard to say and not to say—and what was not heard at all then but is reaching qualified audition now. Following this story also, and not coincidentally, reveals a certain unsettledness about these questions in Hemans's poetry itself—what she says, what she muffles, what she cannot say.

In this essay I measure the culturally preferred doors of Hemans's reception and then look at the challenges of some potentially heterodox, critically potent texts: a mad mother in *Tales, and Historic Scenes, in Verse* (1819) and two disparate, but deeply related scenes in her political-domestic play, *The Siege of Valencia* (1823). In the tale, a wife takes stark revenge on a husband who has proven both a domestic and a national traitor. In the play, a similarly anguished wife discovers that domestic affections are both inextricable from and radically vulnerable to political emergency. Her anguish is an outcry that every contemporary review notes and quotes, usually with acclaim for Hemans's "exquisite" rendering of "maternal" passion, but also with simultaneous deafness to the ideological crisis.

One strikingly fugitive element appears in the sixth scene of this play, when the ordinary citizens and laborers of Valencia discuss the wasting effects of the extended siege, one citizen even voicing a bitter critique of the luxuries and privileges of the ruling class and noting the perverse democratic leveling that only the extremity of the siege can produce—a phenomenon that in the 1790s Mary Wollstonecraft, Thomas Paine, and Charlotte Smith remarked in similar tones about the plight of the French aristocracy. Not only did no contemporary reviewer comment on this scene, let alone hear its republican echoes or register their implications, but even recent critics have not found a way to coordinate their preferred focus on gender with Hemans's brief, truncated, but sharp attention to the questions of class privilege that underwrite the maternal claims.

"Feminine"/ Not "Unfeminine"

That Hemans is not a poet of uninterrupted sweetness and light has long been recognized: along with the beauties of nature, the paradise of home, and the domestic affections, her themes are female suffering, abandonment, desperate suicides, love-longing, mourning, and death. Nineteenth-century readers tended in their imaginary investments to read these shadows as a particular "Hemans melancholy" or to theorize them, if there was such an impulse, as an excess that was still "female" and that could even be recruited to a feminine heroic, limned in figures of patience, suffering, forbearance, faith, and martyrdom.[4] This heroism, moreover, could serve patriotism in its repeated striving to reconcile the tensions of modern life—social, political, and domestic—under the sign of these quintessential "feminine" and essentially "female" virtues, a sign that also covered any liability in Hemans's "unfeminine" success and financial independence as a professional writer.

Her "delicacy of feeling," crooned *Quarterly Review* in 1820, in a virtual hymn of praise, is "the fair and valued boast of our countrywomen"—all that is best in "an English lady"; "she never ceases to be strictly *feminine* in the whole current of her thought and feeling," chimed *Edinburgh Monthly* in the same year (its italics); her subjects evince "the delicacy which belongs to the sex, and the tenderness and enthusiasm which form its finest characteristic." In a preface to the posthumous English edition of Hemans (put together by her sister, Harriett Hughes), Lydia Sigourney sums the tenor of this discourse: "Critics and casual readers have united in pronouncing her poetry to be essentially feminine. The whole sweet circle of the domestic affections,—the hallowed ministries of woman, at the cradle, the hearth-stone, and the death-bed, were its chosen themes . . . the disinterested, self-sacrificing virtues of her sex."[5] Hughes graced her edition with a reprint of Francis Jeffrey's review of 1829, which gave the imprimatur of the literary establishment to this essentialism.

Jeffrey's essay was first published at the height of Hemans's fame in *Edinburgh Review*, probably the most influential quarterly of the day.[6] "We think the poetry of Mrs Hemans a fine exemplification of Female Poetry," he declared (34). He invoked the authority of nature to underwrite this literary culture. "Women, we fear cannot do every thing; not even every thing they attempt," he begins, in one of his characteristically sweeping judgments, this one inaugurating a two-and-a-half-page exfoliation before turning to Hemans herself. What women cannot do, he explains, is "represent naturally the fierce and sullen passions of men . . . nor even scenes of actual business or contention—and the mixed motives, and strong and faulty characters, by which affairs of moment are usually conducted on the great theatre of the world" (32). With the separate spheres thus mapped and gendered, and with a noticeable elision of *The Siege of Valencia* in this account, Jeffrey contends that women are "disqualified" from such representations not only by the "delicacy of their training and habits," but "still more" by the "disabling delicacy which pervades their conceptions and feelings" (32).

As Wollstonecraft noted long before, praise for delicacy is usually a bauble strung on a negative chain. Jeffrey's negatives are precisely those that negate power or political efficacy. The year before, the *London Literary Gazette* displayed such a trade-off in the midst of a hymn of praise whose themes were so well-known that a few bars were sufficient: "Of the fair writer's talents and peculiar qualities, it is now unnecessary to speak: her tenderness, fine feeling, moral beauty, and melodious versification, are justly appreciated by the public, and have long placed her in the front rank among the female ornaments of English literature." The *Gazette* giveth and the *Gazette* taketh away: ornaments are lovely and the front rank is an honor, but these elements are not part of the canonical architecture. This is also Jeffrey's qualification: Under the combined force of both nature and culture, women "are excluded by their actual inexperience of the realities they might wish to describe"—among these, "the true nature of the agents and impulses that give movement and direction to the stronger currents of ordinary life" (32). What women can do is nonpublic and nonpolitical: women's "proper and natural business is the practical regulation of private life, in all its bearings, affections, and concerns" (32)—cultural values again authorized by nature.[7]

Within this delimiting to "private life," Jeffrey means to praise "female genius" (34), even "to encourage women to write for publication" (33), but this public sphere, for Jeffrey, is only a more liberal tracing of the separate spheres: "No *man*, we will venture to say, could have written the Letters of Madame de Sevigné, or the Novels of Miss Austin [*sic*], or the Hymns and Early Lessons of Mrs. Barbauld, or the Conversations of Mrs. Marcet. These performances, too, are not only essentially and intensely feminine, but they are, in our judgment, decidedly more perfect than any masculine productions with which they can be brought into comparison" (33). Jeffrey's italicized differential, set in terms of "essential" talents, is doubly loaded: men will muddle the performance of masculinity if they venture "feminine" productions, whereas women will only embarrass themselves in venturing anything else. His review concludes in this very measure, urging Hemans to respect that "tenderness and loftiness of feeling, and an ethereal purity of sentiment, which could only emanate from the soul of a woman." In practical terms, this means sticking with "occasional verses" and not attempting to "venture again on any thing so long" and awkward as *The Forest Sanctuary* (47), an epic romance of 169 quasi-Spenserian stanzas that Hemans herself thought "almost, if not altogether, the best of her works."[8]

When Jeffrey's initial discussion finally turns to Hemans, it is to situate her with gender properties and propriety and to read her as an embodiment of their symbolic essence: "We think the poetry of Mrs Hemans a fine exemplification of Female Poetry." Like the praise of delicacy, this language of "exemplification" is necessarily and, reassuringly for the integrity and prestige of a masculine literary tradition, a qualified one: "Female Poetry . . . may not be the best imaginable poetry, and may not indicate the very highest or most commanding genius" (34). The praises come trailing the disabilities and qualifications already established in the prefacing discussion. Hemans's poetry is "infinitely sweet, elegant, and tender—touching, perhaps, and contemplative, rather than vehement and overpowering; and not only finished throughout with an exquisite delicacy, and even serenity of execution, but informed with a purity and loftiness of feeling, and a certain sober and humble tone of indulgence and piety, which must satisfy all judgments, and allay the apprehensions of those who are most afraid of the passionate exaggerations of poetry" (34). It is within this differentiated and diminished realm—distinct from the writing of "the stronger sex" (33)—that Hemans wins admiration. "Female Poetry" is continuous with female cultural function, not only to uphold serenity, delicacy, elegance, and tenderness, but also to refrain from incitements to social disorder: the vehement and overpowering, what might stir apprehensions in, say, representing a political grievance, or even a domestic grievance with political implications. Jeffrey's summary praise of Hemans is exactly in this key, setting her poetry against the "fiery passion, and disdainful vehemence, which seemed for a time to be so much more in favour with the public. . . . If taste and elegance, however, be titles to enduring fame, we might venture securely to promise that rich boon to the author before us" (47).

Henry Chorley, Hemans's friend and later her biographer, recognized this cultural system in his *Memorials,* calling on Anna Jameson's "rightly" saying that Hemans's poems "could not have been written by a man," before rendering his own encomium to their "essentially womanly" character: "Their love is without selfishness—their passion pure from sensual coarseness—their high heroism . . . unsullied by any base alloy of ambition. In their religion, too, she is essentially womanly—fervent, trustful, unquestioning, 'hoping on, hoping ever'—in spite of a painfully acute consciousness of the peculiar trials of her sex" (1:138). This is a text of positive values defined by negatives, of character that is *without, pure from, un-* (but at least with a tacit sense of the pain and peculiar trials that invade these purifying negatives). When Chorley calls on Hemans's friend Maria Jane Jewsbury for a further gloss, she, too, plays this double key: if "other women might be more commanding, more versatile, more acute," she says, no one was "so exquisitely feminine" as Hemans (1:187).[9]

The reiterated representation of an ultrafeminine-and-not-anything-else Hemans was as culturally potent as the voice of her poetry, shaping how it was and was not read. Related to this syntax of "not" is the diminutive "poetess," a separate and secondary gender. Hemans's writing reflects "the life at once of a woman and a poetess," writes George Gilfillan in 1847, echoing Chorley's conclusion to *Memorials*—"the woman and the poetess were in her too inseparably united to admit of their being considered apart from each other"—and stressing the genre difference: "We are reluctantly compelled . . . to deny her, in its highest sense, the name of poet—a word often abused, often misapplied in mere compliment or courtesy." Likewise, William Michael Rossetti's prefatory notice, having already suggested "the deficiency which she, merely as a woman, was almost certain to evince," accords "Mrs. Hemans . . . a very honorable rank among poetesses," reserving "poet" for "he."[10]

"Poetess" is not only a diminutive, but also a negative wrapped in faint praise. Even Gilfillan says as much: "A *maker* she is not. . . . Mrs. Hemans's poems are strictly effusions. And not a little of their charm springs from their unstudied and extempore character . . . in fine keeping with the sex of the writer" (360-61; his italics). Gilfillan more than half creates the "keeping" he perceives, wielding, as Jeffrey had, laws of culture reified as nature. As "an extension and refinement of that element of female influence," emanating from "the proper sphere and mission of woman" (361), women's writing, he insists, is not to be confused, in production or in effect, with the intellect, rigor, and real labor of men's writing. If the "charm" of Hemans's poems is that they are "strictly effusions," the stricture of this genre is confirmed in Wordsworth's dismissive use of the noun, and Hemans's use without praise in her regret over "the waste of [her] mind in . . . mere desultory effusions," instead of the "noble and more complete work" that would confirm her as "a British poetess."[11] Gilfillan frankly concedes the demotion: it is "not because we consider her the best, but because we consider her by far the most feminine writer of the age," he explains, that he has made her the "first specimen" in his 1847 series in *Tait's Edinburgh* on "Female Authors": "All the woman in her shines. You could not . . . open a page of her writing without feeling this is written by a lady. Her inspiration always pauses at the feminine point" (360).

The chiaroscuro of charms bound to deficiencies marks the doors of reception as much as the overt gendering. In the decade after Gilfillan, Frederic Rowton admired Hemans for representing and uniting "the peculiar and specific qualities of the female mind": "Her works are . . . a perfect embodiment of woman's soul: . . . *intensely* feminine. The delicacy, the softness, the pureness, the quick observant vision, the ready sensibility, the devotedness, the faith of woman's nature find in Mrs. Hemans their ultra representative."[12] This "ultra" is wed to the negatives familiar from Gilfillan: "Female writing" is marked by "the absence of original genius, or of profound penetration, or of wide experience"; "we dare not say that we consider [lady authors] entitled to speak with equal authority on those higher and deeper questions, where not instinct nor heart, but severe and tried intellect is qualified to return the responses" (359). It is with noticeably less gallantry that Rossetti deploys the language of gender in his prefatory notice, a decidedly desultory tone crossing the occasion of establishing merit: "Sentiment without passion, and suffering without abjection—these, along with a deep religious sense, and with the gifts of a brilliant mind taking the poetical direction through eager sympathy and some genuine vocation, constitute the life of Mrs. Hemans" (11). By the end of this preface, he concedes the negative judgment: if the "tone" of Hemans's mind is "feminine in an intense degree," the weakness of her poetry is exactly this difference, and doubly so: "it is not only 'feminine' poetry (which under the circumstances can be no imputation, rather an encomium) but also 'female' poetry: besides exhibiting the fineness and charm of womanhood, it has the monotone of mere sex" (24). Well before Rossetti, Elizabeth Barrett frankly confided to her and Hemans's friend, Mary Russell Mitford, her weariness with this monotone, hearing it less as the voice of "mere sex" than of the class and gender (de)formation of being "too ladylike." "I admire her genius—love her memory—respect her piety & high moral tone," she writes, deploying a syntactic suspense that predicts the qualification: "But she always does seem to me a lady rather than a woman, & so, much rather than a poetess. . . . She is polished all over to one smoothness & one level, & is monotonous in her best qualities." The slip from celebration to near contempt is confirmed by a recent critic, Virgil Nemoianu, who cites Hemans as a reminder of how replete now-marginalized literature is "with acquiescence, formalized harmonies, and translations of obsolete ideologies"; it "is *par excellence* the domain of conservatism."[13]

As these frames of excellence make clear, another culturally potent way of saying what Hemans and her poems were "not" was to say that "Mrs. Hemans" is not unfeminine—not, that is, of the sorority sensationally lambasted by Reverend Richard Polwhele in "The Unsex'd Females" (1798), neutered thus by the masculinizing exercise of a public voice and political opinion:

> Survey with me, what ne'er our fathers saw,
> A female band despising NATURE's law,
> As "proud defiance" flashes from their arms,
> And vengeance smothers all their softer charms.
>   I shudder at the new unpictur'd scene,
> Where unsex'd woman vaunts the imperious mien.[14]

What Hemans was "not" was an unfilial, denatured, Amazonian, defiant, unpatriotic, immodest daughter of Wollstonecraft—the double negatives shaping a positive cultural syntax cherished from the end of the eighteenth century right into the end of the nineteenth. In 1820 the *Edinburgh Monthly* enforced the equation of nonpolitical, nonassertive, and the feminine, praising "the modesty of Mrs. Hemans, for whose gentle hands the auxiliary club of political warfare, and the sharp lash of personal satire are equally unsuited," and admiring her for "scrupulously abstaining from all that may betray unfeminine temerity."[15] A "Prefatory Memoir" in one popular edition of her poems (1889) urges "lady readers" to peruse Jeffrey's review (which it quotes lavishly) "in its entirety, as it commences with an estimate of womanly powers which appears to us to answer many of the vexed questions of the present day"; and a later edition from the same publisher (1900) amplifies this advice by way of a telling complaint: the waning popularity over the course of the century of Hemans's "essentially feminine" genius seems due to a "lamentable change in the tone of modern society. The age that gave birth to the cry of 'Women's Rights,' and to the unfeminine imitators of masculine habits, was not likely to appreciate the voice of the *true* woman that spoke in Felicia Hemans."[16]

Admiration for Hemans under the sign of "not" operated throughout the century as a tactical front for a more pervasive discipline, "a stick to beat other women writers," as Norma Clarke nicely puts it. This function was nearly synonymous with "Hemans." Here is Gilfillan again: "You are saved the ludicrous image of double-dyed Blue, in papers and morning wrapper, sweating at some stupendous treatise or tragedy from morn to noon, and from noon to dewy eve. . . . [T]he transition is so natural and graceful, from the duties or delights of the day to the employments of her desk, that there is as little pedantry in writing a poem as in writing a letter, and the authoress appears only the lady in *flower*."[17] In the mystique of natural instinct ("the lady in *flower*"), women's writing has to seem an "unstudied" "charm." Both the title "poet" and the spectacle of sweaty labor he casts as female travesties, an abuse and misapplication in the former case, and a farce in the latter. Such transgression demands reproof, a task Gilfillan gleefully undertakes in his mock-heroic comparison of the span of a Blue's labors to the fall of the Satanically confederate architect, Mulciber, from Heaven ("from Morn / To Noon he fell, from Noon to dewy Eve" [*Paradise Lost*, book 1, lines 742-43]).

Reflecting on Reception

If the exemption of Hemans from the stigma of Blue confirms her success in maintaining a "feminine" character in her public fame, it also shows a resistance in the reception of women poets to noticing critical deviations, except in the form of dramatically "unsex'd" extremes. What is missed between the extremes is a middle ground of equivocation, of poignant protest, and of shadowy critique—in many ways the haunt and main region of Hemans's song. Encased in a culturally orthodox language of the domestic affections, the emotional and affective center of her poems frequently exposes women's devastating struggles against the structures, both domestic and national, in which these struggles are set. Although the stages are typically not contemporary England (rather, ancient Carthage or medieval Valencia), this is not a distancing and de-realizing displacement. The very fictions effect a strategy for presenting disturbingly familiar scenes, and the foreign stage returns a sign of a universal condition.[18]

This reflexive force sometimes even registers unwittingly in the rhetoric of reception that would recruit Hemans to the project of ideological reconciliation. Take, for instance, the uncanny deafness (or willful forgetfulness, or partial reading) of Gilfillan's statement that she "is no Sibyl, tossed to and fro in the tempest of furious excitement, but ever a . . . calm mistress of the highest and stormiest of her emotions," and the similar effect of this "no" in Agnes Mary Robinson's late-century headnote on Hemans for Ward's *English Poets:* "Fifty years ago few poets were more popular than Mrs. Hemans; her verses were familiar to all hearts. . . . [Y]et now they are chiefly forgotten, and without injustice. . . . Sprung from a talent expressive but not creative, her verses are stamped with feminine qualities. . . . [N]o Pythian enthusiasm fills the poet and compels us to forget her womanhood."[19] Yet more than a few poems show Hemans involved in the tempest of furious excitement and Pythian enthusiasm, fascinated by it, and representing it in historically displaced figures that are all the more resonant for suggesting a transhistorical veracity—a dynamic nowhere more obvious than in "The Wife of Asdrubal," in *Tales, and Historic Scenes in Verse* (1819).[20]

This is a patriotic woman with a vengeance. In exchange for his life, Asdrubal, governor of Carthage, has secretly ceded the city to the invading Romans. The betrayed citizens, including his wife and children, retreat to the citadel, and as conquest becomes imminent, they torch it and die in the immolation. Before this spectacular suicide, Asdrubal's wife berates him from the roof, stabs their sons before his eyes, and throws their bodies down into the blaze. Preempting the boys' inevitable execution by the Roman conquerors, this infanticide is a conflation of desperate maternal affection and bitter revenge against Asdrubal, who, the wife sneers, though he is "in bondage safe," will see himself "expire" in his sons. Declining any poetics of delicacy and tender sentiment, Hemans casts this mother as a figure of "wild courage," a radically patriotic self-determination in the face of defeat.

> She might be deem'd a Pythia in the hour
> Of dread communion and delirious power;
> A being more than earthly, in whose eye
> There dwells a strange and fierce ascendency.

> The flames are gathering round—intensely bright,
> Full on her features glares their meteor-light,
> But a wild courage sits triumphant there,
> The stormy grandeur of a proud despair;
> A daring spirit, in its woes elate,
> Mightier than death, untameable by fate.
> The dark profusion of her locks unbound,
> Waves like a warrior's floating plumage round;
> Flush'd is her cheek, inspired her haughty mien,
> She seems th' avenging goddess of the scene.
> [lines 19-32]

The comparison of her unbound locks to a warrior's plumage tropes Pythian fervor as a politicized travesty of gender, a transformation with domestic as well as political import:

> Are those *her* infants, that with suppliant-cry
> Cling round her, shrinking as the flame draws nigh,
> Clasp with their feeble hands her gorgeous vest,
> And fain would rush for shelter to her breast?
> Is that a mother's glance, where stern disdain,
> And passion awfully vindictive, reign?
> [lines 33-38, emphasis in original]

In the spectacle of a mother whose "towering form" has become less (or more) than maternal, domestic affection turns fatal, political, and sensational all at once. "Think'st thou I love them not?" (line 59) this Wife taunts Asdrubal:

> 'Tis mine with these to suffer and to die.
> Behold their fate!—the arms that cannot save
> Have been their cradle, and shall be their grave.
> [lines 60-62]

The poem closes in a lurid scene of the promised act:

> Bright in her hand the lifted dagger gleams,
> Swift from her children's hearts the life-blood streams;
> With frantic laugh she clasps them to the breast;
> Whose woes and passions soon shall be at rest;
> Lifts one appealing, frenzied glance on high,
> Then deep midst rolling flames is lost to mortal eye.
> [lines 63-68]

The infanticide-suicide is patriotic, heroic, and a devastating comment on the gothic form these commitments are forced to take in a culture of imperialist confrontation. The gendering of the betrayed city itself as feminine extends a convention into a political statement whereby the wife's actions cannot be as-cribed to the mere, though frightening, spectacle of individual pathology.

No wonder that the *Quarterly,* only too happy to conclude its essay with accolades for and generous quotations of Hemans's *Stanzas to the Memory of the Late King* (prefaced by its own eulogy), omitted mention of this poem in its earlier remarks on *Tales and Historic Scenes.* Views of Hemans as Tory fellow traveler, from her day to our own, tend not to cross such paths. But the deeper force of Hemans's representations, especially in their exposure of contradic-tions between the ideals of the feminine and women's social fate, explains why her most attentive readers find her poetry only tenuously conservative and far from replete. Both Tricia Lootens and Anne Mellor see the celebrations of the domestic affections as "precarious" and "threatened" and (in Mellor's words) situated in "a corpus that constantly reminds us of the fragility of the very domestic ideology it endorses"; to Jerome McGann, this is a corpus consciously "haunted by death and insubstantiality"; and Cora Kaplan suggests that the array of "proper sentiments," "normative morality" and "the emerging stereo-type of the pure, long-suffering female" are more than haunted by their oppo-sites; they are symbolic representations that mask anger turned inward.[21]

These tensions of understanding, and their tension with how the military patriotism of the nineteenth century understood Hemans's feminine patrio-tism, mark the aesthetic and ideological reception of *The Siege of Valencia* (1823).[22] The play's meaning is not limited to a crisis from a medieval chivalric past. By force of Spain's recent history of "chivalric" resistance to Napoleon and of England's shifting involvement in it (Hemans's brothers and future husband served in the Peninsular Campaign), this play also stages, if not ex-actly an intervention, then a critical reflection on questions of contemporary British nationalism and its imperialist expressions. A brief summary may be useful. The setting is late medieval Spain, and the political conflict, cast in terms of Christian versus Moslem, is tested against an affectional conflict of national honor versus human life. The Christian city-state has been under a prolonged and wasting siege by the Moslem Moors. In the opening scene, Gonzalez, governor of Valencia and descendant of the national hero El Cid, informs his wife Elmina that their young sons have been taken hostage by Abdullah, the Moorish prince and general; the boys, "eager to behold / the face of noble war," says the proud papa, got too close and were captured. To ransom their lives, he must "yield the city," a "disgrace" he and, he assumes, Elmina cannot contemplate. The "noble" martyrdom of the sons is inevitable. Their daughter, "heroic" Ximena (bearing the name of El Cid's wife), agrees, refusing to join her anguished mother in an unexpected plea for her brothers' lives at this cost. In anger and despair, Elmina seeks out the priest Hernandez for counsel and support, not knowing that, some time before, he had killed a Moor in battle who turned out to be his own son (he had deserted the Christians to be with his beloved Moorish maid). Hernandez upbraids Elmina's frailty and counsels to her to accept the martyrdom of her sons for the glory of Christian Spain. In desperation she gains entry in disguise to the Moors' camp, both to see her sons (the eldest is brave, the other is frightened) and to make a deal, agreeing to unlock the gates of the city in exchange for their lives. She soon feels remorse, however, and confesses to Gonzalez and Ximena; Gonzalez scorns her, and Ximena, dying in grief for a lover already fallen in battle, pities her and rallies the citizens to save her brothers. When Gonzalez refuses to surrender the city, Abdullah has his eldest son (a willing martyr) slain before his eyes. Gonzalez rushes into battle to try to save his remaining son and receives a fatal wound. Ximena soon dies, but Gonzalez hangs on long enough to behold the king of Castile's army come to the rescue. The Moors are routed, Abdullah is slain, Valencia is delivered, and Elmina, left with a life "uprooted" and an "unpeopled earth," supervises Gonzalez's funeral as a noble hero's ascent to "that last home of glory."

Although the architecture of Hemans's plot absorbs and suppresses the conflict of values by saving the city for Christianity, the most important effect of her play is to represent the ideological network of social existence: one that constrains, even annihilates, the claims of domestic affection. The play's languages are saturated with national myths, codes of honor, definitions of masculine patriotism, and religious sanctions that govern political and domestic life. Showing this structure of values in supposedly opposed cultural systems—Moslem Africa and Christian Spain—Hemans exposes a common patriarchal ideology in which fathers behave with disturbing consistency, especially in the noble martyrdom of sons: both "the sons of Afric" and the sons of Valencia revere the patriarch Abraham, who would willingly sacrifice his son on divine command. The plot concludes with the honor of Spain vindicated on the Christian refraction of this model (God's sacrifice of His Son to save mankind); but in the language of the play, the mother Elmina has the last words, and they are not about national or Christian honor but about a world of death in which her best hope is to anticipate her own.

The sensitivity of Georgian Tory reviews to this implicit challenge to military patriotism in post-Napoleonic England is etched in the negative rhetoric of their praise. The *British Critic and Quarterly Theological Review* announces its negative investment—antipathy to poetry of political critique, or any poetry that advertised the critical authority of women—with a review that opens not with a discussion of the play, but with a diatribe against female claims to a voice of intellectual and political critique. The scandal of Wollstonecraft had not, it seems, put this imp to bed, and the *British* meant to invoke every counterauthority, from divine creation to the legacy of forefathers, to modern science, to Shakespeare, to sneers of ridicule and disgust:

> We heartily abjure Blue Stockings. We make no compromise with any variation of the colour, from sky-blue to Prussian blue, blue stockings are an outrage upon the eternal fitness of things. . . . We would fain make a fire in charing-Cross, of all the bas blus in the kingdom, and albums, and commonplace books, as accessaries before or after the fact, should perish in the conflagration.
>
> Our forefathers never heard of such a thing as a Blue Stocking, except upon their sons' legs; the writers of Natural History make no mention of the name. . . . Shakspeare, who painted all sorts and degrees of persons and things, who compounded or created thousands, which, perhaps, never existed, except in his own prolific mind, even he, in the wildest excursion of his fancy never dreamed of such an extraordinary combination as a Blue Stocking! No! it is a creature of modern growth, and capable of existing only in such times as the present. . . .
>
> A Blue Stocking is the natural product of an age in which knowledge is lost in accomplishments. It is the vapoury offspring of ignorance, impregnated by conceit. It is the epicene *tertium aliquid* between a fool and a coquette. . . . Without being positively criminal, a Blue Stocking is the most odious character in society; nature, sense, and hilarity fly at her approach; affectation, absurdity, and peevishness follow in her train; she sinks, wherever she is placed, like the yolk of an egg, to the bottom, and carries the filth and the lees with her. . . .
>
> We thought it becoming the sound principles, and manly character, of our Review, to declare ourselves thus openly upon this subject; and we hereby give notice to all whom it may concern, that it is our intention henceforth, to visit enormities of this description, with the severity they so justly deserve.
>
> We now turn to Mrs. Hemans, and we do so with pleasure and confidence. [50–52]

It is Hemans's appearance of weakness, her accord with conservative views of women's claims—a tone emotional and affectional rather than intellectual and critical—that spares her the lash:

> She is especially excellent in painting the strength, and the weaknesses of her own lovely sex, and there is a womanly nature throughout all her thoughts and her aspirations. . . . There is a fineness of apprehension, and a subtlety of feeling, peculiar to the weaker sex, and perhaps the result of that very weakness, which enables them to set some subjects in such lights, and to paint them in such colours, as the more robust intellect of men could never have imagined. A woman is so much more a creature of passion than man; her virtues and her failings flow so much more directly and visibly from the impulse of affection; her talent and her genius, her thoughts and her wishes, her natural qualities and her acquired accomplishments are so interchangeably blended, and all but identified with each other, that there results a

wholeness of conception, and a vividness and reality of colouring in her mental efforts which advantageously distinguishes them from the most powerful productions of men on the same subjects.
[52-53, emphasis in original]

This praise is everywhere gender-marked in the double of positive negative. Hemans's strength is her weakness and her fidelity to that of her sex, all endorsed by the authority of nature: she is a "creature" of passion, in whom an indistinguishable blend of "natural qualities" and cultural acquisition simultaneously distinguishes her art from "the most powerful productions of men."

It has "stormed no hearts," Gilfillan said of *The Siege*. Indeed, the passages favored for admiring quotation are Ximena's inspirational, patriotic, and elegiac songs, Hemans's own acclaimed genres. *The Monthly Review* loved their "high chivalric poetry," especially as they speak to "a sentiment of degradation and shame" at the fate of Spain.[23] The other sign of Hemans in the play, however, is the mother who resists the spiritual solaces and inspirations voiced by her daughter's songs and who keeps returning to the pain of material suffering and loss. The reviews noticed this voice, too, but usually to recuperate it to the repertoire of Hemans-song. One stormy scene early on, noticed by everyone, is Elmina's plea to Gonzalez for their sons' lives. He tells her that martyrdom is inevitable, indeed divinely sanctioned:

Gonzalez   We have but   [420]
      To bow the head in silence, when Heaven's voice
      Calls back the things we love.
Elmina   Love! love!—there are soft smiles and gentle words,
      And there are faces, skilful to put on
      The look we trust in—and 'tis mockery all!   [425]
      —A faithful mist, a desert-vapour, wearing
      The brightest of clear waters, thus to cheat
      The thirst that semblance kindled!—There is none,
      In all this cold and hollow world, no fount
      Of deep, strong, deathless love, save that within   [430]
      A mother's heart.—It is but pride, wherewith
      To his fair son the father's eye doth turn,
      Watching his growth. Aye, on the boy he looks,
      The bright glad creature springing in his path,
      But as the heir of his great name, the young   [435]
      And stately tree, whose rising strength ere long
      Shall bear his trophies well.—And this is love!
      This is *man's* love!—What marvel?—*you* ne'er made
      Your breast the pillow of his infancy,
      While to the fulness of your heart's glad heavings   [440]

His fair cheek rose and fell; and his bright hair
Waved softly to your breath!—*You* ne'er kept watch
Beside him, till the last pale star had set,
And morn, all dazzling, as in triumph, broke
On your dim weary eye; not *yours* the face   [445]
Which, early faded thro' fond care for him,
Hung o'er his sleep, and, duly, as Heaven's light,
Was there to greet his wakening! *You* ne'er smooth'd
His couch, ne'er sung him to his rosy rest,
Caught his least whisper, when his voice from yours   [450]
Had learn'd soft utterance; press'd your lip to his,
When fever parch'd it, hush'd his wayward cries,
With patient, vigi'lant, never-wearied love!
No! these are *woman's* tasks!—In these her youth,
And bloom of cheek, and buoyancy of heart,   [455]
Steal from her all unmark'd!—My boys! my boys!
Hath vain affection borne with all for this?
—Why were ye giv'n me?
Gonzalez   Is there strength in man
Thus to endure?—That thou couldst read, thro' all
Its depths of silent agony, the heart   [460]
Thy voice of woe doth rend!
Elmina   Thy heart?—*thy* heart?—Away! It feels not *now*!
But an hour comes to tame the mighty man
Unto the infant's weakness; nor shall Heaven
Spare you that bitter chastening!—May you live   [465]
To be alone, when loneliness doth seem
Most heavy to sustain!—For me, my voice
Of prayer and fruitless weeping shall be soon
With all forgotten sounds; my quiet place
Low with my lovely ones, and we shall sleep,   [470]
Tho' kings lead armies o'er us, we shall sleep,
Wrapt in earth's covering mantle!—you the while
Shall sit within your vast, forsaken halls,
And hear the wild and melancholy winds
Moan thro' their drooping banners, never more   [475]
To wave above your race.
[1:420-76]

Hemans's italics underscore the gender difference that influences political judgment: castigating the father's claim of love as self-reflecting, patriarchal egotism, she urges against it, both as counterclaim and exposure, a maternal love based on the intimacy of a physical bond and the labor of care. Elmina even goes so far as to suggest a maternal martyrdom in this labor, a sacrifice of her youth and beauty that is nowhere credited in the official language that sanctions a hollow, life-destroying commitment to patriotic-religious-racial honor.

In recognizing the critical power of this moment, Chorley was perhaps unique in Hemans's century. Quoting Elmina, lines 423-58, he heard the "grief of [a] mother . . . broken down but not degraded, by the agony of maternal affection"; he understood the "treachery" it tempted, and he admired the "strong, fervid, indignant" inspiration. He was also shrewd enough to see the play itself driven by "a thrilling conflict between maternal love and the inflexible spirit of chivalrous honour," and he preferred this to the merely monotonous Ximena, "all glowing and heroic" but in sum "too spiritual, too saintly, wholly to carry away the sympathies" (*Memorials* 1:111). "Indignant," "fervid," "conflict," the relative value of "inflexible . . . honour," the militant authority of "maternal" values: these terms might punctuate praise of Wollstonecraft but are quite anomalous inside the doors of Hemans's reception.

The reviews, by contrast, opened the usual doors. Quoting the same passage, the Tory *British Critic* heard a maternal voice that was only "exquisitely beautiful," the "weaker sex" impelled by "passion" and "affection" to utter a kind of extended song: a "deep and passionate strain of eloquence" that a "mother *only* could have poured forth." *Monthly Review*, preferring the actual songs to the dramatic story (the political stage), nonetheless liked the dialogue above enough to quote it from "There is none . . ." (line 428) to "all unmark'd!" (line 456). And they too heard the diatribe as a song—a "singularly pleasing passage"—that they linked in this aesthetic to Hernandez's statement of radical solitude, his conviction that there is no "chain" of affection not ultimately broken by "Death," which "Knows no companionship" (2:26-43). *New European Magazine* quoted Elmina from "There is none . . ." to Gonzalez's interruption (line 458) and, also favoring the genre of song, called these lines "sweetly poetical." Not only did they not notice its politics of the grievance, but their review began by naming "the fair Authoress of this elegant little volume" as a writer distinguished by "purity of taste, a correctness of sentiment, and an elegance of expression, truly feminine." *British Review* cooperated, quoting from "*You* ne'er kept watch" (line 442) to line 476, to admire the "ardent spirit" of Hemans's "elegant pen."[24]

The resistance to hearing an assault on the system of values for which Gonzalez is at once exemplar and synecdoche is amplified in the reviewers' special pleading for his merits, even taking his own voice ("Think'st thou *I* feel no pangs?" [1:301]) as a cue: "Gonzalez is brave, dignified, faithful, calm, and kind; exhibiting the honour and integrity of a soldier. . . . Wherever he appears he obtains our love, esteem, and sympathy," said the *British Review* (200); and they admired the perpetuation of this masculine integrity in his male offspring: "Alphonso, his eldest son, is a boy of high, and unbending spirit, full of pride and impetuosity." Their only criticism is deflected into a modern British antipathy to the severity of medieval Catholicism, Spanish style, embodied in and limited to the priest Hernandez: "In Hernandez we find a total destitution of all kindly feeling . . . severe and vehement, with nothing of the sanctity of affliction, and nothing of the sacredness of a priest" (200).

Literary Gazette presents the most obvious example of a special pleading that circumvents, or suppresses to the point of distortion, the issue of gender difference in commitments to patriotic honor. Noting Hemans's fame for "sweet thoughts," "harmonious numbers," "classical allusiveness," "female feeling, grace and pathos . . . also some want of force," they print Ximena's opening "Ballad" (1:1-64).[25] Then, on the question of sons' lives versus national honor, they, too, quote Elmina (1:428-58), preceding this with earlier dialogue from the scene:

Elmina	Oh! I have stood	
	Beside thee through the beating storms of life,	[340]
	With the true heart of unrepining love,	
	As the poor peasant's mate doth cheerily,	
	In the parch'd vineyard, or the harvest-field,	
	Bearing her part, sustain with him the heat	
	And burden of the day;—But now the hour,	[345]
	The heavy hour is come, when human strength	
	Sinks down, a toil-worn pilgrim, in the dust,	
	Owning that woe is mightier!—Spare me yet	
	This bitter cup, my husband!—Let not her,	
	The mother of the lovely, sit and mourn	[350]
	In her unpeopled home, a broken stem,	
	O'er its fall'n roses dying!	
Gonzalez	Urge me not,	
	Thou that through all sharp conflicts has been found	
	Worthy a brave man's love, oh! urge me not	
	To guilt, which through the midst of blinding tears,	[355]
	In its own hues thou seest not!—Death may scarce	
	Bring aught like this!	
Elmina	All, all thy gentle race,	
	The beautiful beings that around thee grew,	
	Creatures of sunshine! Wilt thou doom them all?	
	—She too, thy daughter—doth her smile unmark'd	[360]
	Pass from thee, with its radiance, day by day?	
	Shadows are gathering round her—seest thou not?	
	The misty dimness of the spoiler's breath	
	Hangs o'er her beauty, and the face which made	
	The summer of our hearts, now doth but send,	[365]

With every glance, deep bodings through the soul,
Telling of early fate.
[1:339-67]

To the ear of the *Literary Gazette*, this and the later outcry are as texts of "a mother's feelings" only (407-8), with no resonance of political critique. Yet, Elmina sees what Gonzalez cannot—that the war has already killed his children, that the contest for victory is not between Moor and Spaniard but between life and death, and that the spoiler is winning. At the end of the play, Hemans stresses this economy: Elmina's cry to be spared an "unpeopled home" is not only defeated but multiplied into an "unpeopled earth" (9:225). It is telling that the *Gazette* declines to comment on the passage it presents, and more telling that it suppresses the critique that is specifically Elmina's as it moves on to quote, with equalizing sympathy, Elmina's and Gonzalez's grief over their sons' death. Elmina, they say, shows "powerfully natural feeling" and Gonzalez, a "distress . . . pourtrayed with almost equal skill" (408).

Elmina   The clouds are fearful that o'erhang thy ways,
         Oh, thou mysterious Heaven!—It cannot be
         That I have drawn the vials of thy wrath,
         To burst upon me through the lifting up
         Of a proud heart, elate in happiness!   [5]
         No! in my day's full noon, for me life's flowers
         But wreath'd a cup of trembling; and the love,
         The boundless love, my spirit was form'd to bear,
         Hath ever, in its place of silence, been
         A trouble and a shadow, tinging thought   [10]
         With hues too deep for joy!—I never look'd
         On my fair children, in their buoyant mirth,
         Or sunny sleep, when all the gentle air
         Seem'd glowing with their quiet blessedness,
         But o'er my soul there came a shuddering sense   [15]
         Of earth, and its pale changes; even like that
         Which vaguely mingles with our glorious dreams,
         A restless and disturbing consciousness
         That the bright things must fade!—How have I shrunk
         From the dull murmur of th' unquiet voice,   [20]
         With its low tokens of mortality,
         Till my heart fainted midst their smiles!—their smiles!
         —Where are those glad looks now?—Could they go down,
         With all their joyous light, that seem'd not earth's,
         To the cold grave?—My children! . . . (8:1-25)
     . . . .

Gonzalez   Alas! This woe must be,
        I do but shake my spirit from its height
        So startling it with hope!—But the dread hour   [180]
        Shall be met bravely still. I can keep down
        Yet for a little while—and Heaven will ask
        No more—the passionate workings of my heart;
        —And thine—Elmina?
Elmina   'Tis—I am prepared.
        I *have* prepared for all.
Gonzalez   Oh, well I knew   [185]
        Thou wouldst not fail me!—Not in vain my soul,
        Upon thy faith and courage, hath built up
        Unshaken trust.
Elmina (*wildly*)   Away!—thou know'st me not!
        Man dares too far, his rashness would invest
        This our mortality with an attribute   [190]
        Too high and awful, boasting that he knows
        One human heart! (5:178-92)

But there is a serious distortion. Elmina's grief, which the *Gazette* quotes first, is uttered after the sons have been killed, and Gonzalez's, which it quotes second, as if voiced at the same or even subsequent moment, is made to seem equivalent. The scene numbers (which the *Gazette* does not include, because they would reveal the manipulation) show Hemans's significantly different arrangement. Gonzalez's "Alas!" is uttered while his sons still live—declaring a "must be" that is not inevitable. The *Gazette*'s reverse order equalizes what is a temporal difference and does Gonzalez the further favor of italicizing "I do but shake my spirit from its height / So startling it with hope!"

This diminishment of the mother's claim is also evident in the way the *British Review* manages to be sympathetic to her, but only after she has lost everything, only after her worst imaginings are realized. And even then, they hint at something too Wollstonecraftian: "Elmina principally appears in the character of a distressed mother, overwhelmed with grief, and losing, in the prevalence of maternal affection, all sight and sense of rectitude and propriety. But we also see in her a peculiar spirit of pride and loftiness, even after the death of her sons, after her own reconciliation with her husband, and his death" (200). The implication of their glimpsing that "peculiar spirit of pride and loftiness" is that Elmina has not been made to suffer enough, that even her devotion to her husband's honor is encouraging an unfeminine pride, another version of rectitude and propriety compromised.

This is a failing, they hint, that lurks in Hemans herself: "Still there is too much vehemence, too much effort in our authoress, especially when she enters on scenes that require the exhibition of tender or ardent feeling; but it is in the latter that she puts forth her energy most conspicuously. . . . [S]he has a strong predilection for warlike affairs, for bold, fervid, and daring characters. We must, however, remark, that the military spirit that breathes and glows in many of her pages, does not add to their real excellence. We do not like Bellona as a Muse" (202). Bellona as a Muse is both a gender problem and, relatedly, a political one. The gender trouble is that her acolytes are traditionally male erotic subjects, men whom she espouses (recall Ross's description of Macbeth as "Bellona's bridegroom" [*Macbeth* 1.2.54]). A woman who espouses Bellona is courting unnatural combinations, a hyperfeminine that may turn against men altogether. In Hemans's play, "the military spirit that breathes and glows in many of her pages" (her fervor, indignation), as Chorley recognized, is less apparent in Ximena's chivalric songs than in Elmina's critique. Is it this unpredictable combination that repels the *British Review*?

Notwithstanding his disdain of the feminine and of female sensibility, Rossetti is the hardest on Elmina, not liking her insurrection, and he is the quickest to read in her miserable survival an apt retribution and poetic justice:

As the reader approaches the *dénouement,* and finds the authoress dealing death with an unsparing hand to the heroically patriotic Gonzalez and all his offspring, he may perhaps at first feel a little ruffled at noting that the only member of the family who has been found wanting in the fiery trial—wanting through an excess of maternal love—is also the only one saved alive: but in this also the authoress may be pronounced in the right. Reunion with her beloved ones in death would in fact have been mercy to Elmina, and would have left her undistinguished from the others, and untouched by any retribution: survival, mourning, and self-discipline, are the only chastisement in which a poetic justice, in its higher conception, could be expressed. [prefatory notice, 17]

Another way to sort out the evidence, however, is to observe that "the authoress dealing death with an unsparing hand to the heroically patriotic Gonzalez and all his offspring" is siding with Elmina's bitterly prophetic curse on Gonzalez, which she knows, tragically, will redound to her:

> May you live
> To be alone, when loneliness doth seem
> Most heavy to sustain! . . .
> . . . .
> Aye, then call up
> Shadows—dim phantoms from ancestral tombs,
> But all—all *glorious*—conquerors, chieftains, kings—
> To people the cold void!
> [1:465–67, 476-79]

The chastisement, though it is dramatically visited on her, is ideologically aimed at Gonzalez. *British Critic* had it right when it said it would not analyze the play "minutely": "A poem is valuable or worthless, according to its poetry; the mere *story* can have little to do with it" (54).

The question that the nineteenth-century reviews feel the pressure of (and with which recent criticism addresses) is whether Hemans's literary aesthetics—her displacements and containments—prevail over what they contain: a critique of imperialism, of class privilege, of the way gender is used to sentimentalize warfare and to demonize pacifism. What no review was able to quote is Hemans's sharpest attack, her siege on the masculine ideology of warfare, honor and national glory:

<pre>
Elmina   Then their doom is seal'd!   [265]
            Thou wilt not save thy children?
Gonzalez   Hast thou cause,
            Wife of my youth! to deem it lies within
            The bounds of possible things, that I should link
            My name to that word—*traitor?*—They that sleep
            On their proud battle-fields, thy sires and mine,   [270]
            Died not for this!
Elmina   Oh, cold and hard of heart!
            Thou shouldst be born for empire, since thy soul
            Thus lightly from all human bonds can free
            Its haughty flight!—Men, men! too much is yours
            Of vantage; ye, that with a sound, a breath,   [275]
            A shadow, thus can fill the desolate space
            Of rooted up affections, o'er whose void
            Our yearning hearts must wither!—So it is,
            Dominion must be won!—Nay, leave me not—
            My heart is bursting, and I *must* be heard!
            [1:265-80]
</pre>

This is the story that is not heard, even as it is voiced.

British Critic even managed to quote, seemingly without hearing, an entire poem from the same volume, "Elysium," which Hemans prefaces with a bitter headnote from Chateaubriand's *Génie du Christianisme* about the poverty of classical notions of glory: "In the Elysium of the ancients, we find none but heroes and persons who had either been fortunate or distinguished on earth; the children, and apparently the slaves and lower classes, that is to say, Poverty, Misfortune, and Innocence, were banished to the infernal regions"—a sentiment echoed in the poem:

<pre>
            The peasant, at his door
Might sink to die, when vintage-feasts were spread
</pre>

. . . .
    The slave, whose very tears
Were a forbidden luxury, and whose breast
Shut up the woes and burning thoughts of years,
As in the ashes of an urn compress'd;
    He might not be thy guest!
["Elysium" 57-58; 64-67]

This is a class difference with which Hemans is willing to confront her readers, and it also informs *The Siege*, briefly but quite potently, in a scene of conversation among Valencia's citizens. Hemans sounds the anxieties and potential for class rebellion articulated in the 1790s and renewed in the 1820s— the decade that pushed toward the reform bills of the early 1830s to deflect the potential for a domestic French Revolution:

An Old Citizen   The air is sultry, as with thunder-clouds.
    I left my desolate home, that I might breathe
    More freely in heaven's face, but my heart feels
    With this hot gloom o'erburthen'd. I have now
    No sons to tend me. Which of you, kind friends,   [5]
    Will bring the old man water from the fount,
    To moisten his parch'd lip? [*A citizen goes out.*
Second Citizen   This wasting siege,
    Good Father Lopez, hath gone hard with you!
    'Tis sad to hear no voices through the house,
    Once peopled with fair sons!
Third Citizen   Why, better thus,   [10]
    Than to be haunted with their famish'd cries,
    E'en in your very dreams!
Old Citizen   Heaven's will be done!
    These are dark times! I have not been alone
    In my affliction.
Third Citizen (*with bitterness*)   Why, we have but this thought
    Left for our gloomy comfort!—And 'tis well!   [15]
    Aye, let the balance be awhile struck even
    Between the noble's palace and the hut,
    Where the worn peasant sickens!—They that bear
    The humble dead unhonour'd to their homes,
    Pass now I' th' streets no lordly bridal train,   [20]
    With its exulting music; and the wretch
    Who on the marble steps of some proud hall
    Flings himself down to die, in his last need
    And agony of famine, doth behold
    No scornful guests, with their long purple robes,   [25]

To the banquet sweeping by. Why, this is just!
These are the days when pomp is made to feel
Its human mould!
[6:1-28]

In the Third Citizen, Hemans patently echoes the sarcastic retorts to Burke's
tragedy of aristocratic fall in *Reflections of the Revolution in France* (1790), re-
torts voiced, for example, by Wollstonecraft's and Paine's refutations and the
more bitter passages of Smith's *The Emigrants,* all saying, in one way or an-
other, "Why, this is just! / These are the days when pomp is made to feel / Its
human mould!" Wollstonecraft's *Vindication of the Rights of Men* (1790) chal-
lenges Burke in remarkably similar terms: "What is this mighty revolution in
property? The present incumbents only are injured"; "did the pangs you felt for
insulted nobility, the anguish that rent your heart when the gorgeous robes
were torn off . . . deserve to be compared with the long-drawn sigh of melan-
choly reflection when . . . the sick wretch, who can no longer earn the sour
bread of unremitting labour, steal to a ditch to bid the world a long good night."
Paine famously sneers in his *Rights of Man* that Burke "pities the plumage, but
forgets the dying bird": "Not one glance of compassion, not one commiserat-
ing reflection . . . has he bestowed on those who lingered out the most wretched
of lives, a life without hope, in the most miserable of prisons"; and with a sharp
critique of Burke's aesthetic ideology, he adds, "His hero or his heroine must be
a tragedy-victim expiring in show, and not the real prisoner of mystery, sinking
into death in the silence of the dungeon." Smith, with equivocal sympathy for
emigrant clergy and aristocrats, sees a kind of moral correction in their fall
from privilege, a leveling of the aristocrat's pride: "[T]hat high consciousness
of noble blood, / Which he has learn'd from infancy to think / Exalts him o'er
the race of common men" now finds itself among one company of "Poor va-
grant wretches! outcasts of the world! / Whom no abode receives, no parish
owns; / Roving like Nature's commoners."[26]

It seems a short Paineful step from the Third Citizen's "Aye, let the bal-
ance be awhile struck even / Between the noble's palace and the hut" (6:16-17)
to forming the Citizens of Valencia into a counterinsurgent force, or even more
threateningly, into an organized class that will, beyond the interval of "awhile,"
claim and press its political rights against the lordly train. Although Hemans
writes this scene of complaint to set the stage for the renewed patriotism of
Valencia, the dramatic structure does not mute its contemporary rhetoric. And
she knows it. Through the heterodox political voice of her Third Citizen, she
addresses the English public of the 1820s with a mordant editorial on the
general waste of sons to insure an aristocracy normally indifferent to the labor-
ing classes that sustain their luxury; she also admonishes aristocratic arrogance
about the resentment below. This theme is amplified in the 1823 volume by its

echo of "Elysium," even as Hemans suppresses it when Ximena enters to rally the citizenry to battle. Along with Elmina's bitter denunciations and protests in scene 1, this brief moment in scene 6 opens up a powerful form of what McGann describes as "double perspectivism": "two dialectically functioning historical frames of reference," that of the plot or story, and that of the writer's own historical moment.[27]

This dialectic of reference and the critical voices that shape it, once put into play, are not containable by the plot's own disciplinary and didactic apparatus. This is organized to heal conflicts between "patriarchal" honor and "maternal" affection, between political and domestic values, and finds symmetry of the reviews: an eagerness to reduce the play to the tragedy of an errant, then penitent mother. Such fables of healing and resolution spell a quintessential "Romantic Ideology."[28] But Hemans's play disarms, even breaks, the spell by marking its harmonizing structure as too-artificial-by-half, a patently overformalized determination against elements that resist its legislation. The arrival of the king of Castile to deliver Valencia from imminent annihilation is a blatant deus ex machina that she motivates to expose the ideological problem: the device of a last-minute rescue is not a devastating refutation of Elmina's values and a vindication of Gonzalez's, but an admission that the ideological conflicts between patriotism and maternal affection, between aristocratic honor and common misery, are not soluble by historical process. *The Siege of Valencia* dramatizes how domestic affections, in both the family and the state, get caught up in national self-determination, the larger *domus* that paradoxically excludes such affections and, in class terms, violates them as it conscripts the sacrifice of the anonymous many to the fame of a few. The ultimate symbolic coherence of Hemans's play finds its emblem not in the chivalric rescue of Valencia, but in the ravaged city, its dying citizenry, and its destroyed families.

If Hemans's readers in the nineteenth century could not or did not want to read this information, it has emerged in our own post-Vietnam skepticism about the idealism of warfare and the necessary sacrifice of sons and daughters to national honor. Hemans writes as part of this debate. Does *The Siege* bring ideological conflicts into an aesthetic resolution, or does the form of such resolution report a persistent dissonance? To Marlon Ross, Hemans serves and serves up a double conservatism: the lesson that Elmina learns about patriotic honor is the same one that Hemans transmits to her readers. Elmina "realizes that her heroic attempt to save her children, though empowered by the right affection, has been misplaced. Her affection is then transferred to the state as she comes to realize the continuity between political freedom and domestic happiness"; she returns "to domesticity now cognizant of the continuity between the hearth and the state, between the state and the heart." Mellor, by contrast, sees these linkages strained into a powerful critique: Elmina is the center of a story of alienated, and ultimately annihilated, domestic values, and the play "is finally the story of *her* suffering, *her* tragedy—the tragedy of a woman whose 'feminine' love and virtue [have] been rejected by a patriarchal state religion."[29]

The strongest difference between Hemans's historical moment and our own may be this skepticism, and it is no coincidence that the contemporaneous "Casabianca," a sentimental favorite throughout the nineteenth century, is now the focus of similar questions. Hemans's imaginative power is to push patriotism to a radical consequence—for example, the willing martyrdom of children in filial obedience—and to stage this consequence in ways that put pressure on the whole ideology. It is not that Hemans's culture valued honor over life, whereas our post-Vietnam moment is inclined to question "national honor" ransomed by the lives of children or the nonelite. Hemans shaped this question in the midst of overt and deeply sentimental commitments to national honor. Hers may have been a culture in which every schoolboy idolized Nelson and Wellington, but it was also a culture in which Charles Wolfe's morbidly dark and borderline-skeptical-of-"glory" dirge, "The Burial of Sir John Moore at Corunna" (1817)—the retreat in which one of her brothers participated—was memorized almost as soon as it was published, and a culture in which Byron's mordant critiques of military glory—most famously in *Childe Harold's Pilgrimage, Cantos I and II* (1812) and continuing to *Don Juan, Canto VII* (published the same year as Hemans's *Siege,* 1823, by Byron's former publisher John Murray)—were widely broadcast. Hemans's most important cultural work is no facile elaboration of a nationalist ideology of honor-at-any-and-all-costs; it is her testing of its elements to reveal their interaction with differences of gender, class, race, and religion. *The Siege,* like "The Wife of Asdrubal," emerges from the conflicts of reception it provokes, conflicts solicited by extreme events and consequences and achieving forms of closure only in displays of motives and devices. Hemans's figures of female resistance, including their resistance to the ideology of the "feminine" that she is so often credited with sustaining and perpetuating, embody the issue of reception, insofar as they bear and struggle with received forms of understanding. If the story of Hemans's reception, both in her texts and of her texts, is marked by sociocultural gate-keeping, it is also one shaped by the force of her seemingly proper texts in provoking a critical reflection on who is keeping the gates, then and now.

Notes

1. Even Ellen Moers's massive scholarly recovery and critical intervention, *Literary Women: The Great Writers* (1963) had very little to say about Hemans, other than citing her as a cautionary example of "precocious" yet ultimately "facile" talent (301).

Ross's *Contours of Masculine Desire* (1989) has a ground-breaking discussion of Hemans (232-310), as does Clarke's *Ambitious Heights* (1990).

2. In *The Longman's Anthology* see Wolfson and Manning, "The Romantics and Their Contemporaries." Reprints of the first editions of Hemans's lifetime volumes have been issued by Garland Press (Westport, Conn.) and, less comprehensively, by Woodstock Books (Oxford, England).

3. For a sharp review of the tensions in this binding, sometimes nearly unraveling the domestic text, see Lootens, "Hemans and Home." An exemplary case of this unstable mixture, Lootens shows, is the anthology and parlor favorite "Casabianca": "setting the tactically unnecessary death of a child at the heart of Britain's victory in the Battle of the Nile, the poem suggests the powerful, unstable fusion of domestic and military values that helped render Hemans's poetry influential"; despite the "idealistic emphasis on filial loyalty and chivalric family honor," the poem "never fully defuses the horror of the history it evokes" (241). "Casabianca," I would add, heightens this tension by figuring the filial "heroic" in the form of the enemy French admiral's son: this battle was Nelson's first important, widely celebrated victory, one trophy of which was the mast from *L'Orient,* Commodore Casabianca's ship.

4. For relevant discussion, see Leighton, *Victorian Women Poets: Writing Against the Heart,* 11-12.

5. Quarterly Review 24 (October 1820): 131; review of *The Sceptic,* by Hemans, *Edinburgh Monthly Review* 3 (1820): 374; Sigourney, "The Genius of Mrs. Hemans," xv.

6. Jeffrey, review of *Records of Woman,* by Hemans (Oct. 1829), 32-47. By force of its reissue in Harriett Hughes's *The Works of Mrs. Hemans* (1839), this review became canonical; it is quoted generously in *The Poetical Works of Mrs. Hemans* (Chandos Classic), xxiii.

7. See Wollstonecraft, *Vindication of the Rights of Woman* (1792): "women . . . act contrary to their real interest on an enlarged scale, when they cherish or affect weakness under the name of delicacy" (47). Review of *Records of Woman,* by Hemans, *London Literary Gazette* 590 (10 May 1828): 289.

8. Hemans is paraphrased by Chorley, *Memorials of Mrs. Hemans,* 1:123.

9. Chorley quotes Jewsbury's Hemans-coded portrait of Egeria in *History of a Nonchalant,* 193. The reference became a standard: Jane Williams deems it "obviously true" for Hemans (*The Literary Women of England,* 479-80); W.M. Rossetti quotes it lavishly to convey her character (prefatory notice, 22-23); and George Gilfillan uses Egeria as a synonym ("Female Authors, No. I," 361, 363).

10. Gilfillan, "Female Authors, No. I," 360; Chorley, *Memorials,* 2:355; W.M. Rossetti, prefatory notice, 16, 24.

11. Hemans, quoted in Hughes, *Memoir,* 300. Wordsworth described some "Elegiac Stanzas" to Coleridge as "effused" rather than "*composed* . . . the mere pouring out of my own feeling" (*Letters, Middle Years,* part 1, 219, emphasis in original); and he represented other poems to John Scott as having "sprung" forth as "Effusions rather than Compositions" (*Middle Years,* part 2, 284). For a related reading of Gilfillan's remarks, see Leighton, *Victorian Women Poets: Writing Against the Heart,* 28-30.

12. Rowton, *Female Poets of Great Britain* (1853), 136.

13. Elizabeth Barrett to Mary Russell Mitford, 23 Nov. 1842, in [Browning], *Let-*

ters, ed. Raymond and Sullivan, 1:88. Nemoianu, "Literary Canons," 240. Cautioning that "anticanonical movements" may "backfire in the case of feminine literature," Nemoianu cites the case of Hemans: "public, prominent, and popular in her own day, slowly declining into obscurity later," she epitomizes the "marginalized feminine" that "turns out to be a repository of and tireless extoller of the values of family, tradition, stability, religion, and hierarchy" (240). My thanks to Tricia Lootens for alerting me to this remark.

14. Polwhele, "The Unsex'd Females," lines 11-16, in Mellor and Matlak, *British Literature,* 42. Polwhele's footnote glosses the quoted phrase: "'A troop came next, who crowns and armour wore, / And proud defiance in their looks they bore.' Pope. The Amazonian band—the female Quixotes of the new philosophy, are, here, too justly characterised." The quotation is from Alexander Pope's *The Temple of Fame* (1711; lines 342-43), the troop answering "the direful trump of Slander."

15. Review of *The Sceptic,* by Hemans, *Edinburgh Monthly Review* 3 (1820): 373, 375.

16. "Prefatory Memoir," in Hemans, *Poetical Works,* Chandos Classics ed., xxiii-xiv; "Prefatory Memoir," in Hemans, *Poetical Works,* Albion ed., xv-xvi; my thanks, again, to Tricia Lootens for alerting me to this second passage.

17. Clarke, *Ambitious Heights,* 33; for the durable view of Hemans's complicity with conservative idealizings of women's place in hearth and home, see p. 55 and passim; Kaplan, *Salt and Bitter and Good,* 93-95, makes a similar point but sees this complicity strained. For informative discussions of the cultural constraints on publishing women writers, see Clarke's first two chapters, "Contrary to Custom" and "The Pride of Literature," and Poovey, *The Proper Lady and the Woman Writer.* Gilfillan, "Female Authors, No. I," 361.

18. For my fuller discussion of this dynamic, see Wolfson, "Domestic Affections," 128-66.

19. Gilfillan, "Female Authors," 360; Robinson, "Felicia Hemans" (1880-94), 4:334.

20. Quotations follow the first edition (1819); this poem is also in Mellor and Matlak's *British Literature.*

21. Lootens, "Hemans and Home"; Mellor, *Romanticism and Gender,* 124 (see her excellent discussion, 124-43); [McGann] et al., "Literary History," 228; Kaplan, *Salt and Bitter and Good,* 93-95.

22. Quotations follow the first edition, identified by scene and line numbers. Mellor and Matlak's *British Literature* includes the play (1190-225), but lines are misnumbered beginning at 1:70; a major erratum in the first printing interpolates later text (their 1:354-415) into an earlier part of the first scene, making a hash of its sequence. For readers for whom theirs is the only available text, I supply approximate line numbers, with the difference that I count an iambic pentameter unit, even when shared by different speakers, as a single line, as is standard in the editing of plays.

23. Gilfillan, "Female Authors, No. I," 361; Review of *The Siege of Valencia,* by Hemans, *Monthly Review,* 180. The recent fate of Spain involved a futile revolution to restore constitutional liberties, and the restoration of a repressive monarchy. In *The Contours of Masculine Desire,* Marlon Ross discusses Ximena's ballads in this perspec-

tive (282), and Chorley sees Hemans's identification with Ximena in the deathbed language of chivalric delivery (*Memorials*, 2:324).

24. Review of *The Siege of Valencia*, by Hemans, *British Critic*, 52-53; Review of *The Siege of Valencia*, by Hemans, *Monthly Review*, 180-81; "Contemporary Poets, No. I," *New European Magazine* 3 (1823), 120-22; *British Review and Critical Journal*, 31 (August 1823), 201.

25. Review of *The Siege of Valencia*, by Hemans, *Literary Gazette*, 385 and 407.

26. Wollstonecraft, *Vindication of the Rights of Men*, 121, 152-53; Paine, *The Rights of Man*, 288; Smith, *The Emigrants*, 1:235-37, 303-5.

27. McGann, *The Beauty of Inflections*, 266.

28. I am, of course, invoking the title term of Jerome J. McGann's *The Romantic Ideology*, but I apply McGann's resonant term to the reception discourse with this qualification: I resist his view that "the poetry of Romanticism" participates in this ideology in the way that he says—that it is "everywhere marked by extreme forms of displacement and poetic conceptualization whereby the actual human issues with which the poetry is concerned are resituated in . . . idealized localities," and that it is only the critic, the sole locus of critique, who may expose "these dramas of displacement" (1).

29. Ross, *The Contours of Masculine Desire*, 275, 282, Mellor, *Romanticism and Gender*, 137, 140-41.

Receiving the Legend, Rethinking the Writer

Letitia Landon and the Poetess Tradition

❦

Tricia Lootens

> *Alas! hope is not prophecy,—we dream,*
> *But rarely does the glad fulfillment come:*
> *We leave our land, and we return no more.*

What happens if one sets out to read Letitia Elizabeth Landon as something other than a poet of ideal femininity or a primary source of the poetess tradition? At first, such a project may seem perverse: for it is as a feminine poet that L.E.L. has been rescued from near oblivion. Read as "a woman poet who situated her self and her work wholly *within* the Burkean-Rousseauian categories of the beautiful and the domestic" and as a writer who "accepted and reflected in her work the dominant views concerning how, what and why a woman wrote," Landon has opened up new understandings of feminine poetry's relations to the aesthetic, philosophical, and political preoccupations of her time.[1] Her work has offered a revealing access point for explorations of "the hermeneutic problem of discerning a feminine discourse";[2] her reception has provided a rich source of material on the construction and marketing of poetic femininity and "feminine desire."[3] Why challenge an approach that has been so successful?

One answer lies precisely in that success. For what critics rescue, we partly create; and the construction of our generation's "Letitia Landon" is at a crucial stage. Consigned to near oblivion only a few years ago, Landon's work now appears not merely in reprint editions or in the pages of a canonical text such as the *New Oxford Book of Romantic Period Verse*, but in its own ambitious selected teaching edition. As certain of her poems are becoming increasingly well-known, however, other works, including her novels and many periodical pieces, are scarcely read.[4] Now, before accounts of her career have been fully institutionalized, we need to test our own reception of her work against earlier readings and analyze that work as flexibly and completely as possible.[5] For canonization proceeds, in part, through de-canonization; and we need to ensure that whole categories of Landon's writing are not once more lost almost before they are found.[6]

Landon herself lies behind the literary legend of L.E.L., of course; and it is she who elevated audience response to a central position in that legend. Many of her most famous poems elaborate upon a tragic romance of literary reception: an account of the fall of a female poet who is flattered, seduced, and ultimately betrayed by her public. In the life of a Landon heroine such as Erinna or Eulalie, as in those of imaginary Sapphos and of Corinne before her, fame implicitly corresponds to unhappy sexual (and specifically, heterosexual) love: the first awakening of desire, which catalyzes passion and power, almost inevitably precedes a fall.[7] Was such writing to be read as confessional? Nineteenth-century critics could never entirely agree; and indeed, the ironies and ambiguities suggested by L.E.L.'s famous characterization as a "snub-nosed Brompton Sappho" remain irresolvable.[8] In the wake of Landon's mysterious death at Cape Coast Colony, Africa, however, L.E.L.'s chroniclers could easily read her accounts of doomed female poetry and passion as eerily prophetic.[9] Some transformed Cape Coast Castle into the home of Bluebeard, replete with "all the horrors" of the "mysterious castle" of gothic fiction or folktales.[10] Others envisioned Landon herself as an unquiet spirit.[11] And thus, in part, the literary legend that grew up around Letitia Landon did not develop into the secular equivalent of a saint's life. Rather, it became what Germans term a *Sage:* that is, a disturbing legend whose physical location is often crucial and whose moral, though perhaps unclear, is quite likely unpleasant.

More recent narratives often echo this tendency to cast Landon's life as feminine poetic fall. Now, however, the instrument of her fate is not literary genius, but femininity. Still naive, still seduced by praise, this Landon remains ultimately doomed by dependence on the approval of her audience, condemned to failure as a poet through her drive to enact and market a conventional feminine ideal.[12] Such accounts are deeply compelling—and with reason. Yet their resonance with earlier narratives of the fall of feminine genius can endow them with a canonical force to which they do not necessarily even aspire. Read alone, they can render it almost too easy to forget that Letitia Landon did more than write or enact poetic femininity, too easy to assimilate the trajectory of her literary career to the fates of her own characters.

Consider, for example, this essay's opening lines, which reprint the epigraph of Emma Roberts's 1839 edition of *The Zenana and Other Poems.*[13] Early idealism—disillusionment—exile from "the impassioned land" of romantic dreams:[14] few passages could seem to offer so concise an evocation of the fate of feminine love and genius in L.E.L.'s verse. In fact, however, Roberts drew her epigraph from a poem entitled "Shuhur, Jeypore," which had been inspired by the death of a "young acquaintance" in India.[15] "Golden idols," not fame or love, are the seducers here: driven by attempts to "win the wealth of worlds beyond the wave," the nameless masculine subject of "Shuhur, Jeypore" is left to "pine and perish 'neath a foreign sky" (lines 28, 32-33).

De-center femininity, then, and Landon's evocation of one who can "return no more" comes to seem more complex. So, too, may her reception. For Emma Roberts had reason to remember the colonial source of the epigraph she chose. She had lived in India and would return there; she died in Poonah in 1840.[16] Could Roberts have implicitly identified Landon with the Englishman buried in Shuhur, Jeypore? Certainly in many accounts, what killed "England's own dearly loved and gifted daughter" was not merely love, fame, or poetry.[17] It was also Africa—whether conceived as a "Land of Death" in itself or as embodied in its inhabitants.[18]

The British had reason to fear West Africa. In 1836, the year that Landon and her future husband George Maclean met, Dr. Henry Marshall and Lt. Alexander Tulloch began a parliamentary survey that would eventually establish military mortality rates on the Gold Coast as the highest in the empire. A posting to Cape Coast was "equivalent to a death sentence," their findings were to reveal. Maclean's very troops were comprised chiefly of "men whose sentences for military crimes had been commuted in return for 'volunteering' for West African duty in what were appropriately called 'condemned corps.'"[19] Do accounts of L.E.L.'s marriage metaphorically cast her as a feminine counterpart to members of the "condemned corps"? Certainly narratives of a female poet betrayed by love mingle with stories of a persecuted Englishwoman driven to fatal exile, or an English dreamer doomed by a lifelong fascination with "African habits, African horrors, and African wonders."[20]

Where the dangers of the "Land of Death" took human form, George Maclean's former common-law wife was their most sensational representative. Casting her as a woman scorned, biographers played upon terror, not only of West Africans' alleged "hot blood and . . . fierce habits," but of the "horrible spirit of female vengeance."[21] Local servants also proved easy targets.[22] Suggestively, however, belief in Africa's victimization of L.E.L. shaped even portrayals of her Scottish widower. Laman Blanchard, for example, compares L.E.L. to Shakespeare's "'gentle Lady,' afterwards 'married to the Moor,'" whereas R.R. Madden suggests that Maclean had "become, by long privation of the humanizing influence of the society of educated women previously to his marriage, selfish, coarse-minded, cynical—a colonial sybarite." Such a husband might easily drive a sensitive Englishwoman to suicide, Madden made clear.[23]

No cultural glory was to be gained from serving as what one 1874 article termed the "solitary literary and feminine association" of a "pestilential coast" whose colonial history presented "a long dreary vista of innumerable deaths; of miserable defeats interspersed with trumpery victories . . . ; and of British mercantile cupidity overriding the dictates not of patriotism alone, but of common honesty." Already shaped by sexual scandal, Landon's reputation could only suffer from its connection with imperial scandal. And such connection was inevitable: for despite Roberts's praise for "the chivalric energy with which" Maclean "strove to put an end to the slave-trade," by the time L.E.L. agreed to marry him, George Maclean was thoroughly embroiled in controversy over enforcement of the Slave Trade Abolition Act.[24] Madden, who investigated Landon's mysterious death, actually traveled to Cape Coast Colony as commissioner of inquiry on the western coast of Africa, charged with investigating Maclean's alleged complicity in profiteering from trade with known slavers.[25]

Apparently, attempts to downplay accounts of European mortality caused by the West Africa climate or fever may have inadvertently sparked part of the scandal surrounding Landon's death.[26] Could her decline in popularity later in the century be equally inseparable from British anxieties concerning the colonies in general and slavery in particular? Certainly the Landon legend is anchored on descriptions or images of the poet's solitary Cape Coast Castle burial place.[27] "Surrounded by the dungeons (well filled with human pawns by Mr. Maclean) which had formerly been used for slave barracones," and "daily trampled over by the soldiers of the fort," L.E.L.'s parched grave rises as an image of colonial hell.[28]

Though Landon's burial site marks a woman and a poet, then, it also memorializes one of England's dead. This last phrase points directly back to the issue of feminine poetic tradition; for however out of place a work such as "Shuhur, Jeypore" may seem among L.E.L.'s narratives of passion, sorrow, and song, it resonates strongly with the patriotic poetry of Felicia Hemans. "Wave may not foam, nor wild wind sweep, / Where rest not England's dead," exults the speaker of Hemans's "England's Dead."[29] "Many are the tombs that scatter'd lie / Alone neglected, o'er the Indian plains—" answers "Shuhur, Jeypore": "Alas! we do mistake, and vainly buy / Our golden idols at too great a price" (lines 17-18, 27-28).

Thus, by reading Landon as English first, rather than as feminine, we may establish new relationships between her work and that of other women poets. The paradox is only apparent: for though L.E.L. may come as close as any writer to representing what her generation considered a purely feminine poet, in practice the concept of pure femininity is an illusion. No human being is thoroughly and consistently gendered; no gender exists in isolation from other constructions of cultural identity. Focusing on sexual politics through the lens of national identity (as, say, of ethnicity or religion) can help us see past the monolithic mirage of femininity in the abstract: it can open up our reading of specific writers, even as it challenges the implicit identification of "abstract" femininity with cultural privilege. Landon's influential portrayals of feminine suffering might look very different, for example, if we set class issues in the center: among other things, the mother of "The Factory" might take her place next to the heirs of Sappho and Corinne.[30]

One way to rethink the works and reception of L.E.L. as a woman poet, then, is to read her primarily as something other than a woman. Another is to read her as something other than a poet. Significantly entitled *Romance and Reality,* Landon's first novel appeared in 1831, transforming the outlines of both her literary career and her public presence. "We ask the poetry of the authoress," wrote an *Athenaeum* reviewer, "where, till now, dwelt the brave good sense—the sarcasm bitter with medicine, not poison . . . ?"[31] The authoress might have answered that such qualities had been there all along, though in person rather than in print. Henceforth, her career would be a far more public performance of dissonance: in multiple genres, it would dramatize the shifting, ambiguous relations between what Landon herself liked to call "romance and reality." And it would not always privilege the former term.

Apparently, some readers felt that Landon's fiction unveiled the "real" woman—a perception that could not hold, as Glennis Stephenson notes. Neither, however, can attempts to separate L.E.L. the poet from Landon the novelist.[32] For the severity and satire of L.E.L.'s novels opened up compelling ways of reading—and rereading—not only Landon's "character" but also her previous verse. Whether in terms of criticism or of reception, the poet, the person, and the novelist could no more be separated than they could be conflated. Poetry and prose jostled in the annuals as, finally, in the collected "Works"; and Landon's epigraphs to her final completed novel, *Ethel Churchill,* reprinted under the title "Fragments," won rapid inclusion among her most powerful verse.[33]

In *Ethel Churchill,* as in so much of Landon's poetry, the tragic romance of reception is never far from the surface. Seduced and betrayed by casual flattery, increasingly wearied by frantic attempts to please, two of the novel's central characters fall—from innocence, health, joy, creativity, and ultimately from life. Where L.E.L.'s prose differs from the poetry, however—and the difference is crucial—is that Landon's doomed woman is not a poet, and her doomed poet is not a woman.

Henrietta enters *Ethel Churchill* as an unmistakable Landon heroine. Raven-haired, passionate, alternately despairing and feverishly brilliant, she is already world-weary when the novel opens. Where a heroine of Landon's verse might unwittingly trade her poetic genius for flattery or her bloom for romantic passion, however, Henrietta enacts a more conventional feminine bargain. She loves the young poet Walter Maynard (who loves Ethel Churchill), but she sells herself in marriage to Lord Marchmont. Behind her mask of cynical frivolity, however, she remains deeply vulnerable to dreams of ideal love; and she thus falls prey to the advances of Sir George Kingston. Shortly after her husband discovers her intrigue with Kingston and declares his intention to repudiate her, she learns that Kingston is a heartless rake. In a series of vivid, highly charged scenes that provoked one reviewer of *Ethel Churchill* to delighted quotation and others to expostulation, Henrietta takes revenge.[34] She poisons her husband, displays his corpse to her would-be lover, and then offers Kingston a cup of coffee. Unwisely, Kingston drinks; and in the lengthy scene that follows, the details of his death agony are graphically—even lovingly—described.

Like "Shuhur, Jeypore," *Ethel Churchill* can serve as a lens for reading back through L.E.L.'s verse. By flying in the face of critical attempts to underplay "violent, vengeful impulses" in Landon's work, for example, the novel's portrayal of Lady Marchmont can help draw attention to the sinister splendor of a poem such as "A Supper of Madame de Brinvilliers"—and thus to a possible instance of Landon's influence on Elizabeth Barrett Browning.[35] Even more significant in terms of Landon's reception, however, is the fate of the young poet Walter Maynard: for it recapitulates and drastically alters Landon's recurrent representation of her own career—and of women poets' careers in general—in terms of the tragic romance of reception.

Like Lady Marchmont, Maynard sells himself. Desperate from exhaustion and poverty, he accepts the post of personal secretary to Sir George Kingston and, with it, duties that include writing love letters for a seducer too busy to do all his own courting. Too late, Maynard discovers to whom his letters have been delivered: to Lady Marchmont, whose responses innocently reveal that "but for your letters, I should never have known you; therefore, never have loved you as I do!" In this sinister anticipation of *Cyrano de Bergerac*, Maynard recognizes his own fall: "To think that this earnest, this sorrowful love, has been a toy—an amusement—the result of such heartless treachery! . . . I stand amazed now at my own recklessness . . . ; but I am so accustomed to invent an existence, that I forget the consequence in the interest of the composition."[36] He can and does reveal the plot, but it is too late to avert its tragic consequences. Already consumptive, Maynard is wounded in a dual with Sir George and soon dies. After murdering her husband and Kingston, Henrietta goes mad.

Stephenson asserts that Landon "is not as concerned with self-projection in the novels"; and indeed, by portraying the poet of *Ethel Churchill* as male, Landon goes beyond her verses' conventional references to the poet as "he" to effect an explicit reinscription of traditional associations of poetic creativity with masculinity.[37] Walter Maynard's unrequited love for Ethel Churchill, for example, clearly replays a traditional heterosexual poet/muse model. If one grants L.E.L. the possibility of projecting something other than a feminine self, however, the fictional form of a male poet may also afford her a new posi-tion—a masculine position—from which to reconsider certain of the central preoccupations of her literary career. Given powerful nineteenth-century im-pulses to identify writers with their characters, for instance, Maynard's open expressions of desire for Ethel, his human Muse, inevitably become associated with the author herself.[38] By echoing Landon's own notoriously lingering heroine descriptions, Maynard underscores their intensity and erotic ambiguity:[39] he reminds us that though luscious pictorial representations of intertwined "beau-ties" are thoroughly conventional in Landon's period (and our own), they need be no less homoerotic for that reason.[40]

"Solitary, chilled, and weary," pent up in stark quarters whose barren dis-comfort inescapably calls up a certain legendary attic room at Hans Place,[41] Maynard speaks for his author in more explicit ways as well. Most signifi-cantly, he inspires a series of meditations on the mundane agonies of literary labor—meditations that easily shift into first-person accounts.[42] Thus allied with her masculine subject, Landon's writer/narrator emerges as what Adrienne Rich has called an "absorbed, drudging, puzzled, sometimes in-spired creature . . . who sits at a desk trying to put words together":[43] she claims her place as a writer among writers, a professional whose struggles are inflected and intensified, not fully created, by her gender.[44]

In *Ethel Churchill,* to be a writer is not merely to follow a calling: it is to engage in what would come to be called alienated labor. "I cannot help," Maynard thinks at one point, "reading my fate in one of those little boats now rocking on the tide, only fastened by a rope, scarcely visible to the passer by . . . seemingly free, yet, in reality, fettered by the strong, though slight chain of circumstances. For a small sum, any passenger may enter that boat and direct its course."[45] "So free we seem, so fettered fast we are!" Even as many of Landon's contemporar-ies and immediate successors sought to evade or deny the dilemmas posed by the professionalization of art, Landon insisted upon them. Indeed, L.E.L.'s self-representation can be read as a constant reminder that her audience is buying, and thus constructing, her performance both as woman and as poet. "Now society is a market-place, not a temple," she instructs the reader of *Ro-mance and Reality,* for example. What is more, "there is nothing people are so much ashamed of as truth."[46]

Landon was concealing truth in order to succeed in the marketplace, she continually insisted: but what truth? Was she the devoted victim of her audience's whims, or the manipulator of their desires? Did her love poetry confess the passion of a real Sappho, albeit in snub-nosed Brompton form, and incom-pletely disguised as a "professional"? Or was it actually the work of a hypocrite, an adept at emotional artifice who marketed expressions of a passion she did not feel?[47] Such questions were intrinsic to the "mystery" of L.E.L. At the first extreme, she could be seen as ridiculous or pitiable, but an "honest" woman; at the second, as a competent literary businesswoman, but emotionally disingenuous. In either case, her insistence on writing as an economic project, combined with the evocations of the romance of reception, clearly provoked anxieties over literary chastity. Landon "will pardon us for asking," William Makepeace Thackeray writes, for example, "if she does justice to her great talent by employing it" to fill the pages of annuals such as *Fisher's Scrap-Book*. "It is the gift of God to her—to watch, to cherish, and to improve: it was not given her to be made over to the highest bidder, or to be pawned for so many pounds per sheet. An inferior talent . . . must sell itself to live—a *genius* has higher duties; and Miss Landon degrades hers, by producing what is even indifferent."[48] Was it only the sale of Landon's talent that disturbed Thackeray, one wonders? Or was it also her openness about that sale?

Ethel Churchill is suggestive in this context: for even as Landon's novel replays the tragic romance of reception, it reverses certain of that narrative's key elements. Above all, with *Ethel Churchill* Landon creates a story in which seductive relationships between writer and readers can cut both ways. For though part of Maynard's audience, Sir George, exploits him by soliciting the prostitution of his art, another part, Lady Marchmont, is solicited by the power of the writing that results. To what extent does Maynard stand for his author? Does his complicity in literary betrayal represent an indirect confession, an insistence that Landon's sins are even worse than those named by her critics? Prostituting one's art is bad enough, the novel makes clear, but discovering that one has unknowingly pimped with it is worse. Or do Maynard's misleading love letters represent the sort of writing Landon refrains from marketing: writing, that is, which seduces women through false promises of romantic happy endings? In either case this story of the fall of a poet and a woman radically destabilizes Landon's familiar accounts of transactions between erotic and literary desires and between artist and audience. "I never saw any one reading a volume of mine without almost a sensation of fear," she wrote toward the end of her life, in words that resonate with many of Maynard's. "I write every day more earnestly and more seriously."[49]

Reception has its own legends. Influenced, perhaps, by modernist dismissals such as D. E. Enfield's account of Landon's novels as nothing but "prose L.E.L." and thus as merely "readable, voluptuous, sentimental, verbose, and delightfully silly," few critics have taken Landon's fiction into serious account in assessing the development of her literary reputation. Biographies of Thackeray, for example, commonly mention his youthful parody of Landon's "Violets, deep blue violets!" as "Cabbages, bright green cabbages!"[50] His strictures concerning the sale of her art also receive some attention. What remains to be acknowledged, however, is the intensity of his response to *Ethel Churchill*. "We are not going to praise Miss Landon's novel," Thackeray writes in an 1838 *Fraser's*—having already offered a lengthy quotation and an assurance that "we mistake if there is any thing in modern English literature more sparkling or beautiful."[51] Landon's "very painful journal of misery, and depression, and despair" is "not written in a healthy and honest tone of sentiment," he writes; yet he also insists that "no one can read it without admiring the astonishing qualities of the authoress. . . . The wit of it is really startling; and there are occasional remarks which shew quite a fearful knowledge of the heart."[52] Startling wit and fearful knowledge: thus speaks the future author of *Vanity Fair*.

And indeed, the creator of Rebecca Sharp owes a great deal to *Ethel Churchill*. As C.I. Johnstone noted in 1838, a character named Lavinia Fenton emerges as a real star of *Ethel Churchill*.[53] "Shrewd, careless, clever; ready to meet any difficulty, however humiliating, that might occur; utterly without principle; confident in that good fortune which she scrupled at no means of attaining—" Lavinia is what Landon terms "the very type of the real." She may honor romantic idealism, but she is not about to attempt to put it into practice. "Do you know, Walter," she confesses, "that, though I know what you are saying is great nonsense, I cannot help liking you for the deep, true feeling, you carry into every thing. Still, even you only confirm me in my creed; the warm emotion, the generous faith, only place you in the power of others, and power is what we all abuse."[54]

Lavinia does not fall: she dives. Like virtually everyone in *Ethel Churchill*, she is hopelessly in love. Instead of pining, however, she runs off to become a dramatic star. She may fail to win Walter Maynard's heart, but she succeeds at rendering his first play a success; at easing his decline, partly through pawning her own belongings; at saving him from Sir George's brutality; and at bringing Ethel Churchill and her true love to Walter's deathbed, where everyone who is still sane can be reconciled. Unlike Lady Marchmont, who falls in love with the villain, or Walter, who panders for him and falls at his hand, Lavinia sees through Sir George from the beginning. She becomes his mistress; and after taking his money, revealing his plot against Lady Marchmont, and spiriting the wounded Walter out of his clutches, she exacts her revenge—not through poison, but through savage insults, brilliantly and casually delivered. In short, without justifying any claims to conventional virtue, Lavinia Fenton operates as the novel's sole effective agent for good. Like Becky Sharp, she begins as a servant. She ends as a duchess.[55] If the doom of Eulalie or Erinna stands at one pole of Landon's influence in terms of creating heroines, the exuberant, cynical triumph of Lavinia may stand at another.

Thus, focusing on *Ethel Churchill* does more than encourage new readings of Landon's verse or of her tragic romance of reception: it also suggests grounds for rethinking the legend of L.E.L.'s career as a poetic fall that replicates those of her heroines. Up to this point I have emphasized only our vulnerability to a continuing tendency to read Landon's career in terms of her own plots. In fact, however, such an account of the effects of the Landon legend is too simple. For in many ways, I think, that legend may have rendered us hesitant to stress key aspects of her work—aspects that are perhaps most unmistakable in her prose, as in its reception. Witness, for example, Thackeray and William Maginn's comment on *Francesca Carrara:* "There is, in truth, a tone of sorrow and melancholy diffused through the book, amounting at times to complete depression, which we know not how to account for. . . . A sterner goddess never presided over the destinies of a novel." Such responses speak to a powerful, deeply disturbing, strain in Landon's writing: a bleak vision conceived in cosmic, not merely feminine terms. Though Landon's contemporaries fully recognized this aspect of her work, for the most part we have not.[56] Perhaps we have not yet read her novels carefully enough; perhaps, too, anxiety over the Landon legend has encouraged us to shy away from the topic. We fear once more reducing the poet's career, both personal and poetic, to one grand foreshadowing of suicide. In fact, however, we do not know that Landon killed herself. What is more, even when a writer does commit suicide, we cannot assume either that the decision to do so was inevitable or that its origins need be transparently inscribed in that writer's work. Had Landon died in her sleep after a joyous old age, we would presumably have faced the bleakness and violence of much of her writing. That her death was a mystery should be no reason to accord her work any less frank analysis.

Once one allows oneself to envision Landon's writing persona as something other than a Sappho, Corinne, or Erinna—as, say, a Lavinia—one may be better prepared to face what Thackeray calls the "stern goddess" who presides over her bleaker moments. In so doing, one may find that one's sense of her influence expands—not least with respect to Thackeray himself. When Becky Sharp lies crushed on the floor of her home, "in a brilliant full toilette," for example, with "serpents, and rings, and baubles" glittering on her arms and hands, her figure and impending fate echo Lady Marchmont's, beginning in a chapter entitled "The Masked Ball."[57] The following poem, "Stern Truth" was originally the epigraph for that chapter:

> Life is made up of vanities—so small,
> So mean, the common history of the day,—
> That mockery seems the sole philosophy.
> Then some stern truth starts up—cold, sudden, strange;
> And we are taught what life is by despair:—

> The toys, the trifles, and the petty cares,
> Melt into nothingness—we know their worth;
> The heart avenges every careless thought,
> And makes us feel that fate is terrible.

Vanity, vanity: the refrain echoes throughout Landon's work.[58] The vanity of love; that of poetic fame—these we have already grown accustomed to consider as her themes. Yet there are vanities beyond these, and those, too, have their place in L.E.L.

Often in her prose and occasionally, as here, in her verse, Landon evokes the universe of Blaise Pascal's "miserable man"—perhaps without the "great wager" of Christian faith in the offing. One "admission is necessary," writes Sarah Sheppard, in the only full-length nineteenth-century study of Landon's work: "that all her gloomy representations belong to human nature in its unchanged state, destitute of the light of Christianity. . . . Her views and estimate of life . . . are correct, inasmuch as she represents life unsanctified by religion,—."[59] Sheppard's assessment inevitably calls to mind Thackeray's own description of the characters of *Vanity Fair* as a "set of people living without God in the world."[60]

Femininity in Landon is not only suffering; suffering is not merely feminine. L.E.L. is known for proclaiming her unfitness to write verses about war, much as is Thackeray for his refusal to portray Waterloo in *Vanity Fair*.[61] Yet both go onto the field after the victory—Thackeray in a single, unforgettable sentence,[62] and Landon in the following poem:

The Battle Field

> It was a battle field, and the cold moon
> Made the pale dead yet paler. Two lay there;
> One with the ghastly marble of the grave
> Upon his face; the other wan, but yet
> Touch'd with the hues of life, and its warm breath
> Upon his parted lips.
>
> He sleeps,—the night wind o'er the battle field
>   Is gently sighing;
> Gently, though each breeze bear away
>   Life from the dying.
>
> He sleeps,—though his dear and early friend
>   A corpse lies by him;
> Though the ravening vulture and screaming crow
>   Are hovering nigh him.

He sleeps,—where blood has been pour'd like rain,
　　Another field before him;
And he sleeps as calm as his mother's eyes
　　Were watching o'er him.

To-morrow that youthful victor's name
　　Will be proudly given,
By the trumpet's voice, and the soldier's shout,
　　To the winds of heaven.

Yet, life, how pitiful and how mean
　　Thy noblest story;
When the high excitement of victory,
　　The fullness of glory,

Nor the sorrow felt for the friend of his youth,
　　Whose corpse he's keeping,
Can give his human weakness force
　　To keep from sleeping!

And this is the sum of our mortal state,
　　The hopes we number,—
Feverish waking, danger, death,
　　And listless slumber.

No lush sentiment, no heaping up of luxuriant metaphors here: even the fairly restrained poetic diction of the epigraph and opening stanzas gives way to straightforward verse whose simplicity recalls the folk ballads of which L.E.L. was fond.[63] The youth on the battlefield, sleeping as if under his mother's eyes, may be a woman's vision. Yet his obliviousness to both loss and glory is not merely masculine: it is mortal. That life's most glorious stories are "pitiful and . . . mean"; that the "sum of our mortal state" is "feverish waking, danger, death, / And listless slumber": such assertions may be inflected by the politics of gender, but they cannot be contained by them.

　　If this Landon—the writer concerned with mortality, triviality, and terror—takes her place within twentieth-century criticism, we may gain a different sense both of L.E.L's prose and of its place in her career. Angela Leighton, for example, reads the achievement of the "Fragments," including "Stern Truth," as evidence of a "new, desolating sense of reality" in Landon's work. Once L.E.L. had attained such a vision, Leighton suggests, "as a poet, she had nowhere to go."[64] Yet as Leighton herself implicitly acknowledges, the sense of desolate reality that she perceptively identifies forms a crucial groundwork for Landon's novels. Even L.E.L.'s earlier verse, when reread with the novels in mind, reveals evocations of human desolation embedded within narratives of poetic or romantic passion.[65] What if the relatively plain diction and epigrammatic wit of Landon's prose had begun to transform her verse? If, indeed, the voices of L.E.L.'s poetry and her prose—of the "Fragments" and of *Ethel Churchill*—were beginning to merge, who knows where such developments might have led?[66]

Perhaps, then, we should attend more carefully to those of Landon's contemporaries for whom her career did not represent a decline. Consider, for example, the following summation, from the January 1840 *Fraser's:* "In her poems there are unquestioned indications of genius. . . . At the period of her death, she was rapidly rising in all that could gratify a lady and an authoress—in general estimation, in public honour, in increasing respect—as well as in the more matured development of her genius, made evident in her prose compositions. *Ethel Churchill* is, indeed, a work of beauty and talent, for which it would be hard to find a parallel in the history of female authorship. And then, when the prospect of her taking a place in her land's language was within her sight—*then* she died."[67]

It was as a writer, not merely a poet, that Landon lived; and considered in such terms, her career could appear as a crescendo cut short.[68] Rather than casting her death as the ironic culmination of a lifetime's commitment to the poetess's role, then, we might consider reading it as the collapse of a more complicated public persona—a developing persona capable of creating and claiming the power, as well as the moral ambiguity, of figures such as Lady Marchmont, Lavinia Fenton, and Walter Maynard. Landon had already rendered her own account of the feminine poetic fall deeply problematic; given more time, she might have transformed it altogether.

Such speculations can never be proved, of course. What can be known are more of the complexities of audience response to a many-layered literary career—as well as the joys of reading Landon's "reality" alongside her "romance." "Truly," reads an aside in *Romance and Reality*, "sorrow hath no more substance than a sandwich. . . . Affections are as passing as the worthless life they redeem."[69] Sorrow and a sandwich; relish for "remarks that, beginning in levity, die off into reflection"[70]—such are the qualities of Landon the satirist and moralist. A certain sort of gallows humor, of grim zestfulness in the evocation of human (and perhaps universal) triviality, is part of Landon's literary heritage. Accessible primarily through her prose, such ironic self-reflection emerges in her poetry as well. In certain of the poems written as epigraphs for *Ethel Churchill*, for example, as in "A Battle Field," her verse attains an unsparing matter-of-factness of tone, as well as—surprisingly, given her reputation—an economy of language, that may foreshadow such works as Christina Rossetti's "From the Antique" or "Later Life."[71] This L.E.L., whose indulgence in cosmic weariness and in epigrammatic, often bleak humor sets her apart from the poetess tradition, may come to claim her own sort of successors among a group as disparate as Thackeray, Christina Rossetti, Emily Dickinson, Oscar Wilde, Dorothy Parker, and Sylvia Plath. She should certainly claim the attention of Landon's critics today; and she may do so, in part, through closer attention to the critics of the past.

Notes

1. Mellor, *Romanticism and Gender*, 110; Stephenson, *Letitia Landon*, 3.

2. I. Armstrong, *Victorian Poetry*, 339.

3. Mellor, *Romanticism and Gender*, 110-14, 120-23; M.B. Ross, *The Contours of Masculine Desire*, 7-14, 295-97, 299-302. Stephenson's work is invaluable in this context.

4. See McGann, *Romantic Period Verse*, xxiii, 699-700, and Landon, *Selected Writings*. Landon has yet to break into that most canonical of U.S. teaching texts, the *Norton Anthology of English Literature*. Greater attention to Landon's periodical pieces, many of which have yet to be identified, may significantly alter readings of her work. See, for example, Landon, *Critical Writings* and *Selected Writings*, and Leighton, *Victorian Women Poets*, 50. Many of Landon's poems also have not been reprinted. See Glenn Dibert-Himes and Cynthia Lawford's invaluable though inevitably incomplete bibliography in Landon, *Selected Writings*, 387-506.

5. See [Sheppard], *The Genius and Writings of L.E.L.*, 11.

6. Foucault, "What Is an Author?"; Lootens, *Lost Saints*, 8-9, 15-44.

7. See, for example, Landon, "Erinna," or "A History of the Lyre."

8. See, for example, Jack, *English Literature 1815-1832*, 169. Benjamin Disraeli, to whom the Landon legend credits this phrase, actually wrote that L.E.L. "looked the very personification of Brompton—pink satin dress and white satin shoes, red cheeks snub nose, and her hair a la Sappho." Disraeli, *Letters: 1815-1834*, 247.

9. Landon appears as "another Cassandra," possessed by an "irresistible annunciation . . . of woe and desolation." Howitt, *Homes and Haunts*, 2:158. See, for example, Blanchard, *Life and Literary Remains of L.E.L.*, 1:213, 247; [Maginn,] "Preface to Our Second Decade," 24.

10. [Thomson], "Memorials of the Departed Great," 186. See Disraeli, *Letters: 1838-1841*, 132; and Metcalfe, *Maclean of the Gold Coast*, 238. Maclean, who claimed that rumors had made him a "monster" (Blanchard, *Life and Literary Remains of L.E.L.*, 1:208), also appears as a "ghost-like" figure akin to a demon lover ([Thomson], "Memorials of the Departed Great," 189; Thomson, *Recollections of Literary Characters*, 89). Maclean's status as *homme fatal* was intensified by reports that he had spurned an earlier fiancée, who accidentally burned to death while sealing a farewell letter to him. "L.E.L.," *Living Age* 190 (1891): 376; see Stephenson, *Letitia Landon*, 182.

11. Kenealy, E.V.H., "William Maginn," 100-101; R.R. Madden, *The Countess of Blessington*, 2:64-65. See also Stephenson, *Letitia Landon*, 183, 197 nn 10-11.

12. Greer, "The Tulsa Center," 19-23; Mellor, *Romanticism and Gender*, 110-23 (see esp. 123); Leighton, *Victorian Women Poets*, 57, 71, 74.

13. Landon, "Shuhur, Jeypore," lines 8-10; punctuation follows the epigraph's original source.

14. I. Armstrong, *Victorian Poetry*, 324-26.

15. Landon, "Shuhur Jeypore," 578 n. "The picture of a lonely burying-ground in India," Sheppard writes, seems to have "called forth" the poem. *The Genius and Writings of L.E.L.*, 49. First printed in *Fisher's Drawing-room Scrap Book* for 1834, it appears in the appendix to F.J. Sypher's 1990 facsimile reprint of the 1873 *Poetical Works*.

16. T.C. Croker, *A Walk from London to Fulham*, 34.

17. R.R. Madden, *The Countess of Blessington*, 2:63.

18. [Thomson], "Memorials of the Departed Great," 189; Thomson, *Recollections of Literary Characters*, 88.

19. The study, which covered 1817 to 1836, began publication in 1838, the year Landon died. P. Burroughs, "The Human Cost of Imperial Defence," 9, 13-14. Mortality rates on the Gold Coast were 668 per thousand: half of all arrivals to the Cape Coast "perished within three months and few survived fifteen" (14).

20. Blanchard, *Life and Literary Remains of L.E.L.*, 1:116; see also 1:9, 1:23. See I. Armstrong, *Victorian Poetry*, 324, on Africa as Landon's "impassioned land." L.E.L.'s own jokes about African travel scarcely suggest a sense of predestined exile. See Blanchard, *Life and Literary Remains of L.E.L.*, 1:36; Landon, *Romance and Reality*, 88.

21. Blanchard, *Life and Literary Remains of L.E.L.*, 1:181. See also Metcalfe, *Maclean of the Gold Coast*, 238; Hall, *Retrospect of a Long Life*, 396; Hall, "Memories of Authors," 339; "L.E.L.," *Living Age* 190 (1891): 378. Such stories may implicitly associate Landon with figures such as her own Edith, in "The Venetian Bracelet."

22. See especially Thomson's expanding speculations in "Memorials of the Departed Great," 191, and in *Recollections of Literary Characters*, 95-96. Madden, who claims that he himself was nearly poisoned by Maclean's servants (*The Countess of Blessington*, 2:65-66), also quotes similar, if less sensational views by Lady Blessington (2:72).

23. Blanchard, *Life and Literary Remains of L.E.L.*, 1:116; R.R. Madden, *The Countess of Blessington*, 2:46, 64. See also Forbes's 1874 reference to rumors that Maclean had kept a "harem of black women." Forbes, "A Gold Coast Tragedy," 699. For metaphoric associations of L.E.L. with slavery, see [Thomson], "Memorials of the Departed Great," 186. See also P.G. Patmore, *My Friends and Acquaintance*, 3:230.

24. Forbes, "A Gold Coast Tragedy," 697. See also "L.E.L. and the Gold Coast," 657. Roberts, "Memoir," 29; on Maclean and the slave trade, see Metcalfe, *Maclean of the Gold Coast*, 35-36, 69-70, 134-40, 204-5, 281-84. On Roberts's attitude toward Maclean, see Stephenson, *Letitia Landon*, 195.

25. R.R. Madden, *The Countess of Blessington*, 2:46-47; Metcalfe, *Maclean of the Gold Coast*, 249-54, 259-68, 280-83. Madden ruled out foul play in L.E.L.'s death. *The Countess of Blessington*, 2:59. Though Maclean's relations to abolition were justifiably controversial (Metcalfe, *Maclean of the Gold Coast*, 134-35, 219-86, 311-14), he seems also to have been the victim of malicious rumors (191-95, 204-5, 216-21).

26. Metcalfe, *Maclean of the Gold Coast*, 237.

27. See, for example, Blanchard, *Life and Literary Remains of L.E.L.*, 1:211-13, 244, 247; Howitt, *Homes and Haunts*, 2:145, 166; Hall, *Retrospect of a Long Life*, 395,

Receiving the Legend ~ 257

397-98; Hall, "Memories of Authors," 340; Fitzgerald, "The Story of L.E.L.," 53; Forbes, "A Gold Coast Tragedy," 697; [Maginn,] "Preface to Our Second Decade," 24-25; Cruickshank, *Eighteen Years on the Gold Coast,* 1:229-30; Metcalfe, *Maclean of the Gold Coast,* illustration after page 208. Stephenson offers a revealing detailed analysis of several contemporary accounts of Landon's death. *Letitia Landon,* 175-98.

28. R.R. Madden, *The Countess of Blessington,* 2:56-57; see also 53.

29. Hemans, "England's Dead," lines 7-8, 55-56.

30. Landon, "The Factory." Browning's "The Cry of the Children," for example, echoes and revises Landon, in terms of both argumentative structure and concern with maternal complicity in the continuation of child labor. For contemporary praise of L.E.L.'s social criticism, see [Sheppard], *The Genius and Writings of L.E.L.,* 50; Howitt, *Homes and Haunts,* 2:156-57. Rufus Griswold opens Landon's section of his successful anthology with this poem. "Mrs. Maclean," 389.

31. "Reviews: *Romance and Reality*," 793.

32. Stephenson, *Letitia Landon,* 40. "L.E.L. is above all a *poetic* persona," Stephenson asserts (19-20 n. 3): "readers and critics . . . soon dismissed the new voice" offered by the novels (40). Elsewhere, Stephenson clearly argues against reducing Landon to the figure she calls "L.E.L." (195).

33. Blanchard, *Life and Literary Remains of L.E.L.,* 2:240-76; Landon, *Poetical Works,* 420-53. For contemporary praise, see Moir, *Sketches,* 275; Browning, *Letters,* ed. Kenyon, 1:232; Thackeray, "Our Batch of Novels," 91.

34. For praise, see "Ethel Churchill," 423; for criticism, see Blanchard, *Life and Literary Remains of L.E.L.,* 1:135, and [Sheppard], *The Genius and Writings of L.E.L.,* 140-42. See also [Johnstone], "The New Novels," 755.

35. Sypher, introduction to *Ethel Churchill,* 16 n. 11. See Landon, "The Head" and "A Scene in the Life of Nourmahal" for more evidence of Landon's taste for violent storytelling. At points, the poisoning in *Ethel Churchill* has entered discussions of Landon's death. Howitt, *Homes and Haunts,* 2:158-63; Stephenson, *Letitia Landon,* 193-94. "I wonder if Brinvilliers suffered more / In the water-torture," Aurora asks of her dreary girlhood education. Browning, *Aurora Leigh,* book 1, 467-68. Clearly, Browning knew the court case; but Landon could well have helped bring this particular murderess to mind.

36. Landon, *Ethel Churchill,* 206, 208, 213.

37. Stephenson, *Letitia Landon,* 19-20 n. 3. The novel as a genre scarcely inhibited Landon's treatment of sexual politics, however. See, for example, *Romance and Reality,* 24-25, 103-4. In her unfinished last book, *Lady Anne Granard; or, Keeping Up Appearances,* Landon still satirizes gender relations: see her ironic praise of wedding guests (153), or her suggestion that young wives use cookbooks as manuals on managing husbands: "Your roasted husband is subdued by the fire of fierce words and fiercer looks— . . . — your boiled husband dissolves under the watery influences, while your confectionized husband goes through a course of the blanc mange of flattery" (112-13).

38. L.E.L. herself wryly notes this tendency. *Romance and Reality,* 122. For critics' identification of characters in *Ethel Churchill* with Landon, see Howitt, *Homes and Haunts,* 2:158, and Thackeray, "Our Batch of Novels," 91.

39. See L.E.L.'s own playful responses to criticism of excessive attention to char-

acters' looks. *Romance and Reality,* 62, 102. Suggestively, Katherine Thomson also adopted the persona of a male admirer describing the personal charms of L.E.L. herself: see "Memorials of the Departed Great." She did so, she wrote later, "in order that, by better disguising myself, I might . . . express myself the more unreservedly." Quoted in Stephenson, *Letitia Landon,* 185.

40. Even if such figures fawn on each other for the voyeuristic pleasure of the spectator, how much does that spectator's pleasure have to do with imagining theirs? Moreover, given the assumed readership of annuals, can one assume that the spectator in question is male?

41. Landon, *Ethel Churchill,* 162-63. On Landon's room at Hans Place, see T.C. Croker, *A Walk from London to Fulham,* 33-34.

42. See, for example, Landon, *Ethel Churchill,* 99-101. Such passages were further circulated by quotation. See "Reviews: *Ethel Churchill*"; [Sheppard], *The Genius and Writings of L.E.L.,* 12. For earlier writing in a similar vein, see Landon, *Romance and Reality,* 36-37.

43. Rich, "When We Dead Awaken," 39.

44. When George Gilfillan later praises Felicia Hemans for sparing him "the ludicrous image of a double-dyed Blue, in papers and morning wrapper, sweating at some stupendous treatise or tragedy" (*Modern Literature,* 234), one cannot help wondering whether he is referring to the unladylike (if indirect) self-representations of L.E.L.

45. Landon, *Ethel Churchill,* 150.

46. Landon, *Romance and Reality,* 36, 37.

47. Howitt, *Homes and Haunts,* 2:154.

48. Thackeray, "A Word on the Annuals," 763.

49. Quoted in Blanchard, *Life and Literary Remains of L.E.L.,* 1:132.

50. Enfield, *L.E.L.,* 83, see, however, the preceding paragraph. Enfield's work summarized and consolidated the modernist Landon legend on Thackeray's parody—see, for example, Cunliffe, *Leaders of the Victorian Revolution,* 88-89; Ray, *Thackeray,* 90-91; [Benjamin], *Life of Thackeray,* 1:30-31. See also Saintsbury, *Nineteenth-Century Literature,* 119.

51. Thackeray, "Our Batch of Novels," 91. See Thackeray, *Letters and Private Papers,* ed. Harden, 1:26; see also Sypher, introduction to *Ethel Churchill,* 11.

52. "—of that particular heart," he continues, ". . . which beats in the bosom of Miss Landon." "Our Batch of Novels," 91.

53. [Johnstone], "The New Novels," 745 (this review quotes virtually every scene in which Lavinia appears). See also Blanchard, *Life and Literary Remains of L.E.L.,* 1:135. Landon, *Ethel Churchill,* 105.

54. Landon, *Ethel Churchill,* 105, 202.

55. Landon follows history here: the actual Lavinia Fenton, who first brought Polly Peachum to the stage in John Gay's *The Beggar's Opera,* ended her life as the duchess of Bolton. See Highfill, Burnim, and Langhans, *A Biographical Dictionary,* 5:221-25.

56. [Thackeray and Maginn], "A Quintette of Novels," 480. Contemporaries consistently express unease at her work's pessimism. For a sampling of such comments over a period of years, see "The Troubadour and Other Poems," 385; Thackeray, "Our Batch of Novels," 91-92; [Maginn,] "Preface to Our Second Decade," 23-24; Blanchard, *Life*

and Literary Remains of L.E.L., 1:33-34, 125-26; "Memoir of Letitia Elizabeth Landon," 81-82.

57. Thackeray, *Vanity Fair,* 675. Dressed in black velvet, with "a serpent of precious stones" winding through her braid, Lady Marchmont returns from a ball. She begins "unfastening the glittering bands of her hair even while going up stairs; but her hands [sink] down, and she [stands] fixed on the threshold" (173, 188). Her husband is inside, waiting to confront her. Landon, *Ethel Churchill,* 172-73.

58. See [Sheppard], *The Genius and Writings of L.E.L.*, 27-29, 163, 165. Much of this essay was composed before I gained access to Sheppard's work; discovering the extent to which she had anticipated my readings was both exhilarating and unnerving.

59. [Sheppard], *The Genius and Writings of L.E.L.*, 164-65. Landon's literary professions of Christian faith include the volume *An Easter Offering,* of which she wrote in private, "Now do you think I could collect sin, sorrow, and sanctitude enough for a whole volume of sacred poetry?" "Really," she complained later, "it is not so easy to be pious as people think." T.F.D. Croker, "Landon's Correspondence," 67. For differing opinions of her attitude toward religion, see [Sheppard], *The Genius and Writings of L.E.L.*, 165; Leighton, *Victorian Women Poets,* 57, 68-69.

60. "Of course you are quite right about Vanity Fair . . ." he wrote in July 1847. "Dont you see how odious all the people are in the book (with exception of Dobbin)—behind whom all there lies a dark moral I hope." Thackeray, *Letters and Private Papers,* ed. Ray, 309.

61. See Landon, *The Golden Violet,* 187-88; and Thackeray, *Vanity Fair,* 361.

62. "Darkness came down on the field and city: and Amelia was praying for George, who was lying on his face, dead, with a bullet through his heart." Thackeray, *Vanity Fair,* 406.

63. Roberts, "Memoir," 7. For a more conventional battlefield poem attributed to Landon, see "The Sword," which was anthologized by an 1831 American textbook for "young ladies."

64. Leighton, *Victorian Women Poets,* 70-71.

65. See the introduction to "The Pilgrim's Tale" or "The Rose," both from Landon, *The Golden Violet,* 153-54, 174.

66. Since Landon died before *Lady Anne Granard* was completed, there is no way of knowing whether this final work, too, would have contained poetic epigraphs.

67. [Maginn,] "Preface to Our Second Decade," 25; quoted in Blanchard, *Life and Literary Remains of L.E.L.*, 1:243.

68. Sheppard devotes nearly half her study to Landon's prose. See, too, for example, a popular account such as "Celebrated Authoresses and their Works," (103). For accounts of a rising career cut short, see [Sheppard], *The Genius and Writings of L.E.L.*, 52; [Chorley], "Mrs. Maclean"; "Memoir of Letitia Elizabeth Landon," 81-82; Howitt, *Homes and Haunts,* 2:157. In contrast, see Chorley, *Autobiography, Memoir, and Letters,* 1:249-54; Martineau, *The Thirty Years' Peace,* 4:75-76. Griswold, in "Mrs. Maclean," manages to include both versions, as does R.R. Madden, *The Countess of Blessington,* 2:42, 44.

69. Landon, *Romance and Reality,* 196.

70. "Reviews: *Romance and Reality,*" 793.

71. In "Later Life," see esp. Sonnet 17, lines 9-14.

Works Cited

Aaron, Jane. *A Double Singleness: Gender and the Writings of Charles and Mary Lamb.* Oxford: Clarendon Press, 1991.

———. "A Modern Electra: Matricide and the Writings of Charles and Mary Lamb." In *Reviewing Romanticism,* edited by Philip W. Martin and Robin Jarvis, 1-13. Basingstoke, Eng.: Macmillan, 1992.

———. "'On Needlework': Protest and Contradiction in Mary Lamb's Essay." In Mellor, *Romanticism and Feminism,* 167-84.

Abrams, Meyer H. "English Romanticism: The Spirit of the Age. In *Romanticism and Consciousness,* edited by Harold Bloom, 91-119. 1963; New York: Norton, 1970.

———. *The Mirror and the Lamp.* London: Oxford Univ. Press, 1953.

———. "Structure and Style in the Greater Romantic Lyric." In *Romanticism and Consciousness,* edited by Harold Bloom, 201-29. New York: Norton, 1970.

Aikin, Charles Rochemont. Letter to A.L. Barbauld, 6 Dec. 1792. MS, Lady Rodgers (private collection).

Aikin, Lucy. *Epistles on Women, Exemplifying their Character and Condition in Various Ages and Nations, With Miscellaneous Poems.* London: J. Johnson, 1810.

———. Letter to William Roscoe, 20 Jan. 1823. MS 920 ROS 67, Liverpool Record Office, Liverpool, Eng.

———. "Memoir." In *The Works of Anna Letitia Barbauld,* edited by Lucy Aikin, 1:v-lxxii. London: Longman, Hurst, Rees, Orme, Brown, and Green, 1825.

Aikin-Sneath, Betsy. "Mrs. Barbauld." *Times Literary Supplement,* 25 Aug. 1932, 592.

Ainger, Alfred. "Mrs. Barbauld." In *Lectures and Essays,* by Alfred Ainger. 1:367-81. London: Macmillan, 1905.

Albergotti, Charles Dantzler, III. "Byron, Hemans, and the Reviewers, 1807-1835: Two Routes to Fame." Ph.D. diss., Univ. of South Carolina, 1995.

Alexander, Meena. *Women in Romanticism.* New York: Macmillan, 1989.

Anderson, John M. "'The First Fire': Barbauld Rewrites the Greater Romantic Lyric." *Studies in English Literature* 34 (1994): 719-38.

Anthony, Katherine. *The Lambs: A Story of Pre-Victorian England.* London: Hammond, Hammond, and Co., 1948.

Appleton, Miss [Elizabeth]. *Edgar; A National Tale.* 3 vols. London: Henry Colburn, 1816.

Arden, John. "Uses of Iron." *Cogs Tyrannic: Four Stories.* London: Methuen, 1991.

Arliss, George. Introduction to *On the Stage,* by Frances Anne Kemble. New York: Dramatic Museum of Columbia Univ., 1926.

Armstrong, Isobel. "Caterpillar on the Skin." *Times Literary Supplement,* 12 July 1996, 27.

———. "The Gush of the Feminine: How Can We Read Women's Poetry of the Romantic Period?" In Feldman and Kelley, *Romantic Women Writers,* 13-32.

———. "'A Music of Thine Own': Women's Poetry—An Expressive Tradition?" Chap. 12 in *Victorian Poetry: Poetry, Poetics and Politics.* New York: Routledge, 1993.

Armstrong, Nancy. *Desire and Domestic Fiction: A Political History of the Novel.* Oxford: Oxford Univ. Press, 1987.

Armstrong, Nancy, and Leonard Tennenhouse. "Introduction: Representing Violence, or 'How the West Was Won.'" In *The Violence of Representation: Literature and the History of Violence,* edited by Nancy Armstrong and Leonard Tennenhouse. 1-26. New York: Routledge, 1989.

Arnold, Matthew. *Complete Prose Works.* Edited by Robert Henry Super. Vols. 3, 5, 9, 10. Ann Arbor: Univ. of Michigan Press, 1962, 1965, 1973, 1974.

Ashfield, Andrew. Introduction to *Romantic Women Poets 1770-1838: An Anthology,* edited by Andrew Ashfield, xi-xviii. Manchester, Eng.: Manchester Univ. Press, 1995.

Ashton, Helen, and Katherine Davies. *I Had a Sister: A Study of Mary Lamb, Dorothy Wordsworth, Caroline Herschel, Cassandra Austen.* London: Lovat Dickson, 1937.

Auerbach, Nina. *Private Theatricals: The Lives of the Victorians.* Cambridge, Mass.: Harvard Univ. Press, 1990.

Baker, H. Barton. "Mrs. Barbauld." *Argosy* 17 (1881): 303-8.

Balfour, Clara. *Working Women of the last Half Century: The Lesson of their Lives.* London: Cash, 1854.

Balle, Mary Blanchard. "Mary Lamb: Her Mental Health Issues." *Charles Lamb Bulletin,* n.s., 93 (Jan. 1996): 2-11.

Bannerman, Anne. *Tales of Superstition and Chivalry.* London: Vernor and Hood, 1802.

Barbauld, Anna Letitia. *An Address to the Opposers of the Repeal of the Corporation and Test Acts.* 2d ed. London: J. Johnson, 1790.

———. "Mrs. Charlotte Smith." Vol. 36 of *The British Novelists.* 50 vols. London: F.C. and J. Rivington, 1810.

———. *A Legacy for Young Ladies.* Edited by Lucy Aikin. London: Longman, Hurst, Rees, Orme, Brown, and Green, 1826.

———. *The Poems of Anna Letitia Barbauld.* Edited by William McCarthy and Elizabeth Kraft. Athens: Univ. of Georgia Press, 1994.

Barrell, P. *The Test of Virtue, and Other Poems.* London: C. Chapple and T. Boosey, 1811.

Barrett [Browning], Elizabeth. *The Letters of Elizabeth Barrett Browning to Mary Russell Mitford, 1836-1854.* Edited by Meredith B. Raymond and Mary Rose Sullivan. 3 vols. Winfield, Kans.: Wedgestone Press, 1983.

Barton, Bernard. "The Daughter of Herodias." *A New Year's Eve.* London: John Hatchard and Son, 1828. English Poetry Full Text Database (online). Available: Chadwyck-Healy, 5 Feb. 1998.

Bataille, Georges. "The Use Value of D.A.F. de Sade." In *Visions of Excess: Selected Writings 1927-1939,* translated by Allan Stoekl, 91-102. Minneapolis: Univ. of Minnesota Press, 1985.

Beard, Charles. "Anna Letitia Barbauld." *Theological Review* 11 (1874): 388-406.

Beers, Henry A. *A History of Romanticism in the Nineteenth Century.* New York: Henry Holt, 1901.

Beeton, S.O., ed. *Beeton's Great Book of Poetry.* 2 vols. London, 1871.

Behrendt, Stephen C. "British Women Poets and the Reverberations of Radicalism in the 1790s." In *Romanticism, Radicalism, and the Press,* edited by Stephen C. Behrendt, 83-102. Detroit: Wayne State Univ. Press, 1997.

———. "Placing the Places in Wordsworth's 1802 Sonnets." *Studies in English Literature 1500-1900* 35 (1995): 641-67

[Benjamin, Lewis S.]. *The Life of William Makepeace Thackeray.* Chicago: Herbert S. Stone, 1909.

Bennett, Betty T., ed. *British War Poetry in the Age of Romanticism: 1793-1815.* New York: Garland, 1976.

Bernhardt-Kabisch, Ernest. *Robert Southey.* Boston: Twayne, 1977.

Bethune, George W. *The British Female Poets: With Biographical and Critical Notices.* Philadelphia: Lindsay and Blakiston, 1848.

Blackburne, E. Owens [Elizabeth Casey, pseud.]. *Illustrious Irishwomen. Being Memoirs of Some of the Most Noted Irishwomen from the Earliest Ages to the Present Century.* 2 vols. London: Tinsley Brothers, 1877.

Blain, Virginia. *Caroline Bowles Southey, 1786-1854: The Making of a Woman Writer.* Brookfield, Vermont: Ashgate, 1998.

Blain, Virginia, Isobel Grundy, and Patricia Clements, eds. *The Feminist Companion to Literature in English.* New Haven, Conn.: Yale Univ. Press, 1990.

Blanchard, Laman. *Life and Literary Remains of L.E.L.* 2 vols. Philadelphia: Lea and Blanchard, 1841.

Bloom, Harold. "The Internalization of Quest-Romance." In *Romanticism and Consciousness,* edited by Harold Bloom, 3-24. New York: Norton, 1970.

Bloomfield, Robert. *The Farmer's Boy; a Rural Poem.* London: Vernor and Hood, 1800.

Booth, Alison. "From Miranda to Prospero: The Works of Fanny Kemble." *Victorian Studies* 38, no. 2 (1995): 227-54.

Boswell, James. *The Life of Samuel Johnson.* Edited by George Birkbeck Hill and Lawrence Fitzroy Powell. Oxford: Clarendon Press, 1934.

Bowles, Caroline. *The Birthday and Other Poems.* Edinburgh: Blackwood, 1836.

———. *Chapters on Churchyards.* Edinburgh: Blackwood, 1829; 2d ed., 1841.

———. *Solitary Hours.* Edinburgh: Blackwood, 1826; 2d ed., 1839.

———. *Tales of the Factories.* Edinburgh: Blackwood, 1833.

———. *The Widow's Tale.* London: Longmans, 1822. Reprint, New York: Woodstock Books, 1996.

Brantlinger, Patrick. "Victorians and Africans: The Genealogy of the Myth of the Dark

Continent." In *"Race," Writing, and Difference,* edited by Henry Louis Gates Jr., 185-222. Chicago: Univ. of Chicago Press, 1986.

Bratton, Jacky. "Working in the Margin: Women in Theatre History." *New Theatre Quarterly* 10, no. 38 (1994): 122-31.

Brightwell, Cecilia Lucy. *Memorials of the Life of Amelia Opie.* London: Longman and Brown, 1854.

Bristow, A[melia]. *The Maniac, a Tale; or, A View of Bethlem Hospital; and The Merits of Women, a Poem from the French: with poetical pieces on various subjects, original and translated.* London: J. Hatchard, 1810.

British Critic (Apr. 1806): 428-29.

British Critic (June 1809): 618-23.

British Public Characters of 1800-1801. Vol. 3. London: Richard Phillips, 1807, 43-65.

British Review (Jan. 1820): 299-300.

[Brodribb, C.W.] "'Life, I Know Not': Mrs. Barbauld, 1743-1825." *Times Literary Supplement,* 19 June 1943, 298.

[Browne, Felicia Dorothea (later Hemans)]. *The Domestic Affections.* London: T. Cadell and W. Davies, 1812.

Browning, Elizabeth Barrett. *Aurora Leigh.* In Browning, *Complete Works,* vols. 4 and 5.

———. *Complete Works of Elizabeth Barrett Browning.* Edited by Charlotte Porter and Helen A. Clarke. New York: Thomas Y. Crowell, 1900.

———. "Cry of the Children." In Browning, *Complete Works,* 3:53-59, 362-63.

———. *The Letters of Elizabeth Barrett Browning.* Edited by Frederic G. Kenyon. 2 vols. New York: Macmillan, 1898.

Bryant, William Cullen, ed. *A New Library of Poetry and Song.* New York, 1877.

Burroughs, Catherine B. *Closet Stages: Joanna Baillie and the Theater Theory of British Romantic Women Writers.* Philadelphia: Univ. of Pennsylvania Press, 1997.

Burroughs, Peter. "The Human Cost of Imperial Defence in the Early Victorian Age." *Victorian Studies* 24 (1980): 7-32.

Butler, Judith. *Bodies That Matter: On the Discursive Limits of Sex.* New York: Routledge, 1993.

Butler, Marilyn. "Revising the Canon." *Times Literary Supplement,* 4-10 Dec. 1987, 1349.

———. *Romantics, Rebels and Reactionaries: English Literature and its Background, 1760-1830.* New York: Oxford Univ. Press, 1981.

Byron, George Gordon, Lord. *Byron's Letters and Journals.* Edited by Leslie Marchand. 12 vols. Cambridge, Mass.: Harvard Univ. Press, 1973-82.

The Cambridge Book of Poetry and Song. Charlotte Fiske Bates, ed. New York: Crowell, [1882].

Cameron, Sharon. *Lyric Time: Dickinson and the Limits of Genre.* Baltimore: Johns Hopkins Univ. Press, 1979.

Campbell, D[orothea] P[rimrose], of Zetland, *Poems.* London: Baldwin, Craddock, and Joy, 1816.

Campbell, Thomas. *The Pleasures of Hope; with Other Poems.* Edinburgh: Mundell; London: Longman, 1799.

Carlson, Julie. *In the Theatre of Romanticism: Coleridge, Nationalism, Women.* Cambridge: Cambridge Univ. Press, 1994.

"Caroline Southey." *Athenaeum* (5 Aug. 1854), 969-70.

Castle, Terry. "Unruly and Unresigned." *Times Literary Supplement,* 10-16 Nov. 1989, 1227-28.

"Celebrated Authoresses and Their Works." *Englishwoman's Domestic Magazine* 26 (1878): 52-54, 101-5.

Charriére, Isabelle de. *Œuvres complètes.* Edited by Jean-Daniel Dandaux. 10 vols. Amsterdam: G.A. Van Oorschot, 1979-81.

Choice Poems and Lyrics. London, 1867.

Chorley, Henry F. *Autobiography, Memoir, and Letters.* Compiled by Henry G. Hewlett. Vol. 1. London: Richard Bentley and Son, 1873.

———. *Memorials of Mrs. Hemans, with Illustrations of her Literary Character from her Private Correspondence.* 2 vols. London: Saunders and Otley, 1836.

[———]. "Mrs. Maclean." *Athenaeum* (5 Jan. 1839): 14.

Clare, John. *The Natural History Prose Writings of John Clare.* Edited by Margaret Grainger. Oxford: Clarendon Press, 1983.

Clarke, Norma. *Ambitious Heights: Writing, Friendship, Love--The Jewsbury Sisters, Felicia Hemans, and Jane Welsh Carlyle.* London: Routledge, 1990.

Coleman, Deirdre. "Conspicuous Consumption: White Abolitionism and English Women's Writing in the 1790s." *English Literary History* 61 (1994): 341-62.

[Coleridge, Hartley Nelson]. "Modern Poetesses." *Quarterly Review* 66 (July/Sept. 1840): 374-418.

Coleridge, Samuel Taylor. "Introduction to the Sonnets." In *The Complete Poetical and Dramatic Works,* edited by James Dykes Campbell. 572-644. 1796. Reprint, London: Macmillan, 1938.

———. *Lectures 1808-1819 on Literature,* edited by R.A. Foakes. Princeton, N.J.: Princeton Univ. Press, 1987.

———. *Letters, Conversations and Recollections.* London: Moxon, 1836.

———. *Notebooks.* Edited by Kathleen Coburn. Vol. 2, New York: Pantheon, 1961; vol. 3, Princeton, N.J.: Princeton Univ. Press, 1973.

———. *Table Talk.* Edited by Carl Woodring. Princeton, N.J.: Princeton Univ. Press, 1990.

"Contemporary Poets. No. I." *New European Magazine* 3 (1823): 120-33.

Coppée, Henry, ed. *A Gallery of English and American Women Famous in Song.* Philadelphia, 1875.

Corbett, Mary Jean. *Representing Femininity: Middle-Class Subjectivity in Victorian and Edwardian Women's Autobiographies.* New York: Oxford Univ. Press, 1992.

Courtney, Janet E. *The Adventurous Thirties: A Chapter in the Women's Movement.* 1933. Reprint, Freeport, N.Y.: Books for Libraries Press, 1967.

Cowper, William. *The Correspondence.* Edited by Thomas Wright. 4 vols. London: Hodder and Stoughton, 1904.

———. *The Poems of William Cowper.* Vol. 3, edited by John D. Baird and Charles Ryskamp. Oxford: Clarendon Press, 1995.

Cox, Jeffrey. *Seven Gothic Dramas, 1789-1825.* Athens: Ohio Univ. Press, 1992.

Critical Review (Aug. 1811): 419.

Critical Review (Nov. 1812): 554.

Croker, T.F. Dillon, ed. "Miss Landon's Correspondence with Thomas Crofton Croker, 1831-1838." *Sharpe's London Magazine* 35 (Feb. 1862): 64-67.

Croker, Thomas Crofton. *A Walk from London to Fulham*. London: William Tegg, 1860.

Crookshank, C.H. *Memorable Women of Irish Methodism of the Last Century*. London: Wesley-Methodist Book-Room, 1882.

Crowell, Thomas Young, ed. *Red Letter Poems by English Men and Women*. New York, 1885.

Cruickshank, Brodie. *Eighteen Years on the Gold Coast of Africa*. 2 vols. 1853. Reprint, London: Frank Cass, 1966.

Culler, Jonathan. *Structuralist Poetics*. Ithaca, N.Y.: Cornell Univ. Press, 1975.

Cummings, E.E. *Complete Poems: 1904-1962*. Edited by George J. Firmage. New York: Liveright, 1944.

Cunliffe, John W. *Leaders of the Victorian Revolution*. New York: D. Appleton, [1934].

Cunningham, Valentine. *Everywhere Spoken Against: Dissent in the Victorian Novel*. Oxford: Clarendon Press, 1975.

Curran, Stuart. *Poetic Form and British Romanticism*. New York: Oxford Univ. Press, 1986.

———. "Romantic Poetry: The 'I' Altered." In Mellor, *Romanticism and Feminism*, 185-207.

———. "Romantic Poetry: Why and Wherefore?" In *The Cambridge Companion to British Romanticism*, edited by Stuart Curran, 216-35. Cambridge: Cambridge Univ. Press, 1993.

———. "Women Readers, Women Writers." In *The Cambridge Companion to British Romanticism*, edited by Stuart Curran, 177-95. Cambridge: Cambridge Univ. Press, 1993.

Curry, Kenneth, ed. *New Letters of Robert Southey*. 2 vols. New York: Columbia Univ. Press, 1965.

Dacre, Charlotte. *Hours of Solitude*. 2 vols. in 1. London: Hughes and Ridgeway, 1805. Facsimile ed., edited by Donald H. Reiman, New York: Garland, 1978.

Davie, Donald. *A Gathered Church: The Literature of the English Dissenting Interest, 1700-1930*. New York: Oxford Univ. Press, 1978.

Davis, David Brion. "The Quaker Ethic and the Antislavery Internation." In *The Antislavery Debate: Capitalism and Abolitionism as a Problem in Historical Interpretation*, edited by Thomas Bender, 27-64. Berkeley: Univ. of California Press, 1992.

de Lauretis, Teresa. "The Violence of Rhetoric: Considerations of Representation and Gender." In *The Violence of Representation: Literature and the History of Violence*, edited by Nancy Armstrong and Leonard Tennenhouse, 239-58. New York: Routledge, 1989.

Dennis, John. ed. *Robert Southey: The Story of His Life Written in His Letters*. London: George Bell and Sons, 1894.

Derrida, Jacques. *Of Grammatology*. Translated by Gayatri Spivak. Baltimore: Johns Hopkins Univ. Press, 1976.

———. *Writing and Difference*. Translated by Alan Bass. Chicago: Univ. of Chicago Press, 1978.

Dictionary of National Biography. S.v. "Opie, Amelia." Vol. 42., 1921-22.

Dictionary of National Biography. S.v. "Southey, Caroline." Vol. 53., 283.

Dictionary of National Biography. S.v. "Tighe, Mary." Vol. 56., 388-89.

Disraeli, Benjamin. *Benjamin Disraeli Letters: 1815-1834.* Edited by John Alexander Wilson Gunn, John Matthews, Donald M. Schurman, and M.G. Wiebe. Toronto: Univ. of Toronto Press, 1982.

———. *Benjamin Disraeli Letters: 1838-1841.* Edited by M.G. Wiebe, J.B. Conacher, and John Matthews. Toronto: Univ. of Toronto Press, 1987.

Doane, Mary Ann. *Femmes Fatales: Feminism, Film Theory, Psychoanalysis.* New York: Routledge, 1991.

Dobson, Meaghan Hanrahan. "(Re)considering Mary Lamb: Imagination and Memory in *Mrs. Leicester's School.*" *Charles Lamb Bulletin,* n.s., 93 (Jan. 1996): 12-21.

[Dorset, Catherine Ann]. *The Peacock "At Home": A Sequel to the Butterfly's Ball.* London: J. Harris, 1807.

Dorset, Mrs. [Catherine Ann]. *The Peacock "At Home"; and Other Poems.* London: John Murray, J. Harris, 1809.

Dowden, Edward, ed. *The Correspondence of Robert Southey with Caroline Bowles.* London: Longmans Green, 1881.

———. *Southey.* English Men of Letters Series. 1879. Reprint, New York: Harper, 1902.

The Earlier British Drawings. Compiled by David Blayney Brown. Vol. 4 of *Ashmolean Museum Oxford: Catalogue of the Collection of Drawings.* Oxford: Clarendon Press, 1982.

Eberle, Roxanne. "Amelia Opie's *Adeline Mowbray:* Diverting the Libertine Gaze: or, The Vindication of a Fallen Woman." *Studies in the Novel* 26, no. 2 (1994): 121-52.

Ellis, Grace. *A Memoir of Mrs. Anna Letitia Barbauld.* Boston: Osgood, 1874.

Enfield, D.E. *L.E.L.: A Mystery of the Thirties.* London: Hogarth Press, 1928.

"Ethel Churchill." *New Monthly Magazine* (Nov. 1837): 421-24.

Ezell, Margaret J.M. *Writing Women's Literary History.* Baltimore: Johns Hopkins Univ. Press, 1993.

Feldman, Paula R., ed. *British Women Poets of the Romantic Era: An Anthology.* Baltimore: Johns Hopkins Univ. Press, 1997.

Feldman, Paula R. "The Poet and the Profits: Felicia Hemans and the Literary Marketplace." *Keats-Shelley Journal* 46 (1997): 148-76.

Feldman, Paula R., and Theresa M. Kelley, eds. *Romantic Women Writers: Voices and Countervoices.* Hanover, N.H.: Univ. Press of New England, 1995.

Felman, Shoshana. "Narrative as Testimony: Camus's *The Plague.*" In *Reading Narrative: Form, Ethics, Ideology,* edited by James Phelan, 250-61. Columbus: Ohio State Univ. Press, 1989.

Ferguson, Moira. *Subject to Others: British Women Writers and Colonial Slavery, 1670-1834.* New York: Routledge, 1992.

Fields, James T., and Edwin P. Whipple, eds. *The Family Library of British Poetry from Chaucer to the Present Time.* Boston, 1881.

Finney, Claude Lee. *The Evolution of Keats's Poetry.* 2 vols. Cambridge, Mass.: Harvard Univ. Press, 1936.

Fitzgerald, Percy. "The Story of L.E.L." *Gentleman's Magazine.* Reprint, *Living Age* 156 (Jan. 1883): 47-53.

Fladeland, Betty. *Men and Brothers: Anglo-American Cooperation.* Urbana: Univ. of Illinois Press, 1972.

Flowerdew, A[lice]. *Poems, on Moral and Religious Subjects.* London: H.D. Symonds, Mrs. Gurney, E. Vidler, 1803.

———. *Poems on Moral and Religious Subjects: To Which are Pefixed, Introductory Remarks on a Course of Female Education.* 3d ed. London: Sherwood, Neely, and Jones, 1811.

Folger Collective, ed. *Women Critics, 1660-1820: An Anthology.* Bloomington: Indiana Univ. Press, 1995.

Forbes, Archibald. "A Gold Coast Tragedy." *St. Paul's.* Reprint, *Living Age* 120 (March 1874): 697-701.

Foucault, Michel. *Discipline and Punish: The Birth of the Prison.* Translated by Alan Sheridan. New York: Vintage, 1979.

———. *The History of Sexuality.* Vol. 1, *An Introduction,* translated by Robert Hurley. New York: Vintage, 1980.

———. "Tales of Murder." In *I, Pierre Rivière, having slaughtered my mother, my sister, and my brother . . . : A Case of Parricide in the 19th Century,* edited by Michel Foucault, translated by Frank Jellinek, 199-212. 1975. Reprint, Lincoln: Univ. of Nebraska Press, 1982.

———. "What Is an Author?" In *Language, Counter-Memory, Practice: Selected Essays and Interviews,* edited by Donald F. Bouchard, translated by Donald F. Bouchard and Sherry Simon, 113-38. Ithaca, N.Y.: Cornell Univ. Press, 1992.

Fox-Genovese, Elizabeth. Foreword to *Fanny Kemble: Journal of a Young Actress,* edited by Monica Gough, ix-xx. New York: Columbia Univ. Press.

Fried, Michael. *Absorption and Theatricality: Painting and Beholder in the Age of Diderot.* Chicago: Univ. of Chicago Press, 1980.

Friedman, Leslie Joan. "Mary Lamb: Sister, Seamstress, Murderer, Writer." 2 vols. Ph.D. diss., Stanford Univ., 1976.

Frye, Northrop. *Anatomy of Criticism.* Princeton, N.J.: Princeton Univ. Press, 1957.

———. "Approaching the Lyric." In *Lyric Poetry: Beyond New Criticism,* edited by Chaviva Hosek and Patricia Parker, 31-37. Ithaca, N.Y.: Cornell Univ. Press, 1985.

———. *A Study of English Romanticism.* Chicago: Univ. of Chicago Press, 1968.

Fryer, Peter. *Staying Power: Black People in Britain since 1504.* Atlantic Highlands, N.J.: Humanities Press, 1984.

Fuseli, Henry. *Woman with a Stiletto, Man's Head with a Startled Expression* (1810-20). In *Henry Fuseli, 1741-1825,* 134. London: Tate Gallery Publications Dept., 1975.

Gardner, Martin. *The Annotated Ancient Mariner.* New York: Clarkson Potter, 1965.

Gaskell, Elizabeth. *The Life of Charlotte Brontë.* London: Smith, Elder, and Co., 1857. Reprint, New York: Penguin, 1980.

Gates, Henry Louis, Jr. *Figures in Black: Words, Signs, and the 'Racial' Self.* New York: Oxford Univ. Press, 1987.

Gibbon, Charles, ed. *The Casquet of Literature: being a Selection in Poetry and Prose from the works of the most admired authors.* 4 vols. London, 1874-75.

[Gifford, William]. "Mrs. Hemans's Poems." *Quarterly Review* 24 (1820): 130-39.

Gilbert, Sandra, and Susan Gubar. *The Madwoman in the Attic: The Woman Writer and the Nineteenth-Century Literary Imagination.* New Haven, Conn.: Yale Univ. Press, 1979.

Gilchrist, Mrs. *Mary Lamb.* London: W.H. Allen, 1883.

Gilfillan, George. "Female Authors. No. I--Mrs. Hemans." *Tait's Edinburgh Magazine,* n.s., 14 (1847): 359-63.

———. "Mrs. Hemans." In *Modern Literature and Literary Men: Being a Gallery of Literary Portraits,* 229-39. New York: D. Appleton, 1850.

Gooch, Elizabeth Sarah. *Sherwood Forest; or, Northern Adventures. A Novel.* London: S. Highley, 1804.

Greer, Germaine. "The Tulsa Center for the Study of Women's Literature: What We Are Doing and Why We Are Doing It." *Tulsa Studies in Women's Literature* 1 (1982): 5-26.

Grigson, Geoffrey, ed. *A Choice of Southey's Verse.* London: Faber, 1970.

Griswold, Rufus W. "Mrs. Maclean." In *The Poets and Poetry of England, in the Nineteenth Century.* Edited by Rufus W. Griswold. 388-89. Philadelphia: Carey and Hart, 1846.

Gutwirth, Madelyn. *The Twilight of the Goddesses: Women and Representation in the French Revolutionary Era.* New Brunswick, N.J.: Rutgers Univ. Press, 1992.

Halbersleben, Karen. *Women's Participation in the British Antislavery Movement, 1824-1865.* Lewiston, N.Y.: Edwin Mellen Press, 1993.

Hale, Sarah Josepha. *Woman's Record; or, Sketches of all Distinguished Women, from the Creation to A.D. 1854.* 2d ed. New York: Harper, 1855.

Hall, Samuel Carter. *A Book of Memories of Great Men and Women of the Age.* London: Virtue, 1871.

———. "Memories of Authors." *Atlantic Monthly* (March 1865): 330-40.

———. *Retrospect of a Long Life: From 1815 to 1883.* New York: D. Appleton, 1883.

[Hamilton, Lady Anne]. *The Epics of the Ton; or, The Glories of the Great World: A Poem.* London: C. and R. Baldwin, 1807.

Hamilton, C[atherine] J[ane]. *Notable Irishwomen.* Dublin: Sealy, Bryers, and Walker, 1904.

Harvey, Arnold D. *English Poetry in a Changing Society, 1780-1825.* New York: St. Martin's Press, 1980.

Hazlitt, W. Carew, ed. and commentator. *Mary and Charles Lamb: Poems, Letters and Remains.* London: Chatto and Windus, 1874.

Hedrick, Joan D. *Harriet Beecher Stowe: A Life.* New York: Oxford Univ. Press, 1994.

Heinzelman, Kurt. "The Uneducated Imagination." In *At the Limits of Romanticism: Essays in Cultural, Feminist, and Materialist Criticism,* edited by Mary Favret and Nicola Watson, 101-24. Bloomington: Indiana Univ. Press, 1994.

Hemans, Felicia. "England's Dead." In *Works of Mrs. Hemans,* 6 vols., 5:127-29. Edinburgh: Blackwood, 1839.

———. *The Poetical Works of Felicia Dorothea Hemans.* Oxford Edition. Oxford: Humphrey Milford, 1914.

————. *The Poetical Works of Mrs. Hemans.* Albion Edition. London: Frederick Warne, 1900.

————. *Poetical Works of Mrs. Hemans.* Chandos Classics. London: Frederick Warne, [ca. 1875].

————. *Records of Woman.* London: Cadell, 1828.

————. *The Restoration of the Works of Art to Italy: A Poem.* London: J. Murray, 1816.

————. *The Sceptic; a Poem.* London: John Murray, 1820.

————. *The Siege of Valencia; A Dramatic Poem; The Last Constantine: With Other Poems.* London: John Murray, 1823.

————. *Tales, and Historic Scenes, in Verse.* London: John Murray, 1819.

Henchy, Patrick. *The Works of Mary Tighe, Published and Unpublished.* The Bibliographic Society of Ireland 6.6. Dublin: At the Sign of the Three Candles, 1957.

Heyrick, Elizabeth. *Immediate, Not Gradual Abolition; or, An Inquiry into the Shortest, Safest, and Most Effectual Means of Getting Rid of West Indian Slavery.* 1824. Philadelphia: Merrihew and Gunn, 1836.

Hickok, Kathleen. *Representations of Women: Nineteenth-Century British Women's Poetry.* Westport, Conn.: Greenwood Press, 1984.

Highfill, Philip H., Kalman A. Burnim, and Edward A. Langhans. *A Biographical Dictionary of Actors, Actresses, Musicians, Dancers, Managers and Other Stage Personnel in London, 1660-1800.* Chicago: Southern Illinois Univ. Press, 1978.

Hoeveler, Diane Long. *Romantic Androgyny: The Women Within.* University Park: Pennsylvania State Univ. Press, 1990.

Hofkosh, Sonia. "The Writer's Ravishment: Women and the Romantic Author--the Example of Byron." In Mellor, *Romanticism and Feminism,* 93-114.

Homans, Margaret. *Bearing the Word: Language and Female Experience in Nineteenth-Century Women's Writing.* Chicago: Univ. of Chicago Press, 1986.

————. "Keats Reading Women, Women Reading Keats." *Studies in Romanticism* 29 (1990): 341-70.

————. *Women Writers and Poetic Identity: Dorothy Wordsworth, Emily Brontë, and Emily Dickinson.* Princeton, N.J.: Princeton Univ. Press, 1980.

Horwood, E. *Instructive Amusements for Young Minds.* London: A.K. Newman and Co., 1815.

Howitt, William. "L.E.L." In *Homes and Haunts of the Most Eminent British Poets,* 2:145-66. New York: Harper, 1847.

————. "Mrs. Tighe, the Author of Psyche." In *Homes and Haunts of the British Poets,* 281-91. London: Routledge, 1894.

————. *The Northern Heights of London.* London: Longmans, 1869.

Hoyle, Charles. *Exodus: An Epic Poem.* London: J. Hatchard, 1807.

Hughes, Harriett. *The Works of Mrs. Hemans; with a Memoir of her Life, by her Sister.* 7 vols. London: Thomas Cadell; Edinburgh: William Blackwood and Sons, 1839.

————. *Memoir.* In *The Works of Mrs. Hemans.* London: Thomas Cadell; Edinburgh: William Blackwood and Sons, 1839, 1:1-315.

Hunt, Bishop C., Jr. "Wordsworth and Charlotte Smith." *Wordsworth Circle* 1 (1970): 85-103.

Hunt, Leigh. *The Book of the Sonnet.* Edited by Leigh Hunt and S. Adams Lee. Boston: Roberts Brothers, 1867.

————. "Specimens of British Poetesses." In *Men, Women, and Books: A Selection of Sketches, Essays, and Critical Memoirs From His Uncollected Prose Writings.* New York: Harper, 1847, 2:95-136; London: Smith, Elder, 1891, 257-86.

Hunt, Lynn. *The Family Romance of the French Revolution.* Berkeley: Univ. of California Press, 1992.

Hussey, Cyril. "Fresh Light on the Poems of Mary Lamb." *Supplement to the Charles Lamb Bulletin* 213 (Jan. 1972): 1-12.

Inglis, Robert, ed. *Gleanings from the English Poets.* Edinburgh, [ca. 1882].

Jack, Ian. *The Oxford History of English Literature, 1815-1832.* Edited by F.P. Wilson and Bonamy Dobree. Oxford: Oxford Univ. Press, 1963.

Jackson, James Robert de Jager. *Poetry of the Romantic Period.* London: Routledge, 1980.

————, ed. *Annals of English Verse, 1779-1835: A Preliminary Survey of the Volumes Published.* New York: Garland Press, 1985.

————, ed. *Romantic Poetry by Women: A Bibliography, 1770-1835.* Oxford: Clarenden Press, 1993.

James, Henry. *The American Scene.* 1907. Reprint, Bloomington: Indiana Univ. Press, 1968.

[————]. "The Schönberg-Cotta Family." *Nation,* 14 Sept. 1865, 344-45.

Jeffrey, Francis. Review of *Records of Woman* (2d ed.) and *The Forest Sanctuary* (2d ed.), by Hemans. *Edinburgh Review, or Critical Journal* 50 (Oct. 1829): 32-47.

Jerdan, William. *Men I Have Known.* London: George Routledge and Sons, 1866.

Jewsbury, Maria Jane. *The History of a Nonchalant.* In *The Three Histories. The History of an Enthusiast. The History of a Nonchalant. The History of a Realist.* 1830. Reprint, Boston: Perkins, and Marvin, 1831.

Johnson, Samuel. "Milton." In *Lives of the English Poets,* edited by George Birkbeck Hill, 1:84-194. Oxford: Clarendon Press, 1905.

[Johnstone, C.I.] "The New Novels. No. 1.--Ethel Churchill." *Tait's Edinburgh Magazine* (1837): 745-56.

Jones, Alun R., ed. *Wordsworth's Poems of 1807.* Atlantic Highlands, N.J.: Humanities Press International, 1987.

Kahan, Gerald. "Fanny Kemble Reads Shakespeare: Her First American Tour, 1849-50." *Theatre Survey* 24, nos. 1-2 (1983): 77-98.

Kaplan, Cora. *Salt and Bitter and Good: Three Centuries of English and American Women Poets.* New York: Paddington, 1973.

Karl, Frederick R. *George Eliot, Voice of a Century: A Biography.* New York: Norton, 1995.

Keats, John. *The Letters of John Keats.* Edited by Robert Gittings. London: Oxford Univ. Press, 1970.

Kelley, Theresa M., and Paula R. Feldman. Introduction to *Romantic Women Writers: Voices and Countervoices,* edited by Paula R. Feldman and Theresa M. Kelley, 1-10. Hanover, N.H.: Univ. Press of New England, 1995.

Kemble, Frances Anne. *An English Tragedy, Plays.* London: Longman, Green, Longman, Roberts, and Green, 1863.

————. *Fanny Kemble: Journal of a Young Actress*. Edited by Monica Gough. New York: Columbia Univ. Press, 1990.

————. *Journal of a Residence on a Georgia Plantation in 1838-39, by Frances Anne Kemble*. Edited by John A. Scott. New York: Alfred A. Knopf, 1961.

————. *Notes Upon Some of Shakespeare's Plays*. London: Richard Bentley and Son, 1882.

————. *Poems*. London: Edward Moxon and Co., 1866.

————. *Records of a Girlhood*. 3 vols. London: Richard Bentley and Son, 1878.

————. *Records of Later Life*. New York: Henry Holt and Company, 1882.

Kenealy, E.V.H. "William Maginn." *Dublin University Magazine* 23 (1844): 72-101.

Kramerae, Cheris. *Women and Men Speaking*. Rowley, Mass.: Newbury House, 1981.

Kucich, Greg. "Gender Crossings: Keats and Tighe." *Keats-Shelley Journal* 44 (1995): 29-39.

Kunitz, Stanley, and Howard Haycraft, eds. *British Authors of the Nineteenth Century*. New York: Wilson, 1936.

Lamb, Mary. "On Needlework." *New British Ladies' Magazine* 1 (1815): 257-60.

Lamb, Charles, and Mary Lamb. *The Letters of Charles and Mary Lamb*. Edited by Edwin Marrs. 3 vols. Ithaca, N.Y.: Cornell Univ. Press, 1975.

————. *The Works of Charles and Mary Lamb*. Edited by E.V. Lucas. New York: G.P. Putnam's Sons; London: Methuen, 1903.

Landon, Letitia Elizabeth. "The Battle Field." In Landon, *Poetical Works*, 337.

————. *Critical Writings*. Edited by F.J. Sypher. Delmar, N.Y.: Scholars' Facsimiles and Reprints, 1996.

————. *Ethel Churchill*. Edited by F.J. Sypher. Delmar, N.Y.: Scholars' Facsimiles and Reprints, 1992.

————. "Erinna." In Landon, *Poetical Works*, 214-22.

————. "The Factory." In Landon, *Poetical Works*, 569-71.

————. *The Golden Violet*. In Landon, *Poetical Works*, 113-88.

————. "The Head." In *The Keepsake for 1834*, edited by Frederic Mansel Reynolds. London: Longman, 93-117.

————. "A History of the Lyre." In Landon, *Poetical Works*, 223-31.

————. *Lady Anne Granard; or, Keeping Up Appearances*. London: Henry Colburn, 1842.

————. "Miss Landon's Correspondence with Thomas Crofton Croker, 1831-1838." Edited by T.F. Dillon Croker. *Sharpe's London Magazine* 35 (Feb. 1862): 64-67.

————. *Poetical Works of Letitia Elizabeth Landon*. 1873. Reprint, with additional poems, edited by F.J. Sypher, Delmar, N.Y.: Scholars' Facsimiles and Reprints, 1990.

————. *Romance and Reality*. In Landon, *Works*, 1:7-201.

————. "A Scene in the Life of Nourmahal." *Heath's Book of Beauty* (1837): 232-40.

————. *Letitia Elizabeth Landon: Selected Writings*. Edited by Jerome McGann and Daniel Riess. Peterborough, Ontario: Broadview Press, 1997.

————. "Shuhur, Jeypore." In Landon, *Poetical Works*, 577-78.

————. "A Supper of Madame de Brinvilliers." In Landon, *Poetical Works*, 381-83.

————. "Stern Truth." In Landon, *Poetical Works*, 448.

————. "The Sword." In *The Young Ladies' Class Book: A Selection of Lessons for Reading*, edited by Ebenezer Bailey, 399-400. Boston: Gould, Kendall, and Lincoln, 1831.

————. "The Venetian Bracelet." In Landon, *Poetical Works,* 199-213.

————. *The Works of L. E. Landon.* 2 vols. Philadelphia: Jesper Harding, 1850.

Landry, Donna. "Figures of the Feminine: An Amazonian Revolution in Feminist Literary History?" In *The Uses of Literary History,* edited by Marshall Brown, 107-28. Durham, N.C.: Duke Univ. Press, 1995.

————. *The Muses of Resistance: Laboring-Class Women's Poetry in Britain, 1739-1796.* Cambridge: Cambridge Univ. Press, 1990.

Lang, Andrew, ed. *The Blue Poetry Book.* 2d ed. London, 1896.

Lawrence, Rose D'Aguilar. *The Last Autumn at a Favorite Residence with Other Poems; and Recollections of Mrs. Hemans.* Liverpool: G. and J. Robinson, 1836.

Lazarus, Rachel Mordecai. Letter to Maria Edgeworth, 24 June 1827. In *The Education of the Heart: The Correspondence of Rachel Mordecai Lazarus and Maria Edgeworth,* edited by Edgar E. MacDonald, 128-29. Chapel Hill: Univ. of North Carolina Press, 1977.

Leadbeater, Mary. *Poems.* Dublin: Martin Keene; London: Longman, Hurst, Rees, and Orme, 1808.

LeBreton, Anna Letitia. *Memoir of Mrs. Barbauld.* London: Bell, 1874.

Leighton, Angela. *Victorian Women Poets: Writing against the Heart.* Charlottesville: Univ. Press of Virginia, 1992.

Leighton, Angela, and Margaret Reynolds, eds. *Victorian Women Poets.* Oxford: Blackwell, 1995.

"L.E.L." *Belgravia.* Reprint, *Living Age* 190 (Aug. 1891): 372-78.

"L.E.L. and the Gold Coast." *Athenaeum.* Reprint, *Living Age* 37 (June 1853): 657-61.

Lincoln's Inn. Minutes of Lincoln's Inn Council, vol. 46. MS, Lincoln's Inn, London.

————. Rent Roll, 1940. MS, Lincoln's Inn, London.

"Lines to the Memory of Anna Lætitia Barbauld," 1845. MS 24.81. (40), Dr. Williams's Library, London.

Linkin, Harriet Kramer. "Romantic Aesthetics in Mary Tighe and Letitia Landon: How Women Poets Recuperate the Gaze." *European Romantic Review* 7 (1997): 159-88.

————. "Romanticism and Mary Tighe's *Psyche:* Peering at the Hem of Her Blue Stockings." *Studies in Romanticism* 35 (1996): 55-72.

Liu, Alan. *Wordsworth: The Sense of History.* Stanford, Calif.: Stanford Univ. Press, 1989.

Looser, Devoney. "Scolding Lady Mary Wortley Montagu? The Problemantics of Sisterhood in Feminist Criticism." In *Feminist Nightmares: Women at Odds: Feminism and the Problem of Sisterhood,* edited by Susan Ostrov Weisser and Jennifer Fleischner, 44-61. New York: New York Univ. Press, 1994.

Lootens, Tricia. "Hemans and Home: Victorianism, Feminine 'Internal Enemies,' and the Domestication of National Identity." *PMLA* 109 (1994): 238-53.

————. *Lost Saints: Silence, Gender, and Victorian Literary Canonization.* Charlottesville: Univ. Press of Virginia, 1996.

Lorimer, Douglas. "Black Resistance to Slavery and Racism in Eighteenth-Century England." In *Essays on the History of Blacks in Britain,* edited by Jagdish S. Gundara and Ian Duffield, 58-80. Aldershot, Eng.: Avebury, 1992.

Lyotard, Jean-François. *The Differend: Phrases in Dispite.* Minneapolis: Univ. of Minnesota Press, 1988.

Macgregor, Margaret Eliot. *Amelia Alderson Opie: Worldling and Friend.* Smith College Studies in Modern Language, vol. 14, nos. 1-2, Northhampton, Mass., 1933.

Mackay, Charles, ed. *A Thousand and One Gems of English Poetry.* London, 1869.

Mackintosh, Sir James. *Memoirs of the Life of the Right Honourable Sir James Mackintosh.* 2 vols. London: Moxon, 1835.

Madden, Lionel, ed. *Robert Southey: The Critical Heritage.* Boston: Routledge and Kegan Paul, 1972.

Madden, Richard R. *The Literary Life and Correspondence of the Countess of Blessington.* 2 vols. New York: Harper and Brothers, 1855.

[Maginn, William.] "Preface to Our Second Decade." *Fraser's Magazine* 21 (1840): 19-31.

Magnuson, Paul. "The Politics of 'Frost at Midnight.'" *Wordsworth Circle* 22 (1991): 3-11.

Mahl, Mary R., and Helene Koon, eds. *The Female Spectator.* Bloomington: Indiana Univ. Press, 1977.

Marren, Susan. "Between Slavery and Freedom: The Transgressive Self in Olaudah Equiano's Autobiography." *PMLA* 108, no. 1 (1993): 94-106.

Marsden, Jean. "Letters on a Tombstone: Mothers and Literacy in Mary Lamb's *Mrs. Leicester's School.*" *Children's Literature* 23 (1995): 31-44.

Marshall, David. *The Surprising Effects of Sympathy: Marivaux, Diderot, Rousseau, and Mary Shelley.* Chicago: Univ. of Chicago Press, 1988.

Martin, Mrs. Herbert (Mary Emma LeBreton). Preface to [A.L. LeBreton], *Memories of Seventy Years,* iii-vi. London: Griffith and Farran, 1883.

Martin, Philip W. *Mad Women in Romantic Writing.* Sussex: Harvester Press, 1987.

Martineau, Harriet. *Autobiography.* Vol. 1. 1877. Reprint, London: Virago Press, 1983.

———. *A History of the Thirty Years' Peace, 1816-1846.* 4 vols. 1877-78. Reprint, Shannon, Ireland: Irish Univ. Press, [1971].

Marx, Karl. *Capital.* Vol. 1, translated by Samuel Moore and Edward Aveling. 1867. Reprint, New York: Modern Library, n.d.

Massé, Michelle. *In the Name of Love: Women, Masochism and the Gothic.* Ithaca, N.Y.: Cornell Univ. Press, 1992.

McGann, Jerome J. *The Beauty of Inflections: Literary Investigations in Historical Method and Theory.* Oxford: Clarendon Press, 1988.

———. *The Poetics of Sensibility: A Revolution in Literary Style.* Oxford: Clarendon Press, 1996.

———. "Poetry, 1785-1832." In *The Columbia History of British Poetry,* edited by Carl Woodring, 353-80. New York: Columbia Univ. Press, 1994.

———. *The Romantic Ideology: A Critical Investigation.* Chicago: Univ. of Chicago Press, 1983.

———, ed. *The New Oxford Book of Romantic Period Verse.* Oxford: Oxford Univ. Press, 1994.

[McGann, Jerome J.], Anne Mack, J.J. Rome, and Goerg Mannejc, "Literary History,

Romanticism, and Felicia Hemans." *Modern Language Quarterly* 54, no. 2 (June 1993): 215-35. Reprinted under McGann's name in *Re-Visioning Romanticism: British Women Writers, 1776-1837,* edited by Carol Shiner Wilson and Joel Haefner (Philadelphia: Univ. of Pennsylvania Press, 1994), 210-227; reprinted as "Literary History, Romanticism, and Felicia Hemans: A Conversation between A. Mack, J. J. Rome, and G. Mannejc," in *The Poetics of Sensibility: A Revolution in Literary Style* (Oxford: Clarendon Press, 1996), 174-94.

Mellor, Anne K. "A Criticism of Their Own: Romantic Women Literary Critics." In *Questioning Romanticism,* edited by John Beer, 29-48. Baltimore: Johns Hopkins Univ. Press, 1995.

———. "'Am I not a Woman, and a Sister?': Slavery, Romanticism, and Gender." In *Romanticism, Race, and Imperial Culture,* edited by Alan Richardson and Sonia Hofkosh, 311-29. Bloomington: Indiana Univ. Press, 1996.

———. "The Female Poet and the Poetess: Two Traditions of British Women's Poetry, 1780-1830." *Studies in Romanticism* 36, no. 2 (1997): 261-76.

———. *Romanticism and Gender.* New York: Routledge, 1993.

———, ed. *Romanticism and Feminism.* Bloomington: Indiana Univ. Press, 1988.

Mellor, Anne K., and Richard Matlak, eds. *British Literature 1780-1830.* Fort Worth: Harcourt Brace, 1996.

"Memoir of Letitia Elizabeth Landon." *Colburn's* 50 (1837): 78-82.

"Memoir of Mrs. Anna Letitia Barbauld." *Imperial Magazine* 7 (1825): 397-411.

"A Memoir of Mrs. Barbauld." *The Lady's Magazine,* n.s., 6 (1825): 237-38.

[Merivale, Herman.] Review of *Poetical Works of Robert Southey. Edinburgh Review* 68 (Jan. 1839): 354-76.

Metcalfe, George E. *Maclean of the Gold Coast: The Life and Times of George Maclean, 1801-1847.* London: Oxford Univ. Press, 1962.

Miles, Alfred H. "Caroline (Bowles) Southey." In *The Poets and the Poetry of the Century,* edited by Alfred H. Miles, 7:39-52. London: Hutchinson, 1892.

Moers, Ellen. *Literary Women: The Great Writers.* 1963. Reprint, New York: Oxford Univ. Press, 1976; Garden City, N.Y.: Anchor/Doubleday, 1977 (page citations are to the 1977 edition).

Moir, David M. *Sketches of the Poetical Literature of the Past Half-Century.* 3d ed. London: Blackwood, 1856.

Montgomery, James. *Lectures on General Literature.* New York: Harper, 1833.

Monthly Review (April 1811): 380-81.

Moore, Catherine. "The Literary Career of Anna Letitia Barbauld." Ph.D. diss., Univ. of North Carolina, Chapel Hill, 1969.

Morgan, Peter F. "Southey on Poetry." *Tennessee Studies in Literature* 16 (1971): 80-81.

Morley, Edith J. *The Life and Times of Henry Crabb Robinson.* London: Dent, 1935.

"Mr. C. W. Brodribb." *Times* (London), 22 June 1945, 7d.

"Mr. Matthew Arnold and Isaiah of Jerusalem." *The Inquirer,* 14 April 1883, 225.

"Mrs. Barbauld." *Christian Reformer* 11 (1825): 141-44.

"Mrs. Barbauld." *The Lady's Own Paper,* 25 Jan. 1868, 49.

"Mrs. Barbauld." *The Times* (London), 11 Mar. 1925, 15e.

"Mrs. Barbauld and the Aikin Family." *Leisure Hour* 33 (1884): 158-62.

"Mrs. Barbauld, 1743-1825." *The Inquirer,* 7 Mar. 1925, 147-48.

Murch, Jerom. *Mrs. Barbauld and Her Contemporaries.* London: Longmans, 1877.

Myers, Mitzi. "Of Mice and Mothers: Mrs. Barbauld's 'New Walk' and Gendered Codes in Children's Literature." In *Feminine Principles and Women's Experience in American Composition and Rhetoric,* edited by Louise Wetherbee Phelps and Janet Emig, 255-88. Pittsburgh: Univ. of Pittsburgh Press, 1995.

Nemoianu, Virgil. "Literary Canons and Social Value Options." In *The Hospitable Canon: Essays on Literary Play, Scholarly Choice, and Popular Pressures,* edited by Virgil Nemoianu and Robert Royal. 215-47. Philadelphia: John Benjamins, 1991.

Nietzsche, Friedrich. *The Gay Science.* Translated by Walter Kaufmann. New York: Vintage, 1974.

Northcote, Stafford Harry, Viscount St. Cyres. "The Sorrows of Mrs. Charlotte Smith." *Cornhill Magazine,* n.s., 15 (1903): 683-96.

Notes and Queries, ser. 12, 7 (4 and 11 Sept. 1920): 181-84, 201-03.

O'Keeffe, Adelaide. *Original Poems; Calculated to Improve the Mind of Youth, and Allure It to Virtue.* London: J. Harris, 1808.

Oldfield, John R. "The 'Ties of soft Humanity': Slavery and Race in British Drama, 1760-1800." *Huntington Library Quarterly* 56, no. 1 (1993): 1-14.

Oliphant, Margaret. *The Literary History of England in the End of the Eighteenth and Beginning of the Nineteenth Century.* 1882. Reprint, New York: AMS Press, n.d.

O'Malley, Ida B. *Women in Subjection: A Study of the Lives of Englishwomen before 1832.* London: Duckworth, 1933.

Opie, Amelia. Amelia Opie to Elizabeth Fry, 19 Jan. 1824, Opie Papers, OP 48, Huntington Library, San Marino, Calif.

———. *The Black Man's Lament; or, How to Make Sugar.* London: Harvey and Darton, 1826.

———. *Lays of the Dead.* London: Longman, Rees, Orme, Brown, Green and Longman, 1834.

———. *The Negro Boy's Tale: a poem, addressed to children.* London: Harvey and Darton; Norwich: S. Wilkin, 1824.

———. *The Negro Boy's tale: a poem / by Amelia Opie; to which are added, The Morning Dream / by William Cowper, and other poems.* New York: S. Wood and Sons, 1825[?].

———. *Poems.* 4th ed. London: Longman, Hurst, Rees, and Orme, 1804.

Opie, Mrs. [Amelia]. *Poems by Mrs. Opie.* London: T.N. Longman and 0. Rees, 1802.

Paine, Thomas. *The Rights of Man.* 1791-93. *Two Classics of the French Revolution,* 267-515. New York: Anchor, 1973.

Palgrave, Francis T., ed. *The Golden Treasury, Selected from the Best Songs and Lyrical Poems in the English Language.* London: Macmillan, 1929.

Parsons, Mrs. Letitia. *Verses, Hymns and Poems, on Various Subjects; Composed under a Long Series of Affliction and Deprivation of Sight.* Hawkshurst: John Parsons, 1806; reprinted with 2d vol. added, Hawkshurst: John Parsons, 1808.

Pascoe, Judith. *Romantic Theatricality: Gender, Poetry, and Spectatorship.* Ithaca, N.Y.: Cornell Univ. Press, 1997.

Patmore, P.G. *My Friends and Acquaintance.* 3 vols. London: Saunders and Otley, 1854.

[Peabody, William B.O.]. Review of Barbauld, *Works. Christian Examiner* 3 (1826): 299-315.

Perkins, David, ed. *English Romantic Writers.* 2d ed. Fort Worth: Harcourt Brace, 1995.

Pickering, Sam. "Mrs. Barbauld's *Hymns in Prose:* 'An Air-Blown Particle' of Romanticism?" *Southern Humanities Review* 9 (1975): 259-68.

Pinch, Adela. *Strange Fits of Passion: Epistemologies of Emotion, from Hume to Austen.* Stanford, Calif.: Stanford Univ. Press, 1996.

Plimpton, Pamela. "Anna Letitia Barbauld: Editorial Agency and the Ideology of the Feminine." Paper presented at the annual meeting of the Modern Language Association, Chicago, 28 Dec. 1995.

Plumb, John H. Review of *Georgian Chronicle,* by Betsy Rodgers. *The Listener,* 8 Jan. 1959, 73.

Poetical Register (1810-11): 553.

[Polwhele, Richard]. *The Unsex'd Females: A Poem.* London: Cadell and Davies, 1798.

Poovey, Mary. *The Proper Lady and the Woman Writer: Ideology as Style in the Works of Mary Wollstonecraft, Mary Shelley, and Jane Austen.* Chicago: Univ. of Chicago Press, 1984.

Porden, Miss [Eleanor]. *The Veils; or the Triumph of Constancy. A Poem, in Six Books.* London: John Murray, 1815.

Prince, Mary. *The History of Mary Prince: A West Indian Slave, Related by Herself.* 1831. Reprint, edited and with an introduction by Moira Ferguson, Ann Arbor: Univ. of Michigan Press, 1993.

Pryde, Ambrose. "Letitia Barbauld." *Time and Tide,* 19 June 1943, 498.

Raimond, Jean. "Robert Southey. " In *A Handbook to English Romanticism,* edited by Jean Raimond and John Richard Watson, 262-69. New York: St. Martin's Press, 1992.

Rajan, Tilottama. *The Supplement of Reading: Figures of Understanding in Romantic Theory and Practice.* Ithaca, N.Y.: Cornell Univ. Press, 1990.

Ray, Gordon N. *Thackeray: The Uses of Adversity.* New York: McGraw-Hill, 1955.

Raysor, Thomas M. "Coleridge's Comment on the Moral of 'The Ancient Mariner.'" *Philological Quarterly* 31 (1952): 88-91.

Reiman, Donald H. Introduction to *Hours of Solitude,* by Charlotte Dacre. New York: Garland, 1978.

———. Introduction to *Poems, by Amelia Opie.* 1802. Reprint, New York: Garland, 1978.

Review of *The Banished Man,* by Charlotte Smith. *Analytical Review* 20 (1794): 254-55.

Review of *The Banished Man,* by Charlotte Smith. *British Critic* 4 (1794): 621-23.

Review of *The Banished Man,* by Charlotte Smith. *European Magazine* 26 (1794): 273-77.

Review of *Beachy Head, with Other Poems,* by Charlotte Smith. *British Critic* 30 (1807): 170-74.

Review of *Elegiac Sonnets*, vol. 2, by Charlotte Smith. *Analytical Review* 26 (1797): 156-59.

Review of *Elegiac Sonnets*, 3d ed., by Charlotte Smith. *Gentleman's Magazine* 56 (1786): 333-34.

Review of *The Emigrants*, by Charlotte Smith. *British Critic* 1 (1793): 403-6.

Review of *Legacy for Young Ladies*, by Anna Letitia Barbauld. *Eclectic Review*, n.s., 25 (1826): 79-85.

Review of *Letters of a Solitary Wanderer*, vols. 1-3, by Charlotte Smith. *Anti-jacobin* 10 (1801): 318.

Review of *Letters of a Solitary Wanderer*, vols. 1-3, by Charlotte Smith. *Critical Review* 32 (1801): 35-42.

Review of *Memoir of Mrs. Anna Letitia Barbauld*, by Grace Ellis, unidentified newspaper clipping, ca. 1874. Vassar College Library.

Review of *Poems, 1802*, by Amelia Opie. *Critical Review* 52 (1802).

Review of *Poems, 1802*, by Amelia Opie. *Edinburgh Review* 1 (Oct. 1802).

Review of *Poetry for Children*, by Charles and Mary Lamb. *Monthly Review* 64 (1811): 102.

Review of *Psyche, with other Poems*, by the late Mrs. Henry Tighe. *British Critic* 38 (1811): 631-32.

Review of *Psyche, with other Poems*, by the late Mrs. Henry Tighe. *British Review* 1 (June 1811): 277-98.

Review of *Psyche, with other Poems*, by the late Mrs. Henry Tighe. *Critical Review, or, Annals of Literature* 4 (1812): 606-9.

Review of *Psyche, with other Poems*, by the late Mrs. Henry Tighe. *Eclectic Review* 9 (1813): 217-29.

Review of *Psyche, with other Poems*, by the late Mrs. Henry Tighe. *Gentleman's Magazine* 82 (1812): 464-67.

Review of *Psyche, with other Poems*, by the late Mrs. Henry Tighe. *Monthly Review* 66 (1811): 138-52.

Review of *Psyche, with other Poems*, by the late Mrs. Henry Tighe. *New Annual Register, or, General Repository of History, Politics, and Literature* 32 (1811): 364-72.

Review of *Psyche, with other Poems*, by the late Mrs. Henry Tighe. *Quarterly Review* 5, no. 10 (1811): 471-85.

Review of *Records of Woman*, by Felicia Hemans. *London Literary Gazette, Journal of Belles Lettres, Arts, Sciences, & c.*, no. 590 (10 May 1828).

Review of *The Sceptic*, by Felicia Hemans. *Edinburgh Monthly Review* 3 (1820): 373-83.

Review of *The Siege of Valencia; A Dramatic Poem; The Last Constantine: With Other Poems*, by Felicia Hemans. *London Literary Gazette, Journal of Belles Lettres, Arts, Sciences, & c.*, no. 335 (21 and 28 June 1823): 385-86, 407-8.

Review of *The Siege of Valencia; A Dramatic Poem; The Last Constantine: With Other Poems*, by Felicia Hemans. *Monthly Review or Literary Journal* 102 (1823): 177-81.

Review of *The Siege of Valencia and The Last Constantine, with Other Poems,* by Felicia Hemans. *British Critic and Quarterly Theological Review,* n.s., 20 (1823): 50-61.

Review of *The Siege of Valencia and the Last Constantine, with Other Poems,* by Felicia Hemans. *British Review and Critical Journal* 31 (August 1823): 196-202.

Review of *Works,* by Anna Letitia Barbauld. *Literary Gazette* (London), no. 453, 24 Sept. 1825, 611-12.

Review of *Works,* by Anna Letitia Barbauld. *Monthly Repository* 20 (1825): 484-89, 558-62.

Review of *Works,* by Anna Letitia Barbauld. *Monthly Review,* n.s., 107 (1825): 294-312.

"Reviews: *Ethel Churchill.*" *Athenaeum* (30 Sept. 1837): 713-14.

"Reviews: *Romance and Reality.*" *Athenaeum* (10 Dec. 1831): 793-95.

Rich, Adrienne. "When We Dead Awaken: Writing as Re-Vision." In *On Lies, Secrets, and Silence: Selected Prose 1966-1978,* 33-49. New York: W.W. Norton, 1979.

Richardson, Charlotte Caroline. *Harvest, A Poem in two parts, with other Poetical Pieces.* London: Sherwood, Neely, and Jones, 1818.

Richardson, Sarah. *Original Poems, Intended for the Use of Young Persons.* London: Vernor, Hood, and Sharpe, 1808.

Ridgway, Mrs. "An Address Delivered to the Warrington Society, on the Unveiling of a Tablet in Memory of Mrs. Barbauld, on the 18th of April 1912." *Warrington Guardian,* 20 Apr. 1912.

Ritchie, Anne Thackeray. *A Book of Sybils.* London: Smith, Elder, 1883.

Robbins, Sarah. "*Lessons for Children* and Teaching Mothers: Mrs. Barbauld's Primer for the Textual Construction of Middle-Class Domestic Pedagogy." *The Lion and the Unicorn* 17 (1993): 135-51.

Roberts, Emma. "Memoir." In *The Zenana and Minor Poems of L.E.L., with a Memoir by Emma Roberts,* 5-33. London: Fisher, [1839?].

Robertson, Eric S. *English Poetesses: A Series of Critical Biographies.* London: Cassell, 1883.

Robinson, Agnes Mary F. "Felicia Hemans." In *The English Poets: Selections with Critical Introductions,* 5 vols, edited by Thomas Humphry Ward, 4:334. London: Macmillan, 1880-94, 1909.

———. "Mrs. Barbauld." In *The English Poets: Selections with Critical Introductions,* 5 vols, edited by Thomas Humphry Ward, 3:576-77. London: Macmillan, 1880-94, 1909.

Robinson, Henry Crabb. *Diary, Reminiscences, and Correspondence,* edited by Thomas Sadler. 3d ed. London: Macmillan, 1872.

Rogers, Katharine M. "Anna Barbauld's Criticism of Fiction--Johnsonian Mode, Female Vision." In *Studies in Eighteenth-Century Culture,* edited by Patricia B. Craddock and Carla M. Hay, 27-41. East Lansing, Mich.: Colleagues Press, 1991.

Roper, Derek. *Reviewing before the Edinburgh, 1788-1802.* London: Methuen, 1978.

Rose, June. *Elizabeth Fry.* London: Macmillan, 1980.

Ross, Ernest. *The Ordeal of Bridget Elia: A Chronicle of the Lambs.* Norman: Univ. of Oklahoma Press, 1960.

Ross, Marlon B. "Configurations of Feminine Reform: The Woman Writer and the Tradition of Dissent." In Wilson and Haefner, *Re-Visioning Romanticism,* 91-110.

———. *The Contours of Masculine Desire: Romanticism and the Rise of Women's Poetry.* New York: Oxford Univ. Press, 1989.

Rossetti, Christina. *The Complete Poems of Christina Rossetti,* edited by Rebecca W. Crump. Baton Rouge: Louisiana State Univ. Press, 1979, 1986, 1990.

———. "From the Antique." In Rossetti, *Complete Poems,* 3:231.

———. "Later Life: A Double Sonnet of Sonnets." In Rossetti, *Complete Poems,* 2:138-50.

Rossetti, William Michael. Prefatory notice to *The Poetical Works of Mrs. Hemans.* New York: Thomas Y. Crowell; Philadelphia: J.B. Lippincott, 1881.

Rowton, Frederic, ed. *The Female Poets of Great Britain, Chronologically Arranged with Copious Selections and Critical Remarks.* 1853. Facsimile ed., edited by Marilyn L. Williamson, Detroit: Wayne State Univ. Press, 1981.

———, ed. *The Female Poets of Great Britain, Containing the Choicest Poems of Our Female Poets, From the Time of Lady Juliana Berners to the Present Day, including those of the Hon. Mrs. Norton, Mrs. Hemans, Joanna Baillie, Miss Landon, Eliza Cook, etc., with Memoirs and Critical Remarks.* London, 1848.

S.A.A. "Notable North Londoners. No. VI. Anna Lætitia Barbauld." *North Londoner,* 13 Mar. 1869, 83.

Sackville-West, Vita. Introduction to *The Annual: Being a Selection from the Forget-Me-Nots, Keepsakes, and Other Annuals of the Nineteenth Century,* edited by Dorothy Wellesley. London: Cobden-Sanderson, 1930.

———. "The Women Poets of the Seventies." In *The Eighteen-Seventies,* edited by Harley Granville-Barker. 112-34. New York: Macmillan, 1929.

Saintsbury, George. *A History of Nineteenth-Century Literature.* New York: Macmillan, 1899.

Sallust. *The Jugurthine War/Conspiracy of Catiline.* Translated by Stanley A. Handford. Harmondsworth, Eng.: Penguin Books, 1963.

Sanchez-Eppler, Karen. *Touching Liberty: Abolition, Feminism, and the Politics of the Body.* Los Angeles: Univ. of California Press, 1993.

Satirist, March 1809, 273-76.

Schofield, Mary Anne, and Cecelia Macheski, eds. *Fetter'd or Free? British Women Novelists, 1670-1815.* Athens: Ohio Univ. Press, 1986.

Scott, John A. Introduction to *Journal of a Residence on a Georgia Plantation, in 1838-39, by Frances Anne Kemble,* edited by John A. Scott. New York: Alfred Knopf, 1961.

Scott, Sir Walter. *The Miscellaneous Prose Works of Sir Walter Scott.* 28 vols. Edinburgh: Robert Cadell, 1849.

Scrivener, Michael. *Poetry and Reform: Periodical Verse from the English Democratic Press 1792-1824.* Detroit: Wayne State Univ. Press, 1992.

Select Works of the British Poets. Philadelphia: Hart, 1850.

Sewell, Mrs. G. [Mary]. *Poems.* Egham, Eng.: R. Wetton and Sons, 1803.

Shakespeare, William. *A Midsummer Night's Dream.* In *Shakespeare: The Complete Works,* edited by G.B. Harrison. New York: Harcourt, Brace, 1968.

Sharpe, Jenny. *Allegories of Empire: The Figure of Woman in the Colonial Text.* Minneapolis: Univ. of Minnesota Press, 1993.

Shattock, Joanne, ed. *The Oxford Guide to British Women Writers.* New York: Oxford Univ. Press, 1993.

Shelley, Percy Bysshe. *The Complete Poetical Works of Percy Bysshe Shelley,* edited by Thomas Hutchinson. Oxford: Humphrey Milford, 1923.

Shelley, Percy Bysshe. *Shelley's Poetry and Prose.* Edited by Donald Reiman and Sharon Powers. New York: Norton, 1977.

[Sheppard, Sarah.] *Characteristics of the Genius and Writings of L.E.L., with Illustrations from her Works and from Personal Recollection.* London: Longman, Brown, Green, and Longman, 1841.

Shore, John, Lord Teignmouth. *Memoirs of The Life, Writings and Correspondence of Sir William Jones.* London: John Hatchard, 1806.

Showalter, Elaine. *Sexual Anarchy: Gender and Culture at the Fin de Siècle.* New York: Penguin, 1991.

Shyllon, Folarin. *Black People in Britain, 1555-1833.* London: Oxford Univ. Press, 1977.

Sigourney, Mrs. [Lydia]. "Essay on the Genius of Mrs. Hemans." In Harriett Hughes, *Memoir of the Life and Writings of Felicia Hemans: By Her Sister; with an Essay on her Genius: By Mrs. Sigourney.* New York: C.S. Francis; Boston: J.H. Francis, 1845, v-xxvi.

Simmons, Jack. *Southey.* New Haven, Conn.: Yale Univ. Press, 1948.

"Sketch of Anna Letitia Barbauld." *Godey's Lady's Book and Magazine* 16 (1838): 18.

Smith, Charlotte. *The Banished Man.* 4 vols. London: T. Cadell Jr. and W. Davies, 1794.

———. *Beachy Head; With Other Poems.* London: J. Johnson, 1807.

———. *Conversations Introducing Poetry: Chiefly on Subjects of Natural History. For the Use of Young Persons.* London: J. Johnson, 1804.

———. *Marchmont.* 4 vols. London: Sampson Low, 1796.

———. *The Poems of Charlotte Smith,* edited by Stuart Curran. New York: Oxford Univ. Press, 1993.

"Sonnet to Mrs. Smith." *European Magazine* 10 (1786): 125.

"Sonnet, to Mrs. Smith, on reading her Sonnets lately published." *Universal Magazine* 78 (1786): 328.

Southey, Caroline. *Autumn Flowers and Other Poems.* Boston: Saxton, Pierce, and Co., 1844.

———. *Chapters on Churchyards.* New York: Wiley and Putnam, 1842.

———. *Select Literary Works.* Hartford, Conn.: S. Andrus and Son, 1851.

Southey, Caroline Bowles. *Poetical Works.* Edinburgh: Blackwood, 1867.

———. *Solitary Hours.* New York: Wiley and Putnam, 1846.

Southey, Charles Cuthbert, ed. *The Life and Correspondence of the Late Robert Southey.* 2d ed. 3 vols. London: Longman, Brown, Green and Longmans, 1849-50.

Spivak, Gayatri Chakravorty. "Three Women's Texts and a Critique of Imperialism." In *Race, Writing, and Difference*, edited by Henry Louis Gates Jr., 262-80. Chicago: Univ. of Chicago Press, 1986.

Stanton, Judith Phillips. "Charlotte Smith's 'Literary Business': Income, Patronage, and Indigence." In *The Age of Johnson*, edited by Paul J. Korshin, 375-401. New York: AMS Press, 1987.

———. Introduction to *The Old Manor House*, edited by Anne Henry Ehrenpreis, vii-xxiii. Oxford: Oxford Univ. Press, 1989.

Stephenson, Glennis. *Letitia Landon: The Woman behind L.E.L.* New York: Manchester Univ. Press, 1995.

Stevens, Wallace. *Collected Poems*. New York: Knopf, 1954.

Stockdale, Mary. *The Family Book; or, Children's Journal. Consisting of Moral and Entertaining Stories . . . From the French of M. Berquin. Interspersed with Poetical Pieces, Written by the translator.* Translated by Miss Stockdale. London: John Stockdale, 1798.

———. *The Mirror of the Mind, Poems*. London: John Stockdale, 1810.

Storey, Mark. *Robert Southey: A Life*. New York: Oxford Univ. Press, 1997.

Substance of the Debates on a Resolution for Abolishing the Slave Trade which was moved in the House of Commons 10th June, 1806 and in the House of Lords 24th June, 1806. 1806. Reprint, London: Dawsons of Pall Mall, 1968.

Sullivan, Alvin. *British Literary Magazines: The Romantic Age, 1789-1836.* Westport, Conn.: Greenwood Press, 1983.

Swingle, L.J. "The Romantic Emergence: Multiplication of Alternatives and the Problem of Systematic Entrapment." *Modern Language Quarterly* 39, no. 3 (Sept. 1978): 264-84.

Sypher, F.J. Introduction to *Ethel Churchill*, by Letitia Elizabeth Landon, edited by F.J. Sypher, 5-18. Delmar, N.Y.: Scholars' Facsimiles and Reprints, 1992.

Tayler, John James. *Letters*. Edited by John Hamilton Thom. London: Williams and Norgate, 1872.

Taylor, Ann, and Jane Taylor. *Original Poems for Infant Minds*. London: Darton and Harvey, 1804.

Thackeray, William Makepeace. *The Letters and Private Papers of William Makepeace Thackeray*. Edited by Edgar F. Harden. Vol. 1. New York: Garland, 1994.

———. *The Letters and Private Papers of William Makepeace Thackeray*. Edited by Gordon N. Ray. Cambridge, Mass.: Harvard Univ. Press, 1945.

———. "'Our Batch of Novels for Christmas' 1837: Landon's 'Ethel Churchill.'" *Fraser's* (1838): 89-92.

———. *Vanity Fair*. Edited by John Sutherland. New York: Oxford Univ. Press, 1987.

———. "A Word on the Annuals." *Fraser's* 16 (1837): 757-63.

[Thackeray, William Makepeace, and William Maginn]. "A Quintette of Novels." *Fraser's* 11 (1835): 465-90.

[Thomson, Katherine]. "Memorials of the Departed Great." *Bentley's Miscellany* 17 (1845): 182-91.

———. *Recollections of Literary Characters and Celebrated Places*. 2 vols. London: Richard Bentley, 1854.

Thornbury, Walter, ed. *Two Centuries of Song; or, Lyrics, Madrigals, Sonnets, and Other Occasional Verses of the English Poets of the Last Two Hundred Years.* New York, 1867.

Tighe, Mary. Journals and family histories. In Wicklow Papers, MS 4810, National Library of Ireland, Dublin.

[Tighe, Mary]. *Mary, a Series of Reflections during Twenty Years.* Edited by William Tighe. Roundwood, 1811.

———. *Psyche; or, the Legend of Love.* London: [James Carpenter], 1805.

———. *Psyche, with Other Poems.* By the Late Mrs Henry Tighe. Edited by William Tighe. London: Longman, Hurst, Rees, Orme, and Brown. 1811. Facsimile reprint, edited by Jonathan Wordsworth, Oxford and New York: Woodstock Books, 1992.

Todd, Janet. *Sensibility: An Introduction.* London: Methuen, 1986.

Trench, Richard Chenevix, ed. *A Household Book of English Poetry.* London, 1868.

Trilling, Lionel. *Sincerity and Authenticity.* Cambridge: Harvard Univ. Press, 1971.

"The Troubadour and Other Poems." *Museum of Foreign Literature and Science* 7 (1826): 381-91.

Turley, David. *The Culture of English Antislavery, 1780-1860.* London: Routledge, 1991.

Turner, Elizabeth. *The Daisy; or, Cautionary Stories in Verse. Adapted to the Ideas of Children from Four to Eight Years Old.* London: J. Harris and Crosby and Co., 1807.

Turner, William. "Mrs Barbauld." *Newcastle Magazine,* n.s., 4 (1825): 183-86.

Vargo, Lisa. "'Mistress Bare and Bald': 'To Mr. C' and Coleridge's Agency." Paper presented at the annual meeting of the Modern Language Association, Chicago, 28 Dec. 1995.

Walpole, Horace. *Correspondence.* Edited by Wilmarth S. Lewis. Vols. 11 and 41. New Haven, Conn.: Yale Univ. Press, 1948, 1980.

Walvin, James. *Black and White: The Negro and English Society, 1555-1945.* London: Allen Lane, 1973.

———. *The Black Presence: A Documentary History of the Negro in England, 1555-1860.* New York: Schocken Books, 1972.

Ward, William S. *Literary Reviews in British Periodicals 1798-1820: A Bibliography.* 2 vols. New York: Garland, 1972.

Warrington Academy. "Minute-Books." Vol. 1. MS, Manchester College Library, Oxford.

Watson, Mary Sidney. "When Flattery Kills: Barbauld and the Anthologies." Paper presented at the annual meeting of the Modern Language Association, Chicago, 28 Dec. 1995.

Weintraub, Stanley. *Victoria: An Intimate Biography.* New York: Truman Talley Books, 1987.

West, Jane. *The Mother: A Poem, in Five Books.* London: Longman, Hurst, Rees, and Orme, 1809; 2d ed., London: Longman, Hurst, Rees, and Orme, 1810.

West, Mrs. [Jane]. *Miscellaneous Poetry . . . Written at an Early Period of Life.* London: W.T. Swift, 1786.

Wilde, Oscar. "English Poetesses." In *The Artist as Critic: Critical Writings of Oscar Wilde,* edited by Richard Ellmann, 101-8. Chicago: Univ. of Chicago Press, 1969.

———. *The Importance of Being Earnest.* London: Smithers, 1899.

Williams, Jane. *The Literary Women of England.* London: Saunders, Otley, 1861.

Williamson, Marilyn. "Who's Afraid of Mrs. Barbauld? The Blue Stockings and Feminism." *International Journal of Women's Studies* 3 (1980): 89-102.

Wilmott, Robert Aris, ed. *The Poets of the Nineteenth Century.* New York, 1860.

Wilson, Carol Shiner, and Joel Haefner, eds. *Re-Visioning Romanticism: British Women Writers, 1776-1837.* Philadelphia: Univ. of Pennsylvania Press, 1994.

Wilson, John, William Maginn, John Lockhart, and James Hogg. *Noctes Ambrosianae.* Edited by R. Shelton Mackenzie. 4th ed. 5 vols. 1819-35; New York: Redfield, 1855.

Wilson, Mona. *Jane Austen and Some Contemporaries.* 1938. Reprint, Port Washington, N.Y.: Kennikat Press, n.d.

Wimsatt, William K., Jr. *The Prose Style of Samuel Johnson.* New Haven, Conn.: Yale Univ. Press, 1941.

Wimsatt, William K., Jr., and Cleanth Brooks. *Literary Criticism: A Short History.* 1957. Reprint, New York: Vintage, 1967.

Wolfson, Susan J. "Domestic Affections and the Spear of Minerva." In *Re-Visioning Romanticism: British Women Writers, 1776-1837,* edited by Carol Shiner Wilson and Joel Haefner, 128-66. Philadelphia: Univ. of Pennsylvania Press, 1994.

———. "Feminizing Keats." In *Critical Essays on John Keats,* edited by Hermione de Almeida, 317-56. Boston: G.K. Hall, 1990.

Wolfson, Susan J., and Peter J. Manning, eds. "The Romantics and Their Contemporaries." Vol. 2 of *The Longman's Anthology of British Literature,* edited by David Damrosch. New York: Longman, 1998.

Wollstonecraft, Mary. *Vindication of the Rights of Men, in a Letter to the Right Honourable Edmund Burke; Occasioned by his Reflections on the Revolution in France.* 2d ed. 1790. Reprint, Gainesville, Florida: Scholars' Facsimiles and Reprints, 1960.

———. *A Vindication of the Rights of Woman.* 1792. Edited by Carol H. Poston. New York: Norton, 1988.

Women of Worth: A Book for Girls. New York: Townsend, 1860.

Woof, Pamela. "Dorothy Wordsworth and Mary Lamb, Writers (part 1)." *Charles Lamb Bulletin,* n.s., 66 (1989): 41-52.

———. "Dorothy Wordsworth and Mary Lamb, Writers (part 2)." *Charles Lamb Bulletin,* n.s., 67 (1989): 82-93.

Woolf, Virginia. *The Common Reader.* First Series. New York: Harcourt Brace, 1925.

———. *Orlando.* New York: Harcourt Brace, 1928.

———. *A Room of One's Own.* 1929. Reprint, New York: Penguin, 1972.

Wordsworth, Christopher. *Memoirs of William Wordsworth.* Edited by Henry Reed. Boston: Ticknor, Reed, and Fields, 1851.

Wordsworth, Jonathan. "Ann Yearsley to Caroline Norton: Women Poets of the Romantic Period." *Wordsworth Circle* 26 (1995): 114-24.

———. Introduction to *The Widow's Tale,* by Caroline Bowles. 1822. Reprint, New York: Woodstock Books, 1996.

Wordsworth, William. *The Letters of William and Dorothy Wordsworth.* Edited by Alan G. Hill. 2d ed. Vols. 5 and 8. Oxford: Clarendon Press, 1979, 1993.

———. *The Middle Years, 1806–1820; Part 1, 1806–1811. The Letters of William and Dorothy Wordsworth,* 2d ed. Rev. by Mary Moorman, edited by Ernest de Selincourt. Oxford: Clarendon Press, 1969.

———. *The Middle Years, 1806–1820; Part 2, 1812–1820. The Letters of William and Dorothy Wordsworth,* 2d ed. Rev. by Mary Moorman and Alan G. Hill, edited by Ernest de Selincourt. Oxford: Clarendon Press, 1970.

———. *The Poetical Works of William Wordsworth.* Edited by William Knight. Vol. 7. London: Macmillan, 1896.

———. *The Poetical Works of William Wordsworth.* Edited by Ernest de Selincourt and Helen Darbishire. 5 vols. Oxford: Clarendon Press, 1940–49.

———. *William Wordsworth.* Edited by Stephen Gill. Oxford: Oxford Univ. Press, 1984.

Wu, Duncan, ed. *Romanticism: An Anthology.* London: Blackwell, 1994.

———. *Romantic Women Poets: An Anthology.* London: Blackwell, 1997.

Yeats, William Butler. *Autobiographies.* London: Macmillan, 1961.

Yellin, Jean Fagan. *Women and Sisters: The Antislavery Feminists in American Culture.* New Haven, Conn.: Yale Univ. Press, 1989.

Zall, Paul M. "Wordsworth's 'Ode' and Mrs. Barbauld's *Hymns.*" *Wordsworth Circle* 1 (1970): 177–79.

Zimmerman, Sarah. "Charlotte Smith's Letters and the Practice of Self-Presentation." *Princeton University Library Chronicle* 53 (1991) : 50–77.

Contributors

Stephen C. Behrendt is George Holmes Distinguished Professor of English at the University of Nebraska, Lincoln, and author of *Shelley and His Audiences* (1989), *Reading William Blake* (1992), and *Royal Mourning and Regency Culture: Elegies and Memorials of Princess Charlotte* (1997). He has edited *History and Myth: Essays on English Romantic Literature* (1990), *Approaches to Teaching Shelley's Frankenstein* (1990), and *Romanticism, Radicalism, and the Press* (1997) and has coedited *Approaches to Teaching British Women Poets of the Romantic Period* (1997).

Catherine B. Burroughs is the author of *Closet Stages: Joanna Baillie and the Theater Theory of British Romantic Women Writers* (1997) and a coeditor of *Reading the Social Body* (1993).

Adriana Craciun, assistant professor at Loyola University, Chicago, has published articles on Mary Wollstonecraft, Mary Robinson, and Charlotte Dacre and is currently completing a manuscript on femmes fatales in women's writing from the Romantic period, as well as coediting a collection of essays on British women writers and the French Revolution.

Roxanne Eberle, assistant professor of English at the University of Georgia, is writing a book on representations of sexual trangression, chastity, and feminism in nineteenth-century literature by British women writers.

Paula R. Feldman, professor of English at the University of South Carolina, Columbia, is a coeditor of *The Journals of Mary Shelley* (1987) and *Romantic Women Writers: Voices and Countervoices* (1995) and the editor of *British Women Poets of the Romantic Era: An Anthology* (1997); she is currently editing an edition of the poetry of Felicia Hemans.

Kathleen Hickok is associate professor of English and Women's Studies at Iowa State University, where she also directs the graduate program in English. Her book *Representations of Women: Nineteenth-Century British Women's Poetry* (1984) helped establish the new and expanding canon of rediscovered Romantic and Victorian women poets.

Harriet Kramer Linkin, associate professor of English at New Mexico State University, coedited *Approaches to Teaching British Women Poets of the Romantic Period* and has published articles on Romanticism, gender, and women's literature. She is completing a full-length study on Mary Blachford Tighe.

Tricia Lootens, associate professor of English at the University of Georgia, is the author of *Lost Saints: Silence, Gender, and Victorian Literary Canonization* (1996). She is currently writing a study of nineteenth-century British and American women's patriotic poetry.

William McCarthy, professor of English at Iowa State University, is the author of *Hester Thrale Piozzi: Portrait of a Literary Woman* (1985) and coeditor of *The Poems of Anna Letitia Barbauld* (1994) and *Selected Poems and Prose of Anna Letitia Barbauld* (in preparation). Since 1987 he has been gathering material for a new biography of Barbauld; his newly researched account of her school at Palgrave appeared in *The Age of Johnson* in 1997.

Susan Wolfson is professor of English at Princeton University. Her most recent books include *Formal Changes: The Shaping of Poetic Form in British Romanticism* (1997) and *Figures on the Margin: The Language of Gender in British Romanticism* (1998). In addition to coediting an anthology of Romantic literature, she continues her research in poetic form, aesthetic ideology, and gender in Romantic writing.

Sarah M. Zimmerman is assistant professor of English at the University of Wisconsin, Madison, where she teaches British Romanticism. She has published *Romanticism, Lyricism and History* and is at work on a study of the public literary lecture in England, 1790-1820.

Index